.NET System Management Services

ALEXANDER GOLOMSHTOK

.NET System Management Services

ISBN (pbk): 1-59059-058-9

Printed and bound in the United States of America 12345678910

Trademarked names may appear in this book. Rather than use a trademark symbol with every occurrence of a trademarked name, we use the names only in an editorial fashion and to the benefit of the trademark owner, with no intention of infringement of the trademark.

Technical Reviewer: Yefim Nodelman
Editorial Directors: Dan Appleman, Gary Cornell, Jason Gilmore, Simon Hayes, Martin Streicher, Karen Watterson, John Zukowski
Managing Editor: Grace Wong
Project Manager: Nicole LeClerc
Copy Editor: Rebecca Rider
Compositor: Impressions Book and Journal Services, Inc.
Indexer: Valerie Perry
Cover Designer and Illustrator: Kurt Krames
Production Manager: Kari Brooks
Manufacturing Manager: Tom Debolski

Distributed to the book trade in the United States by Springer-Verlag New York, Inc., 175 Fifth Avenue, New York, NY, 10010 and outside the United States by Springer-Verlag GmbH & Co. KG, Tiergartenstr. 17, 69112 Heidelberg, Germany.

In the United States, phone 1-800-SPRINGER, email orders@springer-ny.com, or visit http://www.springer-ny.com.

Outside the United States, fax +49 6221 345229, email orders@springer.de, or visit http://www.springer.de.

For information on translations, please contact Apress directly at 2560 Ninth Street, Suite 219, Berkeley, CA 94710. Phone 510-549-5930, fax 510-549-5939, email info@apress.com, or visit http://www.apress.com.

The source code for this book is available to readers at http://www.apress.com in the Downloads section. You will need to answer questions pertaining to this book in order to successfully download the code.

We write what we observe. What we don't observe we don't write.
—Faddei Faddeevich Bellinsgausen, Russian Explorer and Naval Officer

Contents at a Glance

Contents

About the Author

ALEXANDER GOLOMSHTOK first laid his hands on a computer keyboard in 1984—as soon as he became a computer science student. Strictly speaking, it wasn't even a computer keyboard, rather it was a keyboard of an IBM card-punching machine. Although he doesn't consider himself a dinosaur, those punched cards were, for a while, his primary interface into the world of computing. He admits that just ten years ago, he was able to read through a stack of cards as easily as he could now read through, say, a C++ source listing.

In his third year of college, Golomshtok landed a job as a programmer for a major shipyard, developing computer simulations for ships' power sources. At work, he spent most of his time writing crude computer games and playing geek jokes on his colleagues and coworkers.

In 1990, right after receiving his MS in Computer Engineering, Golomshtok joined a small software house in NYC, as an application programmer. He soon realized that developing applications might not satisfy his cravings for exploration and adventure, so in 1992 he joined yet another software house—Vista Concepts, Inc.—where, in addition to application development, he got to act as a handyman, supporting all kinds of operating environments including MVS/System 370, CICS, AS 400, and OS/2.

While at Vista Concepts, Golomshtok turned into a real world-traveler, spending most of his time overseas. Even after the company was acquired by a much larger technology consulting outfit—American Management Systems, Inc.—the clientele didn't change much, and he kept accumulating 300,000 frequent-flyer miles every year. However, shortly after the flight attendants of Swiss Air started to recognize him and call him by his first name, Golomshtok opted for preserving his sanity and joined the New York Office of Price Waterhouse Coopers L.L.P. (Coopers and Lybrand L.L.P. at that time). While at PWC, he spent the vast majority of his time building large-scale financial systems for investment institutions such as JP Morgan Chase. But, unable to abandon his passion for system administration and systems management, he often sneaked out of his Wall Street office to participate in some enterprise systems management projects. This continuing fascination with the subject of system administration and management amounted to a small consulting company Cronos Systems Inc., which Golomshtok founded in 1998 to develop custom performance and system management tools for UNIX/Windows platforms.

Currently, Alexander Golomshtok is desperately trying to juggle his full-time job as a project manager and technology specialist at JP Morgan Chase, his responsibilities as a founder of Cronos Systems Inc., and his technical writing hobby.

Acknowledgments

I AM NOT GOING TO SURPRISE ANYONE if I say that writing a book is difficult. Unfortunately, not too many people realize how difficult it really is. After all, experimenting with a new and exciting technology seems like a lot of fun, and hacking around is just about the best thing there is. However, writing a book takes much more than just hacking. It is more like documenting every bit of the code that you write—the worst nightmare of every self-respecting hacker.

Writing a book also takes a lot of discipline and dedication, and, most importantly, it takes more than just one person. It is truly a team effort and, just like any other book, this book is the fruit of a collective endeavor. Luckily, I have been blessed with not only a great editorial team, but also with good friends and supporters who helped me finish this rather lengthy project and remain sane at the same time.

I would like to express my deepest sympathy and gratitude to many different people, directly or indirectly involved in this book project. First and foremost, I want to thank my favorite technical writer and editor, Dan Appleman of Apress, for giving me the idea for the book. Dan is the main reason this book exists. I would also like to thank my project manager, Nicole LeClerc, for not only coping with a disorganized individual such as myself, but also for her patience while teaching me to use the Apress Word template—the task that had the same difficulty rating as building the Eiffel tower.

I also want to thank my copy editor, Rebecca Rider, for the great job she did turning my soup of words into something consumable by a normal human. She is the one who explained to me that, unlike Leo Tolstoy, I should not write sentences that span multiple pages.

I want to express my gratitude to my technical editor, and a very good friend, Yefim Nodelman, who spent countless hours debugging my code. If any of the code samples in this book actually compile, Yefim is the one who should be credited. Conversely, he is the one to blame in case something does not work.

Finally, I would like to thank the rest of the Apress team for making my job as an author so much easier. Everyone I had a pleasure to interact with while working on this book was a top-notch professional, striving to perfect every aspect of the writing and production process.

I also want to thank my boss and good friend, Chris Catania of JP Morgan Chase, for putting up with my crankiness and absentmindedness for the entire duration of this book project. A man cannot wish for a better boss and friend.

I am eternally grateful to Serge Lidin of Microsoft for developing a wonderful IL Disassembler (ILDASM.EXE). For a while, ILDASM has been my only window into the exciting world of .NET internals, and it is certainly one of the reasons why I was able to write this book.

Last but not least, I want to thank my wife Natalie simply for being there. Babe, you are what keeps me going.

Introduction

THE INTRODUCTION OF .NET Framework is, perhaps, one of the most exciting events in the history of software development. Modern, sophisticated, powerful, and sometimes overwhelming, .NET is destined to change the way Windows applications are developed and deployed forever. This new platform is gaining worldwide acceptance by the hour, and today, shortly after its official release to the general public, it has already captured the hearts and souls of many professionals throughout the software development industry.

The Book

Rapidly growing interest in .NET development has given birth to many new books that are designed to cover various aspects of .NET Framework and the languages and tools associated with it. Unfortunately, not all the components and services of the new platform have received equal coverage in these texts. For instance, the new and enhanced .NET languages, such as C# and VB.NET, have attracted the most attention. As a result, the current book market seems to be reaching its saturation point with respect to .NET programming language books.

No doubt, the common language runtime platform and the new programming languages make up the core of .NET Framework. Developers, however, often measure the versatility of a particular programming environment by its ability to provide reusable software components, libraries, and OS interfaces. These elements are crucial to promoting the paradigm of rapid software development, and no modern development system may survive without them. Therefore, the power of .NET Framework comes not only from its language independence, but also from the rich selection of class libraries, or namespaces, with which it is equipped. These namespaces address every aspect of Windows programming, from graphical application development and data access to system management, making .NET development much faster and easier than ever before.

The books on .NET namespaces are just starting to appear. This is most likely because in order to fully understand and use the functionality afforded by these namespaces, one has to master the new .NET language facilities, which takes time; therefore these books are being published at a much slower rate then .NET programming language books. But even those few books on .NET namespaces that are either already on the market or are scheduled for publication in the upcoming year seem to focus mostly on aspects of Windows development such as graphical interfaces, web services, and database interactions. Meanwhile, .NET offers much more than just solutions to these conventional development problems—it is equipped with powerful facilities for application tracing and debugging, performance monitoring, and system management. Unfortunately, such tools are often regarded as secondary and, as a result, they receive much less attention.

System management, especially, is a subject often overlooked by book authors and publishers and, despite recent exciting developments in this field, today's book market has little to offer. One may argue that learning the programming interfaces to system management facilities may not be a useful skill due to wide availability of shrink-wrapped management tools; this argument may explain the lack of good books on the subject. However, such an opinion indicates a narrow view of the problem.

Although off-the-shelf tools are definitely useful and may even be indispensable on occasion, all of them suffer from the same limitation—they lack flexibility. Modern computing environments are so complex and diverse that it is next to impossible to come up with a generalized management approach; hence the tool vendors always fail to solve the problem completely. Every computer system has something special about it, and because of this, most tools come up short, thus leaving a gap to be filled with some, often crude, custom utilities. Yet another problem is that most tool vendors have a bird's eye view of the problem—they attempt to solve it on the global scale rather than by concentrating on the little annoying issues. This approach often results in monstrous enterprise-wide distributed management systems, which cost millions to acquire and maintain and add very little real value.

Often developers can solve such a complex issue with ten lines of scripting code, which could save them countless hours and significant amounts of money. All that they need is a little expertise on programming access to management interfaces.

Microsoft is very well aware of the importance of having a solid system management framework in place, which puts them far ahead of other software vendors. The invention of the Windows Management Instrumentation (WMI) framework was a major milestone toward turning Windows into the best enterprise computing platform in the world. In fact, WMI is no less revolutionary than .NET with respect to how it changed the way people think of system management. Equipped with WMI programming expertise, any Windows developer or maintainer can perform complex management tasks over a large-scale distributed computing environment with minimal effort.

As powerful and exciting as WMI already was, with the introduction of .NET Framework, it has become a premier system management facility for Windows platforms. The .NET system management namespaces are a unique blend of power, simplicity, and elegance where the state-of-the-art system management framework is combined with state-of-the-art development languages and tools. .NET is definitely the ultimate last word in the field of system management and, as such, it deserves special attention.

Although it is likely that many more .NET books will hit the market in the next few months, and some of them will, perhaps, touch on the .NET class libraries, the system management namespaces may not receive adequate coverage for quite some time. After all, .NET Framework comes equipped with a very extensive set of class libraries that are designed to solve all kinds of imaginable programming problems, and most authors will probably provide just a broad overview of these facilities rather than focusing on the system management services. Unfortunately, those of us interested in system management will continue to struggle with Microsoft documentation, spending month after month digging through countless pages of hard-to-decipher material.

The purpose of this book is to change all that by zeroing in on just the system management facilities available through .NET Framework. Due to time and space limitations, I do not mean for this book to be an exhaustive reference on absolutely every aspect of .NET management services—I'd have a tough time trying to keep up with the pace of prolific Microsoft programmers. However, I do intend to provide a very detailed, technical coverage of the most essential elements that constitute the .NET system management namespaces and I plan to lay a solid foundation for building comprehensive management utilities with minimal coding.

Also, I would like this book to stimulate your appetite for developing custom system management solutions and cause you to take full advantage of the power afforded to you by .NET Framework. Hopefully, after reading this book, you, and many other adventurous system administrators and developers, will begin your journey through the maze of .NET namespaces and will discover priceless hidden treasures.

The Scope

Although most of the content in this book deals with WMI, it is not intended to be a primer on this subject. First and foremost, this book is on .NET system management namespaces, and as such, it will only cover those WMI facilities exposed through the .NET Framework. Although the book covers the basic concepts behind WMI and presents an overview of its architecture, no attempt is made to provide any tutorial or reference information on those features that have no direct relationship to .NET system management services. For instance, there is no mentioning of the WMI Scripting API, no reference information on WMI namespaces, and no formal description of WMI Query Language (WQL) language syntax and grammar—instead, WMI classes and objects, as well as the specifics of WQL, are covered in the context of .NET system management features. This book, therefore, is not a replacement for WMI reference information; those readers wishing to find detailed descriptions of WMI namespaces, classes, and methods will have to refer to the latest WMI SDK documentation.

In general, system management is a very broad topic and it may refer to nearly any activity related to monitoring, troubleshooting, and managing computer systems. As a direct reflection of this, .NET management services is designed as a very versatile framework, which enables the user to do almost anything—from performance monitoring to configuring applications. Unfortunately, the scope limitations of this text will not allow me to discuss everything that can be done with .NET management namespaces. For instance, rather than demonstrating how to administer user accounts or monitor disk usage, I will just cover the most common usage patterns. After all, the structure of WMI and .NET is such that enumerating user accounts on a given system is not much different than enumerating disks or processes. Therefore, equipped with a detailed knowledge of .NET management facilities and a little creativity, you should be able to solve pretty much any management problem.

For these same reasons, some of the commonly discussed features of WMI will not be addressed. For instance, although this book has a separate chapter on WMI security, any security-related issues are only discussed in the context of using .NET management namespaces. .NET Framework does not introduce any radical changes in regards to handling WMI security issues, and I feel that it is unnecessary to repeat the WMI SDK documentation, which already provides comprehensive coverage of WMI security.

Although this book contains a discussion of different WMI providers and dedicates nearly an entire chapter to WMI collaboration with the Simple Network Management Protocol (SNMP), I do not attempt to provide an exhaustive reference on all existing WMI providers. For instance, I do not mention WMI interfaces to Active Directory Services Interfaces (ADSI)—ADSI is a very well researched topic and, since neither WMI nor .NET Framework significantly change the ADSI programming model, there is no reason to discuss it again.

The Reader

This book should definitely attract the attention of Windows system administrators who are struggling to get more control over the operations and performance of their systems. However, administrators are not the only group who may potentially benefit from reading the book. Over the last few years, enterprise system management has become a hot issue and has attracted the special attention of corporate technology officers. In fact, numerous professional services firms and technology consulting companies have recognized the potential of this market segment and have attempted to come up with various service and product offerings. Technology consultants, such as myself, have been struggling for years trying to produce powerful, yet inexpensive, management solutions for their clients.

One of my goals for this book is to present a clear path to follow in order to build low cost, effective system management tools that are tailored to the needs of a particular organization—thus providing an attractive alternative to expensive and inflexible off-the-shelf products. Therefore, I hope that many professional consultants who are developing system management solutions will broaden their horizons as a result of reading the book.

As I already mentioned, this is a book on .NET Framework, and therefore, you are expected to be somewhat familiar with the basic principles behind .NET; you should also be fluent in at least one of the most commonly used .NET languages such as C# or VB.NET. However, since the main focus of this book is the functionality afforded by the .NET system management namespaces rather than the intricacies of a particular programming language, it is my intention to keep the coding examples reasonably simple. Thus, even the novice .NET developer should be able to gain some level of expertise in building .NET system management applications.

The programming language used for all examples in this book, is C#. Since the book concentrates mainly on the usage patterns of the .NET system management classes, which are fairly language-agnostic, I felt that the code examples did not warrant duplication in other .NET programming languages such as VB.NET. Instead, on those rare occasions where choice of the programming language does matter, I attempt to pinpoint the differences. Thus, if you are an average reader who is familiar with the fundamental principles of .NET programming, you should be capable of easily translating the examples into your favorite .NET programming language.

After reading this book, you should find that you have acquired a solid understanding of the structure of .NET system management namespaces, functionality afforded by these namespaces, and finally, the most common usage patterns for building sophisticated system management solutions. Armed with this information, the average developer or system administrator should be in a position to develop a custom tool suitable for managing just about any aspect of Windows operations.

The Structure

Although many new books have tricks, tips, and various other text features designed to make skimming through the book easier, I am reluctant to making these part of this book for several reasons. First, this book is mostly about management classes and objects that are designed to work together in order to achieve a certain goal. As a result, it does not promote "skimming" and requires you to read through pretty much the entire chapter to understand the mechanics of a particular object model or feature. Second, tips and tricks are usually designed to attract your attention and they often disrupt the normal flow of text, thus breaking your concentration. Therefore, I feel that having such text features as part of this book may be an annoyance rather than a help.

Case Studies are just another feature that I prefer to avoid. Any case study of a software system usually translates into dozens of pages of code, which are impossible to follow and, for the most part, have little to do with the subject of the book. Most case studies I have seen are terrible crimes committed against the vegetation of our planet and I see very little use in them.

The index, on the other hand, is indispensable when it comes to books on object models and interfaces because it allows you to quickly locate the portion of the book that is pertinent to a particular function or feature of an object system. This book, therefore, is equipped with a very detailed index, which makes it usable as a reference.

It is my intention to provide numerous code examples throughout the text of the book. The purpose of these examples is to illustrate the usage patterns of .NET system management services rather than to provide ready-to-run management scripts. After all, one of my goals is to enable you to create your own custom solutions instead of just trying to shoehorn inflexible off-the-shelf software into doing what you need. As a result, I don't see the need for any kind of supporting CD-ROMs or web pages, the examples throughout the book should suffice.

The Requirements

WMI is fully supported under Microsoft Windows 2000 and Windows XP. Although Windows NT 4.0, as well as Windows 95, 98, and ME provide only a limited support for WMI, most of the examples in this book will run just fine on these platforms. Hence, unless explicitly noted otherwise (there are a few code examples that depend on the software features that are available only under Windows 2000 or XP), you should feel free to compile and run the code on the platform of your choice.

On Windows 2000 and XP platforms, the core components of WMI are installed by default. The core software package for Windows NT 4.0/95/98/ME can be downloaded from MSDN at `http://www.microsoft.com/downloads/release.asp?ReleaseID=18490`. The following minimal configuration is required to run this software:

- Microsoft Internet Explorer 5.0 or better

- A Microsoft Windows NT 4.0/95/98/ME operating system

- A Pentium-class computer

- 32 MB of RAM

- 30 MB of available hard disk space

- Video graphics card support for 256 colors at 800 × 600 resolution

- A network card

WMI SDK, which contains a slew of useful tools such as CIM Studio, WMI Object Browser, and Event Viewer, is an optional software package; it is available for free download from MSDN at `http://download.microsoft.com/download/ platformsdk/sdkx86/1.5/NT45/EN-US/wmisdk.exe`. The software and hardware requirements for WMI SDK are no different from those for the core WMI components.

Certain WMI data providers mentioned in this book are not installed by default and have to be downloaded from MSDN. One such example is the WMI SNMP Provider, which can be found at `http://www.microsoft.com/downloads/ release.asp?ReleaseID=19776`. The SNMP Provider only runs under Windows NT 4.0/SP4 or Windows 2000 and requires SNMP service to be installed. Before you install optional provider packages like this one, you should make sure that WMI core components are installed and configured properly.

The System.Management namespace is part of .NET Framework Class Library (FCL) and is distributed as part of .NET Framework SDK, which is available for free download from MSDN at `http://download.microsoft.com/download/ .netframesdk/SDK/1.0/W98NT42KMeXP/EN-US/setup.exe`. The SDK is all you will need to compile and run the examples presented in this book, although you may want to obtain a good code editor. Obviously, the best development environment for .NET projects is Microsoft Visual Studio .NET, which features not only an excellent editor, but also a number of other indispensable tools and utilities. Visual Studio .NET is not a free product and, although well worth its price, it may remain an unaffordable luxury for some developers. Therefore, it is my intention to make sure that the material presented in this book is self-sufficient and does not depend on a particular development environment.

If you are the lucky owner of Visual Studio .NET, you may want to acquire the WMI Management Extension for Server Explorer Component, available for free download from MSDN at `http://www.microsoft.com/downloads/ release.asp?ReleaseID=31155`. This handy utility lets you browse and modify the management data by invoking WMI methods and it also lets you handle and register for WMI events.

CHAPTER 1

.NET Framework and Windows Management Instrumentation

OVER THE LAST TWO DECADES, the remarkable evolution of the computer and networking technologies has changed our perception of computing forever. The days of monolithic mainframe installations and running operating systems, utilities, and applications from a single vendor are long gone, and simple, straightforward system architectures were forgotten long ago. The rapidly growing popularity of the distributed computing model has turned the vast majority of computing infrastructures into an extremely complex mix of dissimilar hardware devices that are interconnected by spiderwebs of local and wide area networks and are running software from thousands of different vendors. Besides elevating the complexity of the computer installations to a brand new level, this overwhelming technological progress has materialized the most horrible nightmares for many system administrators by making computer and network management painfully challenging.

The issue of system management is quite complex, even for a centralized homogenous computing environment where all software elements share common operational data and expose uniform management interfaces. A distributed, multivendor installation, however, is simply impossible to manage unless a uniform standard for presenting the operational and statistical data exists and a common protocol for managing the resources is available. That is why, over the years, numerous system engineers have attempted to standardize system management techniques.

In the late 1980s, the Simple Network Management Protocol (SNMP) was designed to address the issue of multi-vendor network management. However, the initial SNMP specification failed to address all the critical network management needs; as a result, SNMP needed a few enhancements. In 1991 the Remote Network Monitoring specification (RMON) was released to overcome SNMP's local area network management limitations. In 1993 an enhanced version of SNMP, widely known as SNMPv2, was released and was subsequently revised in 1995. SNMPv2 augmented the original SNMP specification to provide extended functionality and enhanced its performance. Finally, in 1998 SNMPv3 was issued, primarily to deal with the security capabilities of SNMP and to define the overall architecture for future enhancements. Today, SNMP remains the most popular standard for managing TCP/IP-based internets.

In 1994, another standard, the Desktop Management Interface (DMI), was developed in an attempt to deal with the consequences of the PC revolution. The first DMI specification (DMI v1.0) outlined the ground rules for hardware and software manufacturers; these rules allowed manageable networked desktop systems to be built. In April 1996, this specification was extended to offer remote manageability in networked environments. This extended DMI specification, known as DMI v2.0, was adopted as the industry-standard, and it included a set of operating system-independent and protocol-independent application programming interfaces (APIs) that provided a uniform desktop management framework.

Although SNMP, DMI, and other standards for management instrumentation are a major step forward in the field of system management, they still fail at completely solving the problem. Perhaps the main limitation of these standards is their fairly narrow specialization—each offers just a partial solution and does not provide the unified end-to-end view of the entire management domain. Individual elements or groups of elements are still managed in isolation, and there is little or no integration between management standards and techniques; hence we still need data duplication and specialized management front-ends.

The Birth of WBEM

In 1996 a few industry leaders—BMC Software, Cisco Systems, Compaq, Intel, and Microsoft—set out to address the limitations of the existing management standards and protocols by sponsoring a brand new initiative: Web-Based Enterprise Management (WBEM). The companies' main goal was to develop a uniform way to share management information and control management resources within an entire management domain, irrespective of the underlying platforms, networking technologies, and programming languages. In order to turn this vision into reality, three major design principles were employed:

> **The Common Information Model (CIM):** This uniform, platform, and language independent model represents the managed elements in the enterprise. In addition to covering all major aspects and areas of system management, this model was designed to be open and extensible so that it could describe environment and platform-specific managed elements.

The easy and seamless integration of existing management standards such as SNMP and DMI: WBEM implementations were to allow management information to be translated between the formats utilized by the existing management tools and the CIM.

A standard method for accessing the management information from a variety of distributed managed nodes over different transports: Since the WBEM initiative came in the midst of the Internet revolution, the Web seemed like a natural transport vehicle for sharing and controlling the management information, hence the name Web-Based Enterprise Management.

In June of 1998, in order to achieve industry-wide acceptance and provide an open public forum for ongoing development of WBEM technologies, the founders of WBEM transferred the ownership of this initiative to an organization called the Distributed Management Task Force (DMTF). DMTF, which was founded in 1992 by a group of leading PC manufacturers, is still the industry consortium that leads the development and promotes the adoption of desktop, network, and Internet management standards.

DMTF leadership further accelerated the progress of the WBEM initiative and ensured the wide acceptance of its first standard—the CIM specification. In the next few years, DMTF, along with many participating companies, not only revised and enhanced the CIM specification, but also produced numerous other standards to describe and define uniform protocols for publishing and exchanging the management information. One of the standards that deserves special attention is the XML Encoding Specification, which allows CIM schemas to be encoded in XML. The first draft of this specification was proposed in October 1998, and it replaced the original WBEM data publishing standard, which was called the HyperMedia Management Protocol (HMMP).

Today, DMTF remains fully committed to promoting the WBEM technology as a premier vehicle for accessing the management information in the enterprise environment and lowering the total cost of ownership (TCO) associated with computer hardware and software configuration, deployment, and maintenance. Some software vendors, such as Microsoft and Sun Microsystems, already ship WBEM-compliant management frameworks, and extensive interest in this technology throughout the industry indicates that many more vendors are preparing to incorporate WBEM-based management solutions into their product offerings in the near future.

Introducing the Common Information Model

The *Common Information Model (CIM)* is the centerpiece of the WBEM technology. CIM is a well-defined, conceptual, object-oriented model, designed to serve as a framework that describes all aspects of a managed environment. The management information within CIM is organized into a hierarchy of classes that represent logical and physical elements in the enterprise. The object-oriented modeling approach provides several benefits such as data abstraction, inheritance, and polymorphism. Grouping related objects into classes based on common properties and behavior, for instance, allows the complexity of the model to decrease, while modularity and extensibility are promoted. Inheritance is the ability to construct classes from one or more other parent classes so that derived, or child, classes inherit the characteristics and behavior of the parent. Inheritance upholds the principles of generalization, specialization, and modular design. Finally, polymorphism is the ability of different classes within the same hierarchy to provide specialized responses to the same external message. This promotes extensibility and simplifies the development and maintenance of the management schema.

Management schemas are the primary building blocks of CIM. *CIM Schema* is a named collection of elements that describes a particular functional area within a managed environment, such as device configuration or performance management. CIM is organized as a system of interrelated schemas that cover every aspect of the managed enterprise.

To describe the individual entities within a managed environment, CIM utilizes the generalization technique—it factors common properties and behaviors of the managed elements into sets of classes so that each class reflects a single unit of management. A *CIM class* is essentially a template that describes a particular type of a managed element. These classes can contain properties, also known as data elements, that describe the state of the class instance, and methods that express the behavior of the class. Listing 1-1 presents a partial definition for one of the CIM core classes—CIM_LogicalDevice. This class is designed to serve as a high-level abstraction for a hardware element in a managed environment.

Listing 1-1. Managed Object Format Definition for CIM_LogicalDevice

```
[Abstract, Description (
        "An abstraction or emulation of a hardware entity, that may "
        "or may not be realized in physical hardware...") ]
class CIM_LogicalDevice : CIM_LogicalElement  {
...
[Key, MaxLen (64),
        Description (
```

```
            "An address or other identifying information to uniquely "
            "name the LogicalDevice.") ]
        string DeviceID;
    [Description (
            "LastErrorCode captures the last error code reported by "
            "the LogicalDevice.")]
        uint32 LastErrorCode;
    [Description(
            "SetPowerState defines the desired power state for a "
            "LogicalDevice and when a device should be put into that "
            "state")]
        uint32 SetPowerState([IN] uint16 PowerState, [IN] datetime Time);
        [Description ("Requests a reset of the LogicalDevice")]
        uint32 Reset();
    ...
};
```

The notation used here is called *Managed Object Format (MOF),* which is a DMTF-defined language for specifying management schemas in WBEM. MOF may look a bit intimidating at first, but it is only presented here to provide a context for the discussion—the detailed overview of this language syntax is postponed until Chapter 6.

In this listing, `DeviceID` and `LastErrorCode` are properties that represent the identity and state of a class instance, while `SetPowerState` and `Reset` are methods that express the behavior of the class. Not all classes, however, have methods, especially those defined at the root of the CIM hierarchy. Typically, the root classes represent the highest level of abstraction where it may not always be possible to define any specialized behavioral characteristics.

Another interesting thing you should notice is that MOF definitions do not contain any implementation details for the methods of the class; rather, they specify the method signature. Because MOF is a declarative format for the management data rather than an implementation vehicle, the actual implementation is delegated to so-called data providers (this will be discussed in more detail in Chapter 7). Thus, CIM class specifications are somewhat similar to interface definitions, which are widely used in such frameworks as Component Object Model (COM) and Common Object Request Broker Architecture (CORBA) as well as in some programming languages like Java and C#. Obviously, you can draw a clear parallel between MOF and the Interface Definition Language (IDL).

Even though a class may have one or more methods defined, the implementation for these methods may not necessarily be available. This is because CIM defines a number of classes each of which represent a very high level of abstraction and exist just to serve as parents for more specialized classes. As a result, the actual method implementation is deferred to these respective subclasses. CIM specification requires that all implemented methods be marked with the `Implemented` qualifier in the MOF definition; this allows a class to indicate that a method is actually implemented by a data provider.

All class names must be unique within a particular schema, and the schema name acts as a distinguishing factor that helps differentiate classes with potentially conflicting names. By convention, the fully qualified name of a class always takes the form `<schemaname>_<classname>`, where the underscore serves as a delimiter between the name of the schema and the name of the class. Note that the underscore delimiter may not be a part of the schema name, although it is allowed as part of the class name. This convention limits the scope of the class name to the schema, significantly reducing the chances of name collisions between the classes from different schemas. The CIM classes defined by DMTF have the schema name of "CIM," thus the fully qualified name of the class, which represents an operating system process, is `CIM_Process`. Specific WBEM implementations may provide their own schemas; for instance, the Solaris WBEM SDK defines its own process class, called `Solaris_Process`, while Microsoft Windows Management Instrumentation (WMI) exposes the `Win32_Process` class.

As mentioned earlier, inheritance is another powerful concept of object-oriented design. It is used extensively within the CIM. Simply put, inheritance is a technique that allows class designers to construct a class from one or more other classes, while sharing properties, behavior and, sometimes, constraints.

The process of creating a new class using an existing class as a base is often referred to as *subclassing*. There are a few reasons for subclassing. The first, and perhaps the most obvious one is the ability to inherit some properties and standard methods, thus reducing the effort of building a new class. If you refer back to Listing 1-1, you will see that the `CIM_LogicalDevice` employs `CIM_LogicalElement` as its base class. Although this is not apparent in Listing 1-1, `CIM_LogicalDevice` inherits a few properties, such as `Name`, `InstallDate`, `Description`, and `Caption`.

Another reason why you would use subclassing is if you wanted to specialize some of the class semantics, moving from an abstract base class to a more specific subclass. In addition to adding new properties and methods, a specialized subclass may also redefine some of the existing characteristics of the base class. For instance, a subclass may restate the definition of a particular feature, such as a method description or an informational qualifier. In this case, the subclass overrides the respective characteristic of its base class. Alternatively, a subclass may provide a method or property implementation, different from that of a base class, while inheriting the method signature or property declaration. This process of altering the behavior of an arbitrary method or property is closely related to polymorphism, another fundamental concept of object-oriented design. Polymorphism implies that classes within a certain hierarchy are capable of responding to the same message in a manner specific to a particular class, using a potentially different implementation. This very powerful concept is widely used throughout all areas of the CIM.

Listing 1-2 demonstrates some of these concepts:

Listing 1-2. Inheritance and Method/Property Overriding

```
class CIM_Service : CIM_LogicalElement
{
  ...
  [ValueMap{"Automatic", "Manual"}] string StartMode;
  ...
  uint32 StartService();
  uint32 StopService();
};

class Win32_BaseService : CIM_Service
{
  [ValueMap{"Boot", "System", "Auto", "Manual", "Disabled"},
   Override("StartMode")]
  string StartMode = NULL;
  ...
  [Override("StartService"), Implemented] uint32 StartService();
  [Override("StopService"), Implemented] uint32 StopService();
  [Implemented] uint32 PauseService();
  ...
};
```

Here the base class CIM_Service declares a property, called StartMode, and states that the set of allowed values for this property is limited to Automatic and Manual. The subclass—Win32_BaseService—overrides two aspects of the StartMode property: first it adds a default value of NULL then it redefines the allowed set of values to Boot, System, Auto, Manual, and Disabled.

PauseService, which also appears in Listing 1-2, is a method specific to the Win32_BaseService and it does not exist within the scope of CIM_Service base class. You must realize that not every service can be paused; that is why the CIM_Service class, in an attempt to remain completely implementation-neutral, does not define any such function. The subclass, however, represents a Win32 service, which can be paused; therefore it declares the PauseService method and provides an implementation for it (notice the Implemented qualifier here). The subclass essentially extends the functionality of its base class.

The Win32_BaseService subclass also inherits two method definitions from its parent—StartService and StopService—and it provides its own implement-ation (again, notice the Implemented qualifier). Although the CIM_Service base class does not implement these methods (no Implemented qualifier within the CIM_Service definition), the Win32_BaseService implementation can still be considered polymorphic since it is specific to the subclass. It is conceivable that some other subclass of `CIM_Service` may provide its own implementation for these methods, different from that of `Win32_BaseService`.

Many object-oriented models and languages provide a facility called method overloading where several methods with the same name and different parameter types may coexist. Typically a language processor such as a compiler or an interpreter will select the correct method by inspecting the types of its parameters at the call site. Then a subclass may be able to alter the signature of a method inherited from a base class, thus providing an overloaded method definition. In CIM, however, method overloading is not supported, and a subclass, when overriding a method, must preserve its signature.

Another restriction that CIM imposes is single inheritance. Some object-oriented languages, such as C++, allow a subclass to inherit from more than one parent thus sharing more than one set of characteristics, properties, and methods; this is known as *multiple inheritance.* Although multiple inheritance is a very powerful feature, it typically creates too many problems because there is a great potential for conflicts. For instance, two base classes, A and B, may both implement a method `Foo`, although the `A::Foo` and `B::Foo` implementations may be completely different and not related in any way. Any attempt to create a subclass, C, that inherits from both A and B, will result in a naming conflict between the `A::Foo` and `B::Foo` methods. Although different languages and environments offer various solutions for disambiguating multiple inheritance name conflicts, there is no "silver bullet." The designers of CIM felt that the power of multiple inheritance did not justify the complexity associated with resolving these kinds of naming conflicts; thus CIM inheritance trees are single-rooted.

As we have already established, the CIM is a collection of related classes. Relationships between classes are usually expressed via special properties, called *references.* Essentially a reference is a pointer to an instance of a class; thus, in order to establish a relationship between arbitrary classes A and B, instances of either class may have references that point to a respective instance of another class. CIM relationships are modeled through *associations*—bidirectional semantic connections between related classes. In accordance with their bidirectional nature, all CIM associations are classes that contain references to other classes that are related through the association.

This design approach has several benefits. First, associations may have other properties in addition to references to the classes being associated. CIM designers, for instance, often use an example of a `Marriage` association between a `Male` and a `Female` property. A Marriage not only has links to both `Male` and `Female`, but it also includes other properties such as `Date`. Second, if you model associations as classes, you gain greater design flexibility because you can add an association without changing the interface of the related classes. Thus, adding a `Marriage` association between a `Male` and `Female` does not affect the definition of these two classes in any way (this is, perhaps, where there is a disconnect between the design of CIM and real life); the Marriage association simply ties them together via a pair of references. To enforce this design approach, CIM disallows nonassociation classes that have properties of reference data type.

As I mentioned earlier, classes are just templates for objects or instances; thus an arbitrary class may have one or more instances. For example, the CIM_DataFile class may have hundreds or thousands of instances within a given environment, each representing a single physical data file. To be able to deal with multiple instances of a class in a meaningful fashion, these instances have to be uniquely identifiable within a given system. Numerous instance identification schemes exist, but perhaps the most common scenarios are the following:

Globally Unique Identifiers (GUIDs): GUID-based object identity schemes are used extensively throughout the industry; the most widely known example is the Microsoft Component Object Model (COM). In a GUID-based model, each and every class instance is assigned an artificial identifier, unique across time and space. The benefits of this approach are twofold: GUIDs are guaranteed to be unique, which greatly reduces any chances of collisions; and GUIDs are also relatively cheap to generate. The problem is that GUIDs are intended for machine consumption and are not particularly human-friendly—in fact, they seem quite meaningless and are difficult to memorize.

Natural Keys: In a keyed object model, one or more properties of a class form a unique key that unambiguously identifies an object instance within a given environment. Our example in Listing 1-1, for instance, designates the DeviceID property of CIM_LogicalDevice class as a key (notice the Key qualifier) so that consumers of CIM_LogicalDevice instances (or rather instances of its subclasses) may refer to a particular device instance using the ID string. Obviously, using a keyed approach offers certain benefits for the users of the object model because the natural keys are more easily understood and memorized. Unlike GUIDs, however, the natural keys are only unique within a given scope—for instance, if a file is identified by its name or path, the object instance representing C:\BOOT.INI will only be unique within a single Windows system.

As I already implied, CIM is a keyed object model. Since CIM must be capable of handling the management data across multiple environments and possibly across multiple physical implementations, object keys alone may not be sufficient to uniquely identify an instance. There has to be a way to identify an environment or implementation or, in other words, provide a scope, within which the objects keys are unique. Thus, every object within CIM is uniquely identified by an object path, as outlined in Listing 1-3.

Listing 1-3. Object Naming

```
object_path ::= <namespace_path><model_path>

where:
    namespace_path ::= <namespace_type><namespace_handle>
    model_path ::= <object_name>.<key>=<value>,[<key>=<value>]

example:
    HTTP://CIMHOST/root/CIMV2:CIM_DataFile.Name="C:\BOOT.INI"

where:
    namespace_type = HTTP
    namespace_handle = CIMHOST/root/CIMV2
    object_name = CIM_DataFile
    key = Name
    value = C:\BOOT.INI
```

A *namespace path* is essentially a unique identifier for a namespace that hosts CIM objects, thus acting as a scope for these objects. Although a namespace path is implementation-specific, it typically provides at least two pieces of information: the type of implementation, or namespace, being referenced, and a handle for this namespace. The *namespace type* defines an access protocol used by the implementation to import, export, and update the management data. In a sense, the namespace type is similar to a protocol specification used in URLs, such as http or ftp. It is conceivable that a particular implementation may define several protocols or APIs for accessing the data, and in this case, each of these protocols must have an associated unique namespace type defined. A *namespace handle* defines an instance of a namespace within a given implementation. Although the details of the namespace handles are implementation-specific, these handles often include an identifier of a computer system ("CIMHOST" in our example) that hosts the namespace instance. If an implementation supports multiple namespace instances, a handle may also include an identifier for a particular instance within a given system ("root/CIMV2" in our example).

The purpose of the model path is to uniquely identify an object within its respective namespace. A *model path* consists of the name of the class to which the object belongs and one or more key-value pairs, such that each property designated as a key in the class definition is supplied with a value. Thus in our example, the object of type "CIM_DataFile" is uniquely identified within its respective namespace (CIMHOST/root/CIMV2) by the value of its Name property.

The entire CIM Schema is divided into three areas: the core model, the common model, and the extension schemas. The *core model* is a relatively small set of classes and associations that provides a foundation for describing any kind of managed environment and is applicable to all areas of system management. The core model serves as a basis from which to define more specialized extension schemas that are applicable to concrete management domains. In particular, the core model provides abstract base classes; these allow you to classify all managed objects within a system as either physical or logical. Thus, the CIM_PhysicalElement class is used as a base for modeling those managed objects that have some kind of physical representation, while the CIM_LogicalElement class is used to build abstractions, typically representing the state of a managed system or its capabilities. The core model also provides a set of abstract association classes that are used to model containment and dependency relationships between classes.

The *common model* is a set of classes that define various areas of system management while remaining completely implementation-neutral. This model is detailed enough to serve as a solid foundation for building the technology-specific extension models that are suitable for developing all kinds of system management applications. The common model describes the following aspects of a managed environment:

The systems schema: The systems schema addresses various top-level objects that make up the managed environment, such as computer systems and application systems.

The devices classes: This part of the common model is designed to represent the discrete logical elements of a system that possess basic capabilities, such as processing, input/output, and so on. Interestingly, CIM device classes are descendants of the CIM_LogicalElement class as opposite to CIM_PhysicalElement class. Although the system devices may appear as physical rather than logical elements, the reason for deriving the device classes from CIM_LogicalElement is the fact that management systems deal with the operating system view of the device rather than its physical incarnation.

The networks model: The networks model defines the classes that are necessary to model various aspects of a networked environment, including various network services, protocols, and network topologies.

The applications model: The intent of this model is to provide a basis for managing various software packages and applications. The applications model is fairly flexible and can easily be used to represent not only stand-alone desktop software components, but also complicated distributed application systems that may run on multiple platforms or be deployed via the Internet.

The physical model: The physical model is designed to reflect all aspects of the actual physical environment. As I already mentioned, the vast majority of managed elements may and should be modeled as logical elements because any changes within the physical environment are likely to be just the consequences of some events happening within the logical "world." For example, rotations of a physical disk platter come as a result of an I/O request that originates within a logical environment—the operating system. Also, the physical elements are unable to directly feed the management data into CIM and their state can only be determined through some controlling logical elements, such as device drivers. Yet another problem is that physical elements differ dramatically from environment to environment due to the difference in the underlying hardware technologies; thus they do not lend themselves easily to any generalized modeling techniques. For all these reasons, the aspects of a physical environment are not a direct concern of CIM designers.

Finally, the *extension schemas* are sets of classes that are specific to a particular CIM implementation and are dependent on the characteristics of a given managed environment. As part of their WBEM product offerings, various vendors typically provide extension schemas. Thus, the Microsoft WMI framework ships with a set of extension classes that represent the managed elements specific to Win32 platforms, and Solaris WBEM SDK exposes classes that are only relevant to the specific management aspects of Solaris systems.

Windows Management Instrumentation

In addition to being one of the founders and key contributors to the WBEM initiative, Microsoft was also one of the first software vendors to ship a fully WBEM-compliant instrumentation framework for its Windows platforms. The Microsoft WBEM implementation, called Windows Management Instrumentation (WMI), is the core of Windows management infrastructure. It was designed to facilitate maintenance and greatly reduce the total cost of ownership (TCO) of Windows-based enterprise systems.

WMI provides the following benefits to system managers, administrators, and developers:

A complete and consistent object-oriented model of the entire management domain: The Microsoft WMI implementation is fully CIMv2.0-compliant and as such, it fully supports all management data abstractions defined by the CIMv2.0 specifications of the core and common models. Additionally, WMI exposes a number of extension schemas that cover aspects of system management specific to Windows platforms.

A single point of access to all management information for the enterprise: WMI exposes a powerful COM-based API, which allows the developers of management applications to retrieve and modify virtually any kind of Windows configuration and status data.

An extensible architecture that allows for the seamless integration of existing management solutions and facilitates the instrumentation of third-party software products: WMI is equipped with a number of adapters that make the management data maintained by legacy systems, such as SNMP, accessible through standard WMI interfaces. Additionally, through WMI, the software vendors are afforded the flexibility of extending the management schema and exposing the specific management data for their software applications and hardware devices.

A robust event mechanism: WMI supports an event-driven programming model where management events, such as changes to system configuration or system state, can be intercepted, analyzed, and acted upon. Once registered as an event consumer, a management application can receive various management events, originating from a local or remote system.

A simple yet powerful query language: One of the most remarkable features of WMI is the WMI Query Language (WQL), which allows the developers of custom management applications to navigate through the WMI information model and retrieve the information in which they are interested. WQL is a subset of standard American National Standards Institute (ANSI) SQL (Structured Query Language) with some minor semantic changes that were necessary to accommodate the specifics of WMI.

WMI Overview and Architecture

Figure 1-1 presents a high-level view of the WMI Architecture.

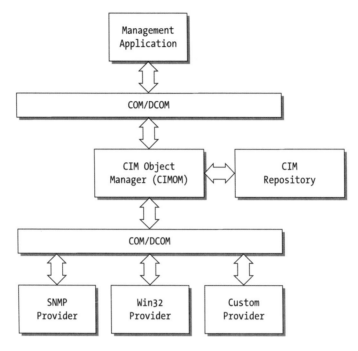

Figure 1-1. The WMI Architecture

Conceptually, the key component of the WMI is the CIM Object Manager (CIMOM). In compliance with the main goal of WBEM—providing a uniform, centralized way of manipulating the management data—CIMOM acts as a single point of access to the entire universe of managed objects that are of interest to management applications. Although all client requests for management data go through CIMOM, it is not responsible for actually collecting this data. Instead, depending on the nature of the information requested, CIMOM may either retrieve the data from its repository (the CIM Repository) or if the data is not available in the repository, route the request to an appropriate data provider. In the latter case, the data provider may retrieve or generate the requested information on demand and return it back to CIMOM, which in turn will return the data to the client application that initiated the request.

The CIM Repository, managed by CIMOM, is a central storage area, intended primarily for storing the WMI schema information. In some cases, however, the repository may also hold the static instance data—mainly the instances of WMI classes that represent the system configuration information, which is not likely to change often. For example, an instance of the Win32_Bios class, which represents the system BIOS, is static and is not likely to change during the normal operations of a system; thus its data is stored in the CIM Repository and retrieved directly by CIMOM. The Win32_Process class, on the other hand, may have many transient instances—one for every process that the operating system creates. Generally, the large volumes and transient nature of the instance data make it unsuitable for storage in the CIM Repository, and in cases such as this one, the task of providing the data is delegated to the respective data provider. Providers that generate and return the management data on demand are often referred to as *dynamic providers*.

CIMOM Implementation

WMI packages the bulk of the CIMOM functionality as well as the repository management functions in a single executable file, WinMgmt.exe. This executable is installed into the %SystemRoot%\System32\Wbem directory and, on Windows NT/2000 platforms, it runs as a separate service process, which by default has an "Automatic" startup option. Since WinMgmt.exe depends on WinComn.dll (also installed in %SystemRoot%\System32\Wbem), which actually implements most of the WMI functionality, under Windows XP, WMI runs as a service host process. For such processes where the functionality is provided by a DLL, Windows XP supplies a generic svchost.exe service executable, which loads the DLL on startup and exposes its functionality via standard service interfaces. Finally, under Windows 98, WMI runs as a standard executable. It is possible, however, to configure WMI to start automatically, even on Windows 98, by doing the following:

1. Set the HKLM\SOFTWARE\MICROSOFT\OLE\EnableDCOM registry value to "Y."

2. Set the HKLM\SOFTWARE\MICROSOFT\OLE\EnableRemoteConnect registry value to "Y."

3. Add the HKLM\SOFTWARE\MICROSOFT\WBEM\CIMOM\AutostartWin9X registry key with value of "1" (which means that there will be an automatic start).

4. Add WinMgmt.exe to the system startup directory.

The WinMgmt.exe can also be run manually from the command prompt, in which case it may be used to perform certain maintenance tasks. Table 1-1 lists the command line switches available in WinMgmt.exe and explains their purpose.

Table 1-1. WinMgmt.exe Command-Line Options

COMMAND-LINE SWITCH	DESCRIPTION
/exe	This switch makes WinMgmt.exe run as a standard executable rather than as a service. The primary purpose of this switch is to facilitate the debugging of custom WMI data providers.
/kill	This switch shuts down all the WinMgmt.exe processes that are running on a local computer system, including the service processes started by the Service Control Manager as well as the processes started manually with the /exe switch.
/regserver	This switch registers WinMgmt.exe with the Service Control Manager as a Windows service. This is a standard switch that is normally implemented by all services.
/unregserver	This switch unregisters WinMgmt.exe as a Windows service. This is a standard switch that is normally implemented by all services.
/backup <filename>	This is a repository maintenance function that causes WinMgmt.exe to back up its CIM Repository to a file, named by the <filename> argument. Using this flag will lock the repository in exclusive mode and suspend all pending write requests until the backup operation is completed.
/restore <filename>	This is a repository maintenance function that allows for manual restoration of the CIM Repository from the file, named by the <filename> argument. When run with this flag, WinMgmt.exe will delete the existing repository file, lock the repository in exclusive mode (which may necessitate disconnecting all existing client connections to WMI), and load the contents of the backup file into the repository.
/resyncperf <winmgmt service process id>	This flag is only available on Windows 2000 and Windows XP and is used to invoke the AutoDiscovery/AutoPurge (ADAP) mechanism. ADAP is used to transfer the performance counters from registered performance libraries into WMI classes in the CIM Repository so that these counters may be accessed as WMI object properties.
/clearadap	This is another ADAP-related flag that effectively clears all ADAP status and configuration information.

As Figure 1-1 implies, WinMgmt.exe (CIMOM) communicates with the rest of the world through a set of well-defined COM interfaces. In fact, all of the WMI functionality is exposed through COM interfaces; this allows the developers to reap the advantages of component-based programming, such as language and location independence. This means that each of many different WMI objects inherits the interfaces, ultimately derived from IUnknown, and complies with COM-imposed rules for memory management, method call parameter manipulation, and thread handling.

WMI defines many different interfaces that are designed to deal with different aspects of its functionality; most of these are declared in the wbemcli.h header file. In addition to COM API, which is mainly used by C++ developers, WMI supplies a set of automation interfaces; these interfaces enable the scripting clients (for example, programs written in scripting languages such as VBScript, JavaScript, or Perl) to consume most of the WMI functionality. Most of these automation interfaces simply duplicate the functionality available through the primary COM API. For instance, automation interface ISWbemLocator, which is used to obtain a reference to SWSbemServices object (an entry point to WMI), reflects the functionality afforded by the IWbemLocator interface of the primary COM API. Both of these interfaces expose a single method, ConnectServer, which connects to WMI on a given computer system.

Much of the WMI configuration information is stored in the Windows Registry under the key HKLM\SOFTWARE\MICROSOFT\WBEM\CIMOM. Coincidentally, WMI provides the Win32_WMISetting class as part of its schema so that each property of this class maps to a respective configuration value in the system registry. Listing 1-4 shows the MOF definition of the Win32_WMISetting class.

Listing 1-4. Win32_WMISetting Class Definition

```
class Win32_WMISetting : CIM_Setting
{
  string ASPScriptDefaultNamespace  ;
  boolean ASPScriptEnabled  ;
  string AutorecoverMofs[]  ;
  uint32 AutoStartWin9X
  uint32 BackupInterval  ;
  datetime BackupLastTime  ;
  string BuildVersion  ;
  string DatabaseDirectory  ;
  uint32 DatabaseMaxSize  ;
  boolean EnableAnonWin9xConnections  ;
  boolean EnableEvents  ;
  boolean EnableStartupHeapPreallocation  ;
  uint32 HighThresholdOnClientObjects  ;
  uint32 HighThresholdOnEvents  ;
```

```
    string InstallationDirectory  ;
    uint32 LastStartupHeapPreallocation  ;
    string LoggingDirectory  ;
    uint32 LoggingLevel  ;
    uint32 LowThresholdOnClientObjects  ;
    uint32 LowThresholdOnEvents  ;
    uint32 MaxLogFileSize  ;
    uint32 MaxWaitOnClientObjects  ;
    uint32 MaxWaitOnEvents  ;
    string MofSelfInstallDirectory  ;
};
```

Table 1-2 provides an explanation of every property of Win32_WMISetting and indicates the respective registry subkey (relative to HKLM\SOFTWARE\MICROSOFT\WBEM) to which a property maps.

Table 1-2. Win32_WMISetting *Properties*

WIN32_WMISETTING PROPERTY	REGISTRY MAPPING	DESCRIPTION
ASPScriptDefaultNamespace	Scripting\Default Namespace	Contains the default namespace, used by the scripting API calls in case the caller does not explicitly provide the namespace. Usually set to "root\CIMV2".
ASPScriptEnabled	Scripting\Enable for ASP	Determines whether WMI scripting API can be used by Active Server Pages (ASP) scripts. This property is only applicable to Windows NT systems, since under Windows 2000 and later, WMI scripting for ASP is always enabled.
AutorecoverMofs	CIMOM\Autorecover MOFs	Ordered list of MOF file names, used to initialize or recover the WMI Repository.
AutostartWin9X	CIMOM\AutostartWin9X	Determines how Windows 98 systems should start WinMgmt.exe: 0—Do not start 1—Autostart 2—Start on reboot

(continued)

Table 1-2. Win32_WMISetting *Properties (continued)*

WIN32_WMISETTING PROPERTY	REGISTRY MAPPING	DESCRIPTION
BackupInterval	CIMOM\Backup Interval Threshold	Time interval (in minutes) between the backups of the WMI Repository.
BackupLastTime	No registry mapping	Date and time of the last backup of the WMI Repository.
BuildVersion	Build	Version number of the WMI service installed on the system.
DatabaseDirectory	CIMOM\Repository Directory	Directory path of the WMI Repository.
DatabaseMaxSize	CIMOM\Max DB Size	Maximum allowed size (in KB) of the WMI Repository.
EnableAnonWin9xConnections	CIMOM\EnableAnonConnections	Determines whether remote access may bypass security checking. This property is only applicable on Windows 98 systems.
EnableEvents	CIMOM\EnableEvents	Determines whether the WMI event subsystem should be enabled.
EnableStartupHeapPreallocation	CIMOM\EnableStartupHeapPreallocation	If set to TRUE, forces WMI to preallocate a memory heap on startup with the size of LastStartupHeap-Preallocation.

(continued)

Table 1-2. Win32_WMISetting *Properties (continued)*

WIN32_WMISETTING PROPERTY	REGISTRY MAPPING	DESCRIPTION
HighThresholdOnClientObjects differences in	CIMOM\High Threshold On Client Objects	To reconcile the processing speed between the providers and the clients, WMI queues objects before handing them out to consumers. If the size of the queue reaches this threshold, WMI stops accepting the objects from providers and returns an "out of memory" error to the clients.
HighThresholdOnEvents differences in	CIMOM\High Threshold On Events	To reconcile the processing speed between the providers and the clients, WMI queues events before delivering them to consumers. If the size of the queue reaches this threshold, WMI stops accepting the events from providers and returns an "out of memory" error to the clients.
InstallationDirectory	Installation Directory	Directory path of the WMI software installation. By default, set to %SystemRoot%\System32\Wbem.
LastStartupHeapPreallocation	CIMOM\LastStartupHeapPreallocation	Size of the memory heap (in bytes) that was preallocated at startup.
LoggingDirectory	CIMOM\Logging Directory	Directory path to the location of WMI system logs.
LoggingLevel	CIMOM\Logging	Level of WMI event logging: 0—Off 1—Error logging on 2—Verbose error logging on

(continued)

Table 1 2. `Win32_WMISetting` *Properties (continued)*

WIN32_WMISETTING PROPERTY	REGISTRY MAPPING	DESCRIPTION
LowThresholdOnClientObjects	CIMOM\Low Threshold On Client Objects	To reconcile the differences in processing speed between the providers and the clients, WMI queues objects before handing them out to consumers. If the size of the queue reaches this threshold, WMI slows down the creation of the objects to accommodate the client's speed.
LowThresholdOnEvents	CIMOM\Low Threshold On Events	To reconcile the differences in processing speed between the providers and the clients, WMI queues events before delivering them out to consumers. If the size of the queue reaches this threshold, WMI slows down the delivery of the events to accommodate the client's speed.
MaxLogFileSize	CIMOM\Log File Max Size	Maximum size of the log file produced by the WMI service.
MaxWaitOnClientObjects	CIMOM\Max Wait On Client Objects	Length of time a new object waits to be used by the client before it is discarded by WMI.
MaxWaitOnEvents	CIMOM\Max Wait On Events	Length of time an event, sent to the client, is queued before it is discarded by WMI.
MofSelfInstallDirectory	MOF Self-Install Directory	Directory path to extension MOF files. WMI automatically compiles all the MOF files that are placed into a directory that is designated by this property, and depending on the outcome of the compilation, moves the files into a "good" or "bad" subdirectory.

The `Win32_WMISetting` class offers a convenient way to access and modify WMI configuration settings and, for reasons that are obvious, using this class is superior to accessing the WMI-related portion of the registry directly. First, there is no guarantee that future releases of WMI will still keep the configuration data in the system registry, so any management application that relies on the presence of certain registry entries may easily break. Using the interface of the `Win32_WMISetting` class, on the other hand, ensures the data location transparency. Since the interface is immutable, only the underlying implementation of the `Win32_Setting` class would have to change in order to accommodate changes to the storage location of WMI configuration parameters. For example, you may have noticed that one of the properties of `Win32_WMISetting` class, `BackupLastTime`, does not have the corresponding registry entry; instead WMI dynamically determines its value by examining the timestamp of the repository backup file. The advantage of using the `Win32_WMISetting` class is clear—an application interested in retrieving the value of `BackupLastTime` property does not have to be concerned with the implementation details and may simply read the object property. Finally, accessing the registry directly and especially modifying the keys and values is notoriously error-prone and may result in data corruption.

Using WMI-provided interfaces is not only a more elegant approach, but it is also much safer and leaves fewer chances for fatal mistakes. As you will see shortly, reading and manipulating the management data through WMI is not too difficult—in fact, it may even be simpler than programmatically accessing the registry, so writing a small management utility to query and set the WMI configuration data is fairly trivial.

If you are less adventurous and do not find building WMI management utilities too exciting, you can use Microsoft's Management Console (MMC) WMI Control Properties snap-in (see Figure 1-2)—this nice little graphical interface allows you to view and modify most of the WMI-related registry settings.

This snap-in features five tabs, each designed to administer different aspects of WMI behavior.

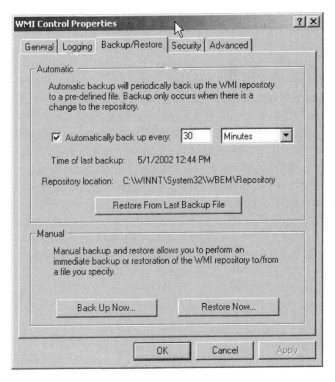

Figure 1-2. The WMI Control Properties MMC snap-in

The General tab: This tab just houses a login prompt that allows you to connect to WMI using the identity of an arbitrary user.

The Logging tab: This tab is a bit more interesting because it controls the logging features of WMI, such as the logging level, the location, and the maximum allowed size of the log file. These controls map to the LoggingLevel, LoggingDirectory, and MaxLogFileSize properties of the Win32_WMISetting class.

The Backup/Restore tab: This tab, shown in Figure 1-2, controls the repository backups. By default, the CIM repository is automatically backed up every 30 minutes. Using this tab, you can perform a manual backup or restore the repository.

The Security tab: This tab lets you set access-level permissions for each WMI namespace. The interface for setting up the permission is similar to the one you use to administer file and directory structure permissions in Windows.

The Advanced tab: This last tab, for some mysterious reason labeled "Advanced," allows you to change the value of the `ASPScriptDefaultNamespace` property of the `Win32_WMISetting`.

The WMI Control MMC snap-in is usually all you need to control most of the WMI configuration parameters; however, there are some important aspects of the WMI behavior that it does not address. For instance, you cannot view or change some properties, such as the size of the heap and various thresholds, with the MMC snap-in; if you are interested in these properties, you will have to use either your registry editor or a custom management utility to alter them.

WMI Repository

As Table 1-2 shows, the location of the CIM Repository is either identified by the DatabaseDirectory property of `Win32_WMISetting` class or pointed to by a key `HKLM\SOFTWARE\MICROSOFT\WBEM\CIMOM\Repository` Directory in the system registry. The repository location is usually set to `%SystemRoot%\System32\WBEM\Repository`. The repository itself is implemented as a single file named `CIM.REP`. As I already mentioned, it contains just the WMI schema information as well as some static instance data, so that the size of the repository file is not very large (usually just a few megabytes).

If you wish to extend the WMI schema you will need to provide the MOF definitions for your classes in a form of text files with the .mof extension. You can then load these files into the CIM Repository using either the command line utility mofcomp.exe (MOF compiler) or the WMI COM API. You also have the option of placing the MOF files for your schema extensions into a specially designated self-install directory, pointed to by the `MofSelfInstallDirectory` property of the `Win32_WMISetting` or the registry key `HKLM\SOFTWARE\MICROSOFT\WBEM\MOF Self-Install Directory`. By default, the location of this self-install directory is set to `%SystemRoot%\System32\Wbem\Mof`. Each MOF file placed into this directory is automatically compiled by WMI. If the compilation yields no errors, the file is acknowledged as "good" and moved to the good subdirectory of the self-install directory. If the compilation fails, the file is moved to the bad subdirectory.

If the repository becomes corrupted, you may have to restore it from the latest backup. However, this backup may not include the definition for those schema extensions that were loaded into the repository after it was last backed up. If this is the case, you may have to manually recompile and load the extension MOFs into the repository. To facilitate the restoration of the extension schemas, the WMI MOF compiler allows you to specify a special preprocessor command—#pragma autorecover in the source MOF file. When it encounters this pragma, the MOF compiler will add the fully qualified name of the MOF file to the autorecover list that was pointed to by the AutorecoverMofs property of the Win32_WMISetting or the registry key HKLM\SOFTWARE\MICROSOFT\WBEM\CIMOM\Autorecover MOFs. Then every time the repository is recovered, WMI will compile all of the MOF files on the autorecover list and load them into the repository, thus ensuring that the repository contains all the latest extension definitions.

When talking about WMI class and object naming conventions, I mentioned that a particular WBEM implementation might have multiple namespace instances, uniquely identified by their respective namespace handles. If you closely examine the WMI repository, you will see that WMI utilizes multiple namespace instances that are organized into a hierarchical structure. WMI documentation simply refers to these namespace instances as namespaces, so in order to avoid confusion, I will use the same terminology from now on. Multiple namespaces within WMI serve the purpose of logically grouping related classes and they do nothing more than just provide the scope for name resolution. A typical WMI installation has the following namespaces:

> **root**: This namespace is at the very top of the WMI namespace hierarchy and its primary purpose is to contain other namespaces.

> **root\DEFAULT**: The DEFAULT namespace holds most of the system classes, most of which are of little interest to a typical application developer.

> **root\CIMV2**: The CIMV2 namespace contains the classes and instances of classes that represent the elements in the managed environment. The name CIMV2 stands for Common Information Model Version 2.0, which implies that this namespace contains all of the classes specified by CIMv2.0 as well as any additional Win32 specific classes and instances. A typical management application will primarily be concerned with the contents of the root\CIMV2 namespace.

A particular WMI installation may also supply some additional namespaces; the extensions schemas, for instance, are often placed in a separate namespace to avoid potential naming conflicts. Thus Microsoft Internet Explorer may provide some WMI classes, such as `MicrosoftIE_InternetExplorer`, which are usually placed into the `Applications\MicrosoftIE` namespace within the `root\CIMV2` namespace. You may also see `ms_409` or other similarly named namespaces within the `root\CIMV2` namespace or within any of the extension namespaces. These namespaces are used to segregate the localized versions of WMI classes; in fact, the name "ms_409" is just a locale identifier. Microsoft locale identifiers take the form of "MS_XXXX" where "XXXX" is a hexadecimal locale string or Locale Identifier (LCID), so that "ms_409" stands for "American English".

Each WMI namespace contains a `__NAMESPACE` system class (notice the double underscore, which is the class naming convention for system classes); this is so that each instance of this class describes a single subordinate namespace. For example, the root namespace will contain at least two instances of the `__NAMESPACE` class: one for `root\DEFAULT` and one for `root\CIMV2`. The `__NAMESPACE` class is very simple and contains just a few useful properties, such as the name of the respective namespace, its full and relative paths, and the name of the computer system on which it resides. Nevertheless, this class is very convenient because it allows the developer to quickly determine the count and the names of all subordinate namespaces by simply enumerating the instances of the `__NAMESPACE` class.

If you closely inspect the objects in the WMI repository, you will see that every object, regardless of its class, has a number of system properties, which, by convention, are prefixed with double underscores. None of the MOF examples presented so far included these properties; in fact, none of the MOF files distributed with WMI include these properties either. Instead, the system properties are automatically added by WMI as part of the object creation process. The main purpose of these system properties is to identify a particular object and determine its place within the WMI class hierarchy. Table 1-3 shows all available system properties.

Table 1-3. WMI System Properties

PROPERTY	DESCRIPTION
__CLASS	The name of the class the object belongs to. This is a read-only property. Example: for an instance of Win32_NTEventlogFile, __CLASS is set to Win32_NTEventlogFile.
__DERIVATION	A list of class names, showing the inheritance hierarchy of a given class. The first element is the immediate superclass; the next one is its parent, and so on. This is a read-only property. Example: for an instance of Win32_NTEventlogFile, __DERIVATION is set to (CIM_DataFile, CIM_LogicalFile, CIM_LogicalElement, CIM_ManagedSystemElement).
__DYNASTY	The name of the top-level class from which the class is ultimately derived. This is a read-only property. Example: for an instance of Win32_NTEventlogFile, __DYNASTY is set to CIM_ManagedSystemElement.
__GENUS	A numeric value that is used to distinguish between classes and instances of a class. The value of '1' represents class and '2' represents instance. This is a read-only property. Example: for an instance of Win32_NTEventlogFIle, __GENUS is set to '2'.
__NAMESPACE	The name of the namespace to which the class belongs. This is a read-only property. Example: for an instance of Win32_NTEventlogFile, __NAMESPACE is set to root\CIMV2.
__PATH	The full path to the class or instance. This is a read-only property. Example: for an instance of the Win32_NTEventlogFile class, __PATH is set to \\machine1\root\CIMV2:Win32_NTEventlogFile.
__PROPERTY_COUNT	A number reflecting the total count of non-system properties, defined for the class. This is a read only property. Example: for an instance of the Win32_NTEventlogFile class, __PROPERTY_COUNT is set to 39.
__RELPATH	A path to the class or instance, relative to the namespace. This is a read-only property. Example: for an instance of the Win32_NTEventlogFile class, __RELPATH is set to Win32_NTEventlogFile.
__SERVER	The name of the server that supplies the class or instance. This is a read-only property. Example: for an instance of the Win32_NTEventlogFile, __SERVER is set to machine1.
__SUPERCLASS	The name of the immediate superclass for a class or instance. This is a read only property. Example: for an instance of Win32_NTEventlogFile, __SUPERCLASS is set to CIM_DataFile.

WMI Data Providers

As powerful and sophisticated as the CIM Object Manager looks, it is just a middle-man whose primary responsibility is to communicate with data providers on behalf of client applications. Thus the task of manipulating the actual managed elements represented via WMI classes, objects, properties, and events, such as retrieving or updating the management information, is left to the data providers. For instance, if a client application asks CIMOM to retrieve a value of the `DatabaseDirectory` property of the `Win32_WMISetting` object, CIMOM delegates the handling of this request to a standard WMI registry provider, which, when the request is acknowledged, reads and returns the value of the `HKLM\SOFTWARE\MICROSOFT\WBEM\CIMOM\Repository Directory` registry entry.

Not all providers are created equal, and depending on the type of functionality exposed and the types of requests serviced, the providers can be categorized as follows:

Instance providers: The instance providers are, perhaps, the most common type of WMI providers; their primary purpose is to supply instances of a given class and support such operations as instance retrieval, enumeration, modification, and deletion, as well as query processing. For instance, the Event Log Provider (which provides access to the Windows Event Log data and event notifications) acts as an instance provider since it supplies the instances of the `Win32_NTEventlogFile` class, which represent the system event log.

Class providers: The only purpose of class providers is to provide applications with class definitions. You only need this if you are going to dynamically generate class definitions and they are affected by factors outside of WMI. In most of the cases, these class definitions are static, and once they are placed into the CIM repository, they never or rarely change; that is why class providers are rare. Yet another reason to avoid class providers is that they have an adverse effect on the performance of WMI; this is because in order to retrieve a definition for a class, CIMOM has to contact the provider rather than just read the repository. Sometimes, however, using class providers is unavoidable; they have to be used despite the performance penalty that they incur. One example of this is when you have to use the Active Directory Services provider dsprov.dll, which enables WMI applications to interoperate with Microsoft Active Directory Service Interfaces (ADSI). Due to the dynamic nature of the information housed by Active Directory, storing the data in the CIM Repository is not practical.

Property providers: As the name implies, the property providers retrieve and modify the values of instance properties. As opposite to instance providers, property providers allow the client to manipulate the values of individual properties rather than modifying the entire instance. The NT Event Log provider is also a property provider because it supports the operations on individual properties of `Win32_NTEventlogFile` instances.

Method providers: The method providers implement the methods of a given class or a collection of classes. For example, the NT Event Log provider is a method provider because it implements the methods of the `Win32_NTEventlogFile` class (and other related classes) such as `Compress` or `Uncompress`.

Event providers: The event providers are responsible for delivering the event notifications that originate from their respective data sources to WMI CIMOM, which forwards these events to the interested applications. The Event Log provider, which is also an event provider, supports the `Win32_NTLogEvent` class that is used to represent the Windows events.

Event consumer providers: The event consumer providers are used to support the permanent event consumer architecture within WMI. Permanent consumer architecture enables the developers to implement permanent event consumers—also known as custom event sinks that are automatically invoked by WMI every time an event of interest is triggered. Thus, the primary responsibility of an event consumer provider is dispatching an event to be handled by the proper consumer sink. One example of an event consumer provider that comes with WMI distribution is the WMI Event Viewer.

In addition to being classified in one of the categories just mentioned, providers may be categorized as push or pull providers, based on the nature of their interactions with the rest of the WMI infrastructure. *Push providers* typically manage the data that is fairly static and does not change frequently. At initialization time, a push provider simply stores its data in the CIM Repository so that each client request can be serviced directly by CIMOM without incurring the overhead that is the result of communicating with the provider. Not only does this push approach significantly simplify the provider development (because providers are not required to implement their own data retrieval or event notification services), but it is also very efficient since CIMOM is optimized for retrieving the data from the repository.

Unfortunately, storing large amounts of frequently changing data in the repository is not practical; therefore, the vast majority of data providers are implemented as pull providers. *Pull providers* respond to requests from CIMOM by either dynamically generating the data or by retrieving the data from some kind of local cache that is maintained by the provider itself. Although this model supports handling large amounts of dynamic data, it lacks the efficiency and significantly complicates the programming of WMI providers.

There are two parts to provider implementation: a section of the WMI schema that describes the managed elements that are supported by the provider; and the provider DLLs that contain the implementation code. The Windows Event Log provider, for example, is implemented as a single DLL, ntevt.dll, and is usually installed in %SystemRoot%\System32\Wbem. The WMI classes supported by this provider, such as Win32_NTEventlogFile, Win32_NTLogEvent, and many more, are defined in ntevt.mof file, which can also be found in the %SystemRoot%\System32\Wbem directory.

As has already been mentioned, CIMOM communicates with providers through a set of well-defined COM interfaces. WMI requires providers to implement different interfaces based on the provider type. Push providers, for instance, are only required to implement the IWbemProviderInit provider initialization interface that is used by CIMOM whenever a provider is loaded. It is the responsibility of a push provider to ensure that the CIM Repository is updated with proper data when its initialization interface is invoked. When the initialization is complete and the repository contains the updated copy of the provider's data, WMI takes over and services all client requests itself, without invoking the provider.

The situation is different, however, for pull providers, which are required to implement a slew of other interfaces, depending on whether they act as instance, property, method, or event providers. A property provider, for instance, is obliged to implement the IWbemPropertyProvider interface, which exposes methods for getting and setting the values of object properties. The methods of this interface are invoked by CIMOM whenever a client issues a property retrieval or modification request. Just like the CIMOM COM interfaces described earlier, most of the provider interfaces are declared in the wbemcli.h header file.

Since COM is the sole communication vehicle between CIMOM and the data providers, the providers are registered with COM just like any other COM objects. However, in order for WMI to dispatch a client request to a proper provider, it has to maintain its own provider registration database. Thus, each WMI provider is described by a static instance of the __Win32Provider system class, which resides in the CIM Repository. Instances of this system class contain just the basic provider identification information, such as the Class Identifier (CLSID) of the COM object and the provider name.

To identify the provider as instance, property, method, or event provider, WMI maintains a collection of class instances that are derived from

__ProviderRegistration. An instance provider, for example, is represented by a static instance of the __InstanceProviderRegistration class; a method provider is represented by __MethodProviderRegistration, and so on. Each of the subclasses of the __ProviderRegistration class has at least one property—a reference to a respective instance of the __Win32Provider class—although some subclasses may have other type-specific properties that indicate whether a provider supports certain functionality. Thus, if WMI knows the name and the type of the required provider, it may quickly look up an appropriate instance of the __ProviderRegistration subclass, determine its capabilities, and follow its provider reference to retrieve the corresponding instance of the __Win32Provider class that contains all the information it needs to invoke the methods of this provider.

Provider-based architecture is, perhaps, the key to the extensibility of WMI. The well-defined interfaces that WMI uses to communicate with providers allow third-party vendors to instrument their applications by providing extension schemas and custom provider DLLs. WMI distribution comes with a number of built-in providers that usually cover the management needs of a rather sophisticated computing environment sufficiently. The following are examples of some of these providers:

NT Event Log Provider: This supplies Windows Event Log data and notifications of Windows events.

Performance Counters Provider: This enables management applications to access the performance counters' raw data.

Registry provider: This provides access to the data stored in the system registry.

Win32 Driver Model (WDM) provider: This provides access to data and events that are maintained by Windows device drivers and conforms to WMI interface specifications.

Win32 provider: This acts as an interface to a Win32 subsystem.

SNMP provider: This enables WMI applications to interoperate with SNMP.

Of these providers, the SNMP provider is especially interesting because it is actually an adapter that allows data and events, maintained by a legacy management system, to be incorporated into WMI.

The main challenge of making WMI interoperate with SNMP is figuring out how to represent the SNMP data in a CIM-compliant fashion. SNMP maintains its own database of managed objects, called Management Information Base (MIB). MIB is a collection of files that describe the management data using the Abstract Syntax Notation (ASN) language, which is quite different from MOF. To address this difference, the developers of an SNMP provider offer two possible approaches. The first is to use the SNMP information module compiler, which transforms the MIBs into a format understood by WMI so that the output of the compilation can be loaded into the CIM Repository. Once the SNMP-managed objects are defined in WMI, SNMP instance and event providers map the WMI requests into SNMP operations and present the SNMP traps as WMI events. The second approach (which is a bit less efficient) is to make use of the SNMP class provider. This provider generates dynamic SNMP class definitions on request from WMI. With this approach, efficiency is sacrificed to increase flexibility because none of the SNMP MIBs need to be manually compiled and loaded into CIM.

Regardless of the integration approach chosen, the SNMP provider makes SNMP-managed objects appear as an integral part of the WMI universe, thus fulfilling the promise of WBEM founders—seamless integration with legacy management standards and protocols.

Introducing System.Management Namespace

From the day WMI was introduced, the developers that wished to access Windows management resources and services had a choice. They could either use the native WMI COM interfaces or they could use its scripting API. Unfortunately, neither of these two options was completely problem-free. Though the COM API offered virtually unlimited power, high performance, and access to even the most obscure features of WMI, it was, after all, just another COM API. As such, it remained completely inaccessible to millions of those poor developers and system administrators who never managed to overcome the COM's steep learning curve.

The scripting API partly solved this problem bringing the joy of WMI to an audience that was much wider than just a bunch of skilled C++ programmers. However, even the scripting, despite its simplicity and adequate power, did not appear to be a complete solution to the problem. First, it was not fast enough. This was because the dispatch interfaces that were necessary for scripting clients did not offer the same speed as the native COM API. Second, the scripting API lacked power and covered only a limited subset of WMI functionality. In fact, certain things, such as provider programming, remained outside the realm of script developers and still required the use of native COM interfaces.

The rollout of the Microsoft .NET Platform took the world of software development by storm. It is rapidly (and hopefully forever) changing the Windows programming paradigm. Programmatic access to WMI was one of the million things that has been radically affected by .NET. Using .NET you can completely replace both the native COM and the scripting APIs. In the true spirit of .NET, the new WMI interface combines the best features of the older APIs; it merges the performance and unlimited power of the native COM API with accessibility and simplicity of the scripting interface.

There are two parts to the .NET Platform: the .NET Framework and the Framework Class Library (FCL). While the Framework, which supports such modern programming concepts as automatic garbage collection, seamless language interoperability, and much more, is definitely the enabling technology behind .NET, it remains fairly transparent to a casual developer.

The FCL, on the other hand, is something that a programmer will immediately appreciate; it exposes thousands of classes or types that address nearly every aspect of Windows programming. There are types that deal with GUI and Web Interface development, types that are designed to make working with structured and unstructured data easier, and, most importantly, there are types that are dedicated solely to interfacing with WMI. The entire FCL is structured so that functionally related types are organized into a hierarchy of namespaces. For instance, types that are used to build Windows GUI applications are grouped into the System.Windows.Forms namespace. The namespace that holds all the types that you need to interact with WMI is called System.Management. The most important types, contained in the System.Management namespace, are the following:

> ManagementObject: This is a fundamental abstraction that is used to represent a single instance of a managed element in the enterprise.

> ManagementClass: This is a type that corresponds to a class of a managed object as defined by WMI.

> ManagementObjectSearcher: This type is used to retrieve collections of ManagementObject or ManagementClass objects that satisfy particular criteria specified by a WQL query or enumeration.

> ManagementQuery: This type is used as a basis for building queries, used to retrieve collections of ManagementObject or ManagementClass objects.

> ManagementEventWatcher: This is a type that allows you to subscribe for WMI event notifications.

Nested inside the System.Management namespace, there is a System.Management.Instrumentation namespace that contains types that are used primarily when you instrument .NET applications. These types allow application developers to use WMI to expose the management data relevant to their applications as well as their application-originated events; this process makes these events and data accessible to a wide variety of management clients.

Because the .NET model used to expose the management applications is mainly declarative, you will not need to use much coding. The System.Management.Instrumentation namespace includes a number of attribute types; developers can use these to describe their managed objects and classes to WMI using simple declarations. In addition to these attributes, this namespace defines a number of schema types that are designed to serve as base types for custom managed classes. These schema types already include all necessary attribution so that WMI immediately recognizes any custom type that uses a schema type as its parent.

As the next few chapters will show, the .NET System.Management types offer enough building blocks to solve nearly any system management problem, and backed by the power and flexibility of the .NET Framework, these types are likely to become the ultimate platform that will be used to develop future management applications. While the Framework addresses such general programming issues as automatic memory management, language interoperability, security, and distribution and maintenance ease, the System.Management namespace of the FCL brings the following benefits to the developers of management applications:

Consistent object-oriented programming model: As is most of the FCL, the System.Management namespace is organized in a very consistent fashion and exposes a well designed object model, which is both natural and easy to understand. The types are well thought-out logical abstractions that are not affected by the peculiarities of the WMI inner workings; as a result they are fairly self-describing and comprehensible. The overall programming paradigm is consistent with the rest of the .NET programming model. This consistency makes it so that .NET developers do not need to learn new skills in order to start programming management applications.

Relative simplicity: Unlike COM programming, in .NET, developers no longer have to take care of the low-level plumbing, such as memory management via reference counting. Instead, they can concentrate on the problem domain. The .NET programming model not only greatly minimizes the amount of boilerplate code for which the developers are responsible, but it also reduces the level of complexity to match that of the legacy WMI scripting API.

Uncompromised performance: When compared to the WMI scripting interface, the .NET System.Management types offer a significant performance enhancement. This is because you no longer a need to use the inefficient dispatch interfaces in order to access the WMI functionality. However, this does not mean that the System.Management types completely solve the performance problems associated with WMI. Unfortunately, some of these performance problems have little to do with the API used by the client applications. The dynamic class providers, for example, are inherently slow and no matter how fast a client application may be able to process the data, the overall efficiency is still hampered by the necessity to generate the class definitions on the fly. Nevertheless, .NET System.Management types offer a significant performance improvement over the less efficient scripting clients.

Tight integration with .NET: The types of System.Management namespace are an integral part of FCL and as a result, they comply with all the .NET programming principles and interoperate seamlessly with the types in other namespaces. Typically, even the simplest management application still has to possess some basic user interface capabilities and may request the operating system or I/O subsystem services. Thus, the FCL offers a complete end-to-end solution to the entire universe of programming problems by making thousands of uniformly designed types available. These types adhere to consistent naming conventions, all use the same error handling protocol, feature the same event dispatching and notification mechanism, and most importantly, are designed to work together.

So with a complete arsenal of powerful tools at their disposal, programmers can build and deploy large-scale enterprise management systems.

As you can see, the .NET System.Management types represent an important step toward turning Microsoft Windows into the number one enterprise-computing platform. However, so far I have still yet to answer a couple of questions: How exactly do these types interact with WMI? Also, did Microsoft intend to replace some or all of the WMI infrastructure with .NET-compliant implementation, or was the System.Management namespace designed to work in concert with the existing WMI components? The best way to answer these questions is by taking a closer look at how the System.Management types are implemented.

As I already mentioned, the main COM interface that the client and provider applications use to access WMI is IWbemServices. This interface exposes a slew of methods that let you issue queries so that you can retrieve collections of classes and instances, create and delete instances, update instance properties, and

execute methods. Thus, perhaps the first thing you would want to do with any
WMI application is make sure that it gets hold of an object that implements the
IWbemServices interface. Listing 1-5 shows a common coding pattern that you
can use to retrieve an IWbemServices interface pointer. Note that for the sake of
simplicity, this example does not implement the proper error checking and does
not include the code necessary to initialize the variables used in the method
calls.

Listing 1-5. Retrieving an IWbemServices *Interface Pointer*

```
IWbemLocator   *pIWbemLocator = NULL;
IWbemServices *pIWbemServices = NULL;

CoCreateInstance(CLSID_WbemLocator,
                 NULL,
                 CLSCTX_INPROC_SERVER,
                 IID_IWbemLocator,
                 (LPVOID *) &pIWbemLocator);
...
pIWbemLocator->ConnectServer(pNamespace,
                 NULL,
                 NULL,
                 0L,
                 0L,
                 NULL,
                 NULL,
                 &pIWbemServices);
```

Here the client application first creates an instance of WbemLocator class,
which you then use to retrieve the IWbemServices interface pointer. The
WbemLocator class implements the IWbemLocator interface, which has a single
method, ConnectServer. The purpose of this method is to establish a connection
to WMI services on a particular host. This method takes several parameters,
namely the full path of the namespace to which the client application wishes to
connect (pNamespace), the address of the memory location that will hold the
IWbemServices interface pointer (pIWbemServices), and a few security-related
arguments, which our example ignores completely. When the ConnectServer
method finishes successfully, the pIWbemServices variable will contain a valid
IWbemServices interface pointer that you can use as a main point of access to
WMI services and resources.

Now let's see how a typical .NET application accomplishes the same task
of connecting to WMI. The type in the System.Management namespace that is
responsible for connecting to WMI is ManagementScope, and Listing 1-6 shows the

disassembly of the class definition and one of its methods, called `InitializeGuts`. The disassembly listing, which contains Microsoft Intermediate Language (MSIL) instructions, was produced using ILDASM.EXE utility, distributed as part of the .NET Framework SDK.. The MSIL instruction sequences may look quite intimidating at first; however, given the limited amount of documentation that comes with .NET, disassembling various parts of FCL is an excellent source of in-depth information, pertinent to the implementation of certain .NET features. Throughout the course of this book, I will occasionally resort to using such disassembly listings to help you better understand the underpinnings of the `System.Management` types. The disassembly listing, presented here, is not a complete implementation of the `ManagementScope` type or its `InitializeGuts` method—for the sake of simplicity, only the code fragments relevant to the WMI connection establishment process are shown.

Listing 1-6. Disassembly of the `InitializeGuts` *Method of the* `ManagementScope` *Type*

```
.class public auto ansi beforefieldinit ManagementScope
        extends [mscorlib]System.Object
        implements [mscorlib]System.ICloneable
{
  ...
    .field private class System.Management.IWbemServices wbemServices
  ...
    .method private hidebysig instance void
            InitializeGuts() cil managed
    {
      // Code size        268 (0x10c)
      .maxstack  9
      .locals init (
                class System.Management.IWbemLocator V_0,
                string V_1,
                bool V_2,
                class System.Management.SecurityHandler V_3,
                int32 V_4,
                class [mscorlib]System.Exception V_5)

        newobj      instance void System.Management.WbemLocator::.ctor()
        stloc.0
  ...
        ldflda      class System.Management.IWbemServices
                System.Management.ManagementScope::wbemServices
        callvirt    instance int32
          System.Management.IWbemLocator::ConnectServer_(
```

```
        string,
        string,
        string,
        string,
        int32,
        string,
        class System.Management.IWbemContext,
        class System.Management.IWbemServices&)
    ...
    }
    ...
}
```

The first important thing you should notice about Listing 1-6 is that there is a private member variable wbemServices of type System.Management.IWbem Services declared using the .field directive at the beginning of the class definition. This variable has been designed to hold what appears to be a reference to an instance of IWbemServices type. Also, at the very beginning of the InitializeGuts method, notice that a local variable of type System.Management.IwbemLocator is declared. This declaration marks a storage location that will hold a reference to the IWbemLocator instance. The first executable instruction of the InitializeGuts method, newobj, creates an instance of the System.Management.IWbemLocator type and invokes its constructor. When this operation finishes, the operands stack will hold a reference to a newly created instance of the IWbemLocator type. The method will now execute its next instruction, stloc.0. This pops the reference off the stack and stores it at the location that is designated by the first local variable declaration—V_0 of type System.Management.IWbemLocator. Then the code loads the wbemServices member variable's address on the stack using the ldflda instruction and calls the ConnectServer method of the IWbemServices type, which passes this address as one of the parameters. When the ConnectServer method returns, the wbemServices variable contains a valid reference to IWbemServices type.

The code described here is very similar to the native COM API code, shown previously in Listing 1-5; in fact, the interface usage pattern is the same! Now, the only thing that remains unclear is how the IWbemLocator and IWbemServices types are implemented in the System.Management namespace. Listing 1-7 should clear this up by showing the complete class declarations for System.Management.IWbemLocator and System.Management.IWbemServices types.

Listing 1-7. IWbemLocator *and* IWbemServices *Class Declarations*

```
.class interface private abstract auto ansi import IWbemLocator
{
  .custom instance void [mscorlib]
  System.Runtime.InteropServices.TypeLibTypeAttribute::.ctor(int16) =
```

```
  ( 01 00 00 02 00 00 )
  .custom instance void [mscorlib]
  System.Runtime.InteropServices.GuidAttribute::.ctor(string) =
  ( 01 00 24 44 43 31 32 41 36 38 37 2D 37 33 37 46 // ..$DC12A687-737F
    2D 31 31 43 46 2D 38 38 34 44 2D 30 30 41 41 30 // -11CF-884D-00AA0
    30 34 42 32 45 32 34 00 00 )                    // 04B2E24..
  .custom instance void [mscorlib]
  System.Runtime.InteropServices.InterfaceTypeAttribute::.ctor(int16) =
  ( 01 00 01 00 00 00 )
}

.class interface private abstract auto ansi import IWbemServices
{
  .custom instance void [mscorlib]
  System.Runtime.InteropServices.InterfaceTypeAttribute::.ctor(int16) =
  ( 01 00 01 00 00 00 )
  .custom instance void [mscorlib]
  System.Runtime.InteropServices.TypeLibTypeAttribute::.ctor(int16) =
  ( 01 00 00 02 00 00 )
  .custom instance void [mscorlib]
  System.Runtime.InteropServices.GuidAttribute::.ctor(string) =
  ( 01 00 24 39 35 35 36 44 43 39 39 2D 38 32 38 43 // ..$9556DC99-828C
    2D 31 31 43 46 2D 41 33 37 45 2D 30 30 41 41 30 // -11CF-A37E-00AA0
    30 33 32 34 30 43 37 00 00 )                    // 03240C7..
}
```

Interestingly, the declarations of both types happen to carry the import flag, which indicates that these types are not implemented in managed code. When the .NET runtime encounters a type marked with the import flag, it identifies a type as COM server and invokes its COM interoperability mechanism. Obviously, COM objects are quite different from the types implemented in managed code—they are allocated from the unmanaged heap and require explicit memory management. Thus, to accommodate a COM server, .NET runtime creates *Runtime Callable Wrappers (RCW)* for each instance of a COM object to be consumed by the managed code. An RCW is a managed object, allocated from the garbage-collected heap, that caches the actual reference-counted COM interface pointer so that .NET code treats it just like any other managed type. To the COM server, however, RCW looks like a conventional well-behaved COM client that adheres to all COM rules and restrictions.

In short, each time an instance of IWbemLocator or IWbemServices types is requested, the runtime silently creates an underlying COM object, allocates the corresponding RCW, and returns the reference to this RCW back to the requestor.

The last question to answer is how the runtime knows which COM object to allocate when the managed code requests an instance of IWbemLocator or IWbem-Services type. As you may have noticed, the declarations of both of these classes are decorated with several attributes—System.Runtime.InteropServices.GuidAttribute is one of these. You can then see that the constructor for this attribute takes a string parameter, which specifies the GUID of the COM server to be created. To no surprise, the inspection of the Windows registry shows that the COM objects, used here, are the same COM objects that are utilized when programming native COM API WMI applications.

As it turns out, the types of the System.Management namespace are by no means a complete reimplementation of the WMI access API. Instead, the entire .NET system management class library is just a clean, managed, object-oriented wrapper that is implemented on top of the existing COM WMI-access API.

Summary

This chapter has provided a comprehensive overview of the latest trends in enterprise system management, defined the main objectives of an ideal management system, and introduced a leading-edge management technology—Microsoft WMI. Although I did not intend to supply an exhaustive technical overview of all components that constitute WMI, I hope that the material presented in this chapter was enough to help you understand its most fundamental concepts. These are essential for grasping the material that I will present in the rest of this book. Armed with this knowledge, you should now be ready to delve into the intricacies of .NET WMI programming.

CHAPTER 2

Using the System.Management Namespace

Dʀɪᴠᴇɴ ʙʏ ᴛʜᴇ ᴅᴇsɪʀᴇ to make the bulk of WMI system management functions easily accessible to .NET developers, the designers of the System.Management namespace built quite a few powerful types that expose all but the most obscure aspects of WMI functionality. Housing more than 40 different classes, this namespace may look complex or even intimidating to a beginner or a casual observer. This seeming complexity, however, is just an illusion; in fact, most of the System.Management types are remarkably easy to use thanks to a well-defined structure and a well-thought-out design. I'm sure that once you spend some time programming .NET management applications, you will quickly overcome any initial confusion and grow to appreciate the elegance and straightforwardness of the System.Management object model.

The first thing that will help you to take the veil of complexity off the System.Management namespace is understanding that most of its types are auxiliary—they do not, by themselves, represent logical abstractions of WMI functionality. In fact, you will soon find yourself spending most of your time with two of the System.Management types: ManagementObject and ManagementClass. These two types reflect WMI objects and schema elements respectively. The rest of the types, although they are very useful and even indispensable at times, are just used to either obtain certain instances of the ManagementObject and ManagementClass types, or affect the behavior of these two types.

Since this chapter zeroes in on the methods and properties of ManagementObject and ManagementClass types, you may want to focus on the material presented here to understand the core of System.Management functionality and to become proficient at programming the management applications. While certain more complex or more specialized aspects of WMI programming are covered in subsequent chapters, the most fundamental concepts, such as navigating the CIM, reading and updating the management data, and analyzing the WMI schema, are presented here. In fact, the contents of this chapter alone should equip you with the skills necessary to build moderately complex system management tools.

ManagementObject: Retrieving the Management Information

The most fundamental type that the System.Management namespace exposes is called ManagementObject. This type represents a .NET view of an arbitrary WMI class instance. In other words, it corresponds to an actual managed element within a given environment. Once created, an instance of the ManagementObject type provides the methods and properties necessary to manipulate the management data associated with an instance of a given WMI class.

Binding to WMI Objects

Creating an instance of the ManagementObject type is remarkably easy. The following line of code produces a single unbound instance of this type using its parameterless constructor:

```
ManagementObject mo = new ManagementObject();
```

This instance of the ManagementObject type is not very useful unless it is linked to an arbitrary WMI class instance. In order to establish this association you must use the type's overloaded constructor; this constructor takes a single parameter of type String, which represents the object path. As outlined in Listing 1-3 of Chapter 1, a full object path consists of the name of the server, which hosts the WMI implementation; the namespace handle; the name of the WMI class; and a key-value pair, which uniquely identifies an instance. Using these components, the following code will create an instance of the ManagementObject type, associated with the instance of the Win32_ComputerSystem WMI class. This class resides in the root\CIMV2 namespace on the BCK_OFFICE machine and it is uniquely identified by the value of its Name property:

```
ManagementObject mo = new ManagementObject(
  @"\\BCK_OFFICE\root\CIMV2:Win32_ComputerSystem.Name='BCK_OFFICE'");
```

Often when you are developing a managed application you will want to work with WMI objects on your local machine. But because hardcoding the server name into a program is not a very flexible solution, you can substitute "." (which stands for the name of the local machine) for the server name. In fact, you don't need to include the name of the hosting server or "." in the object path at all; if you omit it, the local computer system will be the default server.

The namespace portion of the path is also optional and, if you omit it, root\CIMV2 will be the default. In our discussion of WMI settings in Chapter 1, you learned that the default value for the namespace is specified by the HKLM\SOFTWARE\MICROSOFT\WBEM\Scripting\Default Namespace registry setting. You may also recall that changing the registry value does not affect the namespace to which ManagementObject gets bound. This is because the default path is hardcoded in the ManagementPath type's static type constructor so that every time this type is loaded, its static property, DefaultPath, is set to \\.\root\CIMV2. During its initialization sequence, the ManagementObject type examines the supplied object path and, if necessary, it reads the default value from the ManagementPath's DefaultPath property. Hopefully, in future FCL releases, Microsoft will address this issue and make sure that the default namespace for ManagementObject is configurable rather than hardcoded.

Although you must encode a unique object identity into the object path, including the name of the property that functions as an object's key is optional. In other words, you can place an equal sign and the value of the key directly after the name of the class—WMI is smart enough to apply the value to a correct property based on the class definition. Therefore, to create an instance of the ManagementObject type that is bound to the WMI class's Win32_ComputerSystem instance (which resides on the local machine), you would use the following code:

```
ManagementObject mo = new ManagementObject(@"Win32_ComputerSystem='BCK_OFFICE'");
```

Accessing Singletons

Anyone who spends some time playing with WMI will eventually notice that there are some classes that don't seem to have any key properties. For example, the Win32_WMISetting class, discussed in Chapter 1, does not designate any of its properties as a key that uniquely identifies a given instance. The reason behind this is simple—these classes, known in object-oriented parlance as *singletons,* are restricted to having only one instance at a time.

To bind a ManagementObject to an instance of a singleton class such as Win32_WMISetting, you may assume that you can just use the class name as a path and let WMI figure out the rest. However, this approach does not quite work; as a result, the following code throws an ArgumentOutOfRangeException:

```
ManagementObject mo = new ManagementObject("Win32_WMISetting");
```

Appending the equal sign right after the name of the class will not work either; doing so will just cause WMI to throw a `ManagementException`. It turns out that WMI has a special syntax to access singletons. As demonstrated by the following example, you have to use the @ placeholder as a property value:

```
ManagementObject mo = new ManagementObject("Win32_WMISetting=@");
```

During its initialization sequence, `ManagementObject` validates the object path that is passed as a parameter to its constructor. To aid the validation, it uses another type, called `ManagementPath`, which is responsible for parsing the path string and breaking it up into the server, the namespace path, and object path components. The `ManagementPath` is a public type, and as such, you can create it manually and then feed it into an overloaded version of the `ManagementObject` constructor. In fact, this type offers a slew of useful properties and methods and, on occasion, using it may ease the process of binding the `ManagementObject` to a WMI class instance. The following code, for instance, does the same thing as the previous example:

```
ManagementPath mp = new ManagementPath();
mp.Server = "BCK_OFFICE";
mp.NamespacePath = @"\root\CIMV2";
mp.ClassName = "Win32_WMISetting";
mp.SetAsSingleton();
ManagementObject mo = new ManagementObject(mp);
```

Here the properties of the `ManagementPath` instance are explicitly assigned and then the path is marked as a singleton path using the `SetAsSingleton` method. This approach is cleaner and more readable because the `ManagementPath` object takes care of assembling a valid WMI object path and relieves the user of remembering the syntax details, such as separators and placeholder values.

Using the ManagementPath Type

I already mentioned that the `ManagementObject` type constructor creates an instance of `ManagementPath` internally, unless, of course, you pass it as a parameter. In either case, you can access the `ManagementPath` object, which is associated with a given instance of a `ManagementObject`, through the `Path` property of the `ManagementObject` type. Therefore, the code above could be rewritten as follows:

```
ManagementObject mo = new ManagementObject();
mo.Path.Server = 'BCK_OFFICE';
mo.Path.NamespacePath = @"\root\CIMV2";
mo.Path.ClassName = "Win32_WMISetting";
mo.Path.SetAsSingleton();
```

This approach is, perhaps, a little more concise, but otherwise it is no different from the previous one.

One other property of the ManagementPath type, which I already mentioned, is DefaultPath; this property contains the default server and namespace portions of the object path. As you may remember, the initial value of this property is automatically set to a hardcoded string, "\\.\root\CIMV2", when the type is first loaded. Because the DefaultPath is a static property that can be written into, if you set it manually before using the ManagementPath type, you will affect the default namespace settings for all the subsequently created management objects. Thus, to make the default namespace setting configurable via the system registry, you can use code similar to the following:

```
RegistryKey rk = Registry.LocalMachine.OpenSubKey(
    @"SOFTWARE\Microsoft\WBEM\Scripting");
ManagementPath.DefaultPath = new ManagementPath(rk.GetValue(
    "Default Namespace").ToString());
```

This code first reads the static LocalMachine property of the Microsoft.Win32.Registry type to get a reference to an instance of Microsoft.Win32.RegistryKey type that is bound to the HKEY_LOCAL_MACHINE registry key. It then retrieves the reference to the SOFTWARE\Microsoft\WBEM\Scripting subkey using the OpenSubKey method of the RegistryKey. Finally, it assigns the value of the Default Namespace registry entry (obtained with the GetValue method of the RegistryKey type) to the ManagementPath type's static DefaultPath property.

The ManagementPath type has a few other properties that may come in handy when you are analyzing an arbitrary WMI object path. Using these properties, you can determine whether an object path refers to a class or an instance of a class and whether the object at which it points is a singleton. For instance, this snippet of code

```
ManagementPath mp = new ManagementPath("Win32_WMISetting=@");
Console.WriteLine("Class: {0}", mp.IsClass);
Console.WriteLine("Instance: {0}", mp.IsInstance);
Console.WriteLine("Singleton: {0}", mp.IsSingleton);
```

produces the following output on a console:

```
Class: False
Instance: True
Singleton: True
```

Implicit vs. Explicit Binding

Although the `ManagementPath` constructor and property set routines validate the object path, the scope of this validation only ensures that the path is compliant with the WMI object path syntax constraints. So, if a path contains the name of a nonexistent class, the `ManagementPath` type will not throw any exceptions. For instance, if the name of the class in the previous example is mistakenly entered as `Win64_WMISetting` rather than `Win32_WMISetting`, the code will still work perfectly and produce the same results. Moreover, if you try to create an instance of `ManagementObject` type based on an object path that references a nonexistent WMI class, you will succeed. However, the instance you get will be largely unusable and if you invoke its methods, a `ManagementException` will be thrown.

The explanation for this unexpected behavior is simple—instances of the `ManagementObject` type are initialized in a lazy fashion. In an attempt to conserve resources, none of the `ManagementObject` constructors issue WMI COM API calls. Instead, when you first use an instance of `ManagementObject`, its `Initialize` method is called. The `Initialize` method checks whether the instance is already connected to WMI; if it isn't it invokes the initialization sequence of the `ManagementScope` type. Then the `ManagementScope  InitializeGuts` method (briefly discussed in Chapter 1) obtains a pointer to `IWbemLocator` object and calls its `ConnectServer` method to retrieve the `IWbemServices` interface pointer. Once a valid WMI connection is established—or, in other words, when an `IWbemServices` interface pointer is obtained —the instance of `ManagementObject` calls the `IWbemServices::GetObject` method to retrieve an arbitrary instance of WMI class. The resulting WMI object reference (strictly speaking, an `IWbemClassObjectFreeThreaded` interface pointer) is cached in the wbemObject field of the `ManagementObject` instance. From this point on, the instance of the `ManagementObject` is said to be "bound" to WMI and can be used to manipulate the data associated with the corresponding WMI object.

Instead of relying on the `ManagementObject` type to connect to an appropriate WMI object in a lazy fashion, you can use the object's `Get` method to request that it is bound explicitly. For instance, the explicit binding to an underlying WMI object may be achieved as follows:

```
ManagementObject mo = new ManagementObject("Win32_WMISetting=@");
mo.Get();
```

Here, the explicitly initiated `Get` operation invokes the initialization sequence of the `ManagementObject` type and establishes a connection to WMI. In this scenario, it may seem that the `Get` method provides little value over lazy initialization, except perhaps for adding a little code clarity. However, you will find that the overloaded variation of `Get`, which is designed to support asynchronous operations, often comes in very handy. The asynchronous data manipulation techniques will be discussed in detail in "Asynchronous Programming" later in this chapter.

Accessing Properties of WMI Objects

Now that you have created a valid instance of the `ManagementObject` type, you will find it easy to retrieve the properties of a WMI object it represents. In Listing 2-1, you can see a complete implementation of a `PrintWMISettings` class, which binds to a single instance of `Win32_WMISetting` class and prints all its property values on a system console.

Listing 2-1. Printing `Win32_WMISetting` *Properties*

```
using System;
using System.Management;

class PrintWMISettings {

public static void Main(string[] args) {
    ManagementObject mo = new ManagementObject("Win32_WMISetting=@");
    Console.WriteLine("ASPScriptDefaultNamespace : {0}",
        mo["ASPScriptDefaultNamespace"]);
    Console.WriteLine("ASPScriptEnabled : {0}", mo["ASPScriptEnabled"]);
    Console.WriteLine("AutorecoverMofs : {0}", mo["AutorecoverMofs"]);
    Console.WriteLine("AutoStartWin9X : {0}", mo["AutoStartWin9X"]);
    Console.WriteLine("BackupInterval : {0}", mo["BackupInterval"]);
    Console.WriteLine("BackupLastTime : {0}", mo["BackupLastTime"]);
    Console.WriteLine("BuildVersion : {0}", mo["BuildVersion"]);
    Console.WriteLine("Caption : {0}", mo["Caption"]);
    Console.WriteLine("DatabaseDirectory : {0}", mo["DatabaseDirectory"]);
    Console.WriteLine("DatabaseMaxSize : {0}", mo["DatabaseMaxSize"]);
    Console.WriteLine("Description : {0}", mo["Description"]);
    Console.WriteLine("EnableAnonWin9xConnections : {0}",
        mo["EnableAnonWin9xConnections"]);
    Console.WriteLine("EnableEvents : {0}", mo["EnableEvents"]);
    Console.WriteLine("EnableStartupHeapPreallocation : {0}",
        mo["EnableStartupHeapPreallocation"]);
    Console.WriteLine("HighThresholdOnClientObjects : {0}",
        mo["HighThresholdOnClientObjects"]);
    Console.WriteLine("HighThresholdOnEvents : {0}",
        mo["HighThresholdOnEvents"]);
    Console.WriteLine("InstallationDirectory : {0}",
        mo["InstallationDirectory"]);
    Console.WriteLine("LastStartupHeapPreallocation : {0}",
        mo["LastStartupHeapPreallocation"]);
    Console.WriteLine("LoggingDirectory : {0}", mo["LoggingDirectory"]);
```

```
        Console.WriteLine("LoggingLevel : {0}", mo["LoggingLevel"]);
        Console.WriteLine("LowThresholdOnClientObjects : {0}",
            mo["LowThresholdOnClientObjects"]);
        Console.WriteLine("LowThresholdOnEvents : {0}",
            mo["LowThresholdOnEvents"]);
        Console.WriteLine("MaxLogFileSize : {0}", mo["MaxLogFileSize"]);
        Console.WriteLine("MaxWaitOnClientObjects : {0}",
            mo["MaxWaitOnClientObjects"]);
        Console.WriteLine("MaxWaitOnEvents : {0}", mo["MaxWaitOnEvents"]);
        Console.WriteLine("MofSelfInstallDirectory : {0}",
            mo["MofSelfInstallDirectory"]);
        Console.WriteLine("SettingID : {0}", mo["SettingID"]);
    }
}
```

In this code listing, the most interesting thing is the use of the indexer property to retrieve the property values. The indexer, which is defined in the base type
of the ManagementObject—ManagementBaseObject, takes a string property name
index as a parameter and returns the value of the corresponding object property.
If a property associated with a given name cannot be located within a given WMI
object (for instance, if the property name is misspelled), the indexer will throw
a ManagementException.

In this listing, the indexer returns the property value as an object, which can
be easily cast back to its actual data type if need be. Assuming that I am only
interested in printing the property values, this implementation will be sufficient.
This is because the WriteLine method will automatically convert its parameters
to strings using the ToString method's overrides of the respective types; in most
cases, this approach will result in the property value correctly printed on the
console.

To account for those programming languages that do not support the
indexer syntax, the ManagementObject type offers an explicit GetPropertyValue
method, inherited from its base type—ManagementBaseObject. This method, just
like the indexer, takes the string property name as a parameter and returns the
respective property value as object. Truth be told, the Indexer does nothing more
internally than just call the GetPropertyValue method. Thus, the example above
can be rewritten using the following syntax:

```
Console.WriteLine("ASPScriptDefaultNamespace : {0}",
    mo.GetPropertyValue("ASPScriptDefaultNamespace"));
Console.WriteLine("ASPScriptEnabled : {0}",
    mo.GetPropertyValue("ASPScriptEnabled"));
...
```

This involves more typing when you compare it to the indexer syntax, and while some may argue that it adds clarity, it is my opinion that using this method with programming languages that naturally support indexers is overkill.

One thing you may have noticed about the example in Listing 2-1 is that it is easy to misspell the property name, which makes the indexer syntax fairly error prone. A better approach would be to enumerate the properties of an object and print out the values in some generic manner. The example in Listing 2-2 illustrates how to do this.

Listing 2-2. Enumerating Properties of Win32_WMISetting

```
using System;
using System.Management;

class PrintWMISettings {

public static void Main(string[] args) {
   ManagementObject mo = new ManagementObject("Win32_WMISetting=@");
   foreach( PropertyData pd in mo.Properties ) {
      Console.WriteLine("{0} : {1}", pd.Name, pd.Value );
      }
   }
}
```

Here, the ManagementObject type offers a public read-only property, called Properties, which it inherits from its ManagementBaseObject base type. When read, this property returns an object of type PropertyDataCollection. The PropertyDataCollection type by itself is not very interesting—it is just a collection type that implements the standard collection interfaces IEnumerable and ICollection. What is interesting are the contents of the PropertyDataCollection object that is associated with a given instance of the ManagementObject type.

The PropertyDataCollection is a collection of PropertyData type instances that are designed to hold all the information pertinent to a single property of a WMI object. Listing 2-2 demonstrates two of the properties of the PropertyData type: Name and Value. These properties hold the name and the value of the corresponding WMI object property.

Accessing System Properties

If you remember our discussion of WMI system properties in Chapter 1, you may notice that the output produced by the code in Listing 2-2 does not include any of these properties. The reason for this is that system properties are not stored in the same property data collection. Instead, they are in a separate collection that is designed to hold just the WMI system properties. You can access this collection through the SystemProperties property of the ManagementObject type that is inherited from the ManagementBaseObject. Just like the regular properties collection, this collection contains the objects of PropertyData type, but this time, these objects refer exclusively to the system properties of an arbitrary WMI class. Thus, enumerating and printing the system properties is no different from enumerating regular WMI properties:

```
foreach(PropertyData pd in mo.SystemProperties) {
    Console.WriteLine("{0} : {1}", qd.Name, qd.Value);
}
```

Interestingly, the indexers, discussed earlier, as well as the GetPropertyValue method, are capable of retrieving a value of any property, regular or system. In fact, the GetPropertyValue method examines the property name, and depending on whether or not it starts with a double underscore, it retrieves the value from the SystemProperties or Properties collections respectively. Thus, the following code is perfectly valid and will work just fine:

```
Console.WriteLine("__PATH: {0}", mo["__PATH"]);
```

In addition to Name and Value, the PropertyData type exposes a few other properties that greatly simplify the analysis of WMI property data. If you compiled and ran any of the examples in Listing 2-1 or 2-2, you may have noticed that some of the property values of the Win32_WMISetting class were not printed correctly. For instance, instead of printing the value of the AutorecoverMofs property, our PrintWMISettings class prints System.String[]. The reason for it is simple—the ToString method implementation for complex data types, such as an array of strings, returns the name of the type rather than the value of the object. Since some of the WMI properties are arrays, the default ToString implementation does not quite work. The code example in Listing 2-3 shows how to fix this problem.

Listing 2-3. Enumerating Properties of Win32_WMISetting

```
using System;
using System.Management;
using System.Text;

class PrintWMISettings {

public static void Main(string[] args) {
    ManagementObject mo = new ManagementObject("Win32_WMISetting=@");
```

```
    foreach( PropertyData pd in mo.Properties ) {
        Console.WriteLine("{0} : {1}", pd.Name, Format(pd) );
        }
    }
public static object Format(PropertyData pd) {
    if (pd.IsArray) {
        Array pa = (Array)pd.Value;
        StringBuilder sb = new StringBuilder();
        sb.Append(Environment.NewLine);
        for(int i=pa.GetLowerBound(0); i<pa.GetUpperBound(0); i++) {
            sb.Append(pa.GetValue(i));
            sb.Append(Environment.NewLine);
            }
        return sb;
    } else {
        return pd.Value;
    }
    }
}
```

Here I added a public static `Format` function, which is called every time I need a property value printed. First it checks to see if the property value is an `Array` type using the `IsArray` property of the `PropertyData` object. For scalar properties, this function simply returns the property value, which is automatically converted to a string by the `WriteLine` method. If a property is determined to be of `Array` type, the `Format` function casts the property value to an `Array` type and iterates through individual elements of the array using its `GetLowerBound`, `GetUpperBound`, and `GetValue` methods. As an alternative to this, you can use the following code to enumerate the array elements:

```
foreach(object o in (Array)pd.Value) {
    sb.Append(o.ToString()); sb.Append(Environment.NewLine);
}
```

In either case, for array properties, this function returns a new line–delimited list of property values, which it assembles using the `StringBuilder` type from the `System.Text` namespace. Interestingly, the return type of the `Format` function is an object rather than a string. Returning the object from the function helps to avoid checking for null property values; instead, the task of converting values to strings is delegated to the `WriteLine` method.

The `PropertyData` type contains a few other useful properties and the following snippet of code demonstrates all but one of them:

```
PropertyData pd = mo.Properties["AutorecoverMofs"];
Console.WriteLine("IsLocal: {0}", pd.IsLocal);
Console.WriteLine("Origin: {0}", pd.Origin);
Console.WriteLine("Type: {0}", pd.Type);
```

This example produces the following output:

```
IsLocal: True
Origin: Win32_WMISetting
Type: String
```

The IsLocal property returns a Boolean value (TRUE or FALSE) based on whether a particular property is declared in the current WMI class or one of its parents. As shown here, it returns a TRUE value for the AutorecoverMofs property of the Win32_WMISetting, but if it is invoked for the SettingID property, it will return a FALSE value because this property is declared in the parent class of Win32_WMISetting—CIM_Setting. The Origin property contains the name of the declaring class, which in the case of the AutorecoverMofs property, is Win32_WMISetting. For the SettingID property it will return the string "CIM_Setting". Finally, the Type property can be used to determine the CIM data type of the underlying WMI property. The Type property is of type CimType, which is an enumeration that describes all possible CIM types that are used for properties, and qualifier and method parameters. Table 2-1 lists all members of the CimType enumeration.

Table 2-1. CimType *Enumeration*

MEMBER	DESCRIPTION
Boolean	Boolean type
Char16	16-bit character type
DateTime	Date or time value in DMTF string date/time format: yyyymmddHHMMSS.mmmmmmsUUU where: yyyymmdd—year/month/day HHMMSS—hours/minutes/seconds mmmmmm—microsecondss UUU—sign (+/-)/UTC offset
Object	Embedded object type
Real32	32-bit floating point number
Real64	64-bit floating point number
Reference	Reference to another object (string containing the path to another object)

(continued)

Table 2-1. CimType *Enumeration (continued)*

MEMBER	DESCRIPTION
SInt16	Signed 16-bit integer
SInt32	Signed 32-bit integer
SInt64	Signed 64-bit integer
SInt8	Signed 8-bit integer
String	String type
UInt16	Unsigned 16-bit integer
UInt32	Unsigned 32-bit integer
UInt64	Unsigned 64-bit integer
UInt8	Unsigned 8-bit integer

Retrieving Object and Property Qualifiers

The last property of the PropertyData type is a collection of WMI property qualifiers. A *qualifier,* briefly mentioned in Chapter 1, is a special designation that CIM
uses to associate certain qualities with an arbitrary property. For instance, to
identify a property as an object key, a Key qualifier is used. The Qualifiers
property of the PropertyData type is a straightforward collection of the
QualifierDataCollection type, which contains instances of the QualifierData
type. Two of the most important properties that the QualifierData type exposes
are Name and Value, which represent the name and the value of an arbitrary WMI
property qualifier. To iterate through the collection of property qualifiers, you
would use code similar to the following:

```
PropertyData pd = mo.Properties["AutorecoverMofs"];
foreach(QualifierData qd in pd.Qualifiers) {
    Console.WriteLine("{0} : {1}", qd.Name, qd.Value);
}
```

As an alternative to this code, you can access the qualifier values directly
using the GetPropertyQualifierValue method of the ManagementObject type,
which is inherited from the ManagementBaseObject. For example, to print
the value of the CIMTYPE qualifier for the AutorecoverMofs property of the
Win32_WMISetting object, you may use the following code:

```
Console.WriteLine("CIM Type: {0}",
    mo.GetPropertyQualifierValue("AutorecoverMofs", "CIMTYPE"));
```

This method simply takes the property name and qualifier name parameters of type string and returns the value of the qualifier, packaged in an object.

Besides the Name and Value properties, the QualifierData type exposes five other properties, one of which, IsAmended, has to do with the localization capabilities that are built into WMI (these will be discussed in "Localization and Internationalization Issues" later in this chapter). The remaining four properties—IsLocal, IsOverridable, PropagatesToInstance, and PropagatesToSubclass—indicate whether the qualifier is declared in the current class, whether it can be overridden by its subclass, whether it automatically propagates to instances of the class, and whether it propagates to subclasses respectively.

WMI object properties are not the only elements of CIM that may have associated qualifiers. In fact, qualifiers are used extensively to describe the semantics of classes, instances, properties, methods, and method parameters. For example, CIM uses the Singleton qualifier to mark singleton classes as such. Conveniently, the ManagementBaseObject type and its subtype ManagementObject expose a Qualifiers property—a collection that contains the QualifierData objects that refer to the qualifiers defined for an instance of the WMI class. As is shown here, the qualifiers of an object can be iterated through just as easily as the property qualifiers:

```
ManagementObject mo = new ManagementObject("Win32_WMISetting=@");
foreach( QualifierData qd in mo.Qualifiers ) {
    Console.WriteLine("{0} : {1}", qd.Name, qd.Value );
}
```

This example will produce the following output:

```
dynamic : True
Locale : 1033
provider : WBEMCORE
Singleton : True
UUID : {A83EF166-CA8D-11d2-B33D-00104BCC4B4A}
```

As you can see, the Singleton qualifier for the instance of Win32_WMISetting class is set to TRUE, thus marking the instance as a singleton.

If you wanted to enable direct access to the qualifier values, you would use the GetQualifierValue method of the ManagementBaseObject type as follows:

```
ManagementObject mo = new ManagementObject("Win32_WMISetting=@");
Console.WriteLine("Singleton: {0}", mo.GetQualifierValue("Singleton"));
```

This method takes a single parameter of type string—the name of the qualifier—and returns the qualifier value, packaged as an object. Be careful when you are calling this method because it will throw the ManagementException if the qualifier, corresponding to a given name, cannot be found in the qualifiers data collection. For example, if you attempt to retrieve the value of the Singleton qualifier for an instance of the Win32_Process class, you will not get the FALSE qualifier value; instead, the method invocation will result in the ManagementException because the Singleton qualifier is not defined for the Win32_Process class.

If you are an inquisitive reader, the preceding discussion of qualifiers may seem far from exhaustive. There is a good reason, however, for why I did not delve into the gory details here: discussing qualifiers in detail in the current context does not make much sense. Because qualifiers constitute an essential part of WMI class definitions, many of their features and qualities are best understood when talking about classes rather than objects. Therefore, I will present the detailed overview of WMI qualifiers later in this chapter, when I cover the features of ManagementClass type.

ManagementObject: Analyzing the Relationships Between Objects

No WMI object exists in isolation. As we stated in Chapter 1, CIM is an object model that is composed of numerous elements that are related through a set of well-defined associations. Your ability to model and express the relationships between individual managed elements is very important because it is this information—information that describes the object associations—that many management applications rely on in order to function correctly. Windows Service Control Manager, for instance, is a classic example of a management application that requires detailed knowledge about the dependencies between Windows services.

The ManagementObject type features a couple of methods that make the analysis of the object relationships easy and painless. These methods—GetRelated and GetRelationships—allow you to enumerate the instances, related to a given object, and analyze the associations between the individual objects.

Enumerating Related Objects

The following code illustrates how you can retrieve all the objects that are related to an instance of the Win32_Service class, which represents WMI WinMgmt service.

```
ManagementObject mo = new ManagementObject(@"Win32_Service='WinMgmt'");
foreach(ManagementObject o in mo.GetRelated()) {
    Console.WriteLine(o["__PATH"]);
}
```

This snippet of code first binds to an instance of the Win32_Service class that is identified by its name, "WinMgmt", which is the name of the WMI service. Then it calls the GetRelated method of the ManagementObject type to retrieve a collection of ManagementObject instances, each of which represents WMI objects that are related to WMI Service. Finally, it traverses the resulting collection and prints the value of the __PATH property of each object on the console.

This code should be very straightforward. The only thing that you may not readily understand is why I chose to print the __PATH property rather than the Name property. Everything becomes even more clear once you look at the output that this code produces:

```
\\BCK_OFFICE\root\cimv2:Win32_WMISetting=@
\\BCK_OFFICE\root\cimv2:Win32_ComputerSystem.Name="BCK_OFFICE"
\\BCK_OFFICE\root\cimv2:Win32_Service.Name="RpcSs"
```

Now you can see that the GetRelated method retrieves all the objects that are somehow related to the WinMgmt service, not just other instances of Win32_Service class. That is why I used the system __PATH property— all WMI classes have it. If I had attempted to use the Name property (or any other nonsystem property, for that matter) it would have resulted in a ManagementException because the Win32_WMISetting object does not have such a property.

Often you will want to retrieve not just all objects that are related to a given instance, but those that play a certain role in a relationship. The ability to determine the role of an object participating in a relationship may be very handy, especially when you analyze the dependencies between the individual instances of WMI classes. For instance, consider the task of enumerating all Windows services, on which WinMgmt depends. You may attempt to solve this problem by using an overloaded version of the GetRelated method, which takes a single string parameter—the name of the class of related objects:

```
ManagementObject mo = new ManagementObject(@"Win32_Service='WinMgmt'");
foreach(ManagementObject o in mo.GetRelated("Win32_Service")) {
    Console.WriteLine(o["__PATH"]);
}
```

It may look like this code solves the problem. Just one object of type Win32_Service is identified—the Remote Procedure Call (RPC) service, on which WinMgmt is obviously dependent:

```
\\BCK_OFFICE\root\cimv2:Win32_Service.Name="RpcSs"
```

However, if I change the code to retrieve all objects related to the RPC service

```
ManagementObject mo = new ManagementObject(@"Win32_Service='RpcSs'");
foreach(ManagementObject o in mo.GetRelated("Win32_Service")) {
    Console.WriteLine(o["__PATH"]);
}
```

you will see that the output includes WinMgmt Service:

```
\\BCK_OFFICE\root\cimv2:Win32_Service.Name="ProtectedStorage"
\\BCK_OFFICE\root\cimv2:Win32_Service.Name="Schedule"
\\BCK_OFFICE\root\cimv2:Win32_Service.Name="TlntSvr"
\\BCK_OFFICE\root\cimv2:Win32_Service.Name="WinMgmt"
...
```

There is only one conclusion that you can draw from this: both versions of the GetRelated method retrieve related objects regardless of the direction of the relationship and the object role in the relationship.

Fortunately, the ManagementObject type offers another overloaded version of the GetRelated method that provides a finer degree of control over the output of the method. This version of the method is fairly complex and has the following signature:

```
public ManagementObjectCollection GetRelated(
    string              relatedClass,
    string              relationshipClass,
    string              relationshipQualifier,
    string              relatedQualifier,
    string              relatedRole,
    string              thisRole,
    bool                classDefinitionsOnly,
    EnumerationOptions  options
);
```

where the parameters are defined as follows:

relatedClass: Optional string parameter, containing the class name. If specified, this parameter indicates that all returned objects must belong to a given class or a class derived from a given class.

relationshipClass: Optional string parameter, containing the name of the association class. If this parameter is specified, it indicates that the object for which the GetRelated method is invoked, and the resulting objects, must be connected via an association object of a given class or a class that is derived from a given class.

relationshipQualifier: Optional string parameter, containing the name of the qualifier. If this parameter is specified, it indicates that the object for which the GetRelated method is invoked and the resulting objects must be connected via an association object that belongs to a class, which includes a given qualifier.

relatedQualifier: Optional string parameter, containing the name of the qualifier. If this parameter is specified, it indicates that all the returned objects must belong to a class, which includes a given qualifier.

relatedRole: Optional string parameter, containing the name of the role. If this parameter is specified, all the returned objects must play a particular role in the association. The role is defined as the name of the property of an association class, which is a reference property that points to a given object.

thisRole: Optional string parameter, containing the name of the role. If this parameter is specified, it indicates that the object for which the GetRelated method is invoked for must play a particular role in the association. The role is defined as the name of the property of an association class, which is a reference property that points to a given object.

classDefinitionsOnly: Optional Boolean parameter. If this parameter is specified, it indicates whether the method should return schema information (TRUE) or data (FALSE). Enumerating the schema elements will be discussed in "ManagementClass: Analyzing the Schema" later in this chapter.

options: Optional object of type EnumerationOptions. If this parameter is specified, it controls various aspects of the GetRelated method behavior.

This version of the GetRelated method easily solves the problem of enumerating the dependencies for WinMgmt service, as shown here:

```
ManagementObject mo = new ManagementObject(@"Win32_Service='WinMgmt'");
foreach(ManagementObject o in mo.GetRelated("Win32_Service",
  "Win32_DependentService",null,null,"Antecedent","Dependent",false,null)) {
    Console.WriteLine(o["__PATH"]);
}
```

While this may look a bit complex at first, it is really not. In order to understand what is going on here, take a look at the definition for the Win32_DependentService class: it is an association that ties together Win32_Service classes as shown here:

```
class Win32_DependentService : CIM_ServiceServiceDependency
{
    Win32_BaseService ref Antecedent = NULL;
    Win32_BaseService ref Dependent = NULL;
};
```

This class has two properties, marked as references: Antecedent and Dependent. Both of these properties point to instances of the Win32_BaseService class (the parent class of Win32_Service). The Antecedent property refers to a "master" service, and the Dependent property refers to a service that is dependent on the master. Therefore, the preceding code example simply requests all instances of the Win32_Service class that are related to the current instance through an association of type Win32_DependentService such that the current instance is a dependent and the requested instance is a "master." If you wanted to do the opposite—identify all the services that are dependent on a given service—you would reverse the relatedRole and thisRole parameters as follows:

```
ManagementObject mo = new ManagementObject(@"Win32_Service='RpcSs'");
foreach(ManagementObject o in mo.GetRelated("Win32_Service",
  "Win32_DependentService",null,null,"Dependent"," Antecedent ",false,null)) {
    Console.WriteLine(o["__PATH"]);
}
```

For complex scenarios, you can filter the output of the GetRelated method even further by supplying the values for the relatedQualifier and relationshipQualifier parameters, which allow you to include just the instances of those classes where respective qualifiers are defined.

Another interesting and not quite obvious feature of the GetRelated method is its ability to enumerate related objects in a generic fashion using parent class names. Consider the following statement: a directory may contain files as well as other directories. In WMI, a data file is represented by the CIM_DataFile class, while a directory is represented by Win32_Directory. The containment relationship between a directory and a file is expressed via CIM_DirectoryContainsFile association class, which has two properties— GroupComponent and PartComponent, pointing to directory and file objects respectively.

The relationship between a directory and its subdirectories is represented by the Win32_SubDirectory association class with the same properties (GroupComponent and PartComponent) that point to the directory and subdirectory objects respectively. Thus, if you attempt to list the contents of an arbitrary directory, like so

```
ManagementObject mo = new ManagementObject(@"Win32_Directory='C:\TEMP'");
foreach(ManagementObject o in mo.GetRelated("CIM_DataFile",
 null,null,null,"PartComponent","GroupComponent",false,null)) {
    Console.WriteLine(o["__PATH"]);
}
```

you will only get a list of data files and any subdirectories will be ignored since the relatedClass parameter limits the scope to objects of CIM_DataFile class. However, since both CIM_DataFile and Win32_Directory share the same parent class, CIM_LogicalFile, the code can be rewritten as follows:

```
ManagementObject mo = new ManagementObject(@"Win32_Directory='C:\TEMP'");
foreach(ManagementObject o in mo.GetRelated("CIM_LogicalFile",
 null,null,null,"PartComponent","GroupComponent",false,null)) {
    Console.WriteLine(o["__PATH"]);
}
```

Since files and directories are, in fact, instances of subclasses of the CIM_LogicalFile, this last code example will correctly list the contents of C:\TEMP directory, showing not only files, but subdirectories as well.

The last parameter of the GetRelated method, the object of type EnumerationOptions, is fairly interesting. Its purpose is to control certain aspects of the method's behavior, most of which are performance-related. Table 2-2 lists all the public properties of EnumerationOptions type.

Table 2-2. EnumerationOptions *Properties*

PROPERTY	DESCRIPTION
BlockSize	Integer that controls how WMI returns results. When retrieving related instances as a collection of objects, WMI returns objects in groups of size, specified by this parameter.
DirectAccess	Boolean value that indicates whether a direct access to the provider is requested for a given class, without any regard for its superclasses or subclasses.
EnsureLocatable	Boolean value that indicates whether the returned objects have locatable information. If set to true, this ensures that the system properties, such as __PATH, __RELPATH, and __SERVER, are populated. This property is ignored when enumerating related objects.
EnumerateDeep	Boolean value that indicates whether subclasses of a given class should be included in the result set.
PrototypeOnly	Boolean value that controls partial-instance operations. Some classes have dynamic resource-consuming properties that are expensive to retrieve. This property controls whether all or some properties of a WMI class are returned as a result of enumeration.
ReturnImmediately	Boolean value that controls whether an operation is performed synchronously or asynchronously. If set to true, this property causes the method to return immediately and the actual retrieval of results takes place when the returned collection is iterated through.
Rewindable	Boolean value that indicates whether the returned object collection may be enumerated more than once. If set to false, the underlying objects in a collection become unavailable as soon as the enumerator is released.
UseAmendedQualifiers	Boolean value that indicates whether the returned objects should contain localized data. Localization is discussed later in this chapter.
Timeout	Value of type TimeSpan used to set the timeout value for the operation. When a method returns a collection of objects (as the GetRelated method does) the timeout applies to iterating through the collection, rather than just to the method invocation itself. This property is inherited from the ManagementOptions type.

The EnumerationOptions type has a single parameterized constructor, shown here, which allows you to set all of the object properties at once:

```
public EnumerationOptions (
    ManagementNamedValueCollection context ,
    TimeSpan timeout ,
    int    blockSize ,
    bool   rewindable ,
    bool   returnImmediately ,
    bool   useAmendedQualifiers ,
    bool   ensureLocatable ,
    bool   prototypeOnly ,
    bool   directRead ,
    bool   enumerateDeep
);
```

Invoking this constructor is trivial, and the only interesting thing about it is its first parameter—the context parameter of the type ManagementNamedValueCollection. The ManagementNamedValueCollection type is just a simple container that is designed to hold name-value pairs. These name-value pairs are then used to pass additional information to WMI data providers in those cases where standard method parameters are not sufficient. For a SNMP provider, for instance, you may need to pass community strings; this is where the context parameter comes in handy.

You can use the context parameter to initialize the Context property of the ManagementOptions type, which is a parent type for EnumerationOptions and other options types. This parameter provides an excellent generic mechanism for passing provider-specific data as part of method invocations, and it is used extensively by types in the System.Management namespace.

Analyzing Associations Between Objects

Besides inspecting all objects related to a given instance, sometimes you may find it useful to look at the associations that actually link the objects together. As you may remember from Chapter 1, associations are classes that may include properties other than just references to the objects that are related through an association. For instance, the CIM_ProcessExecutable association class, which was designed to express the relationship between an operating system process (Win32_Process) and its components (executable files and dynamic link libraries), has the following definition:

```
class CIM_ProcessExecutable : CIM_Dependency
{
    CIM_DataFile ref Antecedent = NULL;
    CIM_Process ref Dependent = NULL;
    uint32 GlobalProcessCount;
    uint32 ProcessCount;
    uint32 ModuleInstance;
    uint64 BaseAddress;
};
```

In addition to the Antecedent and Dependent properties, which refer to a process and its associated components respectively, the CIM_ProcessExecutable class has a number of other properties:

GlobalProcessCount: This property specifies the total number of processes that have a particular file loaded as part of the process image. For instance, a single in-memory copy of a DLL may be used by several running processes; as a result, the DLLs global process counts will reflect the number of processes that map the DLLs into their process image.

ProcessCount: This property specifies the reference count of the file within the current process. If an application issues a LoadLibrary call against the same DLL multiple times, the DLL is only loaded once and its reference count within the process is incremented for each LoadLibrary call. The process count reflects the reference count for a DLL within a given process.

ModuleInstance: This property specifies the Win32 module handle. When Windows loads a module (DLL) into memory, a module is assigned a unique module handle to the shared code and resources. This module handle is then exposed through the ModuleInstance property.

BaseAddress: This property specifies the base address of the module within the process address space of a given process.

You will most likely find that CIM_ProcessExecutable associations are worth looking at because they contain a wealth of useful information that is unavailable anywhere else. The simplest way to enumerate associations of a class is to use the parameterless version of GetRelationships method of the ManagementObject type. For example, to list all the associations of a process that are identified by its process ID or handle, you can use the following code:

```
ManagementObject mo = new ManagementObject("Win32_Process=269");
foreach(ManagementObject o in mo.GetRelationships()) {
    Console.WriteLine(o["__PATH"]);
}
```

Unfortunately, this code has the same problem as the earlier example for Win32_Service dependencies: it lists all associations regardless of their type. Since a process may be associated with not only executable files and DLLs, but also with the computer system it is running on, and possibly with the threads that comprise the process and other elements, the output of this code fragment is not what you want. To remedy this problem you can use an overloaded version of the GetRelationships method, which takes a single string parameter—the name of the associating class—which should be included in the output:

```
ManagementObject mo = new ManagementObject("Win32_Process=269");
foreach(ManagementObject o in mo.GetRelationships("CIM_ProcessExecutable")) {
    Console.WriteLine(o["__PATH"]);
    Console.WriteLine("GlobalProcessCount: {0}", o["GlobalProcessCount"]);
    Console.WriteLine("ProcessCount : {0}", o["ProcessCount"]);
    Console.WriteLine("ModuleInstance : {0}", o["ModuleInstance"]);
    Console.WriteLine("BaseAddress : {0}", o["BaseAddress"]);
}
```

For more obscure scenarios in which you want to have finer control over the output, the ManagementObject type provides another overload of the GetRelationships method:

```
public ManagementObjectCollection GetRelationships (
    string              relationshipClass ,
    string              relationshipQualifier ,
    string              thisRole ,
    bool                classDefinitionsOnly ,
    EnumerationOptions  options
);
```

where the parameters are defined as follows:

> relationshipClass: This is an optional string parameter that contains the name of the association class. If this parameter is specified, it indicates that the returned association objects must be of a given class or a class derived from a given class.

relationshipQualifier: This is an optional string parameter that contains the name of the qualifier. If this parameter is specified, it indicates that the returned association objects must be of a class that includes a given qualifier.

thisRole: This is an optional string parameter that contains the name of the role. If this parameter is specified, it indicates that the object for which the GetRelationships method is invoked must play a particular role in the association. The role is defined as a name of the property of an association class, which is a reference property that points to a given object.

classDefinitionsOnly: This is an optional Boolean parameter. If this parameter is specified, it indicates whether the method should return schema information (TRUE) or data (FALSE). Enumerating the schema elements will be discussed in detail in "ManagementClass: Analyzing the Schema" later in this chapter.

options: This is an optional object of type EnumerationOptions. If this is specified, it controls various aspects of the GetRelationships method behavior. Refer back to Table 2-2 for detailed description of the properties of EnumerationOptions type.

ManagementObject: Modifying Management Data

If you spend enough time wandering around the WMI object model you will eventually attempt to modify some of the WMI object properties. Although modifying object properties is theoretically possible, there is a caveat of which you should be aware.

Identifying Writable Properties

The problem is that not all properties are writable. One approach you can use to identify writable properties is to inspect the property definitions for write qualifiers. In general, a write qualifier indicates that the property is modifiable, however, the absence of this qualifier does not necessarily mean that the property is read-only. It turns out that WMI qualifiers act in an advisory capacity so that the restrictions associated with a particular qualifier are not enforced by WMI. In fact, when delegating a request for an operation to a data provider, WMI completely ignores any qualifiers, and it is up to a provider to carry out the request. This may change in the future releases of WMI. For instance, CIMOM may start checking the class and property qualifiers before it dispatches the requests to data provider to ensure that none of the constraints, imposed by qualifiers, are accidentally violated.

Thus, identifying the writable properties is somewhat empiric—you may try to change the property value and see if a provider completes the operation. In general, WMI system properties are read-only, except for __CLASS, which is writable, but this is only true when you are programmatically creating a class. The nonsystem properties of the vast majority of WMI classes are also mostly read-only; the most notable exceptions are listed in Table 2-3.

Table 2-3. Writable Properties

CLASS NAME	PROPERTY NAME	DESCRIPTION
Win32_ComputerSystem	SystemStartupDelay	Number of seconds before the computer's default operating system is automatically started
	SystemStartupSetting	Index of boot.ini entry, which contains the computer's default operating system
Win32_Environment	UserName	Identifier of a user, to which a given environment variable applies
	Name	Name of the Windows environment variable
	VariableValue	Value of the Windows environment variable
Win32_LogicalDisk	VolumeName	Name of the volume on a logical disk
Win32_OperatingSystem	ForegroundApplicationBoost	Number of points to be added to an application's priority when that application is brought to the foreground
	QuantumLength	Number of clock ticks before an application is swapped out
	QuantumType	Number that determines whether the system uses fixed or variable length quantums so that foreground applications receive longer quantums

(continued)

Table 2-3. Writable Properties (continued)

CLASS NAME	PROPERTY NAME	DESCRIPTION
Win32_OSRecoveryConfiguration	AutoReboot	Boolean value that specifies whether a system is automatically rebooted during a recovery operation
	DebugFilePath	Path to the debug file that is written if WriteDebugInfo is set to true
	KernelDumpOnly	Boolean value that indicates whether only kernel debug information will be written to the debug log file
	OverWriteExistingDebugFile	Boolean value that determines whether or not to overwrite an existing debug file
	SendAdminAlert	Boolean value that determines whether or not an alert message is sent to the system administrator in the event of an operating system failure
	WriteDebugInfo	Boolean value that determines whether or not debug information will be written to a file
	WriteToSystemLog	Boolean value that determines whether system failure information will be written to a system log file
Win32_PageFileSetting	Name	String that contains the name of the page file
	InitialSize	Number that specifies the size (in MB) of the page file when it is first created
	MaximumSize	Number that specifies the maximum allowed size (in MB) of the page file
Win32_Registry	ProposedSize	Number that specifies the maximum size (in MB) of the registry

One of the classes, besides those mentioned in Table 2-3, that has many modifiable properties is `Win32_WMISetting`. In fact, all of its properties, with the exception of `AutorecoverMofs`, `Caption`, `BuildVersion`, `Description`, `SettingID`, `DatabaseDirectory`, `DatabaseMaxSize`, `InstallationDirectory`, `LastStartupHeapPreallocation`, and `MofSelfInstallDirectory`, are writable. You will find that having read-write access to WMI settings through the instance of `Win32_WMISetting` class is very useful because it allows you to programmatically alter the WMI configuration in a controlled manner—a much better alternative than changing the system registry.

Modifying Properties

Modifying the object properties is surprisingly easy: you may simply assign the properties, which are contained in the `ManagementObject` `Properties` collection, to the values of your choice. The following fragment, for instance, changes the value of the `Win32_WMISetting` object's `BackupInterval` property to 60 seconds:

```
ManagementObject mo = new ManagementObject("Win32_WMISetting=@");
mo["BackupInterval"] = 60;
```

For those programming languages that do not support the indexer syntax, the `ManagementObject` type offers an explicit `SetPropertyValue` method, which it inherits from its base type, `ManagementBaseObject`:

```
ManagementObject mo = new ManagementObject("Win32_WMISetting=@");
mo.SetPropertyValue("BackupInterval", 60);
```

This method takes two parameters: the name of the property and the object that represents the new property value. In fact, when setting the property value via the indexer as in the example above, the indexer set method internally calls the `SetPropertyValue` method to carry out the actual update.

Unfortunately, both code examples above, although absolutely correct, do not have the effect that you want—if you check the registry following the execution of either of these fragments, you will notice that the `BackupInterval` value has not changed. The problem is that, from the WMI prospective, the instance of the WMI object is always in process, or in other words, a client application always operates upon its own local copy of an object. Thus, a read operation always retrieves a property value from a local copy, and a write request always updates the same local copy of the object. In order to propagate the changes to CIM Repository and potentially to a respective data provider, you have to "commit" them. To commit changes to WMI, you must have your application invoke the `Put` method of the `ManagementObject` after any update it performs on the instance:

```
ManagementObject mo = new ManagementObject("Win32_WMISetting=@");
mo["BackupInterval"] = 60;
mo.Put();
```

The fact that WMI always operates on a local copy of an object creates a curious problem. Let's say the current setting of the BackupInterval property of the Win32_WMISetting is 30 minutes (this is the default). What do you think happens when the following code snippet is executed?

```
ManagementObject mo1 = new ManagementObject("Win32_WMISetting=@");
ManagementObject mo2 = new ManagementObject("Win32_WMISetting=@");
Console.WriteLine("BackupInterval (before update) : {0}",
    mo2["BackupInterval"]);
mo1["BackupInterval"] = 60;
mo1.Put();
Console.WriteLine("BackupInterval (after update) : {0}",
    mo2["BackupInterval"]);
```

The output may not be what you expect:

```
BackupInterval (before update) : 30
BackupInterval (after update) : 30
```

Here you see that even though the changes are committed to WMI with the Put method, the value of the BackupInterval property is still being taken from the local copy of the Win32_WMISetting instance, pointed to by the mo2 object reference. And since this local copy has not changed, the value of the BackupInterval remains the same! Potentially, this could lead to all kinds of integrity issues, such as lost updates and various race conditions.

Unfortunately, unlike most database systems, WMI does not implement any locking mechanism, which might have prevented these kinds of problems. Apart from adding complexity, a locking mechanism for WMI would be impractical for a few reasons. First, locking is notoriously expensive and often results in excessive resource consumption. Second, the fundamental concept behind WBEM, and WMI in particular, is its ability to operate via the Internet or a wide area network (WAN) where the principles of stateless programming have to be followed religiously in order to ensure adequate performance. Implementing any kind of locking mechanism in a stateless environment is complicated, to say the least. Thus, the general philosophy of WMI is to limit the number of modifiable properties to a bare minimum. Instead, in order to alter the state of WMI objects, you should invoke object methods where appropriate. The details of method invocation will be discussed later in "Invoking WMI Object Methods."

Controlling the Scope of Modification

Contrary to what you may expect, the key properties that uniquely identify an object within WMI are not necessarily write-protected. Consider the following scenario:

```
ManagementObject mo = new ManagementObject(@"__NAMESPACE='Applications'");
mo["Name"] = "NewNamespace";
mo.Put();
```

This code runs just fine, but the outcome is somewhat unexpected. Instead of renaming the Applications namespace, it creates a brand new namespace, NewNamespace. As confusing as it may look, this behavior is actually logical. The value of the object key property is what uniquely identifies a given instance to WMI. Thus, when the changes are committed, as far as WMI is concerned, the object it is supposed to operate on is identified by the name NewNamespace. Since no such object exists, WMI creates a brand new one.

Although this is a pretty cool way to create new instances of WMI classes, such behavior is a bit unexpected and may lead to obscure and hard-to-find bugs. To reduce the chances of accidentally creating new objects, use the over-loaded version of the Put method that the ManagementObject type offers. This version takes a single parameter of type PutOptions. The PutOptions type has a few properties, one of which, Type, is of immediate interest. The data type of this property is the enumeration PutType, which has three members, described in Table 2-4.

Table 2-4. Members of the PutType Enumeration

PUTTYPE MEMBER	DESCRIPTION
CreateOnly	Allows only those operations that result in creating a new object/class
UpdateOnly	Allows only those operations that result in an existing object being updated
UpdateOrCreate	Allows any kind of operation that results in creating a new object or updating the existing one

The Type property of the PutType object can be set via its constructor or it can be assigned after the object is created. In addition to the default parameterless constructor, there are two overloaded versions:

```
public PutOptions (
    ManagementNamedValueCollection context ,
    TimeSpan timeout ,
    bool   useAmendedQualifiers ,
    PutType   putType
);
public PutOptions (
    ManagementNamedValueCollection context
);
```

Both constructors take the context parameter, which is used to initialize the Context property of the base type, ManagementOptions. The first version also allows you to set the timeout value of the ManagementOptions type, the localization property useAmendedQualifiers, and, finally, the Type property of the PutOptions type.

To illustrate the effect of restricting the scope of the modifications performed on an instance of WMI class, I have altered the previous code example as follows:

```
ManagementObject mo = new ManagementObject(@"__NAMESPACE='Applications'");
mo["Name"] = "NewNamespace";
PutOptions po = new PutOptions();
po.Type = PutType.UpdateOnly;
mo.Put(po);
```

Instead of creating a new namespace NewNamespace, this code will throw the ManagementException because the PutOptions object that controls the Put operation does not allow a new object to be created.

Creating New Objects

In those cases where you want to create a new object instance, you should use the Clone method of the ManagementObject type. When you invoke this method on an existing instance of a WMI class, it stamps out a brand new object, which looks exactly like the original one. However, you should note that the Clone method does not save the resulting object to CIM Repository and you must follow it with the Put method:

```
ManagementObject mo = (ManagementObject) new
    ManagementObject(@"__NAMESPACE='Applications'").Clone();
mo["Name"] = "NewNamespace";
mo.Put();
```

The cast to the ManagementObject is necessary since the Clone method is an override of the Clone of the System.Object base type and, by definition, it returns the result of type System.Object.

Again, make sure to modify the key properties of the cloned object before you save it to the repository. If you fail to do so, the original object will be over-written. To avoid this, use the overloaded version of the Put method, which takes the parameter of type PutOptions as follows:

```
ManagementObject mo = (ManagementObject) new
    ManagementObject(@"__NAMESPACE='Applications'").Clone();
mo["Name"] = "NewNamespace";
PutOptions po = new PutOptions();
po.Type = PutType.CreateOnly;
mo.Put(po);
```

This will ensure that only a creation operation succeeds, since WMI will check to see whether an instance of the class with the same key properties already exists and throw an exception if it does.

Yet another method you can use to create new instances of an object, although in a fairly restrictive fashion, is CopyTo. In its simplest form, CopyTo takes a single string parameter that represents the namespace path for a new instance. However, it is important that you understand that CopyTo only lets you copy objects between namespaces; it does not let you change any of the object properties or the class to which the object belongs. As tempting as the following code may look, it will not work—in fact, it will do nothing:

```
ManagementObject mo = new
    ManagementObject(@"\\.\root:__NAMESPACE='Applications'");
mo.CopyTo(@"\\.\root:__NAMESPACE='NewNamespace'");
```

In this example, it turns out that the class name and the object identity portions of the path that are passed as parameters to the CopyTo method are completely ignored and only the namespace path is used to perform the copy operation. Therefore, the following code will successfully copy the Applications namespace from \root to \root\CIMV2:

```
ManagementObject mo = new
    ManagementObject(@"\\.\root:__NAMESPACE='Applications'");
mo.CopyTo(@"\\.\root\CIMV2");
```

The CopyTo method conveniently returns the object of type ManagementPath, which represents the full object path of a newly created instance:

```
ManagementPath mp = new ManagementObject(
    @"\\.\root:__NAMESPACE='Applications'").CopyTo(@"\\.\root\CIMV2");
Console.WriteLine(mp.Path);
```

This code will produce the following output, which indicates that the
Applications namespace has been successfully copied to the desired location:

```
\\.\root\CIMV2:__NAMESPACE.Name="Applications"
```

When you are copying instances of nonsystem classes between namespaces,
you must make sure that the class definition of the object exists in the target
namespace. For instance, the following code will fail, since the definition for
Win32_Process does not exist in \root namespace:

```
ManagementObject mo = new ManagementObject(@"Win32_Process=269");
mo.CopyTo(@"\\.\root");
```

Finally, to satisfy all developers' tastes, the ManagementObject type offers several overloaded versions of the CopyTo method, three of which are shown below:

```
public ManagementPath CopyTo (
    ManagementPath path
);
public ManagementPath CopyTo (
    string      path ,
    PutOptions options
);
public ManagementPath CopyTo (
    ManagementPath path ,
    PutOptions      options
);
```

Besides providing you with the additional freedom of using the object of type
ManagementPath to specify the destination path rather than the string parameter,
two of these methods also take a PutOptions argument, which may help ensure
the desired semantics of the copy operation.

Removing Objects

If you bothered to compile and execute any of the code above, you must have
a few newly created object instances dangling around your WMI namespaces.

To clean these up, you may want to use a `Delete` method of the
`ManagementObject` type:

```
ManagementObject mo = new
    ManagementObject(@"\\.\root\CIMV2:__NAMESPACE='Applications'");
mo.Delete();
```

The delete operation is atomic and does not have to be followed by the `Put`
method call. However, since `Delete` affects the CIM Repository rather than the
local copy of the object, the object reference is not automatically invalidated following the `Delete`:

```
ManagementObject mo = new
    ManagementObject(@"\\.\root\CIMV2:__NAMESPACE='Applications'");
mo.Delete();
foreach(PropertyData pd in mo.Properties) {
    Console.WriteLine("{0} {1}", pd.Name, pd.Value);
}
```

The preceding code works perfectly, despite the fact that the object no longer
exists in the CIM Repository. To avoid all kinds of hard-to-find bugs, it is probably
the best to set the object reference to null as soon as `Delete` completes.

The `ManagementObject` type offers a few overloaded versions of `Delete`, one
of which takes a parameter of type `DeleteOptions`. The `DeleteOptions` type is
a descendant of the `ManagementOptions` type, and in the current release of FCL, it
does not have any properties of its own. Its only purpose is to hold the provider-
specific context data in those cases where such data is necessary.

Comparing Objects

After you spend some time experimenting with new and existing object
instances, you will eventually find yourself in dire need of some way to compare
them; you can use such a comparison mechanism to determine whether two distinct instances of the `ManagementObject` type refer to the same WMI object. The
basic comparison function, provided by the `ManagementObject` type, is the
`CompareTo` method, which is inherited from its base type `ManagementBaseObject`.
This method takes two parameters: an object of type `ManagementBaseObject` to
compare the current instance to, and a value of type `ComparisonSettings`, which
is an enumeration type. Depending on the outcome of the comparison operation, this `CompareTo` method returns either the Boolean TRUE or FALSE value.

Normally, the comparison operation takes into account all elements that constitute an object: its class, location, values, and the types of its properties and qualifiers. In certain cases, however, you may find it useful to ignore the object's location or qualifier values. This is exactly what the last parameter of CompareTo method, the comparison mode value of type ComparisonSettings, achieves. The ComparisonSettings type is an enumeration with seven members, listed in Table 2-5.

Table 2-5. Members ComparisonSettings *Enumeration*

COMPARISONSETTINGS MEMBER	DESCRIPTION
IncludeAll	This comparison mode takes into account all elements of an object, including its location, class, qualifiers and property values.
IgnoreCase	This mode enables a case-insensitive comparison of property and qualifier values. The names of properties and qualifies are always compared in a case-insensitive manner regardless of this flag.
IgnoreClass	This mode enables the comparison of instance information only, assuming that the objects being compared belong to the same class. Although very efficient in terms of performance, this flag may cause the CompareTo method to produce undefined results if the objects do not belong to the same class.
IgnoreDefaultValues	This mode causes the comparison to ignore the default property values. It is not applicable to instance comparison operations.
IgnoreFlavor	This mode ignores qualifier flavors such as propagation and override restrictions, although the qualifiers are still taken into account.
IgnoreObjectSource	This mode ignores the location of the objects—for instance, the namespace and the server they reside on.
IgnoreQualifiers	This mode causes the qualifiers to be completely ignored by the comparison operation.

To illustrate how the CompareTo method works, I am going to compare the instance of __NAMESPACE class, named Applications (which I created earlier with the CopyTo method underneath the \root\CIMV2), against the original instance of the Applications namespace in \root:

```
ManagementObject mo1 = new
    ManagementObject(@"\\.\root:__NAMESPACE='Applications'");
ManagementObject mo2 = new
    ManagementObject(@"\\.\root\CIMV2:__NAMESPACE='Applications'");
Console.WriteLine(mo1.CompareTo(mo2, new ComparisonSettings()));
```

This code will print the false value on the console because the two name-space instances, although absolutely identical, reside in different namespaces. If you want to ignore the location of the objects, you would modify the code as follows:

```
ManagementObject mo1 = new
    ManagementObject(@"\\.\root:__NAMESPACE='Applications'");
ManagementObject mo2 = new
    ManagementObject(@"\\.\root\CIMV2:__NAMESPACE='Applications'");
Console.WriteLine(
    mo1.CompareTo(mo2, ComparisonSettings.IgnoreObjectSource));
```

You can combine the members of the ComparisonSettings enumeration to achieve the effect that you desire. For instance, if I have two instances of the __NAMESPACE class—\\root\CIMV2:__NAMESPACE='applications' and \\root:__NAMESPACE='Applications'—and the values of their Name properties differ only in case, the following code fragment will print True on the console:

```
ManagementObject mo1 = new
    ManagementObject(@"\\.\root:__NAMESPACE='Applications'");
ManagementObject mo2 = new
    ManagementObject(@"\\.\root\CIMV2:__NAMESPACE='applications'");
Console.WriteLine(
    mo1.CompareTo(mo2, ComparisonSettings.IgnoreObjectSource |
        ComparisonSettings.IgnoreCase));
```

In addition to the CompareTo method, the ManagementBaseObject, which is a base type for the ManagementObject, overrides the Equals method of the System.Object type. The Equals method is implemented so that it calls the CompareTo method inter-nally, passing zero as a comparison mode. Since zero is an equivalent of the ComparisonSettings.IncludeAll member, the following two code snippets produce identical results:

```
mo1.Equals(mo2);
```

or

```
mo1.CompareTo(mo2, ComparisonSettings.IncludeAll);
```

Finally, if you decide to compare two instances of the `ManagementObject` type using a conventional comparison operator, you have to keep in mind that neither the `ManagementBaseObject` nor the `ManagementObject` type provide an overloaded version of this operator, thus such an operation will be treated as a reference rather than an object comparison:

```
ManagementObject mo1 = new
    ManagementObject(@"\\.\root:__NAMESPACE='Applications'");
ManagementObject mo2 = new
    ManagementObject(@"\\.\root:__NAMESPACE='Applications'");
Console.WriteLine(mo1 == mo2);
```

This code will print `False` on the console, since `mo1` and `mo2` are two distinct object references, even though they point to the same WMI object.

ManagementClass: Analyzing the Schema

The CIM object model is complex and programming against it often requires an ultimate understanding of WMI schema—familiarity with class, property, and method semantics as well as detailed knowledge of inter-class relationships.

To facilitate the schema analysis, the `System.Management` namespace of the FCL offers a `ManagementClass` type that is designed to represent the most fundamental element of CIM—a WMI class. The `ManagementClass` type is a subtype of the `ManagementObject`, as I mentioned earlier in this chapter, and as such, it supports much of the same or similar functionality as the `ManagementObject`. Conceptually, there are also similarities between the `ManagementObject` and the `ManagementClass` since both these types represent some aspects of an arbitrary managed element, depicted by some WMI object. This might be why the designers of the `System.Management` namespace chose to use the `ManagementObject` type as a parent for the `ManagementClass`. However, the purpose of the `ManagementClass` type is very different from that of `ManagementObject`; rather than embodying an instance of WMI class, the `ManagementClass` type characterizes the metadata associated with the instance, or, simply put, its class definition. Thus, the purists of object-oriented design would probably argue that the `ManagementClass` is not really a `ManagementObject`. There is some truth to this, and, perhaps a better solution would have been to subclass both `ManagementObject` and `ManagementClass` from a common base type—ManagementBaseObject—so that all their common functionality would have been factored into the shared parent type. However, despite this minor design deficiency, the `ManagementClass` type does its job just fine.

Constructing a ManagementClass Object

Creating an object of type ManagementClass is very similar to creating an instance of the ManagementObject type. In addition to a default parameterless constructor, which creates an unbound instance, the ManagementClass type offers a few other constructors. These, which are just like the constructors of the ManagementObject type, take either a string parameter or an object of type ManagementPath, which represents the respective class path:

```
ManagementClass mc = new
    ManagementClass(@"\\BCK_OFFICE\root\CIMV2:Win32_WMISetting");
```

or

```
ManagementPath mp = new ManagementPath();
mp.Server = "BCK_OFFICE";
mp.NamespacePath = @"\root\CIMV2";
mp.ClassName = "Win32_WMISetting";
ManagementClass mc = new ManagementClass(mp);
```

The only difference between this and constructing an instance of a ManagementObject type here is that the path is a class path rather than the object path, and as such, it does not include the object identity component. In fact, an attempt to create an instance of a ManagementClass type using an object path will fail, as shown in the following:

```
ManagementClass mc = new
    ManagementClass(@"\\BCK_OFFICE\root\CIMV2:Win32_WMISetting=@");
```

The preceding code will throw an ArgumentOutOfRange exception since the constructor is invoked with an object rather than a valid class path parameter.

Retrieving Class Properties

Once created and bound to a respective WMI class definition, an instance of the ManagementClass type provides a convenient vehicle for analyzing the class properties, qualifiers, and methods. Enumerating properties of a WMI class, for instance, is no different from enumerating the properties of an object:

```
ManagementClass mc = new ManagementClass("Win32_WMISetting");
foreach( PropertyData pd in mc.Properties ) {
    Console.WriteLine("{0} : {1}", pd.Name, pd.Value );
    }
}
```

If you compile and execute this code, you may notice that all the properties of the Win32_WMISetting class, except for one—ASPScriptDefaultNamespace—are empty. This should come as no surprise because the code above operates on a class or schema element rather than on a living instance of an object. Since classes are templates for instances and have no state on their own, in most cases, class properties will have no associated values. There are, however, exceptions, as in the case of the ASPScriptDefaultNamespace property of the Win32_WMISetting. This property has a default value assigned to it as part of the class definition:

```
class Win32_WMISetting : CIM_Setting
{
    ...
    string ASPScriptDefaultNamespace = "\\\\root\\cimv2";
    ...
}
```

When such a default value is assigned to a property of a class, all the instances of the class, when created, will have their respective properties set to this default value, unless the instance property value is explicitly modified. The default property values, which are specified within the WMI class definition, are accessible through the Value property of the PropertyData object that is contained in the properties collection of the ManagementClass.

The Value property is the only field that has a different meaning depending on whether it represents the property value of an object or of a class. All other members of the PropertyData type follow exactly the same semantics for the ManagementClass as they do for the ManagementObject.

Accessing Method Definitions

Another constituent element of the WMI class definition is a method. A method represents an action that can be carried out either on an instance of the WMI class, or on the entire class of objects. Not all WMI classes define methods but those that do often employ methods as a primary tool for manipulating the object data. In order to create an operating system process through WMI, for instance, it is not enough to instantiate the object of Win32_Process class. Instead, you must have the management application call a static Create method of the

Win32_Process. By the same token, just deleting an instance of Win32_Process does not terminate the associated process; instead, you should set up the application so it uses the Terminate method of the Win32_Process object.

The fact that a class declares a method does not automatically mean that a data provider supplies an implementation for that method. When subclassing is being performed, method definitions are always being passed from the superclass to its children, but the actual method implementations are not necessarily being inherited. Typically, each method that has an implementation within a class must have the Implemented qualifier associated with it. If this qualifier is not present, this indicates that the method has no implementation. Therefore, if a subclass redeclares a method that it inherited from its superclass and it omits the Implemented qualifier, the method implementation from the superclass will be used at runtime.

Similar to the methods of a class that was built using one of the modern object-oriented programming languages such as C#, WMI methods can have either static or instance methods. *Static methods* operate on the WMI class rather than its instance, and therefore, they can only be invoked through the class rather than an instance reference. An example of a static method is the Create method of the Win32_Process class, which is used to launch new operating system processes. Instance methods, on the other hand, need an instance of the WMI class on which to operate. Thus, the Terminate method of the Win32_Process class, which is used to kill a given operating system process, can only be called for a valid instance of the Win32_Process class, which represents a process to be terminated. In WMI, static methods are designated by the Static qualifier; the absence of this qualifier indicates that a method applies to an instance rather than a class.

A method definition consists of three parts: the method name, the method return type, and the method parameters. Although the name of the method and its return type are fairly self-explanatory, method parameters deserve some explanation. In general, defining parameters for a method is somewhat similar to defining the properties of a class—each parameter has a name and an associated data type and the name and the type are subject to the same restrictions as those of class properties (for a list of CIM data types see Table 2-1). Unlike properties, however, parameters have some additional qualities.

First, all parameters are categorized as input, output, or input-output. In WMI, this is designated by In, Out, or In, Out qualifiers respectively.

Second, parameter lists of a particular method often have a certain order. To enforce the ordering and uniquely identify each method parameter, the WMI MOF compiler automatically adds the ID qualifier to each parameter definition within a method unless the ID attribute is explicitly provided in the method declaration. The ID attribute uniquely identifies each parameter's position within the parameter list for a given method: the first parameter is assigned the ID of zero, the second is assigned one, and so on.

Just like properties, method parameters may have default values assigned to them, and it is these values that are used whenever the calling application does not explicitly supply a value.

In FCL, a WMI method definition is represented by an instance of MethodData type. The MethodData is a simple type that has just a few properties; these are listed in Table 2-6.

Table 2-6. MethodData Properties

PROPERTY	DESCRIPTION
Name	A string that represents the name of the method.
Origin	A string that represents the name of the class that defines the method.
Qualifiers	A collection of QualifierData objects that represent the qualifiers that are defined for the method.
InParameters	An object of type ManagementBaseObject that represents the input parameters for the method.
OutParameters	An object of type ManagementBaseObject that represents the output parameters for the method.

The fact that input and output method parameters are represented by objects of type ManagementBaseObject that are referred to by InParameters and OutParameters properties of MethodData is somewhat interesting. Logically, you might expect method parameters to be described by a collection of PropertyData objects, each representing a single parameter, but instead, these parameters are packaged into the Properties collection of a ManagementBaseObject, which is returned by InParameters and OutParameters properties.

Why would the designers of the System.Management namespace choose to wrap the parameters collection with an instance of ManagementBaseObject, which does not seem to add value? The answer becomes clear once you understand how method parameters are defined in CIM Repository. It turns out that the WMI parameter definitions for a given method are described in a repository by an instance of a system class __PARAMETERS. This is really an abstract class that is used to store method parameter definitions. In its initial form, the __PARAMETERS class has only the standard system properties, but whenever a method with its associated parameter definitions is recorded into the repository, WMI creates an instance of the __PARAMETERS class and dynamically adds properties, each of which represents a single method parameter. This instance of the __PARAMETERS class is embodied by the ManagementBaseObject, which is returned by the InParameters and OutParameters properties of the MethodData type.

Yet, another interesting design choice is the existence of two separate objects of type ManagementBaseObject that are referred to by the InParameters and OutParameters properties of the MethodData instance. Apparently, having a single parameters collection so that each parameter is explicitly marked as input, output, or both, might have been a better approach because it would certainly simplify the coding. It turns out that such design has to do with the way parameters are defined in the repository. For those methods that have both input and output parameters, WMI creates two instances of the __PARAMETERS class that represent the method's input and output respectively. The downside of such a design is the fact that some parameters—those that are used as both input and output—are duplicated. As a result, they appear in the properties collections of both input and output instances of ManagementBaseObject.

Method parameters are identified by name and are specified within the WMI method declaration. As a result, each PropertyData object that represents a single method parameter will have its Name property set appropriately. The method return type, however, does not have an explicit name assigned to it as part of the method definition. To handle the return values, WMI adds a special property, called ReturnValue, to the properties collection of the ManagementBaseObject.

You can access the MethodData objects, which describe the methods of a particular class, through the Methods property of the ManagementClass object, as shown here:

```
ManagementClass mc = new ManagementClass("Win32_Process");
foreach(MethodData md in mc.Methods) {
    Console.WriteLine(md.Name);
}
```

If you have a MethodData object that describes a particular method, it is easy to enumerate all the method parameters:

```
ManagementClass mc = new ManagementClass("Win32_Process");
foreach(MethodData md in mc.Methods) {
    ManagementBaseObject pin = md.InParameters;
    if ( pin != null ) {
        foreach(PropertyData pd in pin.Properties) {
            Console.WriteLine(pd.Name);
        }
    }
    ManagementBaseObject pout = md.OutParameters;
    if ( pout != null ) {
        foreach(PropertyData pd in pout.Properties) {
```

```
        Console.WriteLine(pd.Name);
      }
   }
}
```

Checking for null values here is necessary because for methods with no input parameters, the InParameters property of the MethodData object will be set to null.

Another thing to keep in mind is that input-output parameters will appear in the Properties collections of both input and output ManagementBaseObjects. Thus, there is a chance that the preceding code example will print these parameters twice. To ensure that each parameter is listed only once, you may want to do something like this:

```
using System.Collections;
...
ManagementClass mc = new ManagementClass("Win32_Process");
MethodData md = mc.Methods["Create"];
Hashtable ht = new Hashtable();
ManagementBaseObject pin = md.InParameters;
if ( pin != null ) {
   foreach(PropertyData pd in pin.Properties)
      ht.Add(pd.Name, pd);
}
ManagementBaseObject pout = md.OutParameters;
if ( pout != null ) {
   foreach(PropertyData pd in pout.Properties)
      if ( !ht.ContainsKey(pd.Name) )
         ht.Add(pd.Name, pd);
}
foreach(object o in ht.Values) {
   PropertyData pd = (PropertyData)o;
   Console.WriteLine("{0} {1}", pd.Name, pd.Type);
}
```

First, all the input parameters are loaded into a hash table, which is used here as a temporary container of PropertyData objects. Then, each output parameter is added to the hash table, but only if a parameter with the same name is not already contained in the hash. When this code finishes iterating through the Properties collection of the output ManagementBaseObject, the hash table will contain a single PropertyData object for each of the method parameters. This may not be the most efficient way to eliminate duplicates, but it certainly serves its purpose.

You may find it confusing that the `ManagementObject` type, and therefore, its subtype `ManagementClass`, offers a method called `GetMethodParameters`. This method returns an object of type `ManagementBaseObject` so that the `Properties` collection of the returned object describes the method parameters. Thus, you would imagine that the following is a more concise alternative to the code above:

```
ManagementClass mc = new ManagementClass("Win32_Process");
foreach(MethodData md in mc.Methods) {
  ...
   ManagementBaseObject mb = mc.GetMethodParameters(md.Name);
   if (mb != null ) {
      foreach(PropertyData pd in mb.Properties) {
         Console.WriteLine("{0} {1}", pd.Name, pd.Value);
}
   }
}
```

Unfortunately, this code will not produce the correct results, because the `GetMethodParameters` method returns only the input parameters. The reason for this is that this method is not intended to retrieve the schema information. Instead, it was designed to help invoke the WMI object methods. (Method invocation will be described in details later in this chapter.) Therefore, in order to enumerate all parameters of a given method, you have no other choice but to iterate through both the input and the output property collections.

Retrieving Class, Property, and Method Qualifiers

Finally, the last important elements of the WMI schema, which are easily accessible through an interface that is provided by the `ManagementClass` type, are the class, property, and method parameter qualifier declarations. As was briefly mentioned earlier in this chapter, *qualifiers* are special designations that are attached to various elements of the WMI schema in order to communicate the precise details of an element usage to schema consumers. For instance, in order to specify those properties of a WMI class that uniquely identify its instances, schema designers attach a Key qualifier to each property that makes up the key for that class. In the current release of WMI, qualifiers are strictly informational, meaning that the semantics specified by qualifiers are not enforced by WMI. As an example, Read qualifiers, designating properties of a class as read-only, do not make these properties write-protected, and it is up to the provider to ensure the integrity of the data. Thus, the primary purpose of qualifiers is to communicate some additional schema element usage details to the management applications, which are capable of interpreting the qualifiers.

The qualifier's definition consists of three parts: the qualifier name, the qualifier value, and one or more qualifier flavors. The flavor acts as a "meta-qualifier" providing additional information about an associated qualifier. For instance, a flavor indicates whether a qualifier can be localized. Besides localization, the most important pieces of information communicated by qualifier flavors are the rules for propagating the associated qualifier from the class to its subclasses and instances and the rules that specify whether a subclass or instance can override a qualifier. Table 2-7 lists all the defined qualifier flavors and their meanings.

Table 2-7. Qualifier Flavors

FLAVOR	DESCRIPTION
Amended	Indicates that the associated qualifier is not required as part of the class definition and can be moved to the amendment class. The amendment class is used for localization and will be discussed in detail later in this chapter.
DisableOverride	Indicates that a class, derived from the current class or an instance of the current class, may not override the associated qualifier.
EnableOverride	Indicates that a class, derived from the current class or an instance of the current class, may override the associated qualifier. This is a default.
NotToInstance	Indicates that the associated qualifier is not propagated to the instances of the current class. This is a default.
NotToSubclass	Indicates that the associated qualifier is not propagated to the subclasses of the current class. This is a default.
ToInstance	Indicates that the associated qualifier is propagated to the instances of the current class.
ToSubclass	Indicates that the associated qualifier is propagated to the subclasses of the current class.

Although a qualifier is always assigned a value, it is never explicitly associated with a particular data type. Instead, qualifiers are implicitly typed based on their value and, if no initial value is specified, a qualifier's value is assumed to be the Boolean TRUE value.

Earlier we mentioned that qualifiers are represented in the FCL by the QualifierData type. This is a very simple type that has just a few properties, which are listed in Table 2-8.

Table 2-8. QualifierData *Properties*

QUALIFIERDATA PROPERTY	DESCRIPTION
Name	Name of the qualifier.
Value	Value of the qualifier.
IsLocal	Boolean, indicates whether the qualifier is declared locally or propagated from the base class.
IsAmended	Boolean, indicates whether the qualifier is amended. This corresponds to the Amended qualifier flavor.
IsOverridable	Boolean, indicates whether subclasses and instances of the class are allowed to override the qualifier. This corresponds to EnableOverride/DisableOverride qualifier flavors.
PropagatesToInstances	Boolean, indicates whether the qualifier propagates to instances of the class. Corresponds to ToInstance/NotToInstance qualifier flavors.
PropagatesToSubclasses	Boolean, indicates whether the qualifier propagates to subclasses of the class. Corresponds to ToSubclass/NotToSubclass qualifier flavors.

The QualifierData is a universal type that represents any kind of WMI qualifiers, regardless of whether these qualifiers are associated with a class, a property, a method, or method parameters. In fact, the QualifierData object that represents a property qualifier is indistinguishable from an object that represents, say, a class qualifier. The only thing that sets these two apart is the Qualifiers collection that holds them. Thus, all class qualifiers are contained in the Qualifiers collection of the ManagementClass object and can be enumerated as follows:

```
ManagementClass mc = new ManagementClass("Win32_Process");
foreach(QualifierData qd in mc.Qualifiers) {
    Console.WriteLine("{0} {1}", qd.Name, qd.Value );
}
```

Property qualifiers, on the other hand, relate to a particular property; as a result, they are contained in the Qualifiers collection of their respective PropertyData object, as shown here:

```
ManagementClass mc = new ManagementClass("Win32_Process");
foreach(PropertyData pd in mc.Properties) {
    ...
    foreach(QualifierData qd in pd.Qualifiers) {
```

```
      Console.WriteLine("{0} {1}", qd.Name, qd.Value );
   }
   ...
}
```

By the same token, qualifiers that are associated with methods are contained in the Qualifier collection of their respective MethodData object. The instances of the MethodData type represent individual methods of a WMI class, and they can be accessed through the Methods property of the ManagementClass type:

```
ManagementClass mc = new ManagementClass("Win32_Process");
foreach(MethodData md in mc.Methods) {
   ...
   foreach(QualifierData qd in md.Qualifiers) {
      Console.WriteLine("{0} {1}", qd.Name, qd.Value );
   }
   ...
}
```

Finally, qualifiers for method parameters are held in the Qualifiers collection of the PropertyData object that represents the method parameter. PropertyData objects that describe the parameters of a method can be accessed through the InParameters and OutParameters properties of the MethodData object as shown here:

```
ManagementClass mc = new ManagementClass("Win32_Process");
foreach(MethodData md in mc.Methods) {
   ...
   if (md.InParameters != null ) {
      foreach(PropertyData pd in md.InParameters.Properties) {
         foreach(QualifierData qd in pd.Qualifiers) {
            Console.WriteLine("{0} {1}", qd.Name, qd.Value );
         }
      }
   }
   if (md.OutParameters != null ) {
      foreach(PropertyData pd in md.OutParameters.Properties) {
         foreach(QualifierData qd in pd.Qualifiers) {
            Console.WriteLine("{0} {1}", qd.Name, qd.Value );
         }
      }
   }
   ...
}
```

This code, which is similar to the code that I used earlier to iterate though the collections of method parameters, reads the InParameters and OutParameters properties of the MethodData object and then iterates through the Properties collection of the resulting ManagementBaseObject. There, it prints all the qualifiers that are associated with a given property on the system console. At this point you must check whether InParameters and OutParameters properties point to valid instances of the ManagementBaseObject—if, for instance, a method has no input parameters, the InParameters property of its MethodData object will be set to null.

Just like the property values, qualifier values are not necessarily scalar. Some qualifiers may contain arrays of values—for instance, a standard qualifier ValueMap, which defines a set of allowable values for a given property or method parameter, is obviously an array. Thus, my code snippets, shown earlier, will not be able to correctly print out the values of array qualifiers. Unfortunately, since qualifiers are not explicitly typed, the QualifierData type, unlike the PropertyData type, does not have properties that reflect the underlying data type of the qualifier, nor do they indicate whether it is an array or scalar. Thus, a different approach should be used:

```
ManagementClass mc = new ManagementClass("Win32_Process");
foreach(QualifierData qd in mc.Qualifiers) {
    Console.WriteLine("{0} {1}", qd.Name, FormatQualifier(qd));
}
...
public static object FormatQualifier(QualifierData pd) {
    if (pd.Value.GetType().IsArray) {
        StringBuilder sb = new StringBuilder();
        sb.Append(Environment.NewLine);
        foreach(object o in (Array)pd.Value) {
            sb.Append(o.ToString());
            sb.Append(Environment.NewLine);
            }
        return sb;
    } else {
        return pd.Value;
    }
}
}
```

Here I use the fact that the qualifier value, which is represented by the object of type System.Object, has an underlying type. This type can be accessed via the GetType method of System.Object. The resulting object of type System.Type exposes the IsArray property, which allows me to determine whether the qualifier value is indeed an array.

Analyzing the Schema–A Complete Example

To conclude the discussion of the various elements that constitute a WMI class definition, I will show you a complete example. The example program ClassDef.exe (Listing 2-4) takes a single command line parameter—a path to a WMI class—and prints out the full class definition on the system console. The output bears strong resemblance to MOF class definitions; however, I did not attempt to produce a syntactically correct MOF schema. Frankly, the only reasons I chose to use the MOF-like notation were for readability and brevity—other formats could easily have been either overwhelmingly verbose or too confusing.

The program in Listing 2-4 is fairly straightforward and uses most of the constructs that were discussed earlier in this chapter. The `Main` method of `PrintClassDefinition` class iterates through the qualifiers, properties, and methods of a given class and then it invokes the helper functions `FormatQualifier`, `FormatProperty`, and `FormatMethod` to produce printable representation of the respective elements of WMI class definition. These helper functions are also self-explanatory, and the only one that deserves mentioning, is, perhaps, `FormatMethod`.

As you may remember, enumerating method arguments is a bit tricky because there are two collections that contain input and output parameters respectively. Additionally, there is a chance that some parameters that act as both input and output are duplicated in each of the collections. In one of the code examples above, we used `Hashtable` to temporarily store the `PropertyData` objects representing the parameters, and eliminate duplicates based on the parameter name. `FormatMethod` method takes a different approach. Instead of using `Hashtable`, it loads both input and output parameters into a `SortedList` that is keyed by the value of the `ID` qualifier that is attached to each parameter. Besides eliminating duplicates, this approach has the advantage of automatically sorting the parameter list based on the `ID` qualifier, thus ensuring that parameters are printed out in a correct order. One of the parameters, `ReturnValue`, receives special treatment for two reasons:

First of all, none of its qualifiers are printed as part of the method declaration. Since `ReturnValue` is not a real parameter, but rather a placeholder for method return type, it always has the same qualifiers: a CIM data type, and a designation of an output parameter. Thus, printing these qualifiers does not add any value.

Second, `ReturnValue` does not have an `ID` qualifier, because it is not a part of the formal method parameter list. In fact, its only property of interest is its data type; therefore, instead of storing `ReturnValue` into the `SortedList`, I simply print the value of its `Type` property.

Listing 2-4. Sample Program ClassDef.exe.

```
class PrintClassDefinition {
    static void Main(string[] args) {
        if (args.Length < 1) {
            Console.WriteLine("usage: ClassDef <path>");
            return;
        }
        ManagementClass mc = new ManagementClass(args[0]);
        // process class qualifiers
        foreach(QualifierData qd in mc.Qualifiers)
            Console.WriteLine(FormatQualifier(qd,0));
        Console.WriteLine(@"class {0} : {1} {{",
            mc["__CLASS"], mc["__SUPERCLASS"] );
        // process properties
        foreach(PropertyData pd in mc.Properties)
            Console.WriteLine(FormatProperty(pd,3) + ";");
        // process methods
        foreach(MethodData md in mc.Methods)
            Console.WriteLine(FormatMethod(md,3) + ";");
        Console.WriteLine("}");
    }
    static object FormatQualifier(QualifierData qd, int indent) {
        StringBuilder sb = new StringBuilder();
        sb.Append(' ', indent);
        sb.AppendFormat("[{0}={1}", qd.Name, FormatValue(qd.Value));
        if (qd.PropagatesToInstance)
            sb.Append(" ToInstance");
        if (qd.PropagatesToSubclass)
            sb.Append(" ToSubclass");
        if (qd.IsAmended)
            sb.Append(" Amended");
        if(qd.IsOverridable)
            sb.Append(" Overridable");
        return sb.Append("]");
    }
    static object FormatProperty(PropertyData pd, int indent) {
        StringBuilder sb = new StringBuilder();
        // process property qualifiers
        foreach(QualifierData qd in pd.Qualifiers) {
            sb.Append(FormatQualifier(qd,indent));
            sb.Append(Environment.NewLine);
        }
```

```
        sb.Append(' ',indent);
        sb.AppendFormat("{0} {1}",
            pd.Type.ToString() + (pd.IsArray ? "[]" : string.Empty), pd.Name);
        if ( pd.Value != null )
            sb.AppendFormat("={0}", FormatValue(pd.Value));
        return sb;
}

static object FormatMethod(MethodData md, int indent) {
    StringBuilder sb = new StringBuilder();
    // process method qualifiers
    foreach(QualifierData qd in md.Qualifiers) {
        sb.Append(FormatQualifier(qd,3));
        sb.Append(Environment.NewLine);
    }
    // eliminate duplicate in/out parameters
    SortedList sl = new SortedList();
    if (md.InParameters != null)
        foreach(PropertyData pd in md.InParameters.Properties)
            sl[pd.Qualifiers["ID"].Value] = pd;
    if (md.OutParameters != null)
        foreach(PropertyData pd in md.OutParameters.Properties)
            if (pd.Name != "ReturnValue")
                sl[pd.Qualifiers["ID"].Value] = pd;
    // format method return type and method name
    sb.Append(' ',indent);
    sb.AppendFormat("{0} {1}(",
        ((PropertyData)md.OutParameters.Properties["ReturnValue"]).Type,
        md.Name);
    if (sl.Count > 1 ) {
        sb.Append(Environment.NewLine);
        string[] arr = new string[sl.Count];
        int i = 0;
        foreach(PropertyData pd in sl.Values)
            arr[i++] = FormatProperty(pd, indent+3).ToString();
        sb.Append(string.Join(","+Environment.NewLine, arr));
        sb.Append(Environment.NewLine);
        sb.Append(' ',indent);
    }
    return sb.Append(")");
}
static object FormatValue(object v) {
    if (v.GetType().IsArray) {
```

```
        string[] arr = new string[((Array)v).GetUpperBound(0)+1];
        Array.Copy((Array)v, arr, ((Array)v).GetUpperBound(0)+1);
        return "{" + string.Join(",", arr) + "}";
    } else {
        return v;
    }
  }
}
```

Although quite useful, this program has a few deficiencies. For instance, if you compare the output produced by ClassDef.exe against the MOF class definitions that are output by various WMI tools, such as the CIM Studio MOF generation wizard, you will notice that, for most WMI classes, our program lists more properties and methods than the actual MOF schema. The explanation for this is simple: ClassDef.exe does not differentiate between inherited and locally defined properties and methods. This is easily fixable—all I have to do is check the IsLocal property of each class element and suppress printing if the respective element is not defined locally. Yet another, more involved problem is localizable schema elements, which this program does not take into account. The solution to this one, although fairly simple, will not be shown here. Instead, the in-depth discussion of WMI localization and internationalization issues will be presented in "Localization and Internationalization Issues" later in this chapter.

ManagementClass: Analyzing Relationships Between Schema Elements

As you found out earlier in this chapter, objects related to a given instance of a WMI class can be retrieved using the GetRelated method of the ManagementObject type. Obtaining the class definitions of related classes, however, is slightly more involved than retrieving the instances of these classes.

Retrieving Related Classes

You may remember that the ManagementObject type has an overloaded version of the GetRelated method, which, among other parameters, takes a Boolean flag that specifies whether this method returns live object instances or class definitions. Thus, the definitions of classes, related to Win32_Process class may be retrieved as follows:

```
ManagementObject mo = new ManagementObject(@"Win32_Process=269");
foreach(ManagementBaseObject o in mo.GetRelated(
    null, null, null, null, null, null, true, null)) {
    Console.WriteLine(o["__PATH"]);
}
```

Here, the seventh parameter to the GetRelated method—the Boolean flag—is
set to true, indicating that the method is required to return just the schema information rather than instances.

The output produced by this code verifies that the objects retrieved are
indeed classes rather than instances:

```
\\BCK_OFFICE\ROOT\CIMV2:Win32_ComputerSystem
\\BCK_OFFICE\ROOT\CIMV2:CIM_DataFile
```

Naturally, since the ManagementClass type inherits the GetRelated method
from its parent, ManagementObject, you may assume that the following code will
work just fine:

```
ManagementClass mc = new ManagementClass(@"Win32_Process");
foreach(ManagementBaseObject o in mc.GetRelated(
    null, null, null, null, null, null, true, null)) {
    Console.WriteLine(o["__PATH"]);
}
```

Unfortunately, instead of listing all classes related to Win32_Process, the code
will throw a ManagementException, complaining about an invalid query.

It turns out that in order to retrieve all classes or instances that satisfy a particular criteria (in this case, classes related to Win32_Process), the CIM Repository
must be queried using a special query language, WQL. Thus, when the GetRelated
method is invoked, it constructs an instance of the RelationshipQuery type
(covered in Chapter 3), which in turn assembles a WQL query, based on the
parameters passed to GetRelated. While the detailed coverage of WQL will not be
provided until Chapter 3, I will cover at least the basic WQL query types here to
make sure you understand how the GetRelated method works.

When it comes to querying for related classes, which are often referred to in
WMI documentation as associators, there are several basic types of WQL queries.
You choose the proper query type based on whether a requesting application is
attempting to retrieve WMI classes or instances. Table 2-9 lists all the valid relationship query types.

Table 2-9. Association Query Types

QUERY TYPE	QUERY ENDPOINT	COMMENTS
Normal	Instance or class	Analyzes only the instances of association classes. The result may contain both instances and classes.
ClassDefsOnly	Instance	Analyzes only the instances of association classes. The result contains only class definitions.
SchemaOnly	Class	Analyzes only the association classes. The result set contains only class definitions.

Until now, we have seen only the normal and ClassDefsOnly queries. The problem with these two query types is that in order for them to produce meaningful results, there should be at least one WMI class instance involved. This is not the case with classes, since classes may not relate to instances and may only be associated with other classes. Thus, the only query type that is appropriate for retrieving the definitions of classes that are related to a given class, is a SchemaOnly type. Unfortunately, none of the GetRelated method versions supports the SchemaOnly queries, which renders this method useless for working with classes.

To solve this problem, ManagementClass type defines another method, GetRelatedClasses, which is specifically designed to construct SchemaOnly queries, regardless of its arguments. Thus, using the simplest overloaded form of GetRelatedClasses method, I can rewrite the previous code example as follows:

```
ManagementClass mc = new ManagementClass(@"Win32_Process");
foreach(ManagementBaseObject o in mc.GetRelatedClasses()) {
    Console.WriteLine(o["__PATH"]);
}
```

This code finally works and produces the following output:

```
\\BCK_OFFICE\ROOT\CIMV2:Win32_ComputerSystem
```

Unlike the output of the GetRelated method invoked for an instance of the Win32_Process class, this output does not include the class definition for CIM_DataFile. In order to understand what is happening here, you need to look at the definitions of the WMI association classes involved:

```
class CIM_ProcessExecutable : CIM_Dependency
{
    CIM_DataFile ref Antecedent = NULL;
    CIM_Process ref Dependent = NULL;
    ...
}

class Win32_SystemProcesses : CIM_SystemComponent
{
    Win32_ComputerSystem ref GroupComponent = NULL;
    Win32_Process ref PartComponent = NULL;
}
```

The first association class, CIM_ProcessExecutable, is used to express the relationship between the operating system process and the executable files that make up the process image. The second, Win32_SystemProcess, depicts the connection between a process and a computer system it is running on.

The interesting fact here is that the CIM_ProcessExecutable association does not reference the Win32_Process class; instead, it references its parent, CIM_Process. Strictly speaking, an instance of the Win32_Process class is also an instance of the CIM_Process; that is why, when it is analyzing the actual association objects, the GetRelated method retrieves all the objects that are linked through these associations—regardless of whether the relationship is express via superclass references.

The GetRelatedClasses method, on the other hand, does not analyze the association objects, but rather the association classes. In this case, you will find that considering the relationships at the superclass level is dangerous. This is because it may lead you to include those associations that are never instantiated or, in other words, those that never exist in real life. Therefore, the GetRelatedClasses method would only retrieve classes that are related to the current class through associations that reference the actual classes rather than their superclasses.

Yet another thing to watch out for is duplicate class objects, which GetRelatedClasses method may potentially return. Let us consider the following scenario:

```
ManagementClass mc = new ManagementClass(@"CIM_ComputerSystem");
foreach(ManagementBaseObject o in mc.GetRelatedClasses()) {
    Console.WriteLine(o["__PATH"]);
}
```

You may notice that `CIM_OperatingSystem` is included twice in the output produced by this code:

```
\\BCK_OFFICE\ROOT\CIMV2:CIM_OperatingSystem
\\BCK_OFFICE\ROOT\CIMV2:CIM_SystemResource
\\BCK_OFFICE\ROOT\CIMV2:CIM_DMA
\\BCK_OFFICE\ROOT\CIMV2:CIM_IRQ
\\BCK_OFFICE\ROOT\CIMV2:CIM_MemoryMappedIO
\\BCK_OFFICE\ROOT\CIMV2:CIM_FileSystem
\\BCK_OFFICE\ROOT\CIMV2:CIM_OperatingSystem
\\BCK_OFFICE\ROOT\CIMV2:CIM_SoftwareElement
\\BCK_OFFICE\ROOT\CIMV2:Win32_SoftwareElement
```

The problem here is that there are two different association classes that link the `CIM_ComputerSystem` with the `CIM_OperatingSystem`:

```
class CIM_InstalledOS : CIM_SystemComponent
{
    CIM_ComputerSystem ref GroupComponent = NULL;
    CIM_OperatingSystem ref PartComponent = NULL;
    ...
}


class CIM_RunningOS : CIM_Dependency
{
    CIM_OperatingSystem ref Antecedent = NULL;
    CIM_ComputerSystem ref Dependent = NULL;
}
```

These two associations are designed to express different kinds of relationships between classes. The `CIM_InstalledOS` depicts the containment relationship, while the `CIM_RunningOS` is a dependency association. Fortunately, the `ManagementClass` type provides an overloaded version of the `GetRelatedClasses` method, which allows the output to be filtered based on a certain criteria:

```
public ManagementObjectCollection GetRelatedClasses (
    string relatedClass ,
    string relationshipClass ,
    string relationshipQualifier ,
    string relatedQualifier ,
    string relatedRole ,
    string thisRole ,
    EnumerationOptions options
);
```

where the parameters are defined as follows:

relatedClass: Optional string parameter that contains the class name. If this parameter is specified, it indicates that all returned elements must be of a given class or a class derived from a given class.

relationshipClass: Optional string parameter that contains the name of the association class. If this parameter is specified, it indicates that the class for which the GetRelatedClasses method is invoked and the resulting classes must be connected via a given association class or a class derived from a given class.

relationshipQualifier: Optional string parameter that contains the name of the qualifier. If this parameter is specified, it indicates that the class for which the GetRelatedClasses method is invoked and the resulting classes must be connected via a class, which includes a given qualifier.

relatedQualifier: Optional string parameter that contains the name of the qualifier. If this parameter is specified, it indicates that all returned classes must include a given qualifier.

relatedRole: Optional string parameter that contains the name of the role. If this parameter is specified, it indicates that all returned classes must play a particular role in the association. The role is defined as a name of the property of an association class, which is a reference property that points to a given class.

thisRole: Optional string parameter that contains the name of the role. If this parameter is specified, it indicates that the class for which the GetRelatedClasses method is invoked must play a particular role in the association. The role is defined as a name of the property of an association class, which is a reference property that points to a given class.

options: Optional object of type EnumerationOptions. If this object is specified, it controls various aspects of the GetRelatedClasses method behavior.

Using this version of the GetRelatedClasses method, the preceding code can be rewritten to only return the classes that are engaged in a containment relationship with the CIM_ComputerSystem class so that the latter acts as a container:

```
ManagementClass mc = new ManagementClass(@"CIM_ComputerSystem");
foreach(ManagementBaseObject o in mc.GetRelatedClasses(
    null,"CIM_SystemComponent",null,null,null,"GroupComponent", null)) {
    Console.WriteLine(o["__PATH"]);
}
```

Here we request all classes related to the current class via the containment association CIM_SystemComponent, or an association derived from it, where the current class plays a role of a container—GroupComponent. The output correctly lists the CIM_OperatingSystem class only once:

```
\\BCK_OFFICE\ROOT\CIMV2:CIM_OperatingSystem
\\BCK_OFFICE\ROOT\CIMV2:CIM_SystemResource
\\BCK_OFFICE\ROOT\CIMV2:CIM_DMA
\\BCK_OFFICE\ROOT\CIMV2:CIM_IRQ
\\BCK_OFFICE\ROOT\CIMV2:CIM_MemoryMappedIO
\\BCK_OFFICE\ROOT\CIMV2:CIM_FileSystem
```

Finally, there is another overloaded version of the GetRelatedClasses method that takes a single string parameter, which represents the class name of which the resulting elements should be members, or from which they should be derived:

```
public ManagementObjectCollection GetRelatedClasses (
    string relatedClass
);
```

Although this version of the method has limited usefulness, it may come in handy in certain situations. For instance, when retrieving classes related to Win32_ComputerSystem, the output will include Win32_WMISettings class, which does not really represent a managed element and is usually of no concern to management applications. To ensure that the output contains just those classes that correspond to managed elements in the enterprise, the following code may be used:

```
 ManagementClass mc = new ManagementClass(@"Win32_ComputerSystem");
foreach(ManagementBaseObject o in mc.GetRelatedClasses(
    "CIM_LogicalElement")) {
    Console.WriteLine(o["__PATH"]);
}
```

Since the Win32_WMISettings class is not a subclass of CIM_LogicalElement, it will not be a part of the output produced by this code.

Retrieving Association Classes

Every once in a while, a managed application will be interested in retrieving the class definitions for the association classes used to link the current class to other elements in the CIM model. For reasons outlined earlier, the GetRelationships method inherited from `ManagementObject` will not work for `ManagementClass`. Instead, the `ManagementClass` type provides its own implementation, called `GetRelationshipClasses`, which is capable of issuing `SchemaOnly` queries. Thus, to list all association classes that reference the `CIM_ComputerSystem` class, we can use the following code:

```
ManagementClass mc = new ManagementClass(@"CIM_ComputerSystem");
foreach(ManagementBaseObject o in mc.GetRelationshipClasses()) {
    Console.WriteLine(o["__PATH"]);
}
```

Just like the `GetRelatedClasses` method, `GetRelationshipClasses` has several overloaded versions, two of which are shown here:

```
public ManagementObjectCollection GetRelationshipClasses (
    string relationshipClass
);
```

where the parameter is defined as follows:

> **relationshipClass**: A string parameter that contains the name of the association class. If this parameter is specified, it indicates that the returned associations must be of a given class or a class derived from a given class.

and

```
public ManagementObjectCollection GetRelationshipClasses (
    string relationshipClass ,
    string relationshipQualifier ,
    string thisRole ,
    EnumerationOptions options
);
```

where the parameters are defined as follows:

> **relationshipClass**: Optional string parameter that contains the name of the association class. If this parameter is specified, it indicates that the returned associations must be of a given class or a class derived from a given class.

> **relationshipQualifier**: Optional string parameter that contains the name of the qualifier. If this parameter is specified, it indicates that the returned association classes must include a given qualifier.

thisRole: Optional string parameter that contains the name of the role. If this parameter is specified, it indicates that the class for which the GetRelationshipClasses method is invoked must play a particular role in the association. The role is defined as a name of the property of an association class, which is a reference property that points to a given class.

options: Optional object of type EnumerationOptions. If this object is specified, it controls various aspects of the GetRelationshipClasses method behavior. See Table 2-2 for a detailed description of the properties of EnumerationOptions type.

Thus, the following example will print names of all dependency association classes that reference CIM_OperatingSystem:

```
ManagementClass mc = new ManagementClass(@"CIM_OperatingSystem");
foreach(ManagementBaseObject o in mc.GetRelationshipClasses(
    "CIM_Dependency")) {
    Console.WriteLine(o["__PATH"]);
}
```

And yet another example will list only those dependencies in which the CIM_OperatingSystem class acts as a dependent class:

```
ManagementClass mc = new ManagementClass(@"CIM_OperatingSystem");
foreach(ManagementBaseObject o in mc.GetRelationshipClasses(
    "CIM_Dependency", null, "Dependent", null)) {
    Console.WriteLine(o["__PATH"]);
}
```

Traversing Class Hierarchies

Besides being able to navigate through the relationships in a CIM model, it is sometimes necessary to obtain the definitions of classes, which are either super- or subclasses of a given WMI class. Retrieving the definition of an immediate superclass is easy:

```
ManagementClass mc = new ManagementClass(@"CIM_ComputerSystem");
ManagementClass smc = new ManagementClass(mc["__SUPERCLASS"].ToString());
Console.WriteLine(smc.Path);
```

Here I simply use the fact that the system property __SUPERCLASS of any WMI class contains the name of the immediate superclass. I can even trace the entire inheritance hierarchy for a given class:

```
ManagementClass mc = new ManagementClass(@"CIM_ComputerSystem");
foreach( string s in (string[])mc["__DERIVATION"]) {
    ManagementClass smc = new ManagementClass(s);
    Console.WriteLine(smc.Path);
}
```

Again, another system property, __DERIVATION, which contains a list of all the superclasses for a given class, comes to the rescue.

However, the situation is different when it is required to enumerate the subclasses of a given class since there is no system property that holds the list of subclasses. To solve this problem, the ManagementClass type offers the GetSubclasses method, which, when invoked for a particular class, returns a collection of classes that are derived from this class. In its simplest form, the GetSubclasses method takes no parameters:

```
ManagementClass mc = new ManagementClass(@"CIM_ComputerSystem");
foreach(ManagementClass dmc in mc.GetSubclasses()) {
    Console.WriteLine(dmc["__PATH"]);
}
```

Unfortunately, the output produced by this code may surprise you:

```
\\BCK_OFFICE\ROOT\CIMV2:CIM_UnitaryComputerSystem
```

Here, instead of retrieving all subclasses of CIM_ComputerSystem, the GetSubclasses method only returns its immediate subclass CIM_UnitaryComputerSystem. It turns out that in order to retrieve a complete list of all subclasses, another overloaded version of the GetSubclasses method should be used. If you remember the EnumerationOptions type, described in Table 2-2, you may recall that one of its properties, EnumerateDeep, controls whether the enumeration is recursive. Thus, the following code should do the trick:

```
ManagementClass mc = new ManagementClass(@"CIM_ComputerSystem");
EnumerationOptions eo = new EnumerationOptions();
eo.EnumerateDeep = true;
foreach( ManagementClass dmc in mc.GetSubclasses(eo)) {
    Console.WriteLine(dmc["__PATH"]);
}
```

This code correctly prints the paths of all subclasses of the
CIM_ComputerSystem on the console:

```
\\BCK_OFFICE\ROOT\CIMV2:CIM_UnitaryComputerSystem
\\BCK_OFFICE\ROOT\CIMV2:Win32_ComputerSystem
```

Our discussion of inter-element relationships within the CIM model would
not be complete without pointing out how to enumerate instances of a particular
WMI class. ManagementClass makes the task of retrieving all instances for a given
class surprisingly easy:

```
ManagementClass mc = new ManagementClass(@"Win32_ComputerSystem");
foreach(ManagementObject o in mc.GetInstances()) {
    Console.WriteLine(o["__PATH"]);
}
```

Here the parameterless version of the GetInstances method is used to enumerate the instances of the Win32_ComputerSystem class. The parameterless
GetInstances method behaves similarly to the GetSubclasses method—it only
retrieves objects that are of the same class as the class for which the method is
invoked. For instance, if called for the CIM_ComputerSystem class, the method will
return an empty collection. In order to retrieve all instances that belong to the
current class or a class derived from the current class, the overloaded version of
the GetInstances method should be used:

```
ManagementClass mc = new ManagementClass(@"CIM_ComputerSystem");
EnumerationOptions eo = new EnumerationOptions();
eo.EnumerateDeep = true;
foreach( ManagementObject o in mc.GetInstances(eo)) {
    Console.WriteLine(o["__PATH"]);
}
```

This code will produce the same output as the previous example where the
GetInstances method was invoked for the Win32_ComputerSystem class:

```
\\BCK_OFFICE\ROOT\CIMV2:Win32_ComputerSystem.Name="BCK_OFFICE"
```

Invoking WMI Object Methods

Most of the code examples presented earlier in this chapter dealt mainly with
reading and analyzing the management data that is accessible through WMI

objects and classes. Although the ability to retrieve the data is certainly crucial for virtually any management application, sometimes you may need to alter some information or carry out an action so that your changes are reflected within the management domain. Creating and killing processes, starting and stopping services, and compressing files are all examples of the day-to-day management tasks that any robust management system is expected to support. Although in some cases you will find it possible to create new WMI objects and alter certain management properties, such actions are likely to only affect the CIM Repository and may not be propagated to respective managed elements. Thus, you will find that creating an instance of the `Win32_Process` class will not launch the new operating system process, and setting the `Compressed` property of `CIM_DataFile` object to `True` will not actually compress the file.

The good news is that WMI does support a plethora of management activities that result in physical changes to the underlying managed environment. However, in order to effect these changes, you have to resort to invoking WMI object methods.

Method Fundamentals

Many WMI classes declare methods; however, the implementation for these methods may not always be available. Typically, only the methods marked with the `Implemented` qualifier within a given class are considered to have an implementation. A subclass that inherits an implemented method from its superclass may choose to provide its own implementation, in which case, the subclass's method should be marked as `Implemented`. If you omit the `Implemented` qualifier, the superclass's implementation will be invoked at runtime.

Depending on the semantics of a particular method, you may invoke it against a WMI class or an instance of the class. Methods that are designed to be called through a class are called *static methods,* a concept that should be familiar to anyone who is proficient in at least one mainstream object-oriented programming language, such as C++ or C#. Interestingly, WMI's treatment of static methods is more similar to C# rather than C++—in other words, if you attempt to invoke a static method against an instance of a WMI class, you will get a ManagementException.

To identify a method as static, the method definition should contain the `Static` qualifier. You will find that static methods are often used to construct new instances of a WMI class. For example, using the static `Create` method of the `Win32_Process` class is the only way to create a `Win32_Process` object that is bound to an operating system process. Such static methods, which are responsible for constructing new WMI objects, are similar to the constructors that are used by many object-oriented languages.

If you want to indicate that a method creates new objects, WMI requires that the method definition contain a Constructor qualifier. You may wonder whether CIMOM automatically invokes constructor methods whenever a new WMI class instance is created. Unfortunately, this is not the case—the Constructor qualifier is purely informational and is completely ignored by WMI. Because the construction process for the majority of managed elements is fairly involved, you will find that charging CIMOM with the responsibility of automatically calling object constructors will significantly increase the implementation complexity while providing little value.

To compliment the constructor methods, many WMI classes declare methods, which are responsible for tearing down the unneeded instances. Such methods, often referred to as *destructors,* are functionally very similar to C++ destructors or C# finalizers. A typical destructor is an instance, rather than a static method, because its purpose is to tear down the object against which it is invoked. Just as the constructors are marked with Constructor qualifiers, the destructor methods should have the Destructor qualifier attached to the method declaration. Again, this qualifier is informational and completely ignored by CIMOM.

The method search algorithm, employed by CIMOM at runtime, depends mainly on where a particular method is implemented in the CIM class hierarchy. In order to fully understand how WMI executes static and instance methods, look at the following example:

```
class A {
    sint32 Foo();
}

class B : A {
    [Implemented] sint32 Foo();
}

class C : B {
    sint32 Foo();
}

class D : C {
    [Implemented] sint32 Foo();
}
```

Here, the instance method, Foo, is first declared in class A and implemented in its subclass B. Class C inherits the method from B but does not provide the implementation.

Finally, the last subclass in a hierarchy, D, overrides the method implementation with its own. When the method Foo is called against an instance of one of the classes in this hierarchy, WMI starts with the class of the current instance and continues up the inheritance tree looking for the method implementation. Thus, if the method is invoked against an instance of D, the implementation provided by D is used at runtime. However, if the method is called for an instance of class C, WMI will invoke the implementation supplied by B since C does not provide its own method implementation.

Interestingly, in those cases when an instance for which a method is called is accessed through its superclass, WMI invokes a correct implementation based on the class to which the instance actually belongs. You may remember that the GetInstances method of ManagementClass type may return instances of not only the current class, but also all of its subclasses, if the appropriate enumeration options are specified. Thus, it is entirely possible that an instance of class D is accessed through class A, and in this case, WMI will use the method implementation provided by D. Finally, if the object for which the method is invoked happens to be an instance of class A, the invocation will fail because A does not supply the implementation for Foo and does not have any superclasses that may provide this implementation.

The search algorithm is very different for static methods. In fact, there is no algorithm; instead, WMI always attempts to execute a static method using the implementation provided by the invoking class. Thus, if the class does not supply an implementation, the method invocation will fail. For instance, if Foo above were a static method, it would only be possible to invoke this method for classes B and D, since these are the only classes that supply the implementations for Foo.

Calling Instance Methods

Invoking WMI methods is fairly straightforward. The ManagementObject type offers a convenient, self-explanatory method, InvokeMethod, which, in its simplest form, takes a string parameter that represents the name of the method to invoke and an object array that contains the method parameters.

Before you attempt to execute an arbitrary method, you must know what parameters the method expects. There are many ways to look up a method signature, and one option is to use the ClassDef.exe program that was developed earlier in this chapter. Once you know the method parameter list, invoking the method is trivial:

```
ManagementObject mo = new ManagementObject("Win32_Process=100");
Object r = mo.InvokeMethod("Terminate", new object [] {32} );
Console.WriteLine("Terminate() returned {0}", r);
```

As you may have already guessed, the code above binds to an instance of the Win32_Process class, identified by its process ID, and calls its Terminate method, which effectively kills the process. The Win32_Process Terminate method has the following declaration:

```
[Destructor, Implemented] uint32 Terminate([In] uint32 Reason);
```

It takes a single input parameter—an unsigned integer that represents the exit code for the process to be terminated—and returns an unsigned integer value, which indicates whether the method succeeded or failed. Thus, the preceding code snippet calls the InvokeMethod method, passing the name of the method to invoke and an object array with a single element—a value 32 that will be used as an exit code for the terminated process. Upon completion, InvokeMethod outputs the return status of the Terminate method as a value of type object.

Things get a bit more complicated when a method has output parameters. For instance, consider the declaration for the GetOwner method of the Win32_Process class:

```
[Implemented] uint32 GetOwner([Out] string User, [Out] string Domain);
```

Besides the unsigned integer value that represents the return code of the method, this declaration returns two output parameters: the name of the user to which a process belongs, and the domain of the user. In order to retrieve the values of the output parameters, the method should be invoked as follows:

```
ManagementObject mo = new ManagementObject("Win32_Process=100");
object[] parms = new object [] {null, null};
Object r = mo.InvokeMethod("GetOwner", parms );
Console.WriteLine("GetOwner() returned {0}", r);
Console.WriteLine("User: {0} Domain: {1}", parms[0], parms[1]);
```

Here, the object array is first initialized with two null values that act as placeholders for the user and domain output parameters respectively. This array is then passed as a parameter to GetOwner method, and upon the method completion, it will contain the values of the process owner and the domain. Note that the number of elements in the parameter array must be equal to the number of all input and output method parameters. Thus, the following code will throw an IndexOutOfRangeException:

```
ManagementObject mo = new ManagementObject("Win32_Process=100");
object[] parms = new object [] {};
Object r = mo.InvokeMethod("GetOwner", parms );
```

Calling Static Methods

Executing a static method is not very much different. For instance, given the following declaration of the `Win32_Process` constructor method `Create`:

```
[Constructor, Static, Implemented]
uint32 Create(
    [In]  string CommandLine,
    [In]  string CurrentDirectory,
    [In]  Object ProcessStartupInformation,
    [Out] uint32 ProcessId
);
```

the following code will do the trick:

```
ManagementClass mc = new ManagementClass("Win32_Process");
object[] parms = new object [] {
    @"C:\WINNT\NOTEPAD.EXE C:\BOOT.INI", ".", null, null};
Object r = mc.InvokeMethod("Create", parms );
if ( (uint)r == 0 )
    Console.WriteLine("Process {0} successfully created", parms[3]);
```

The only principal difference here is that the `Create` method is invoked against a class rather than against an instance.

Identifying Method Parameters Programmatically

You will find that having to look up the method declaration in order to determine its parameter list is a bit annoying. In fact, sometimes you might want to identify method parameters programmatically based on some kind of metadata. As you may remember, the `MethodData` object, accessible through the `Methods` collection of the `ManagementClass` type, has two properties: `InParameters` and `OutParameters`. These describe the inputs and outputs of a method, respectively. The `InParameters` and `OutParameters` properties return objects of `ManagementBaseObject` type, which correspond to instances of `WMI __PARAMETERS` system class that is used to describe the formal arguments of a method. Thus, it is possible to iterate through the `Properties` collections of these parameter classes and programmatically construct the object array that represents the method parameters. There is, however, a better way to deal with argument lists. The `ManagementObject` type provides an overloaded version of `InvokeMethod` method, which takes a `ManagementBaseObject` that contains the method parameter values. Therefore, the code above can be rewritten as follows:

```
ManagementClass mc = new ManagementClass("Win32_Process");
ManagementBaseObject parms = ((MethodData)mc.Methods["Create"]).InParameters;
parms["CommandLine"] = @"C:\WINNT\NOTEPAD.EXE C:\BOOT.INI";
parms["CurrentDirectory"] = ".";
ManagementBaseObject r = mc.InvokeMethod("Create", parms, null);
if ( (uint)r["ReturnValue"] == 0 )
    Console.WriteLine("Process {0} successfully created", r["ProcessID"]);
```

This code first reads the InParameters property of the Create method of Win32_Process class. The ManagementBaseObject, returned by the InParameters property, contains one property for each input parameter of the Create method. The code then sets each property of the input object to appropriate values, calls InvokeMethod, and passes it the input ManagementBaseObject, which contains neatly packaged parameter values. The third parameter to the InvokeMethod method is just an object of type InvokeMethodOptions—a derivative of the ManagementOptions type that is used to set the timeout for the operation and pass the context values to the data provider.

Note that the ManagementBaseObject passed to InvokeMethod represents only the input parameters of a method. Upon completion, the InvokeMethod returns another instance of ManagementBaseObject; this time it contains the output parameter values. As I mentioned earlier, every method is guaranteed to return at least one output value: the return code of the invoked method that is identified by the name ReturnValue. The preceding code checks the ReturnValue to ensure that the Create method succeeded, and then it prints out the process ID of a newly created process by reading the value of the ProcessID property of the output ManagementBaseObject.

It is not a good idea to use the ManagementBaseObject, which is pointed to by the InParameters property of the MethodData, to pass input parameters to a method. The purpose of InParameters and OutParameters properties is to describe the method parameter list and help you analyze the class and method definitions. Thus, if you use the InParameters to pass the arguments to a method and forget to clear out its property values when you are finished, the next time you print out the class definition you may be fooled into thinking that some method parameters are assigned default values. A much better way to retrieve the ManagementBaseObject that represents the input parameters of a method is by using the GetMethodParameters method of the ManagementObject type, as shown here:

```
ManagementClass mc = new ManagementClass("Win32_Process");
ManagementBaseObject parms = mc.GetMethodParameters("Create");
parms["CommandLine"] = @"C:\WINNT\NOTEPAD.EXE C:\BOOT.INI";
parms["CurrentDirectory"] = ".";
ManagementBaseObject r = mc.InvokeMethod("Create", parms, null);
if ( (uint)r["ReturnValue"] == 0 )
    Console.WriteLine("Process {0} successfully created", r["ProcessID"]);
```

This method takes a single string argument—the name of the method—and returns a `ManagementBaseObject`, which represents the input parameters of this method. In addition to being cleaner and easier to use, `GetMethodParameters` is also safer because it internally creates a new instance of the `ManagementBaseObject` specifically for the purpose of housing the method parameters.

Until now, I deliberately avoided mentioning the third parameter of the `Create` method of the `Win32_Process` class—`ProcessStartupInformation`. If you are familiar with the Win32 API, you will correctly guess the purpose of this parameter: it specifies the main window properties of a new process. In fact, this parameter directly corresponds to the `STARTUPINFO` structure, which is declared in Winbase.h and used as a parameter to Win32 API `CreateProcess` function:

```
typedef struct _STARTUPINFO {
    DWORD    cb;
    LPTSTR   lpReserved;
    LPTSTR   lpDesktop;
    LPTSTR   lpTitle;
    DWORD    dwX;
    DWORD    dwY;
    DWORD    dwXSize;
    DWORD    dwYSize;
    DWORD    dwXCountChars;
    DWORD    dwYCountChars;
    DWORD    dwFillAttribute;
    DWORD    dwFlags;
    WORD     wShowWindow;
    WORD     cbReserved2;
    LPBYTE   lpReserved2;
    HANDLE   hStdInput;
    HANDLE   hStdOutput;
    HANDLE   hStdError;
} STARTUPINFO, *LPSTARTUPINFO;
```

You may think that in order to specify the startup properties of a process, it is enough to pass a reference to this structure as a parameter to the `Win32_Process` `Create` method:

```
ManagementClass mc = new ManagementClass("Win32_Process");
ManagementBaseObject parms = mc.GetMethodParameters("Create");
STARTUPINFO si = new STARTUPINFO();
si.lpTitle = "Started through WMI";
parms["CommandLine"] = @"C:\WINNT\SYSTEM32\CMD.EXE";
```

```
parms["CurrentDirectory"] = ".";
parms["ProcessStartupInformation"] = si;
ManagementBaseObject r = mc.InvokeMethod("Create", parms, null);
```

Unfortunately, this will not work. First, when you closely inspect the System.Management namespace you will find that it does not reveal the STARTUPINFO type or any other type that bears even a slight resemblance to the STARTUPINFO structure. Even if you define this structure yourself, the code will still fail.

The solution to this problem becomes obvious if you revisit the Create method's declaration:

```
uint32 Create(
    [CIMTYPE=string, In] string CommandLine,
    [CIMTYPE=string, In] string CurrentDirectory,
    [CIMTYPE=object:Win32_ProcessStartup, In]
        object ProcessStartupInformation,
    [CIMTYPE=uint32, Out] uint32 ProcessId
);
```

It turns out that ProcessStartupInformation is expected to be an object of type Win32_ProcessStartup. For this, the CIM Repository contains a class, called Win32_ProcessStartup, that has the following definition:

```
class Win32_ProcessStartup : Win32_MethodParameterClass {
    uint32 CreateFlags;
    uint32 PriorityClass;
    string EnvironmentVariables[];
    string WinstationDesktop;
    string Title;
    uint32 X;
    uint32 Y;
    uint32 XSize;
    uint32 YSize;
    uint32 XCountChars;
    uint32 YCountChars;
    uint32 FillAttribute;
    uint16 ShowWindow;
    uint16 ErrorMode = 0;
};
```

This class matches the STARTUPINFO structure fairly closely. Thus, the following code will correctly set the title of the CMD.EXE window to a "Created through WMI" string:

```
ManagementClass mc = new ManagementClass("Win32_Process");
ManagementBaseObject parms = mc.GetMethodParameters("Create");
ManagementBaseObject si = new
   ManagementClass("Win32_ProcessStartup").CreateInstance();
si["Title"] = "Started through WMI";
parms["CommandLine"] = @"C:\WINNT\SYSTEM32\CMD.EXE";
parms["CurrentDirectory"] = ".";
parms["ProcessStartupInformation"] = si;
ManagementBaseObject r = mc.InvokeMethod("Create", parms, null);
```

Specialized parameter classes, similar to Win32_ProcessStartup, are used extensively throughout the WMI object model. For instance, the Win32_Share Create method that is used to create file shares takes an Access parameter of type Win32_SecurityDescriptor, which represents the permissions, owner, and access capabilities for the shared resource. The Win32_SecurityDescriptor class corresponds to the Win32 SECURITY_DESCRIPTOR structure. The interesting thing about this class is that three of its properties—Group, Owner and SACL—are themselves references to objects of type Win32_Trustee and Win32_ACE respectively.

Asynchronous Programming

WMI can be slow. Not because of its design deficiencies or implementation problems, but simply because it often operates in a vastly distributed environment and handles unwieldy amounts of management data. Just imagine a program that compresses all text files exceeding a certain size limit on hundreds of computers that are connected via a WAN and you will understand why some WMI operations take forever to complete. Although it is possible to optimize the performance of WMI programs, there are still some factors that are beyond the programmer's control, such as the state and the speed of the network. Thus, users of interactive management applications may have to learn how to deal with the frustration that results from staring at the computer screen while waiting for some lengthy WMI action to complete.

Although you will find it difficult to guarantee consistent, subsecond response times for all WMI operations, you may be able to make the problem transparent, or at least less visible to the users. Most WMI operations can be carried out asynchronously, so the main program thread is not tied up until the operation completes. By utilizing the asynchronous programming techniques, you can build a powerful management application that is capable of carrying out multiple actions simultaneously in background and letting the users do other things while the WMI processes their requests.

The following WMI operations can be performed both synchronously and asynchronously:

- Enumerating classes and instances

- Deleting classes and instances

- Updating classes and instances

- Invoking class and instance methods

- Retrieving class and instance definitions

- Registering for WMI events

- Running WMI queries

Therefore, virtually every operation that has been discussed earlier in this chapter, as well as most of the actions discussed in the subsequent chapters, have asynchronous equivalents.

Introducing the ManagementOperationObserver Type

The System.Management type that makes asynchronous operations possible is called ManagementOperationObserver. It is a very simple type, but when you pass it as a parameter to a WMI operation, it monitors the progress and raises events based on the state of the operation. There are four events that are available through the ManagementOperationObserver:

ObjectReady: This event is raised whenever an asynchronous data retrieval operation returns an object.

ObjectPut: This event is raised whenever the changes to an object are successfully committed to the CIM Repository.

Completed: This event is raised when an asynchronous operation completes.

Progress: This event is raised periodically to inform the client of the progress of an asynchronous operation.

The `ObjectReady` is fairly straightforward. To facilitate the handling of this event, the `System.Management` namespace supplies a delegate `ObjectReadyEventHandler`, which takes a parameter of type `ObjectReadyEventArgs`. Every time the event handler is invoked, the `NewObject` property of the `ObjectReadyEventArgs` parameter will point to an object that is returned by the asynchronous data retrieval operation.

To handle the `ObjectPut` event, you should use the `ObjectPutEventHandler` delegate, which takes a parameter of type `ObjectPutEventArgs`. Then when the event handler is invoked, the `Path` property of the `ObjectPutEventArgs` parameter will contain the path to the newly created or updated WMI object.

The remaining two events—Completed and Progress—are intended to communicate the status of the operation back to the client, rather than just deliver the results. Generally, status reporting in WMI is optional and is only enabled if the client application sets the `WBEM_FLAG_SEND_STATUS` flag while issuing an asynchronous call. This flag causes WMI to register the client that receives the intermediate status updates via its implementation of the `IWbemObjectSink::SetStatus` method. You may expect one of the management option types, such as `ObjectGetOptions`, to have a `SendStatus` property that controls whether WMI reports on the operation progress; however, this is not the case. Instead, System.Management seems to enable the intermediate status reporting unconditionally. Thus, you can count on receiving the `Completed` event for every asynchronous operation that you invoke. Raising the `Progress` event, however, is up to the provider, and since not every provider is capable of intermediate status reporting, the `Progress` event is somewhat unreliable.

The handler for the `Progress` event, delegate ProgressEventHandler, receives a parameter of type `ProgressEventArgs`, which houses extended information that describes the progress of the operation. The `ProgressEventArgs` type has three properties: `Current`, `UpperBound`, and `Message`. The first two are integer values that represent the total amount of work to be done and the amount of work already completed, respectively. The last property, `Message`, may contain a textual message that describes the operation's status.

The `Completed` event is a bit more complex. Its handler, represented by delegate CompletedEventHandler, also receives a parameter of type `CompletedEventArgs`, which contains the extended status information about the completion of the asynchronous operation. The `CompletedEventArgs` type has two properties: `Status` and `StatusObject`. The `Status` is simply an error code that is defined by the `ManagementStatus` enumeration. The `StatusObject`, however, is an object of type `ManagementBaseObject` that is bound to an instance of the WMI class `__ExtendedStatus`. The `__ExtendedStatus` class, which is used by WMI to report the detailed status and error information back to the client application, has the following definition:

```
class __ExtendedStatus : __NotifyStatus {
    string ProviderName;
    string Operation;
```

```
    string ParameterInfo;
    string Description;
};
```

Table 2-10 provides a detailed description of each property of the
__ExtendedStatus class.

Table 2-10. __ExtendedStatus *Class Properties*

PROPERTY	DESCRIPTION
ProviderName	A string that represents the name of the WMI data provider that carried out the operation. If the error or status change is not generated by a provider, this property will be set to a string "Windows Management".
Operation	A string that describes the operation that was in progress when an error or status change was raised. Typically, this property will contain the name of the WMI API method that was invoked to carry out the operation, such as ExecQuery.
ParameterInfo	A string that describes the parameters to the operation that was in progress when an error or status change was raised. For instance, when you attempt to retrieve a nonexistent class, this property will be set to the name of the requested class.
Description	A String that provides additional details regarding the error or operation status.

ManagementOperationObserver is capable of monitoring nearly every aspect of
an asynchronous operation and providing rich feedback to the appli-cation clients.

Invoking Asynchronous Operations

Now you will take a look at how an asynchronous operation is invoked. The
following snippet of code demonstrates the mechanics of the simplest asynchronous call: it is used to retrieve a single WMI object:

```
class Monitor {
    bool bComplete = false;
    bool bError = false;
    public void OnCompleted(object sender, CompletedEventArgs ea) {
        if ( ea.Status != ManagementStatus.NoError ) {
            bError = true;
```

```
            Console.WriteLine(
                "Error occurred: {0}", ea.StatusObject["Description"]);
            Console.WriteLine("Provider: {0}",
                ea.StatusObject["ProviderName"]);
            Console.WriteLine("Operation: {0}",
                ea.StatusObject["Operation"]);
            Console.WriteLine("ParameterInfo: {0}",
                ea.StatusObject["ParameterInfo"]);
        }
        bComplete = true;
    }
    public bool IsComplete {
        get { return bComplete; }
    }
    public bool IsError {
        get { return bError; }
    }
    public static void Main(string[] args) {
        Monitor m = new Monitor();
        ManagementOperationObserver ob = new ManagementOperationObserver();
        ob.Completed += new CompletedEventHandler(m.OnCompleted);
        ManagementObject mo = new ManagementObject("Win32_Process=316");
        mo.Get(ob);
        while(!m.IsComplete) {
            // do something while waiting
            System.Threading.Thread.Sleep(1000);
        }
        if(!m.IsError)
            Console.WriteLine("Retrieved {0}", mo["__PATH"]);
    }
}
```

You may remember that instantiating a ManagementObject will not automatically bind it to an underlying WMI object. Instead, the binding occurs
implicitly whenever a property of a ManagementObject instance is first
accessed, or explicitly when a Get method is called. Get has an overloaded version that takes a parameter of type ManagementOperationObserver. When it is
invoked with an instance of ManagementOperationObserver, Get returns immediately, and it's the ManagementOperationObserver that monitors the operation
and raises the Completed event whenever the binding is finished. The
Completed event handler first checks the status of the operation by comparing
the Status field of its CompletedEventArgs parameter object against the NoError
member of the ManagementStatus enumeration. Then it sets the flag to indicate
that the action is completed.

Enumerating Objects Asynchronously

Enumerating through a collection of objects or classes asynchronously is a bit more involved. As opposed to their synchronous counterparts, collection retrieval methods, such as GetInstances, GetRelated, and so on, do not just return a collection of objects when called in asynchronous fashion. Instead, the ManagementOperationObserver, which these methods take as a parameter, raises the ObjectReady event for each object that is returned by the corresponding method:

```
class Monitor {
    bool bComplete = false;
    public void OnObjectReady(object sender, ObjectReadyEventArgs ea) {
        ManagementBaseObject mb = ea.NewObject;
        Console.WriteLine("Retrieved {0}", mb["__PATH"]);
    }
    public void OnCompleted(object sender, CompletedEventArgs ea) {
        if ( ea.Status != ManagementStatus.NoError ) {
            Console.WriteLine(
                "Error occurred: {0}", ea.StatusObject["Description"]);
            Console.WriteLine("Provider: {0}",
                ea.StatusObject["ProviderName"]);
            Console.WriteLine("Operation: {0}",
                ea.StatusObject["Operation"]);
            Console.WriteLine("ParameterInfo: {0}",
                ea.StatusObject["ParameterInfo"]);
        }
        bComplete = true;
    }
    public bool IsComplete {
        get { return bComplete; }
    }
    public static void Main(string[] args) {
        Monitor m = new Monitor();
        ManagementOperationObserver ob = new ManagementOperationObserver();
        ob.Completed += new CompletedEventHandler(m.OnCompleted);
        ob.ObjectReady += new ObjectReadyEventHandler(m.OnObjectReady);
        ManagementClass mc = new ManagementClass("Win32_Process");
        mc.GetInstances(ob);
        while(!m.IsComplete) {
            // do something while waiting
            System.Threading.Thread.Sleep(1000);
        }
```

```
    }
}
```

Here, the ObjectReady event handler is doing most of the work. Whenever the ObjectReady event is raised, its handler is invoked with a parameter of type ObjectReadyEventArgs so that the NewObject property of this parameter points to an object that is returned by the GetInstances method.

Handling Errors

Interestingly, the error handling code that constitutes most of the Completed event handler is actually quite useless. For instance, if you attempt to bind to a nonexistent object, a ManagementException will be thrown and the event handler will never be called. This seems to be the result of a lazy initialization technique employed by types in the System.Management namespace—whenever a method is invoked, the code will always check to see if a requesting object is bound to an underlying WMI object or class. Thus, asynchronous error handling involving the __ExtendedStatus object packaged within the CompletedEventArgs makes most sense when you are running WMI WQL queries. Although the detailed treatment of WQL and System.Management query facilities will be presented in the next chapter, the following code snippet shows a situation when the error handling technique, similar to the one just described, is actually useful:

```
class Monitor {
    bool bComplete = false;
    public void OnObjectReady(object sender, ObjectReadyEventArgs ea) {
        ManagementBaseObject mb = ea.NewObject;
        Console.WriteLine("Retrieved {0}", mb["__PATH"]);
    }
    public void OnCompleted(object sender, CompletedEventArgs ea) {
        if ( ea.Status != ManagementStatus.NoError ) {
            Console.WriteLine(
                "Error occurred: {0}", ea.StatusObject["Description"]);
            Console.WriteLine("Provider: {0}",
                ea.StatusObject["ProviderName"]);
            Console.WriteLine("Operation: {0}",
                ea.StatusObject["Operation"]);
            Console.WriteLine("ParameterInfo: {0}",
                ea.StatusObject["ParameterInfo"]);
        }
        bComplete = true;
    }
```

```
    public bool IsComplete {
        get { return bComplete; }
    }
    public static void Main(string[] args) {
        Monitor m = new Monitor();
        ManagementOperationObserver ob = new ManagementOperationObserver();
        ob.Completed += new CompletedEventHandler(m.OnCompleted);
        ob.ObjectReady += new ObjectReadyEventHandler(m.OnObjectReady);
        ManagementObjectSearcher ms = new ManagementObjectSearcher(
            new SelectQuery("Win64_Process"));
        ms.Get(ob);
        while(!m.IsComplete) {
            // do something while waiting
            System.Threading.Thread.Sleep(1000);
        }
    }
}
```

This code attempts to asynchronously retrieve all instances of the nonexistent `Win64_Process` WMI class using a WQL SELECT query. When run, it will produce the following output on the system console:

```
Error occurred:
Provider: WinMgmt
Operation: ExecQuery
ParameterInfo: select * from Win64_Process
```

Modifying Objects Asynchronously

The technique you would use to modify or delete WMI objects or classes asynchronously is very similar to the one employed for asynchronous data retrieval. The only difference is that `ManagementOperationObserver` will raise a different event (`ObjectPut` rather than `ObjectReady`) when it completes the modification operation. The following code updates the `BackupInterval` property of `Win32_WMISetting` object using the asynchronous version of the `Put` method:

```
class Monitor {
    bool bComplete = false;
    public void OnObjectPut(object sender, ObjectPutEventArgs ea) {
        Console.WriteLine("Updated {0}", ea.Path);
    }
```

```
public void OnCompleted(object sender, CompletedEventArgs ea) {
    if ( ea.Status != ManagementStatus.NoError ) {
        Console.WriteLine(
            "Error occurred: {0}", ea.StatusObject["Description"]);
        Console.WriteLine("Provider: {0}",
            ea.StatusObject["ProviderName"]);
        Console.WriteLine("Operation: {0}",
            ea.StatusObject["Operation"]);
        Console.WriteLine("ParameterInfo: {0}",
            ea.StatusObject["ParameterInfo"]);
    }
    bComplete = true;
}
public bool IsComplete {
    get { return bComplete; }
}
public static void Main(string[] args) {
    Monitor m = new Monitor();
    ManagementOperationObserver ob = new ManagementOperationObserver();
    ob.Completed += new CompletedEventHandler(m.OnCompleted);
    ob.ObjectPut += new ObjectPutEventHandler(m.OnObjectPut);
    ManagementObject mo = new ManagementObject("Win32_WMISetting=@");
    mo["BackupInterval"] = 120;
    mo.Put(ob);
    while(!m.IsComplete) {
        // do something while waiting
        System.Threading.Thread.Sleep(1000);
    }
}
}
```

Here the event handler for the ObjectPut event receives a parameter of type
ObjectPutEventArgs, which has a Path property that is set to the full object path
of the WMI object affected by the update operation.

Calling Methods Asynchronously

Obviously, WMI methods can also be invoked asynchronously. However, what is
not quite obvious is how the output parameter of a method is communicated
back to the client since the asynchronous InvokeMethod returns immediately. It
turns out that asynchronous method invocation will trigger the ObjectReady
event, and the ObjectReadyEventArgs parameter that is passed to the event

handler will house an instance of the __PARAMETERS class that contains the values of the output parameters:

```csharp
class Monitor {
    bool bComplete = false;
    public void OnObjectReady(object sender, ObjectReadyEventArgs ea) {
        ManagementBaseObject mb = ea.NewObject;
        foreach(PropertyData pd in mb.Properties) {
            Console.WriteLine("{0} {1}", pd.Name, pd.Value);
        }
    }
    public void OnCompleted(object sender, CompletedEventArgs ea) {
        if ( ea.Status != ManagementStatus.NoError ) {
            Console.WriteLine(
                "Error occurred: {0}", ea.StatusObject["Description"]);
            Console.WriteLine("Provider: {0}",
                ea.StatusObject["ProviderName"]);
            Console.WriteLine("Operation: {0}",
                ea.StatusObject["Operation"]);
            Console.WriteLine("ParameterInfo: {0}",
                ea.StatusObject["ParameterInfo"]);
        }
        bComplete = true;
    }
    public bool IsComplete {
        get { return bComplete; }
    }
    public static void Main(string[] args) {
        Monitor m = new Monitor();
        ManagementOperationObserver ob = new ManagementOperationObserver();
        ob.Completed += new CompletedEventHandler(m.OnCompleted);
        ob.ObjectReady += new ObjectReadyEventHandler(m.OnObjectReady);
        ManagementClass mc = new ManagementClass("Win32_Process");
        ManagementBaseObject parms = mc.GetMethodParameters("Create");
        parms["CommandLine"] = @"c:\winnt\system32\notepad.exe c:\boot.ini";
        parms["CurrentDirectory"] = ".";
        mc.InvokeMethod(ob, "Create", parms, null);
        while(!m.IsComplete) {
            // do something while waiting
            System.Threading.Thread.Sleep(1000);
        }
    }
}
```

When the ObjectReady event handler is invoked, it will print out the values of output parameters on the system console as follows:

```
ProcessId 247
ReturnValue 0
```

You may remember that there is an alternative version of InvokeMethod method that takes an array of objects that represents both input and output method parameters so that the values of the output parameters are stored in the same array when the method finishes. I also pointed out that you have to supply placeholders for output parameters in order to make sure that InvokeMethod does not throw an exception while it is attempting to store the output values into the array:

```
ManagementObject mo = new ManagementObject("Win32_Process=100");
object[] parms = new object[] {null, null};
mo.InvokeMethod("GetOwner", parms);
Console.WriteLine("User: {0} Domain: {1}", parms[0], parms[1]);
```

You can also call this version of the InvokeMethod asynchronously, but if you do, the output parameter values will not be stored back into the object array. Instead, the operation will trigger the ObjectReady event and provide the values of the output parameters via the instance of the __PARAMETERS class that is packaged into the ObjectReadyEventArgs. Thus, if you assume that ob represents an instance of ManagementOperationObserver, the following code is correct and will produce the results you want:

```
ManagementObject mo = new ManagementObject("Win32_Process=100");
mo.InvokeMethod(ob, "GetOwner", null);
```

Alternatively, you can use this invocation technique:

```
ManagementObject mo = new ManagementObject("Win32_Process=100");
mo.InvokeMethod(ob, "GetOwner", new object[] {});
```

Finally, if an asynchronous method invocation results in an error, the error will be communicated back to the client either through the ReturnValue property of the __PARAMETERS object, which is passed to the ObjectReady event handler; or through the __ExtendedStatus object, which is passed as part of the CompletedEventArgs parameter to the Completed event handler. For instance, if you modify the Monitor class example in an attempt to call the Win32_Process Create method so that its CommandLine parameter refers to a nonexistent executable or does not constitute a valid operating system command:

```
mc.InvokeMethod(ob, "Create",
    new object[] {"C:\notepad.exe", ".", null, null});
```

the ObjectReady event handler will print the following on the console, indicating that the Create method failed:

```
ProcessId
ReturnValue 9
```

However, if you try to execute a static method such as Create against an instance of the WMI class, or an attempt to call an instance method for a class:

```
ManagementClass mc = new ManagementClass("Win32_Process");
mc.InvokeMethod(ob, "GetOwner", new object[] {});
```

the ObjectReady event will never fire and the Completed event handler will print the following on the console:

```
Error occurred:
Provider: WinMgmt
Operation: ExecMethod
ParameterInfo: Win32_Process
```

Lastly, if you call a nonexistent method, the InvokeMethod will throw a ManagementException prior to actually initiating an asynchronous operation.

Localization and Internationalization Issues

Localization is a very popular buzzword that is often thrown around when people are talking about software systems. Generally, to localize an application, you need to translate all the text strings associated with it, such as various labels, messages, and so on, into a format and language that the end user understands, and you need to provide input and output facilities that utilize such format and language. In order to satisfy the localization requirements, software vendors often create localized versions of their products that are suitable for specific cultures.

The concept of *globalization,* which usually presumes that a given software system is capable of supporting multilingual users and data simultaneously, is related to localization. Rather than producing several culture-specific versions of the software, vendors of globalized systems usually offer a single package that configures itself dynamically based on the language and culture preferences of the user. Both localization and globalization are often referred to as *internationalization.*

Just like many other software systems that are marketed and used worldwide, Windows has provisions for supporting multilingual users. The operating system is available in many localized versions, also known as single user interface (SUI) versions, so that the only difference between versions is the language used in the resources section of each binary file. There is also a globalized version of Windows, known as the Multilanguage User Interface (MUI), which allows the users to set up their UI according to their culture and preferences, assuming that the resources that correspond to their language of choice are installed on their system.

WMI and Internationalization

Because WMI is the premier management system for Windows platforms, it is expected to run on both single- and multi-UI versions of the OS, and it has to support both localization and globalization. Simply put, this means that WMI needs to be capable of localizing its schema as well as its object property values, and it needs to have provisions for building globalized management applications.

Generally, localization revolves around those elements of the schema that communicate some information to the end user. Such elements, often referred to as *displayable aspects* of the schema, are typically contained in the qualifiers (such as property of method descriptions, for instance). Thus, localization does not apply to the actual identifier strings that are used to name classes, properties, or methods; instead it is relevant solely to schema qualifiers. Although it would be better if string properties were localizable too, at this time WMI does not provide any direct way to localize the property values.

The idea behind WMI internationalization facilities is based on the concept of a master class. A *master class* is a complete definition for a given class comprised of both localized and locale-neutral elements. At runtime, a master class is dynamically assembled as a union of two distinct class definitions: basic and amendment. All locale-neutral elements of a class definition are segregated into a basic class, while all localizable components constitute an amendment class. As opposed to a basic class, an amendment class is abstract and does not correspond to a real WMI class. Instead, it contains a subset of the properties of a master class that have localizable qualifiers. Since both basic and amendment classes share the same name, all amendment class definitions are placed in a separate namespace that is subordinate to the namespace of a basic class. In fact, there are multiple subordinate namespaces, each corresponding to a particular locale and containing the respective amendment class definitions. The naming convention for these child namespaces is MS_XXXX, where XXXX is a hexadecimal value that represents a particular Win32 Locale ID (LCID). For instance, if a WMI installation contains classes that are amended for German and English locales, its namespace hierarchy may look like the following:

```
\root\CIMV2
\root\CIMV2\ms_409
\root\CIMV2\ms_407
```

where 409 and 407 are locale identifiers for English and German locales respectively.

Retrieving Localized Schema Elements

Such structure makes it easy for the WMI runtime to dynamically merge the localized and locale-neutral elements of a class definition before it returns the information to the client application. However, such merging of basic and amended class definitions does not occur automatically. For instance, most properties have a Description qualifier that provides a textual description, that clarifies the usage or purpose of the property. For apparent reasons, such description is locale-specific and is not part of the basic class definition. Thus, the code, like the following, which attempts to retrieve the value of the Description qualifier for the Handle property of Win32_Process class, will fail:

```
ManagementClass mc = new ManagementClass("Win32_Process");
Console.WriteLine(mc.GetPropertyQualifierValue("Handle", "Description"));
```

The preceding code will throw a ManagementException that complains about a nonexistent qualifier. Obviously, this code retrieves just the basic class definition, which excludes all localizable property qualifiers, such as Description.

To enable the runtime merging of basic and amended class definitions, you must use a special flag, WBEM_FLAG_USE_AMENDED_QUALIFIERS. This flag is exposed through the UseAmendedQualifiers property of the ObjectGetOptions class, which controls the retrieval of the management data:

```
ManagementClass mc = new ManagementClass("Win32_Process");
mc.Options.UseAmendedQualifiers = true;
Console.WriteLine(mc.GetPropertyQualifierValue("Handle", "Description"));
```

Assuming that your locale is set to English (0x409) and that the \root\CIMV2\ms_409 namespace contains the localized definition for the Handle property of the Win32_Process class, this code will correctly print the property description on the system console:

```
A string used to identify the process. A process ID is a process handle.
```

The approach is similar when you iterate through collections of management objects. You may remember that the options object that controls the enumeration operations is called EnumerationOptions. By setting its UseAmendedQualifiers property to true, you can tell WMI to return localizable information for each object output by the enumeration:

```
ManagementClass mc = new ManagementClass("CIM_Process");
EnumerationOptions eo = new EnumerationOptions();
eo.UseAmendedQualifiers = true;
foreach(ManagementClass m in mc.GetSubclasses(eo)) {
    Console.WriteLine(m.GetPropertyQualifierValue("Handle", "Description"));
}
```

It is possible to determine which qualifiers are localizable by inspecting the IsAmended property of the QualifierData type. Thus, the following code prints out all localizable property qualifiers, along with the associated property names, for the Win32_Process class:

```
ManagementClass mc = new ManagementClass(@"Win32_Process");
mc.Options.UseAmendedQualifiers = true;
foreach(PropertyData pd in mc.Properties)  {
    foreach(QualifierData qd in pd.Qualifiers)
        if(qd.IsAmended)
            Console.WriteLine("[{1}] {0}", pd.Name, qd.Name);
}
```

Note that the IsAmended property only returns TRUE for localizable qualifiers if the class definition is retrieved with the UseAmendedQualifiers property set to true. Therefore, if you comment out the line in the preceding code that sets the UseAmendedQualifiers property of ObjectGetOptions, this code will produce no output because IsAmended will always return FALSE.

Updating Localized Schema Elements

If you stumble upon another options type, PutOptions, you may notice that it also has a property named UseAmendedQualifiers. Having to set the flag to get amended qualifier values when you are reading the data is understandable, but what does it have to do with update operations? To find out the answer to this question, consider the following scenario:

```
\root\CIMV2:

[locale(0x409)]
class Foo {
   [key] sint32 fooID;
         string fooName;
}


\root\CIMV2\ms_409:

[amendment, locale(0x409)]
class Foo {
   [Description("This is a key property."):amended]
   sint32 fooID;
   [Description("This is a name property."):amended]
   string fooName;
}
```

Here, the basic class definition for Foo, which has two properties, resides in the \root\CIMV2 namespace. This definition is amended for the English locale with a copy of Foo that is located in the \root\CIMV2\ms_409 namespace so that both of the Foo properties are given localized Description qualifiers. In order to create an instance of Foo and save it to CIM Repository, you may write the following code:

```
ManagementClass mc = new ManagementClass("Foo");
mc.Options.UseAmendedQualifiers = true;
ManagementObject mo = mc.CreateInstance();
mo["fooID"] = 123;
mo["fooName"] = "Foo";
try {
   mo.Put();
} catch(ManagementException ex) {
   Console.WriteLine(ex.Message);
}
```

This legitimate looking code will actually throw a ManagementException and the catch block will print the following message on the system console:

```
An amended object cannot be put unless⏎
   WBEM_FLAG_USE_AMENDED_QUALIFIERS is specified.
```

It turns out that if you retrieve an amended class and spawn its instance, the instance will then contain all the amended qualifiers from the amendment class. This new instance cannot be stored into a namespace that contains the basic class definition unless the amended qualifiers are stripped. This is where the PutOptions type comes in handy:

```
ManagementClass mc = new ManagementClass("Foo");

mc.Options.UseAmendedQualifiers = true;

ManagementObject mo = mc.CreateInstance();

mo["fooID"] = 123;

mo["fooName"] = "Foo";

PutOptions po = new PutOptions();

po.UseAmendedQualifiers = true;

try {

    mo.Put(po);

} catch(ManagementException ex) {

    Console.WriteLine(ex.Message);
}
```

This code snippet will correctly remove the amended qualifiers and save the new instance into the \root\CIMV2 namespace.

Error Handling

All types in the System.Management namespace adhere to the .NET error handling model, which means that all errors are communicated back to the client via exceptions rather than via method return values or error codes. In fact, I should say that WMI errors are communicated via *an* exception since there is only one exception type—ManagementException—that all System.Management types use. ManagementException is a derivative of a standard System.Exception class and, as such, it inherits a few useful properties: Message, Source, TargetSite, and StackTrace. For all intents and purposes, ManagementException behaves just like any other .NET exception type, and that is why I deliberately ignored the subject of error handling up until now. After all, the following boilerplate error handling code should look familiar to just about anyone with some .NET programming experience:

```
try {
    ManagementObject mo = new ManagementObject("Win32_Process=100");
    Console.WriteLine(mo["ExecutablePath"]);
} catch(ManagementException ex) {
    Console.WriteLine("*** ERROR OCCURRED ***");
    Console.WriteLine("Source: {0} Description: {1}",
        ex.Source, ex.Message);
    Console.WriteLine(ex.StackTrace);
}
```

Working with the ManagementException Type

Although these standard exception properties already provide a wealth of useful information, the ManagementException type has additional fields that allow you to look even more deeply into the problem. One of these fields is ErrorCode, which contains the actual WMI return code of an operation that caused an exception. This is a property of type ManagementStatus, which is an enumeration that contains all the currently defined WMI error codes. Second, there is an ErrorInformation property, which refers to an object of type ManagementBaseObject. As you may have guessed, it contains an instance of the __ExtendedStatus class that was described earlier in this chapter (see Table 2-10). Thus, by interrogating the properties of the __ExtendedStatus object, you can obtain very detailed information that is pertinent to what caused the exception. For instance, an attempt to bind to a nonexistent instance of the Win32_Process class:

```
try {
    ManagementObject mo = new ManagementObject("Win32_Process=999999");
    Console.WriteLine(mo["ExecutablePath"]);
} catch(ManagementException ex) {
    foreach(PropertyData pd in ex.ErrorInformation.Properties) {
        Console.WriteLine("{0} {1}", pd.Name, pd.Value);
    }
}
```

will yield the following output:

```
Description
Operation GetObject
ParameterInfo Win32_Process.Handle=999999
ProviderName CIMWin32
StatusCode
```

As opposed to standard exception properties, which present an exception in .NET-centric fashion, __ExtendedStatus object reflects the WMI view of the problem. For instance, its Operation property usually contains a name of a WMI COM API method, which was executing when the exception was thrown.

On those rare occasions when a problem is internal to a given System.Management type and has nothing to do with WMI, some other exception besides ManagementException may be thrown. Thus, if you try to create an instance of the ManagementObject type by providing a class rather than an object path to its constructor, the constructor will throw the all-too-familiar ArgumentOutOfRange exception. Note that in this case, the exception will be thrown by the constructor rather than by any subsequent code that attempts to use a newly created instance. Since all management types use the lazy initialization technique and do not access WMI until first used by a management application, you may deduce that the source of this exception is the constructor code itself rather than WMI. The bottom line is that any exception of a type other than ManagementException is the result of a usage error rather than a system error, and as such, it should not be handled by an application catch block.

Using Strongly Typed Wrappers for WMI Classes

If you have object-oriented programming experience and you have played with System.Management namespace types, you will eventually attempt to build wrappers for the most commonly used WMI classes. Although ManagementClass and ManagementObject types are extremely powerful generic constructs for dealing with all kinds of management data, their generic nature makes programming somewhat more complex. The problem is that these types are late-bound, or, in other words, they are not automatically and permanently associated with arbitrary WMI classes or objects. For instance, a Process class that is bound to the Win32_Process WMI class would significantly simplify the programming model and reduce chances for errors:

```
Process ps = new Process(100);
Console.WriteLine(ps.ExecutablePath);
uint id;
uint r = ps.Create(@"c:\winnt\notepad.exe", ".", null, out id);
```

Thus, if you are striving to reap the benefits of strongly typed programming, you may produce a wrapper for the Win32_Process class that is similar to the following:

```
public class Process {
    private ManagementObject obj;
    public Process(uint Handle) {
        obj = new ManagementObject("Win32_Process=" + Handle);
    }
    public string ExecutablePath {
        get { return (string)obj["ExecutablePath"]; }
    }
    public uint Create(
        string CommandLine,
        string CurrentDirectory,
        ManagementBaseObject ProcessStartupInformation,
        out uint ProcessID) {
        ManagementClass mc = new ManagementClass("Win32_Process");
        ManagementBaseObject parms = mc.GetMethodParameters("Create");
        parms["CommandLine"] = CommandLine;
        parms["CurrentDirectory"] = CurrentDirectory;
        parms["ProcessStartupInformation"] = ProcessStartupInformation;
        ManagementBaseObject r = mc.InvokeMethod("Create", parms, null);
        ProcessID = (uint)r["ProcessID"];
        return (uint)r["ReturnValue"];
    }
}
```

The good news is that building wrappers like this by hand is not necessary. The designers of the System.Management namespace, anticipating the demand for strongly typed management objects, built the powerful tools needed to auto-generate the strongly typed code.

Using MgmtClass.exe to Generate WMI Class Wrappers

Perhaps the easiest way to produce a strongly typed wrapper for an arbitrary WMI class is by using the MgmtClassGen.exe utility that ships as part of the .NET SDK. This is a command line tool that can be invoked as follows:

```
MgmtClassGen.exe <WMI class name> [<options>]
```

When this is invoked with a single parameter—the name of the WMI class for which to generate a strongly typed wrapper—MgmtClassGen.exe simply outputs a file, called <WMI class name>.CS (where <WMI class name> is an actual name of the WMI class less the schema prefix) into the current directory. If you want, you can alter the default behavior of the tool via several command line options, listed in Table 2-11.

Table 2-11. MgmtClassGen.exe Command Line Options

OPTION	DESCRIPTION
/l <language>	Instructs MgmtClassGen.exe to use a particular programming language when generating the strongly typed class definition. Currently, available language options are CS (C#), VB (Visual Basic) and JS (JavaScript). If this option is omitted, C# code is generated by default.
/m <machine>	Specifies the name of the server where the target WMI class is located. By default, MgmtClassGen.exe connects to the local machine.
/n <path>	Sets the path to the WMI namespace that contains the target WMI class. If this option is omitted, the tool assumes that the target WMI class resides in the \root\CIMV2 namespace.
/o <class namespace>	Specifies the name of the .NET namespace into which the generated class should be placed. If this option is omitted, MgmtClassGen.exe generates the namespace prefix using the WMI namespace and class schema prefix. Thus, for the Win32_Process class that resides in \root\CIMV2, the generate namespace prefix will be ROOT.CIMV2.Win32.
/p <file path>	Sets the path to the file to which the generated code should be saved. If this path is omitted, the tool outputs the file into the current directory. By default, the name of the output file is generated based on the name of the target WMI class less the schema prefix. Thus, for the Win32_Process class, the default output file name will be Process.CS.
/pw <password>	When logging on to a remote computer using the /m option, this option specifies a password to be used for establishing the connection.
/u <user name>	When logging on to a remote computer using /m option, this option specifies a user account to be used for establishing the connection.
/?	This option instructs MgmtClassGen.exe to print its usage guidelines on the console and exit.

Using Server Explorer to Generate WMI Class Wrappers

Yet another tool that makes generating the strongly typed wrappers for WMI classes even easier is the Server Explorer Management Extension in Visual Studio .NET, shown on Figure 2-1.

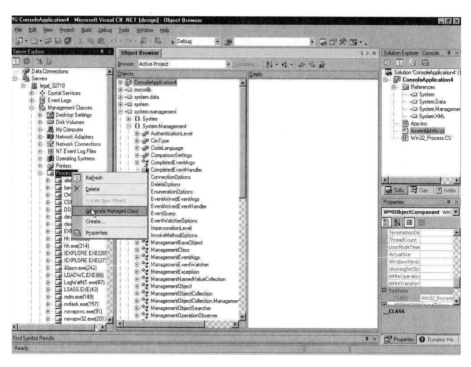

Figure 2-1. Server Explorer Management Extension

This extension can be accessed through the View➤Server Explorer menu option in Visual Studio .NET. In order to generate a wrapper for, say, the Win32_Process class, you should follow these steps:

1. Select a target server using the Tree View of the Server Explorer.

2. Navigate to the Processes node.

3. Right-click on Processes and select Generate Managed Class from the pop-up menu.

The generated class is then added to the current project.

Generating WMI Class Wrappers Programmatically

Although you will find that generating strongly typed wrappers with MgmtClassGen.exe and the Server Explorer extension is very easy and trouble-free, sometimes such an approach lacks flexibility. To satisfy all tastes, the designers of System.Management namespace equipped the ManagementClass type with the GetStronglyTypedClassCode method, which allows you to create the wrappers programmatically. The first form of the GetStronglyTypedClassCode method takes three parameters: a designation for the programming language for which the code is to be generated, the path to the output file, and the .NET namespace into which the newly generated class is to be placed. Thus, to generate a wrapper for the Win32_Process class, you would use the following code:

```
ManagementClass mc = new ManagementClass("Win32_Process");
if(mc.GetStronglyTypedClassCode(CodeLanguage.CSharp,
    @"C:\temp\Process.CS", "WMI"))
    Console.WriteLine("Successfully generated code for Win32_Process");
else
    Console.WriteLine("Failed to generate code for Win32_Process");
```

Here, the first parameter of enumeration type CodeLanguage instructs the method to use C# as an output programming language. Currently, the CodeLanguage enumeration contains just three language designations: CSharp, VB, and JScript (for C#, Visual Basic and JavaScript respectively). The second parameter—path to the output file—is a string that contains either an absolute or a relative file path. If just the file name is supplied, the file will be created in the current working directory. Note that you cannot pass null or an empty string as a file name parameter to GetStronglyTypedClassCode and have the file name defaulted to the name of WMI class. If a valid file name is not supplied, the method will throw ArgumentOutOfRangeException. Finally, the last parameter is a string that represents a .NET namespace into which the resulting wrapper class should be placed. The method accepts an empty string as a placeholder, in which case the namespace will be defaulted to the WMI namespace name plus the schema name. Thus, for the Win32_Process class, which is residing in the \root\CIMV2 namespace, the default .NET namespace name will be ROOT.CIMV2.Win32.

If you are adventurous and looking for even more flexibility, you may want to turn to an overloaded version of the GetStronglyTypedClassCode method. Instead of saving the generated code to a file, this method returns an object of type CodeDom.CodeTypeDeclaration. CodeDom is a .NET namespace that contains a slew of types that are used to generate code in a variety of programming languages. The CodeTypeDeclaration object that is returned by the GetStronglyTypedClassCode method represents a language-independent declaration for a .NET wrapper class that is suitable for being fed to a .NET language compiler or code generator. For instance, the following example does the same thing as the previous code snippet—it saves the generated code to a file—but this time, it does so using the code generation facilities of CodeDom namespace:

```
using System;
using System.Management;
using System.CodeDom;
using System.CodeDom.Compiler;
using Microsoft.CSharp;

...
CodeTypeDeclaration dc = new
    ManagementClass("Win32_Process").GetStronglyTypedClassCode(false,false);
CodeCompileUnit cu = new CodeCompileUnit();
cu.Namespaces.Add(new CodeNamespace("WMI"));
cu.Namespaces[0].Types.Add(dc);
CodeDomProvider prov = new CSharpCodeProvider();
ICodeGenerator gen = prov.CreateGenerator();
System.IO.TextWriter wr = new System.IO.StreamWriter(@"C:\TEMP\Process.cs",
    false, System.Text.Encoding.ASCII, 1024);
CodeGeneratorOptions gco = new CodeGeneratorOptions();
gen.GenerateCodeFromCompileUnit(cu,wr,gco);
```

Although the particulars of the functionality afforded by the CodeDom namespace types are outside the scope of this book, the preceding code sequence is fairly self-explanatory.

1. First, this code creates an instance of the ManagementClass type that is bound to the Win32_Process WMI class.

2. Then it invokes its GetStronglyTypedClassCode method to produce a CodeTypeDeclaration for the wrapper class.

GetStronglyTypedClassCode takes two boolean parameters: a flag that indicates whether a class for managing WMI system properties should be included in the declaration, and another flag that states whether the generated wrapper should be capable of managing the system properties. Once the CodeTypeDeclaration is available, the code follows these steps:

1. It creates the CodeCompileUnit (a unit of compilation) and adds a namespace called WMI to its namespaces collection.

2. After that, it adds the `CodeTypeDeclaration` to the collection of types within that namespace. At this point, the `CodeCompileUnit` contains a complete code graph that is suitable for compilation or code generation.

3. The code example then creates an instance of the code provider. In this case, it is a provider that is capable of generating and compiling the C# code.

4. Finally, the `CodeCompileUnit` is fed into the `GenerateCodeFromCompileUnit` method of the code generator along with an instance of `TextWriter`, which is opened over an output file named C:\temp\Process.cs.

When the `GenerateCodeFromCompileUnit` method finishes, the output file contains a complete source code for the `Win32_Process` wrapper class.

One apparent benefit that you get if you use this version of the `GetStronglyTypedClassCode` method is the ability to manipulate the properties of `CodeTypeDeclaration` and thus analyze or alter the wrapper code before it is generated. A less apparent, but probably even more exciting advantage of this approach is that you get the ability to substitute a custom code provider in place of the standard C#, Visual Basic, or JavaScript provider. Thus, by using the `System.CodeDom.Compiler.CodeDomProvider` abstract class as a base, you can implement a code provider that can generate and compile code in virtually any programming language.

Regardless of how you generate a wrapper class source code for a given WMI class the code is the same. In fact, both the MgmtClassGen.exe and the Server Explorer extension internally use the `GetStronglyTypedClassCode` method of the `ManagementClass` to output the wrapper class definitions. The generated code is fairly straightforward, and it uses primarily the functionality described in this chapter. As a result, you should be able to figure out all implementation details easily. There are, however, a few caveats of which you should be aware:

1. It is entirely possible that the name of a method or property of the generated class is a key (a reserved word) in the target programming language. In this case, the code generation facility will change the name of the respective property or method to avoid the collision.

2. Typically, `GetStronglyTypedClassCode` will generate get and set accessors for each WMI class property that does not have a `Read` qualifier. You may remember that properties marked with `Read` qualifier are considered read-only; therefore, for these properties only the get accessor will be generated.

3. Some WMI class properties may have `Values` or `ValueMap` qualifiers that indicate sets of permissible values for the property. In such cases, `GetStronglyTypedClassCode` will create an enumeration type with individual members that represent each of the values given by the `Values` or `ValueMap` qualifier. The data type of the property will then be set to the generated enumeration type.

4. There is a subtle difference in how the code generation facility handles those WMI classes that are marked in the CIM Repository as singletons. Typically, the generated class will have a default parameterless constructor and a parameterized constructor. The default constructor does nothing. The parameterized constructor takes a parameter that represents a key property of the WMI class and internally creates a bound instance of the `ManagementObject` type. For singletons, however, the default parameterless constructor is coded to bind the class to a single instance of the underlying WMI object.

You will find that generating wrappers for WMI classes is extremely helpful even if you do not intend to use the generated code in your management application. You should definitely look at the generated source code; not only does it significantly simplify the programming, but it can be used as an excellent source of information on System.Management type's usage patterns

Summary

This chapter has provided a comprehensive and detailed overview of the fundamental functionality afforded by the types in `System.Management` namespace. Although some more esoteric details of WMI programming, such as querying the CIM Repository with WQL and handling WMI events, will be covered in subsequent chapters, having studied the material in this chapter, you should be capable of building nearly any kind of management application. More specifically, you should be proficient at

*   Creating instances of the `ManagementObject` type that are bound to WMI objects and retrieving the management data that is exposed through the instance properties

*   Navigating the CIM object model and analyzing the relationships between individual instances of WMI classes

- Updating the management data through the properties of `ManagementObjects` that are bound to WMI class instances and committing those changes to the CIM Repository

- Programmatically retrieving WMI schema information; analyzing class, method, and property definitions; as well as identifying relationships between individual schema elements

- Calling WMI class and instance methods

- Optimizing your programs by using asynchronous programming techniques

- Internationalizing your applications by retrieving localized values of WMI property qualifiers

- Creating and using strongly typed wrappers for WMI classes to simplify programming

Armed with such a thorough understanding of this functionality, you are now ready to delve into the somewhat more complex aspects of System.Management programming that are covered in the next few chapters.

CHAPTER 3

Querying WMI

You will find that navigating through the CIM object model is not always
straightforward and often requires rather elaborate coding. When you know the
identity of a WMI object in question in advance, you can bind to it by just instantiating a ManagementObject with an appropriate object path parameter. The
situation is different, however, if a criterion for retrieving the WMI object is not
based on the object's identity but rather on its other, non-key properties. For
instance, if you are charged with the task of compressing all files that exceed
10 MB in size on a given system, you may crank out the following code:

```
ManagementClass mc = new ManagementClass("CIM_DataFile");
foreach(ManagementObject mo in mc.GetInstances()) {
    if((ulong)mo["FileSize"] > 10490000) {
        uint r = (uint)mo.InvokeMethod("Compress", new object[] {});
        Console.WriteLine("Compressed {0} ({1})", mo["FileName"], r);
    }
}
```

Here the identity of a file—its name, which is necessary in order to bind
the instance of the ManagementObject to a corresponding WMI object directly—
is not known up-front, hence your need to iterate through all objects of type
CIM_DataFile to check whether the FileSize property exceeds the imposed limit.
When you are looking at this code, the first thing that comes to mind is its relative
inefficiency. Even though the number of large files on an average system is fairly
small when compared to the overall count of all file system objects, you still need
to examine all instances of CIM_DataFile to identify those few that match your
search criteria. But before you can inspect the file size, you need to create
a ManagementObject and bind it to an instance of a WMI class, which can be quite
expensive, even for objects on a local system. Worse yet, in a distributed environment, such code is guaranteed to exhibit unacceptable performance, in addition
to generating excessive and unnecessary network traffic.

Another negative factor commonly associated with searching the CIM model
for classes and objects is code complexity. Although the snippet above is not particularly intricate, the level of complexity tends to increase as the criteria you use
to retrieve objects becomes more sophisticated. For instance, if you have a set of

compound selection criteria, based on the non-key properties of several related objects, your code may be extremely convoluted and error-prone.

The good news is that WMI is perfectly capable of doing all the dirty work involved in locating the objects directly based on the values of their non-key properties. The technique for doing this, however, is quite different from the CIM navigation procedures that were outlined in the previous chapter. Specifically, WMI has to be told how to locate the objects in question via a particular notation known as a query.

Clearly, there is a parallel between querying an object model such as CIM and querying a relational database. Just like the relations or database tables, WMI objects have "columns," which are referred to as *properties* in object-oriented parlance, and, just like the tables, the objects are linked together via a well-defined set of relationships. Thus, in theory, you can easily adopt the notation that is used to express relational queries to query the CIM object model. For instance, if you assume that Structured Query Language (SQL), utilized in relational queries, is used to query CIM, the following query may return all objects that represent files with a size exceeding the 10 MB limit:

```
SELECT * FROM CIM_DataFile WHERE FileSize > 10490000
```

This approach is far superior to iterating through a collection of all file objects on a given system. Not only is it more concise, but it is also more efficient, because only the objects that satisfy the search criteria are returned to the caller.

In fact, the query language used by WMI, called WMI Query Language (WQL), is a subset of ANSI SQL. Although it is arguable that the latter is the best query language, especially when it comes to object models, SQL brings quite a few benefits to the table. First, because it is one of the earlier query notations, it enjoys unparalleled popularity and is well understood by software developers. Its straightforward English-like grammar is another factor that makes it easy to learn and use. Finally, SQL has been abused so many times and found in so many unexpected applications, that it would be a sin not to adopt it for WMI.

WQL, when used with the WMI query facilities, is extremely effective and often indispensable, especially when it comes to building sophisticated management tools. The System.Management namespace houses a handful of types that make querying WMI easy while providing almost unlimited flexibility and power. However, to query WMI effectively, you need to understand WQL and the query processing facilities pretty well. This knowledge is exactly what this chapter provides.

WQL Overview

Although the official WMI documentation claims that WQL is a subset of ANSI SQL, this is not entirely true. Even though both query languages are conceptually similar and some WQL constructs bear a strong syntactic resemblance to analogous features of SQL, WQL adds a slew of operators and statements that do not exist in ANSI SQL. Thus, from a syntactical standpoint, WQL is not a subset but rather a variation of SQL; or in other words, it is a SQL-like query language.

Unlike SQL, which offers extensive functionality to support data modification operations, WQL is a *data-retrieval language.* In other words, it is simply not possible to make any changes to either the WMI schema or the management data via WQL because the language does include any data- or schema-manipulation commands. Nevertheless, when it comes to retrieving the data, WQL really shines.

As you learned earlier, two broad classes of information are available through WMI: management data, which is housed by instances of WMI classes, and schema information, which describes the structure of management objects. In reality, WMI maintains an additional category of information—event data, which enables management applications to receive notifications whenever certain changes are made to the management data or schema. WQL, therefore, is designed to facilitate three classes of queries: data queries that return the management data, schema queries that return the schema elements, and, finally, event queries, which register event consumers. Although I will briefly discuss the syntax used for event queries, the primary focus of this chapter is on data and schema queries. I will cover the details of WMI event mechanism, as well as the specifics of how you register and handle events, in Chapter 4.

As you will see shortly, the System.Management namespace offers a range of types that make assembling and processing data, schema, and event queries easier. Although you will find that writing a program to test WQL queries is fairly trivial, sometimes you will want to have a tool that is capable of executing the queries on users behalf and displaying the results. This is exactly what the WQL Query Builder tool, which is included in the WMI CIM Studio that is distributed as part of WMI SDK, is designed to accomplish.

The WQL Query Builder can be accessed by clicking the Query Builder button that is located in the upper-right corner of the CIM Studio screen, just above the object viewer pane. Figure 3-1 shows what the Query Builder looks like, once activated.

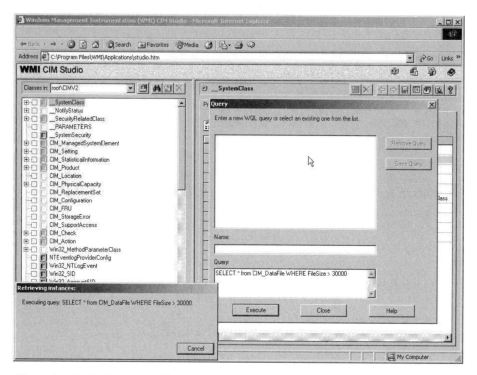

Figure 3-1. WQL Query Builder

To execute a query using WQL Query Builder, simply type the query text into the Query textbox and click the Execute button. The results will appear in the object viewer pane of the CIM Studio. In addition to being a versatile query-testing tool, Query Builder has some basic query management facilities. Thus, you may save a query by assigning a name to it and clicking the Save button. You can recall a saved query later so that you can edit or execute it. Despite its minimalistic user interface, WQL Query Builder is very useful for query debugging or, simply for ensuring the validity of WQL queries before you use them in a management application.

SELECT Statement

Perhaps, one of the qualities of WQL that makes it so attractive is its simplicity. The entire language consists of just three statements: SELECT, ASSOCIATORS OF, and REFERENCES OF. Depending on the syntax options you choose, you may use these to retrieve data, schema, or event information. Out of these three, SELECT is the most powerful and the most versatile data retrieval command; it is typically used to satisfy most of the querying needs. SELECT is also easier to understand, due to its conceptual and syntactic resemblance to its SQL counterpart.

Listing 3-1 shows a semiformal definition of the WQL SELECT statement.

Listing 3-1. WQL SELECT *Statement*

```
statement ::= SELECT <property_list> FROM <class_name> [WITHIN <integer_constant>]
              [WHERE <selection_criteria>]
              [GROUP <grouping_criteria>];
property_list ::= '*' | <property_name>[,<property_name>...];
class_name ::= <class_identifier> | 'meta_class';
property_name ::=
   <property_identifier> | <object_identifier>.<property_identifier>;
selection_criteria ::= <expression> [AND <expression>...] |
                       <expression> [OR <expression>...];
grouping_criteria ::= WITHIN <integer_constant> [BY <property_list>]
                      [HAVING 'NumberOfEvents' <operator> <integer_constant>];
expression ::= <property_name> <operator> <constant>;
operator ::=
   '=' | '!=' | '<>' | '<' | '>' | '>=' | '<=' | 'IS' | 'IS NOT' | 'ISA';
```

SELECT Statement Basics

The following line of code illustrates what a simplest form of the SELECT statement may look like:

```
SELECT ExecutablePath, ProcessID FROM Win32_Process
```

This is a data query, which simply returns the values of the ExecutablePath and ProcessID properties of every Win32_Process object on a given system. In cases when more then just a few object properties are of interest, instead of spelling out the property names, you may use an * as a shortcut—it stands for all properties of a given object:

```
SELECT * FROM Win32_Process
```

However, the SELECT statement is not very useful unless it lets you limit the result set to certain objects or classes that satisfy a given selection criteria. In WQL you achieve this by applying an appropriate WHERE clause to the SELECT statement. Thus, to retrieve a list of Win32_Service objects that have an automatic startup mode, you may use the following query:

```
SELECT * FROM Win32_Service WHERE StartMode = 'Auto'
```

In addition, multiple conditions may be grouped together with AND or OR clauses. For instance, the following query will retrieve all instances of the Win32_Service class that have an automatic startup mode but are not currently running:

```
SELECT * FROM Win32_Service WHERE StartMode = 'Auto' AND State = 'Stopped'
```

Just like in regular SQL, WQL's AND clause has precedence over the OR clause. For example, the following query, which attempts to identify all services with an automatic startup mode that are in either a stopped or an unknown state, will not be processed correctly:

```
SELECT * FROM Win32_Service WHERE StartMode = 'Auto'
AND State = 'Stopped' OR State = 'Unknown'
```

Instead of returning just the autostart services in the stopped or unknown state, the preceding code will return all services that are in the unknown state as well as the autostart services in the stopped state. You can change the precedence of OR and AND clauses by parenthesizing an appropriate expression:

```
SELECT * FROM Win32_Service WHERE StartMode = 'Auto'
AND (State = 'Stopped' OR State = 'Unknown')
```

You may invert the meaning of a particular expression by applying the NOT clause. For instance, the following WQL will produce a list of all Win32_Service objects that do not have an automatic start mode:

```
SELECT * FROM Win32_Service WHERE NOT StartMode = 'Auto'
```

WQL is rather strict when it comes to parsing the expressions that represent the query selection criteria. An arithmetic expression, for instance, may not appear as part of the selection criteria. Thus, the following query will be flagged as invalid:

```
SELECT * FROM Win32_Process WHERE WorkingSetSize >= (1000*5 + 20000)
```

By the same token, evaluating the properties of an object based on an arithmetic expression that involves its other properties is impossible. For example, the following, seemingly innocent query, which attempts to identify those instances of the Win32_Process class where the process working set size exceeds 60 percent of its maximum working set, will fail:

```
SELECT * FROM Win32_Process WHERE WorkingSetSize >= (MaximumWorkingSetSize * 0.60)
```

In general, it is safe to say that any useful WQL search expression should have a property name on one side and a constant on the other. Basically, the data type of a constant should correspond to the data type of a property involved in the expression. Thus, if you attempt to evaluate a condition where a numeric property is compared against a string constant, you will get an error. The comparison operator you choose to use in the expression should also be dictated by the data type of the object property involved. Although it is possible to apply > or < operators to string properties, functionally, it may not make much sense. For instance, the following query retrieves all instances of Win32_Service class where the string that represents the start mode property value is greater than the string 'Auto', when sorted in alphabetical order:

```
SELECT * FROM Win32_Service WHERE StartMode > 'Auto'
```

Although this query parses and even produces results, its functional value is questionable.

All string comparisons in WQL are case-insensitive. Thus, all following queries produce equivalent results:

```
SELECT * FROM Win32_Service WHERE StartMode = 'auto'
SELECT * FROM Win32_Service WHERE StartMode = 'AUTO'
SELECT * FROM Win32_Service WHERE StartMode = 'Auto'
```

When it comes to querying WMI based on the values of Boolean object properties, some restrictions apply. First, you can only use the =, and !=, or <>operators in queries that involve Boolean properties. Using any other operator will make no sense, thus WMI will flag any such query as an error. Second, you can only compare Boolean properties against appropriate constants that represent Boolean values. You can use predefined true and false keywords or the integer constants 1 and 0, where 1 corresponds to true and 0 corresponds to false. Therefore, you can use either of the following two queries to select all currently running services:

```
SELECT * FROM Win32_Service WHERE Started = true
SELECT * FROM Win32_Service WHERE Started = 1
```

Another keyword that can be used to replace a constant in WQL search expression is NULL. A NULL, just like an infamous relation database NULL, represents the absence of a value, and, in the context of WMI, it may be used to identify those properties that are empty. In an attempt to be ANSI-compliant, WQL offers special IS or IS NOT operators that should be used in all expressions that involve NULL values. The alternative syntax, however, which uses an equal sign, is supported as well. Thus, both of the following queries correctly list all disk drives for which the file system cannot be determined:

```
SELECT * FROM Win32_LogicalDisk WHERE FileSystem IS NULL
SELECT * FROM Win32_LogicalDisk WHERE FileSystem = NULL
```

Note that both IS and IS NOT operators may only be used in expressions that involve NULL values. If these operators are applied to constants other than NULL, they cause WMI to reject the query as invalid. For example, the following attempt to find all disk drives that have the NTFS file system will result in error:

```
SELECT * FROM Win32_LogicalDisk WHERE FileSystem IS "NTFS"
```

Now that you have experimented with WQL queries for a while, you may notice that the default behavior for any query is to return not only the instances of the class that are specified in the FROM clause, but also all the instances of its subclasses. The following query, for example, will return objects of type Win32_Service, Win32_ApplicationService, Win32_SystemDriver, and so on, because all of these classes inherit from the CIM_Service class:

```
SELECT * FROM CIM_Service
```

However, sometimes, you do not want this behavior, because the objective of a given query may be to select only those subclasses of a particular class that belong to one or more specified classes. Thus, the intent of the last query example may be only to return those service objects that belong to either Win32_Service or Win32_ApplicationService classes, but not to the Win32_SystemDriver class. To achieve this, you have to resort to using the system properties of a class. As you may remember, a class of an object is identified by its __CLASS system property; therefore, the following query will limit the result set based on the specified class name:

```
SELECT * FROM CIM_Service
WHERE __CLASS = 'Win32_Service' OR __CLASS = 'Win32_ApplicationService'
```

You can query by system properties other than __CLASS. The following query, for instance, will correctly retrieve an instance of the Win32_Process class identified by its __RELPATH system property:

```
SELECT * FROM Win32_Process WHERE __RELPATH = 'Win32_Process.Handle="100"'
```

Note that when you query using __RELPATH, you must spell out the name of the key property of an object (Handle in the example above). When processing WQL queries, WMI will not automatically expand the path string, therefore, unless you supply the fully expanded value, this query will not return any results.

Interestingly, if you try to query using some system properties, such as __PATH or __NAMESPACE, the query will be flagged by WMI as invalid. The reason for such a restriction is that WQL queries operate in a certain namespace to which the client application is connected; or in other words, they are bound to a certain location. Thus, if you allow queries that peruse the object location information, you will introduce ambiguity. The special treatment that __PATH and __NAMESPACE properties receive may seem a bit inconsistent; however, it doesn't really matter because querying by these properties certainly does not make much sense—it is much easier to retrieve the object directly.

Frankly, __CLASS is the only system property that seems to be useful when it comes to querying. If you find yourself attempting to construct a query that retrieves an object based on the values of system properties other than __CLASS, you may want to rethink your approach and see whether querying is really necessary.

Another peculiar aspect of WMI behavior is how it treats the system properties of an object that are returned by a query. Normally, if the * placeholder is used as a property list in a SELECT statement, each object, returned by a query, will have all of its system properties properly populated. However, if a SELECT statement contains a list of nonsystem object properties to be returned, the only system properties that are populated by WMI for each output object are __CLASS, __RELPATH, __GENUS, and __PROPERTY_COUNT. Note that the __PROPERTY_COUNT will reflect the actual number of the properties selected rather than the total number of properties in the class definition. This behavior is logical because * stands for all properties—system and nonsystem. To further illustrate this point, look at the following example:

```
SELECT __PATH FROM Win32_Process
```

Although this query does not use the *, the returned object will contain the correctly populated __PATH property. The only conclusion that you can draw from this is that certain system properties, such as __PATH, __NAMESPACE, and a few more, are only returned when you request them either explicitly or implicitly with *. This is the default behavior of WMI query processing engine, but you may alter it by passing a special flag, WBEM_FLAG_ENSURE_LOCATABLE, to IWbemServices::ExecQuery method. You will see how to set this flag through the EnumerationOptions type later in this chapter (see "Using ManagementObjectSearcher").

Using SELECT for Embedded Object Queries

If you take a close look at Listing 3-1 (which appeared earlier in this section), you may notice that object property names may be prefixed with object identifier names. At first, this may not make much sense, because, unlike SQL, WQL disallows joins between multiple objects. When processing joins, the ability to use prefixes to distinguish between the properties of the multiple objects involved is certainly valuable. However, for WQL queries, which seem to always operate on a single object or class, prefixing property names with object identifiers looks like an unnecessary complication. Moreover, if you attempt to run the following query, WMI will reject it as invalid:

```
SELECT Win32_Process.Name FROM Win32_Process WHERE Win32_Process.Handle = 100
```

It turns out that, even though the joins are disallowed, WMI can process certain queries where multiple objects are involved. It is entirely possible that an arbitrary object contains one or more other objects, often referred to as embedded objects. Consider the following scenario:

```
class Foo {
    [key] string Name;
    string Description;
    uint32 ID;
};
class Bar {
    [key] uint32 ID;
    Foo EmbedObj;
};
```

Here class Bar contains an embedded object of type Foo. If an instance of Bar exists and houses an embedded instance of Foo, such that the ID property of Foo is 1, you may use the following query:

```
SELECT * FROM Bar WHERE EmbedObj.ID = 1
```

This query retrieves the instance of Bar based on the value of the property of its embedded object Foo.

Be careful when you retrieve objects based on the properties of their embedded objects. Normally, WMI ensures the validity of a query by checking on the existence of all properties referenced in the WHERE clause and SELECT property list. These checks, however, are not carried out for the properties of an embedded object. Thus, a query that references the nonexistent properties of an embedded object in its WHERE clause will not fail; it will simply return no results:

```
SELECT * FROM Bar WHERE EmbedObj.Handle = 1
```

The situation is a bit more interesting when properties of embedded objects are referenced in the SELECT property list rather than in its WHERE clause. It turns out that the embedded object property name portion of the fully qualified name is simply ignored. Thus, the following two queries will produce identical results:

```
SELECT EmbedObj FROM Bar
SELECT EmbedObj.ID FROM Bar
```

In both cases, the output object contains a single property, EmbedObj, that refers to an embedded instance of Foo with all its properties fully populated.

Finally, there are cases when you want to retrieve an object based on the class of its embedded object rather than on the values of the embedded object properties. One approach that comes to mind right away is something similar to the following code:

```
SELECT * FROM Bar WHERE EmbedObj.__CLASS = 'Foo'
```

Although querying by the value of the __CLASS system property of an embedded object is a viable solution that will produce the correct results, there is a better tactic for achieving the same goal. In fact, WQL has a special operator, ISA, that solves the problem neatly and effectively. Although ISA has several applications when it comes to data queries, it can be used as follows:

```
SELECT * FROM Bar WHERE EmbedObj ISA 'Foo'
```

In reality, the ISA operator does more then the previous query, which used the __CLASS system property of an embedded object in its search criteria. In addition to retrieving all instances of Bar, which contain embedded objects of type Foo, ISA will also return all Bar objects that are housing embedded objects that are derived from Foo. Let us consider the following situation:

```
class Foo {
    [key] string Name;
    string Description;
    uint32 ID;
};
class FooDerived : Foo {
    uint32 Property1;
    uint32 Property2;
};
class Bar {
```

```
    [key] uint32 ID;
    object EmbedObj;
};
```

Given that multiple instances of `Bar` exist and that some of these instances house an embedded instance of `Foo` while others contain embedded objects of type `FooDerived`, the following query will return all `Bar` objects:

```
SELECT * FROM Bar WHERE EmbedObj ISA 'Foo'
```

Such an effect cannot be achieved by querying based on the value of the `__CLASS` system property of an embedded object. You may be a bit surprised to see fictitious classes `Foo` and `Bar` being used to illustrate the concept of querying by properties of an embedded object. The reason that I do not refer to any of the elements of the standard CIM model is that embedded objects are rarely exploited, and it seems that a typical out-of-the-box WMI installation does not contain any classes that house embedded objects, with the exception of some specialized entities that represent method parameters, events, and status objects. However, if you remember the discussion of object associations, you may disagree with this statement—associations do indeed contain properties that refer to other objects. As a result, it should be possible to issue the following query to retrieve all instances of the `Win32_AccountSID` association based on the `Name` property of its embedded object of type `Win32_Account`:

```
SELECT * FROM Win32_AccountSID WHERE Element.Name = 'Administrator'
```

As attractive as this code may look, it is not going to work; WMI will flag this query as invalid. The problem here is that association objects, such as `Win32_AccountSID`, do not contain embedded objects—they contain object references. An *object reference* is, essentially, a pointer to an instance of another object that exists independently from the association object. Thus, retrieving associations with the `SELECT` statement based on the properties of the associated objects is simply not supported. There is, however, another approach to achieving the same goal, which will be discussed later in this chapter (see `REFERENCES OF` Statement).

Using SELECT for Schema Queries

All the query examples I have shown you this far in this chapter have been data queries that were designed to retrieve instances of certain WMI classes. Although facilitating the retrieval of management data is one of the primary goals of WQL, sometimes retrieving the WMI schema information is of equal importance.

Coincidentally, the very same SELECT statement that you use in data queries is fully equipped for dealing with the schema. As a matter of fact, querying for class definitions is more straightforward than retrieving the management data, although there are a few subtle details of which you should be aware.

Perhaps, the main difference between data and schema queries is the class name used in the FROM clause of the SELECT statement. When you are querying for the schema information rather than using a WMI class name, you should use a special class, meta_class. For instance, the following query returns all class definitions within a given namespace:

```
SELECT * FROM meta_class
```

Just like in data queries, the result set can be limited by applying an appropriate WHERE clause. There is, however, a difference; you may no longer use the property values in your search criteria. This is where the already familiar ISA operator comes to the rescue:

```
SELECT * FROM meta_class WHERE __this ISA 'CIM_Service'
```

Here a special __this keyword is used to designate a target class for the query. In this case, the ISA operator does the same thing it does for data queries—it instructs WMI to return definitions for all classes that are of type CIM_Service as well as those that are its subclasses. Note that you must always use the ISA operator when you are querying using the __this keyword; WMI will complain if you attempt to use the equality operator.

There are cases, when it is necessary to retrieve a definition for a specific class, rather than a class and all its subclasses. The ISA operator is not going to work in this situation; to solve this problem, WQL offers an alternative approach:

```
SELECT * FROM meta_class WHERE __CLASS = 'Win32_Process'
```

It turns out that the system properties of a class can be used in schema queries in the same way that these properties are used in data queries. Thus, the query above retrieves the definition for the Win32_Process class using its __CLASS system property. Conceivably, system properties other than __CLASS can be used to query for class definition. The following query, for instance, selects definitions for all classes that are subclasses of the CIM_Service:

```
SELECT * FROM meta_class WHERE __SUPERCLASS = 'CIM_Service'
```

Just as it is the case with data queries, using system properties such as __PATH or __NAMESPACE in the WHERE clause causes WMI to reject the query as invalid.

If you take another look at Listing 3-1, you will certainly notice that certain elements of the SELECT statement, such as WITHIN, GROUP, and HAVING clauses, have not been discussed here. These constructs are intended to facilitate event queries and are not used to retrieve either management data or schema definitions. Therefore, the detailed discussion of these clauses is deferred to Chapter 4.

ASSOCIATORS OF Statement

As I already mentioned, the WQL SELECT statement does not support joins between multiple objects. At first this may seem to be a severe restriction, but if you think about it, you will realize that it is a necessity when it comes to querying object models such as CIM. In a typical relational database environment, the relationships between individual entities are not very clearly defined. Although it is possible to identify a relationship by defining primary and foreign keys for database objects, this information is of an advisory nature and does not usually affect the behavior of SQL queries. Thus, you can relate two or more seemingly unrelated objects in a single query.

The situation is entirely different for CIM. Here, the relationships between managed entities are modeled as associations, which are themselves objects. As a result, these relationships are very clearly defined and strictly enforced. Thus, you can achieve an effect similar to that of a conventional SQL join, although the mechanics of it are quite different. Rather than using the SELECT statement for this purpose, WQL provides a special construct, ASSOCIATORS OF, which allows you to navigate the association links and retrieve objects or classes that are logically related to a given entity.

If you remember the discussion of the GetRelated and GetRelatedClasses methods from Chapter 2, this prelude may sound familiar. In fact, both these methods internally construct WQL ASSOCIATORS OF query to retrieve classes or instances, related to a given object.

The formal syntax of the ASSOCIATORS OF statement is shown on Listing 3-2.

Listing 3-2. ASSOCIATORS OF *Statement*

```
statement ::= ASSOCIATORS OF {<path>} [WHERE]
              [AssocClass = <class_name>]
              [RequiredAssocQualifier = <qualifier_name>]
              [RequiredQualifier = <qualifier_name>]
              [ResultClass = <class_name>]
              [ResultRole = <property_name>]
              [Role = <property_name>]
              [SchemaOnly]
              [ClassDefsOnly]
```

The most basic form of the `ASSOCIATORS OF` statement is as follows:

```
ASSOCIATORS OF {Win32_Service='WinMgmt'}
```

Without the `WHERE` clause, the `ASSOCIATORS OF` returns all instances of WMI classes that are associated with a given object. For instance, the preceding example returns all objects that are somehow related to an instance of the `Win32_Service` class, which represents the WMI service `WinMgmt`.

Note that, just like the `SELECT` statement, the `ASSOCIATORS OF` statement requires that a relative object path be used to identify an instance for which related objects are retrieved. As I already mentioned, WQL queries exhibit location affinity and cannot retrieve the information that resides in any other namespace than the current one. Thus, the following query, which specifies the full object path, is invalid:

```
ASSOCIATORS OF {\\BCK_OFFICE\root\CIMV2:Win32_Service='WinMgmt'}
```

It is however, perfectly legal to use a relative class path, rather than object path, in the context of the `ASSOCIATORS OF` statement. For example, the following line of code is a valid WQL statement:

```
ASSOCIATORS OF {Win32_Service}
```

The only problem is that this statement will not produce any results. As you may remember from the previous chapter, in order to retrieve WMI instance data, you need to build a query around an object rather than around a class (see Table 2-9). However, if your objective is to retrieve a class definition rather than its instances, a class name may act as a parameter to the `ASSOCIATORS OF` statement. The only caveat is that you need to explicitly inform WMI that your intention is to perform a schema rather than a data query. Thus, in order to produce meaningful output, you should rewrite the preceding query as follows:

```
ASSOCIATORS OF {Win32_Service} WHERE SchemaOnly
```

Here the `SchemaOnly` flag of the `WHERE` clause advises WMI that a query is to be executed against the schema rather than against the data, so the output should include classes that are related to `Win32_Service` rather than instances. Interestingly, there is another flag, `ClassDefsOnly`, that has a similar effect. It instructs WMI to only include the class definitions in the result set. The difference is that `ClassDefsOnly` does not make a query into a schema query; instead, it is just a convenience feature that allows a data query to produce schema output. To see this point further illustrated, consider the following schema query:

```
ASSOCIATORS OF {Win32_Process} WHERE SchemaOnly
```

As expected, this query returns a class definition for Win32_ComputerSystem—the only class that Win32_Process is associated with via a containment association Win32_SystemProcesses. A conceptually similar query using ClassDefsOnly flag may be written as follows:

```
ASSOCIATORS OF {Win32_Process=100} WHERE ClassDefsOnly
```

This query returns two class definitions: Win32_ComputerSystem and CIM_DataFile. This result is quite peculiar because a CIM schema does not contain an association class that links the latter with Win32_Process. However, a superclass of Win32_Process, CIM_Process, is linked to the CIM_DataFile through the CIM_ProcessExecutable association class. Since the second query is really a data query, it analyses instances rather than classes and returns related classes based on actual rather than schema relationships.

These two flags are not interchangeable: you can only use ClassDefsOnly with data queries where the object path points to an instance rather than a class; and SchemaOnly is only valid when you apply the ASSOCIATORS OF statement to a class.

The remaining subclauses of the WHERE clause allow you to further control the behavior of the ASSOCIATORS OF statement and are very similar to the parameters of the GetRelatedClasses method, discussed previously. The AssocClass keyword specifies the name of an association class or the class from which an association is derived. This association connects the current object or class with its related instances or classes. For instance, to retrieve all instances associated with a given instance of Win32_Service through an association of type CIM_SystemComponent, you may use the following query:

```
ASSOCIATORS OF {Win32_Service='WinMgmt'} WHERE AssocClass = CIM_SystemComponent
```

You may use the Role keyword to further restrict the output by specifying the role of the current object or class in an association. Thus, to retrieve just those related objects that act as containers for Win32_Service instances, you would use the following query:

```
ASSOCIATORS OF {Win32_Service='WinMgmt'}
WHERE AssocClass = CIM_SystemComponent Role=PartComponent
```

This query requests WMI to return all the instances that are linked to a given instance of the Win32_Service class via a CIM_SystemComponent containment association so that the Win32_Service object is pointed to by the PartComponent association endpoint, or in other words, the Win32_Service object is being contained. You can express the same query differently using the ResultRole keyword, which specifies the role of the result object or class in an association:

```
ASSOCIATORS OF {Win32_Service='WinMgmt'}
WHERE AssocClass = CIM_SystemComponent ResultRole=GroupComponent
```

Here the output contains all the objects that are connected to a given instance of Win32_Service via the CIM_SystemComponent containment association and act in a capacity of a container—in other words, all those objects that are being pointed to by a GroupComponent endpoint of an association.

The ResultClass keyword requests that the output only include classes or objects that belong to or are derived from a given class. For example, you may remember that Win32_Service objects are associated with an instance of the Win32_ComputerSystem class via containment associations of type CIM_SystemComponent. Thus, to retrieve an instance of the Win32_ComputerSystem that is connected to a given Win32_Service class, you may use the following query:

```
ASSOCIATORS OF {Win32_Service='WinMgmt'} WHERE ResultClass = Win32_ComputerSystem
```

Interestingly, the ResultClass keyword cannot be used with the ClassDefsOnly flag; if you make any attempt to do so, WMI will reject the query as invalid. As restrictive as it may sound, this limitation is actually quite logical—if the result class is known in advance, there are better ways to retrieve its schema.

Finally, the RequiredQualifier and RequiredAssocQualifier indicate that a result class or an association class must have certain qualifiers to warrant inclusion in the result set:

```
ASSOCIATORS OF {Win32_Service='WinMgmt'} WHERE RequiredAssocQualifier = Association
```

Here the query retrieves all objects related to a given instance of the Win32_Service class through an association class, which is explicitly tagged with the Association qualifier.

Thanks to the versatility of the ASSOCIATORS OF statement, relationship queries may grow fairly complex, thus allowing you fine control over the output. However, certain syntax restrictions do apply. First, the only WQL comparison operation allowed in ASSOCIATORS OF queries is =. For instance, the following query, which attempts to use a '!=' operator, will be flagged by WMI as invalid:

```
ASSOCIATORS OF {Win32_Process=100} WHERE RequiredQualifier != Dynamic
```

Second, compound conditionals that contain AND, OR, and NOT operators are disallowed. Furthermore, although it is legal to use several of the above-mentioned keywords in a single query, given that these keywords are not mutually exclusive, the only thing that may appear as a separator between individual criteria is white space. Thus, both queries below are invalid and will be rejected by WMI:

```
ASSOCIATORS OF {Win32_Process=100}
WHERE ResultClass=CIM_DataFile AND Role=Dependent
ASSOCIATORS OF {Win32_Process=100}
WHERE ResultClass=CIM_DataFile, Role=Dependent
```

REFERENCES OF Statement

Just like GetRelationships and GetRelationshipClasses methods discussed in the previous chapter, the REFERENCES OF statement is designed to retrieve instances or definitions of association classes that refer to a given WMI object or class. Truth be told, the REFERENCES OF statement is the underpinning of the GetRelationships and GetRelationshipClasses—both of these methods internally construct the REFECENCES OF query based on the input parameters.

The formal definition of the REFERENCES OF statement is shown on Listing 3-3.

Listing 3-3. REFERENCES OF *Statement*

```
statement ::= REFERENCES OF {<path>} [WHERE]
                 [RequiredQualifier = <qualifier_name>]
                 [ResultClass = <class_name>]
                 [Role = <property_name>]
                 [SchemaOnly]
                 [ClassDefsOnly]
```

The WHERE clause is optional, so the following statement will return all instances of association classes that refer to an instance of Win32_Process:

```
REFERENCES OF {Win32_Process=100}
```

Similar to the ASSOCIATORS OF, the REFERENCES OF may take either an object or a class path as a parameter, as long as it is a relative rather than absolute path. To obtain meaningful results when you are using a class path, you should specify the WHERE clause with SchemaOnly keyword:

```
REFERENCES OF {Win32_Process} WHERE SchemaOnly
```

This will effectively turn this into a schema query so that the association class definitions rather than instances will be returned.

Another way to obtain classes instead of instances is by using the ClassDefsOnly keyword. However, you should remember that using ClassDefsOnly in a data query is not equivalent to using a schema query. Thus, the preceding query, which is a true schema query, will return the definitions for only those associations that have the Win32_Process class as one of their endpoints. In this particular case, the only association class that is returned is Win32_SystemProcesses. The following statement, however, behaves differently; in addition to returning the definition of Win32_SystemProcesses, it also returns the CIM_ProcessExecutable class:

```
REFERENCES OF {Win32_Process=100} WHERE ClassDefsOnly
```

The difference in output is explained by the fact that the latter query examines instance rather than schema data and therefore returns actual associations even though the association endpoints may be defined as superclasses of a given class. Thus, the CIM_ProcessExecutable association has a CIM_Process rather than a Win32_Process as one of its endpoints, but since there are outstanding instances of it that reference subclasses of the CIM_Process, it is picked up by the query.

To further restrict the output, the REFERENCES OF statement offers the ResultClass keyword, which allows you to retrieve only the specified association classes. For instance, to get all instances of the CIM_ProcessExecutable association class or association instances that are derived from this class so that these associations refer to a given instance of Win32_Process, you may use the following query:

```
REFERENCES OF {Win32_Process=100} WHERE ResultClass = CIM_ProcessExecutable
```

The ResultClass keyword is not compatible with the ClassDefsOnly flag and any attempt to use these two keywords together in a single query will be flagged as an error.

Another subclause, which may be used to gain more control over the output of the REFERENCES OF statement, is Role. This keyword indicates that the class or object to which the statement applies should play a certain role in the association. Thus, in order to retrieve all associations where an arbitrary Win32_Process object acts as a dependent, you should use the following query:

```
REFERENCES OF {Win32_Process=100} WHERE Role=Dependent
```

Here the role of an object is identified by the name of the property of an association class that represents an association endpoint. The query returns instances of the CIM_ProcessExecutable association, which links Win32_Process objects with instances of `CIM_DataFile`, so that the `Win32_Process` object is connected to the endpoint that is designated by the `Dependent` property of the association class.

Finally, the `RequiredQualifier` keyword lets you further filter the result set based on the qualifiers that are defined for certain association classes. Hence, the following query returns just the associations that are tagged with `Association` qualifier:

```
REFERENCES OF {Win32_Process=100} WHERE RequiredQualifier = Association
```

Similar to the `ASSOCIATORS OF` statement, the syntax of the `REFERENCES OF` statement is fairly restrictive; compound conditionals are disallowed and the only legal comparison operator is =.

System.Management Query Support Types

To facilitate all aspects of WQL query handling, the designers of the .NET system management framework outfitted the `System.Management` namespace with several query support types. Besides aiding with query-based data retrieval, these types provide backing for other operations such as query assembly, parsing, and analysis. The remainder of this chapter is a comprehensive overview of the WQL query support functionality that is afforded by the System.Management namespace types.

Using ManagementObjectSearcher

`ManagementObjectSearcher` is the centerpiece of the WQL query handling machinery that is available within the `System.Management` namespace. This type is very straightforward and easy to use because it has a single purpose—to execute queries. To see how trivial it is to execute an arbitrary WQL query, take a look at the following snippet of code:

```
ManagementObjectSearcher ms = new ManagementObjectSearcher(
    "SELECT * FROM Win32_Process");
foreach(ManagementObject mo in ms.Get()) {
    Console.WriteLine(mo["__PATH"]);
}
```

This code first creates an instance of `ManagementObjectSearcher` by invoking one of its constructors, which takes a WQL query string as a parameter. Once the `ManagementObjectSearcher` is constructed and ready to use, the code calls its Get method and iterates through the returned ManagementObjectCollection using the foreach loop.

The WQL query, when passed as an argument to the ManagementObjectSearcher constructor, does not have to be a SELECT statement— the ASSOCIATORS OF and REFERENCES OF queries are handled in exactly the same fashion:

```
ManagementObjectSearcher ms =
    new ManagementObjectSearcher("ASSOCIATORS OF {Win32_Process=100}");
foreach(ManagementObject mo in ms.Get()) {
    Console.WriteLine(mo["__PATH"]);
}
```

The same goes for schema queries. The only thing that sets a schema query apart from its data counterpart is the query statement itself, as well as the fact that the ManagementObjectCollection, which is returned by the Get method, will contain classes rather than instances:

```
ManagementObjectSearcher ms = new ManagementObjectSearcher(
    "SELECT * FROM meta_class WHERE __this ISA 'Win32_Process'");
foreach(ManagementClass mo in ms.Get()) {
    Console.WriteLine(mo["__PATH"]);
}
```

As I briefly mentioned before, WQL queries themselves may not include any information, that specifies the location of a WMI class or object of interest. In other words, the only piece of class or object identification allowed in a query is either the relative object path or the class name. Therefore, the earlier examples would always query the \\root\CIMV2 namespace on the local machine, which is not always the behavior you want. One way to overcome this limitation is to use the DefaultPath static property of the ManagementPath type to change the global default namespace path (see Chapter 2 for details):

```
ManagementPath.DefaultPath = new ManagementPath(@"\\BCK_OFFICE\root\CIMV2");
ManagementObjectSearcher ms = new ManagementObjectSearcher(
    "SELECT * FROM Win32_Process");
foreach(ManagementObject mo in ms.Get()) {
    Console.WriteLine(mo["__PATH"]);
}
```

This code does achieve the objective of producing a list of all the processes that are running on the remote system BCK_OFFICE. This approach, however, is less than perfect because the default namespace setting is changed at the global level and will affect not only this query, but all subsequent operations as well. Although you can save the initial default setting and restore it when the query completes, doing something like that is not only error-prone, but also just plain ugly.

There is a much better solution, which comes in a form of an overloaded constructor method for the ManagementObjectSearcher type. This constructor takes two string parameters: a scope, which is essentially a namespace path, and a WQL query. Hence, the previous example can be rewritten as follows:

```
ManagementObjectSearcher ms = new
ManagementObjectSearcher(@"\\BCK_OFFICE\root\CIMV2",
    "SELECT * FROM Win32_Process");
foreach(ManagementObject mo in ms.Get()) {
    Console.WriteLine(mo["__PATH"]);
}
```

The namespace path can also be set using the Scope property of the ManagementObjectSearcher type. This property refers to an object of type ManagementScope, which is used to control the WMI connection establishment process. Since it is not my intention to discuss the functionality afforded by the ManagementScope type until Chapter 8, I will just say that it allows you to set the namespace path for subsequent operations. Thus, the following snippet of code produces exactly the same results as the previous example:

```
ManagementObjectSearcher ms = new ManagementObjectSearcher(
    "SELECT * FROM Win32_Process");
ms.Scope.Path = new ManagementPath(@"\\BCK_OFFICE\root\CIMV2");
foreach(ManagementObject mo in ms.Get()) {
    Console.WriteLine(mo["__PATH"]);
}
```

As you may remember from our discussion of the WQL SELECT statement, queries that explicitly specify object properties to be selected return partially populated objects. Thus, certain system properties of objects returned by such query will not be populated. Let us take a look at the following code:

```
ManagementObjectSearcher ms = new ManagementObjectSearcher(
    "SELECT ExecutablePath FROM Win32_Process WHERE Handle = 100");
foreach(ManagementObject mo in ms.Get()) {
    foreach(PropertyData pd in mo.SystemProperties) {
        Console.WriteLine("{0} {1}", pd.Name, pd.Value);
    }
}
```

The output shows that all system properties that identify the location of a returned object, such as __SERVER, __NAMESPACE, and __PATH, are blank.

You can alter this default behavior by supplying an instance of the EnumerationOptions type to the constructor of the ManagementObjectSearcher. You may recall that the EnumerationOptions type allows you to control different aspects of an enumeration operation such as the block size of the read operation, the inclusion of localized information in the output, and more. Although most of the functionality afforded by this type has already been discussed in Chapter 2, one of its properties, EnsureLocatable, has an interesting effect on the results of a WQL query. By setting this option to the TRUE value, you may instruct WMI to always populate those system properties that identify the location of an object. Hence, the following code correctly prints out the values of location-specific system properties:

```
EnumerationOptions eo = new EnumerationOptions();
eo.EnsureLocatable = true;
ManagementObjectSearcher ms = new ManagementObjectSearcher(null,
    "SELECT ExecutablePath FROM Win32_Process WHERE Handle = 100", eo);
foreach(ManagementObject mo in ms.Get()) {
    foreach(PropertyData pd in mo.SystemProperties) {
        Console.WriteLine("{0} {1}", pd.Name, pd.Value);
    }
}
```

Here the instance of the EnumerationOptions with the EnsureLocatable flag turned on is passed as a last argument to the constructor of the ManagementObjectSearcher. Note that this version of the constructor takes three parameters: a scope string that contains the namespace path, the query string, and the EnumerationOptions object. When you are connecting to a default namespace on a local machine, a null value can be substituted for the scope string.

You can achieve the same result slightly more easily by using the Options property of the ManagementObjectSearcher, which refers to an object of type EnumerationOptions. Thus, the previous example can be simplified as follows:

```
ManagementObjectSearcher ms = new ManagementObjectSearcher(
    "SELECT ExecutablePath FROM Win32_Process WHERE Handle = 100");
ms.Options.EnsureLocatable = true;
foreach(ManagementObject mo in ms.Get()) {
    foreach(PropertyData pd in mo.SystemProperties) {
        Console.WriteLine("{0} {1}", pd.Name, pd.Value);
    }
}
```

Finally, just like the other .NET system management types, the ManagementObjectSearcher has built-in provisions for processing WQL queries in an asynchronous fashion. The usage pattern for an asynchronous query execution is similar to that of a direct object retrieval—it revolves around the ManagementOperationObserver object, passed as a parameter to the overloaded version of the Get method. For example, the following code asynchronously retrieves all instances of the Win32_Process class:

```
class Monitor {
    bool bComplete = false;
    public bool Completed {
        get { return bComplete; }
        set { bComplete = value; }
    }
    public void OnCompleted(object sender, CompletedEventArgs ea) {
        Completed = true;
    }
    public void OnObjectReady(object sender, ObjectReadyEventArgs ea) {
        Console.WriteLine(ea.NewObject["__PATH"]);
    }
    public static void Main(string[] args) {
        Monitor mo = new Monitor();
        ManagementOperationObserver ob = new ManagementOperationObserver();
        ob.Completed += new CompletedEventHandler(mo.OnCompleted);
        ob.ObjectReady += new ObjectReadyEventHandler(mo.OnObjectReady);
        ManagementObjectSearcher ms = new ManagementObjectSearcher(
            "SELECT * FROM Win32_Process");
        ms.Get(ob);
        while(!mo.Completed) {
            System.Threading.Thread.Sleep(1000);
        }
    }
}
```

This code creates an instance of ManagementOperationObserver, sets up the handlers for its Completed and ObjectReady events, and then invokes the asynchronous version of the ManagementObjectSearcher Get method. The results of the SELECT query are delivered one-by-one to the ObjectReady event handler and are accessed through the NewObject property of the ObjectReadyEventArgs object.

Using Query Types

Besides aiding with query execution, the System.Management namespace provides several types for query parsing and analysis. At the root of the type hierarchy there is an abstract type, called ManagementQuery, which is designed to serve as a basis for deriving more specialized management query types. In addition to a few protected methods for parsing the query text, ManagementQuery defines two public properties: QueryLanguage and QueryString. These two properties are all that ManagementObjectSearcher needs to process the query. In fact, if you look at the signature of the IWbemServices::ExecQuery method that is called internally by ManagementObjectSearcher, you will notice that this method expects the language identifier and the query text as its first two parameters. Thus, it seems like implementing a custom query type is a fairly simple matter:

```
class MyQuery : ManagementQuery {
   public MyQuery(string lang, string query) {
      QueryLanguage = lang;
      QueryString = query;
   }
   public override object Clone() {
      return this.MemberwiseClone();
   }
}
```

Note that you need to supply an implementation for Clone method of ICloneable interface, since ManagementQuery, which includes the interface, leaves this method unimplemented.

Theoretically, it should be possible to pass this custom query object to the overloaded constructor ManagementObjectSearcher instead of just the plain query string:

```
MyQuery query = new MyQuery("WQL", "SELECT * FROM Win32_Process");
ManagementObjectSearcher ms = new ManagementObjectSearcher(query);
```

Although ManagementObjectSearcher does have a constructor that takes a query object rather than the plain query string, the code above will not compile. The problem is that this constructor, rather than accepting an object that descends from ManagementQuery directly, expects an instance of ObjectQuery type, which is a subclass of ManagementQuery.

As you may remember, WMI supports three general categories of queries: data, schema, and event queries. ManagementObjectSearcher is designed to handle only those queries that return objects or class definitions—data or schema

queries—and is unsuitable for processing event queries. Thus, the
System.Management namespace offers two specialized subclasses of
ManagementQuery: ObjectQuery and EventQuery. These subclasses are intended to
handle object and event queries respectively. To enforce this separation of duties,
the constructor of ManagementObjectSearcher expects the parameter of type
ObjectQuery, while the constructors of ManagementEventWatcher (a type that is
dedicated to handling WMI events) accept parameters of type EventQuery. The
details of event handling as well as the functionality afforded by EventQuery and
ManagementEventWatcher types, will be discussed in the next chapter.

ObjectQuery is a very simple type that is similar to the MyQuery type shown
earlier. Besides the QueryLanguage and QueryString properties that it inherited
from ManagementQuery, it has three constructor methods: a parameterless one,
one that takes a query string parameter, and another one that takes a string
parameter, which represents the query language, as well as the query string. The
following snippet of code illustrates how ObjectQuery can be used with
ManagementObjectSearcher:

```
ObjectQuery query = new ObjectQuery("WQL", "SELECT * FROM Win32_Process");
ManagementObjectSearcher ms = new ManagementObjectSearcher(query);
foreach(ManagementObject mo in ms.Get()) {
    Console.WriteLine(mo["__PATH"]);
}
```

Note that passing the WQL language identifier to the ObjectQuery constructor
is optional. To save yourself some typing, you may choose to use a single-
parameter constructor, which defaults the language to WQL:

```
ObjectQuery query = new ObjectQuery("SELECT * FROM Win32_Process");
ManagementObjectSearcher ms = new ManagementObjectSearcher(query);
foreach(ManagementObject mo in ms.Get()) {
    Console.WriteLine(mo["__PATH"]);
}
```

Interestingly, the ability to specify the query language has little value because
the only supported language for querying WMI is WQL. It is conceivable, however, that future releases of WMI will support alternative query languages, such as
XPath, for instance. Until then, explicitly setting the query language is not
required and is best avoided. In fact, the only logical reason for having a generic,
language-agnostic object query type seems to be the flexibility of being able to
provide specialized, language-specific query types. In other words, ObjectQuery is
not intended to be used directly and instead, it should serve as a base class for
specialized types, that incorporate features, pertinent to a specific query language. Currently, the only available specialization of ObjectQuery is

WqlObjectQuery, but it is entirely possible that in the near feature the System.Management namespace may include something like XPathObjectQuery.

WqlObjectQuery is not much different from its parent and does not offer any new features. Instead, it restricts the functionality of ObjectQuery by making its QueryLanguage property read-only, thus preventing a user from overriding the default value WQL set by the constructor of ManagementQuery. With that in mind, you can use WqlObjectQuery to rewrite the previous as follows:

```
WqlObjectQuery query = new WqlObjectQuery("SELECT * FROM Win32_Process");
ManagementObjectSearcher ms = new ManagementObjectSearcher(query);
foreach(ManagementObject mo in ms.Get()) {
    Console.WriteLine(mo["__PATH"]);
}
```

As you can see, neither ObjectQuery nor WqlObjectQuery really aid with query parsing or analysis, and as a result, they seem to add little value to query handling. You may find this somewhat puzzling since there is no obvious advantage in using these types versus a plain query string. The reason for their use, once again, is specialization—these types are not intended to be used directly, rather they are designed to serve as base classes for other types that zero in on particular categories of WQL queries.

As mentioned earlier, WQL is a simple language consisting of just three statements. The syntactic structure of two of them, ASSOCIATORS OF and REFERENCES OF, is very similar, so similar, in fact, that you can use a common algorithm to parse. The SELECT statement, on the other hand, is strikingly different and necessitates a special parsing logic. Thus, rather than trying to shoehorn the parsing code for the entire WQL language into a single class, the designers of the System.Management namespace created three separate subclasses of WqlObjectQuery—SelectQuery, RelatedObjectQuery, and RelationshipQuery—each of which is responsible for handling a specific WQL statement.

Using SelectQuery Type

As its name implies, the first of these three types, SelectQuery, is dedicated to handling WQL SELECT queries. SelectQuery makes parsing the query text and breaking it into individual components extremely easy:

```
SelectQuery query = new SelectQuery(
    "SELECT * FROM Win32_Process WHERE Handle = 100");
Console.WriteLine("Class Name: {0}", query.ClassName);
Console.WriteLine("Condition: {0}", query.Condition);
Console.WriteLine("Selected Properties:");
```

```
foreach(string prop in query.SelectedProperties) {
    Console.WriteLine("    {0}", prop);
}
Console.WriteLine("Schema Query: {0}", query.IsSchemaQuery);
```

Here, as soon as the constructor of `SelectQuery` is invoked, it calls the setter routine for the `QueryString` property; this in turns calls the internal method `ParseQuery`, which is responsible for breaking the query text into individual components. Once the `SelectQuery` object is constructed, these components are accessible through its `ClassName`, `Condition`, `SelectedProperties`, and `IsSchemaQuery` properties. The `ClassName` and `Condition` properties are self-explanatory—they contain the name of the WMI class and the query `WHERE` criteria respectively. `IsSchemaQuery` is just a Boolean flag that indicates whether it is a data (FALSE) or schema (TRUE) query. Finally, `SelectedProperties` is a string collection that houses the names of the WMI object properties that are returned by the query. With that in mind, the output, produced by the code above, should come as no surprise:

```
Class Name: Win32_Process
Condition: Handle = 100
Selected Properties:
Schema Query: False
```

Actually, let me take that back—the output is somewhat surprising because the `SelectedProperties` collection seems to be empty. The query uses the * placeholder so that it is logical to expect the `SelectedProperties` collection to contain the names of all properties of `Win32_Process` class. The problem is that the `SelectQuery` type does not interact with WMI by itself and, therefore, it is not capable of fetching the class definition in order to expand the * placeholder. Thus, it is safe to assume that the empty `SelectedProperties` collection implies that all of the object properties are to be returned by the query. Conversely, if you explicitly mention the WMI object properties in the `SELECT` property list, the `SelectedProperties` collection will be correctly populated:

```
SelectQuery query = new SelectQuery(
    "SELECT Handle, ExecutablePath FROM Win32_Process WHERE Handle = 100");
Console.WriteLine("Selected Properties:");
foreach(string prop in query.SelectedProperties) {
    Console.WriteLine("    {0}", prop);
}
```

Thus, this code will produce the following output:

```
Selected Properties:
    Handle
    ExecutablePath
```

The string parameter, taken by the constructor of the `SelectQuery` type, does not necessarily have to be a WQL query. Supplying just a class name will yield the same results, hence the following code will return all instances of `Win32_Process` class:

```
SelectQuery query = new SelectQuery("Win32_Process");
ManagementObjectSearcher ms = new ManagementObjectSearcher(query);
foreach(ManagementObject mo in ms.Get()) {
    Console.WriteLine(mo["__PATH"]);
}
```

If you construct an instance of `SelectQuery` using a class name and then read its `QueryString` property, you will see a valid WQL query:

```
SelectQuery query = new SelectQuery("Win32_Process");
Console.WriteLine(query.QueryString);
```

This code will produce the following output:

```
select * from Win32_Process
```

Judging from the output, you may assume that the constructor of the `SelectQuery` type always assembles a valid WQL `SELECT` statement when it is invoked with the class name parameter. This, however, is not quite the case; the constructor simply sets the `ClassName` property. In fact, the `SELECT` statement only gets built whenever the `QueryString` property is referenced—it is the get property routine of the `QueryString` that invokes the internal `BuildQuery` method that is responsible for assembling a valid `SELECT` statement from individual components.

A query may not necessarily need to be assembled in order for `ManagementObjectSeracher` to process it. Whenever the `Get` method of `ManagementObjectSearcher` is invoked, it analyzes a query to establish the optimum execution strategy. It does this by following these steps:

1. First, it checks whether a query has selection criteria. In other words, it checks whether the query's `Condition` property is populated.

2. Then it looks at the `SelectedProperties` collection to find out whether it is empty (whether all or just some WMI object properties are requested).

3. Finally, it checks the `EnumerationOptions` object associated with `ManagementObjectSeracher` to determine if the `EnumerateDeep` flag is set. In the context of a data query, this flag indicates whether an enumeration operation returns instances of all subclasses of a given class or just the instances of its immediate subclasses.

If a query satisfies all three of these criteria—it has no condition, it selects all properties, and it has its `EnumerateDeep` flag set to TRUE—the `Get` method does not even attempt to execute it via `IWbemServices::ExecQuery`. Instead, it calls the `IWbemServices::CreateInstanceEnum` method. This method, which expects a class name rather than a WQL statement, is just a more efficient way to achieve the same results. In effect, using this method means that even if a `SelectQuery` object is instantiated with a valid WQL `SELECT` statement, this `SELECT` is not used, unless it violates one of the three criteria just mentioned.

Thus, you have probably realized that using data queries without the `WHERE` clause is not such a good idea. There are more efficient and certainly cleaner ways of producing the same results. For instance, you may remember the `GetInstances` method of `ManagementClass` type that was described in the previous chapter. This method does essentially the same thing as the query I was just discussing—it retrieves all instances of a particular WMI class. Interestingly, its implementation is also very similar: it calls `IWbemServices::CreateInstanceEnum` passing it the name of the WMI class. Hence, the following code fragment is functionally identical to the previous example, based on `SelectQuery`, but it is much cleaner and a bit more efficient:

```
ManagementClass mc = new ManagementClass("Win32_Process");
EnumerationOptions eo = new EnumerationOptions();
eo.EnumerateDeep = true;
foreach(ManagementObject mo in mc.GetInstances(eo)) {
    Console.WriteLine(mo["__PATH"]);
}
```

Here the intention is clear because the code is much more readable. A small performance gain is achieved since there is no need to parse and analyze the query string. Note that you must pass the `EnumerationOptions` object with `EnumerateDeep` property set to TRUE to the `GetInstances` method to correctly emulate the behavior of a WQL `SELECT` query. By default, data queries always return instances of all the subclasses of a given class.

You may think that setting the QueryString property to a class name rather than a WQL statement will have an effect similar to that of calling the constructor of SelectQuery with a class name parameter. This, however, is not the case, and the following code will throw ArgumentException:

```
SelectQuery query = new SelectQuery();
query.QueryString = "Win32_Process";
```

Here the exception is thrown by the internal method ParseQuery that is invoked by the property set routine for QueryString. Apparently, a query has to be validated in order to be parsed and a mere class name does not constitute a valid WQL statement. It is, however, perfectly legal to use the ClassName property in the same fashion. Thus, the following code will work, correctly retrieving all instances of the Win32_Process class:

```
SelectQuery query = new SelectQuery();
query.ClassName = "Win32_Process";
ManagementObjectSearcher ms = new ManagementObjectSearcher(query);
foreach(ManagementObject mo in ms.Get()) {
    Console.WriteLine(mo["__PATH"]);
}
```

This effectively means that you can easily construct a query from its individual components without resorting to ugly text manipulation. This may come in very handy, especially when you are building graphical applications where certain controls on the GUI correspond to the elements of a WQL SELECT statement. The following code builds a valid and fairly complex WQL query:

```
SelectQuery query = new SelectQuery();
query.ClassName = "Win32_Service";
query.Condition = "StartMode = 'Auto' AND State = 'Stopped'";
query.SelectedProperties.Add("Name");
query.SelectedProperties.Add("DisplayName");
query.SelectedProperties.Add("StartMode");
Console.WriteLine(query.QueryString);
```

The output, produced by this code will be the following:

```
select Name, DisplayName, StartMode from Win32_Service where StartMode = 'Auto'
AND State = 'Stopped'
```

For convenience, SelectQuery provides a constructor that takes two parameters: the name of the WMI class and the query condition. Thus, the process of assembling a query can be simplified as follows:

```
SelectQuery query = new SelectQuery("Win32_Service",
    "StartMode = 'Auto' AND State = 'Stopped'");
Console.WriteLine(query.QueryString);
```

Yet, another constructor allows you to specify a list of selected properties in addition to the class name and condition:

```
SelectQuery query = new SelectQuery("Win32_Service",
    "StartMode = 'Auto' AND State = 'Stopped'",
    new string[] {"Name", "DisplayName", "StartMode"});
Console.WriteLine(query.QueryString);
```

Contrary to what you may think, SelectQuery does not automatically detect schema queries. This is mildly disappointing since all it takes is scanning the query text for the presence of the meta_class keyword. Unfortunately, if you intend to construct a schema query, it has to be stated explicitly:

```
SelectQuery query = new SelectQuery(true, "__this ISA 'CIM_Process'");
Console.WriteLine(query.QueryString);
```

Here the first parameter to the constructor is a Boolean flag that indicates that a schema query is required. The second argument is not a query, rather it is a query selection criteria. Note that if you attempt to pass a full query instead of just the condition, SelectQuery will assemble an invalid WQL statement since it does not check whether the second argument starts with SELECT.

A schema query does not have to be marked as such in order to produce the expected results. The following code fragment will correctly return all class definitions for the CIM_Process and its descendants, although the IsSchemaQuery property of the SelectQuery object will return FALSE:

```
SelectQuery query = new SelectQuery(
    "SELECT * FROM meta_class WHERE __this ISA 'CIM_Process'");
ManagementObjectSearcher ms = new ManagementObjectSearcher(query);
foreach(ManagementClass mc in ms.Get()) {
    Console.WriteLine(mc["__PATH"]);
}
```

A query can also be marked as a schema query by setting its `IsSchemaQuery` property to TRUE. This very interesting effect is illustrated by the following code snippet:

```
SelectQuery query = new SelectQuery("CIM_Process");
query.IsSchemaQuery = true;
Console.WriteLine(query.QueryString);
```

You may rightfully expect to see a query assembled as follows:

```
SELECT * FROM meta_class WHERE __this ISA 'CIM_Process'
```

Curiously, the output, produced by this code, is totally different and may not seem very logical at first:

```
SELECT * FROM meta_class
```

It turns out that once a query is marked as schema query, the class name passed to the constructor is essentially ignored. Moreover, even if you pass a valid WQL statement with no `WHERE` criteria to the constructor, it will be ignored as well. Thus, the following code will produce exactly the same output:

```
SelectQuery query = new SelectQuery("SELECT * FROM Win32_Process");
query.IsSchemaQuery = true;
Console.WriteLine(query.QueryString);
```

The most interesting thing, however, happens if you create a `SelectQuery` object by passing a WQL `SELECT` with a `WHERE` clause to its constructor. Consider the following code:

```
SelectQuery query = new SelectQuery(
    "SELECT * FROM Win32_Process WHERE Handle = 100");
query.IsSchemaQuery = true;
Console.WriteLine(query.QueryString);
```

Surprisingly, this code is going to output the following query:

```
select * from meta_class where Handle = 100
```

This one is not even a valid schema query and it will generate an exception if you attempt to execute it. However, if a `SelectQuery` object is created with a valid schema query, the output will be a valid schema query:

```
SelectQuery query = new SelectQuery(
    "SELECT * FROM meta_class WHERE __this ISA 'CIM_Process'");
query.IsSchemaQuery = true;
Console.WriteLine(query.QueryString);
```

Whenever the `IsSchemaQuery` property of the `SelectQuery` object is assigned, its set property routine calls an internal function `BuildQuery`, that is responsible for generating a query string. When invoked with the `IsSchemaQuery` property set to TRUE, `BuildQuery` simply strings together the constant string `select * from meta_class` and the contents of the `Condition` property of the `SelectQuery` object. So, you should be careful when you are creating schema queries because the query string that is assembled by the `SelectQuery` type may not always be what you expect. Perhaps, the safest way to achieve the right results is by using a `SelectQuery` constructor, which takes a Boolean `IsSchemaQuery` flag and the query condition as parameters.

Finally, if you are interested in the internals of query processing, you should know that schema queries are processed similarly to data queries. If a query satisfies the same three criteria—it has no `WHERE` clause, it selects all object properties, and it is processed with the `EnumerateDeep` flag set to TRUE—it will not be executed via the `IWbemServices::ExecQuery` method. Just as it is the case with data queries, for the sake of efficiency, `ManagementObjectSearcher` will call the `IWbemServices::CreateClassEnum` method. The `IWbemServices::CreateClassEnum` takes a class name parameter, which specifies a name of the superclass for all returned classes. Thus, theoretically, you should be able to set the `ClassName` property of a schema query object and then retrieve just the subclasses of a given class. In other words, the following code should output just the subclasses of `CIM_Process`:

```
SelectQuery query = new SelectQuery();
query.IsSchemaQuery = true;
query.ClassName = "CIM_Process";
ManagementObjectSearcher ms = new ManagementObjectSearcher(query);
ms.Options.EnumerateDeep = true;
foreach(ManagementClass mc in ms.Get()) {
    Console.WriteLine(mc["__PATH"]);
}
```

However, if you run this code, you will see that it outputs all classes in the current namespace, just as a condition-less schema query does. It turns out that a constructor of `ManagementObjectSearcher` clones the query object by invoking its `Clone` method. `Clone` checks the `IsSchemaQuery` property of its object and ensures that a cloned instance has a blank `ClassName` property in case it is a schema query. This phenomena is illustrated by the following code:

```
SelectQuery query = new SelectQuery();
query.IsSchemaQuery = true;
query.ClassName = "CIM_Process";
ManagementObjectSearcher ms = new ManagementObjectSearcher(query);
query - (SelectQuery)ms.Query;
Console.WriteLine(query.ClassName);
```

The bottom line is that when the Get method of ManagementObjectSearcher
is invoked, it calls IWbemServices::CreateClassEnum with a blank class name
parameter; this results in all classes being returned by the enumeration. As
strange as it may sound, this is done to ensure that the behavior is consistent
with the normal behavior of a schema query without a WHERE clause. After all, if
you want to retrieve just the subclasses of a given class, you should turn to the
GetSubclasses method of the ManagementClass type that was described in
the previous chapter.

The SelectQuery type is, perhaps, the most interesting of the three types
representing the respective WQL statements. The remaining two types—
RelatedObjectQuery and RelationshipQuery—are fairly simple and self-explanatory,
mostly due to the more rigid syntax of the ASSOCIATORS OF and REFERENCES OF statements. Both of these types are structured in such a way that their properties
map one-to-one to the similarly named syntax elements of their respective
WQL statement.

Using the RelatedObjectQuery Type

RelatedObjectQuery represents the WQL ASSOCIATORS OF statement. Just like
a SelectQuery, an instance of RelatedObjectQuery can be created by passing
a query string to its constructor:

```
RelatedObjectQuery query = new RelatedObjectQuery(
 @"ASSOCIATORS OF {Win32_Service='WinMgmt'}
   WHERE ResultClass = Win32_ComputerSystem");
ManagementObjectSearcher ms = new ManagementObjectSearcher(query);
foreach(ManagementObject mo in ms.Get()) {
   Console.WriteLine(mo["__PATH"]);
}
```

Once a query object is created, the query text is parsed and corresponding
object properties are set accordingly. Thus, if you attempt to print out the
SourceObject and RelatedClass properties of the preceding RelatedObjectQuery,
the output will look like the following:

```
Related Class: Win32_ComputerSystem
Source Object: Win32_Service='WinMgmt'
```

Note that, unlike SelectQuery, the RelatedObjectQuery type does not have a Condition property. Instead, the query criteria is broken down into individual elements, such as RelatedClass, RelatedQualifier, RelatedRole, and so on. The QueryString, QueryLanguage, and IsSchemaQuery properties are still available. This time, however, since ASSOCIATORS OF schema queries are unambiguously identified by the SchemaOnly keyword, the IsSchemaQuery property will be correctly set because the query string represents a schema query. Thus, the following code will print TRUE on the console:

```
RelatedObjectQuery query = new RelatedObjectQuery(
    "ASSOCIATORS OF {Win32_Service} WHERE SchemaOnly");
Console.WriteLine(query.IsSchemaQuery);
```

This also holds true for other query elements such as ClassDefsOnly. The following code sample will print TRUE on the console as well:

```
RelatedObjectQuery query = new RelatedObjectQuery(
    "ASSOCIATORS OF {Win32_Service='WinMgmt'} WHERE ClassDefsOnly");
Console.WriteLine(query.ClassDefinitionsOnly);
```

Conversely, the ASSOCIATORS OF query can be assembled out of individual components as follows:

```
RelatedObjectQuery query = new RelatedObjectQuery();
query.SourceObject = "Win32_Service='WinMgmt'";
query.RelatedClass = "Win32_ComputerSystem";
Console.WriteLine(query.QueryString);
```

This code will produce the following output, which represents perfectly a valid ASSOCIATORS OF query:

```
associators of {Win32_Service='WinMgmt'} where resultclass = Win32_ComputerSystem
```

There is more than one way to create an instance of RelatedObjectQuery type. For your convenience, this type offers a few overloaded constructors, which allow you to build a query from its individual components:

```
public RelatedObjectQuery ( string sourceObject , string relatedClass )
```

where the parameters are defined as follows:

sourceObject: A string parameter that represents a relative path to the source object to which the current query applies.

relatedClass: A string parameter that indicates that all returned objects must belong to a given class or a class derived from a given class.

```
public RelatedObjectQuery (
    string sourceObject ,
    string relatedClass ,
    string relationshipClass ,
    string relatedQualifier ,
    string relationshipQualifier ,
    string relatedRole ,
    string thisRole ,
    bool   classDefinitionsOnly
)
```

where

sourceObject: A string parameter that represents the relative path to the source object to which the current query applies.

relatedClass: A string parameter that indicates that all the returned objects must belong to a given class or a class derived from a given class.

relationshipClass: A string parameter that contains the name of the association class. If this parameter is specified, it indicates that the object to which the query applies (sourceObject) and the resulting objects must be connected via an association object of a given class or a class derived from a given class.

relatedQualifier: A string parameter that contains the name of the qualifier. If this parameter is specified it indicates that all the returned objects must belong to a class that includes a given qualifier.

relationshipQualifier: A string parameter that contains the name of the qualifier. If this parameter is specified it indicates that the object to which the query applies (sourceObject) and the resulting objects must be connected via an association object that belongs to a class that includes a given qualifier.

relatedRole: A string parameter that contains the name of the role. If this parameter is specified it indicates that all the returned objects must play a particular role in the association. The role is defined as a name of the property of an association class, which is a reference property that points to a given object.

thisRole: An optional string parameter that contains the name of the role. If this parameter is specified it indicates that the object to which the query applies (sourceObject) must play a particular role in the association. The role is defined as a name of the property of an association class, which is a reference property that points to a given object.

classDefinitionsOnly: A Boolean parameter. If this parameter is specified, it indicates that the method should return schema information (TRUE) or data (FALSE).

and

```
public RelatedObjectQuery (
    bool   isSchemaQuery ,
    string sourceObject ,
    string relatedClass ,
    string relationshipClass ,
    string relatedQualifier ,
    string relationshipQualifier ,
    string relatedRole ,
    string thisRole
)
```

where

isSchemaQuery: A Boolean parameter that, if set to TRUE value, indicates that a query is a schema and as such is only supposed to return schema information.

sourceObject: A string parameter that represents the relative path to the source object to which the current query applies.

relatedClass: A string parameter that indicates that all returned objects must belong to a given class or a class derived from a given class.

relationshipClass: A string parameter that contains the name of the association class. If this parameter is specified, it indicates that the object to which the query applies (sourceObject) and the resulting objects must be connected via an association object of a given class or a class derived from a given class.

relatedQualifier: A string parameter that contains the name of the qualifier. If this parameter is specified, it indicates that all the returned objects must belong to a class that includes a given qualifier.

relationshipQualifier: A string parameter that contains the name of the qualifier. If this parameter is specified the object to which the query applies (sourceObject) and the resulting objects must be connected via an association object that belongs to a class, which includes a given qualifier.

relatedRole: A string parameter that contains the name of the role. If this parameter is specified, all the returned objects must play a particular role in the association. The role is defined as the name of the property of an association class, which is a reference property that points to a given object.

thisRole: An optional string parameter that contains the name of the role. If this parameter is specified, the object to which the query applies (sourceObject) must play a particular role in the association. The role is defined as the name of the property of an association class, which is a reference property that points to a given object.

Using the RelationshipQuery Type

The remaining query type. RelationshipQuery, which embodies REFERENCES OF statement, is very similar to RelatedObjectQuery. Its properties are a one-to-one reflection of the corresponding syntax elements of the REFERENCES OF statement, and its behavior is conceptually the same as the behavior of RelatedObjectQuery.

You can create a fully functional instance of the RelationshipQuery type by calling one of its constructors, which takes a string parameter that represents the REFERENCES OF query:

```
RelationshipQuery query = new RelationshipQuery(
    "REFERENCES OF {Win32_Process=100} WHERE ResultClass = CIM_ProcessExecutable");
ManagementObjectSearcher ms = new ManagementObjectSearcher(query);
foreach(ManagementObject mo in ms.Get()) {
    Console.WriteLine(mo["__PATH"]);
}
```

Once such an instance is created, the query text is parsed and the object properties are set appropriately to reflect respective syntax elements of the query. Thus, if you print out the SourceObject and RelationshipClass properties of the preceding RelationshipQuery object, you will see the following output:

```
SourceObject: Win32_Process=106
RelationshipClass: CIM_ProcessExecutable
```

You can assemble a valid query object by assigning its properties to the appropriate values. Thus, the following code example is equivalent of the previous one:

```
RelationshipQuery query = new RelationshipQuery();
query.SourceObject = "Win32_Process=100";
query.RelationshipClass = "CIM_ProcessExecutable";
ManagementObjectSearcher ms = new ManagementObjectSearcher(query);
foreach(ManagementObject mo in ms.Get()) {
    Console.WriteLine(mo["__PATH"]);
}
```

Finally, the RelationshipQuery type offers several convenience constructors that allow you to build a query from individual components:

```
public RelationshipQuery ( string sourceObject , string relationshipClass )
```

where the parameters are defined as follows:

sourceObject: A string parameter that represents a relative path to the source object to which the current query applies.

relationshipClass: A string parameter that contains the name of the association class. It indicates that the returned associations must be of a given class or a class derived from a given class.

```
public RelationshipQuery (
    string sourceObject ,
    string relationshipClass ,
    string relationshipQualifier ,
    string thisRole ,
    bool   classDefinitionsOnly
)
```

where

> **sourceObject**: A string parameter that represents a relative path to the source object to which the current query applies.

> **relationshipClass**: A string parameter that contains the name of the association class. It indicates that the returned associations must be of a given class or a class derived from a given class.

> **relationshipQualifier**: A string parameter that contains the name of the qualifier. If this parameter is specified, it indicates that the returned association classes must include a given qualifier.

> **thisRole**: A string parameter that contains the name of the role. If this parameter is specified, it indicates that the object to which the query applies (sourceObject) must play a particular role in the association. The role is defined as the name of the property of an association class, which is a reference property that points to a given class.

> **classDefinitionsOnly**: A Boolean parameter. If this parameter is specified, it indicates whether the method should return schema information (TRUE) or data (FALSE).

and

```
public RelationshipQuery (
    bool   isSchemaQuery ,
    string sourceObject ,
    string relationshipClass ,
    string relationshipQualifier ,
    string thisRole
)
```

where

> **isSchemaQuery**: A Boolean parameter that, if set to TRUE, indicates that a query is a schema query and as such is only supposed to return schema information.

> **sourceObject**: A string parameter that represents a relative path to the source object to which the current query applies.

> **relationshipClass**: A string parameter that contains the name of the association class. It indicates that the returned associations must be of a given class or a class derived from a given class.

> **relationshipQualifier**: A string parameter that contains the name of the qualifier. If this parameter is specified, it indicates that the returned association classes must include a given qualifier.

> **thisRole**: A string parameter that contains the name of the role. If this parameter is specified, it indicates that the object to which the query applies (sourceObject) must play a particular role in the association. The role is defined as a name of the property of an association class, which is a reference property that points to a given class.

Alternatives to Query Types

When it comes to parsing queries, RelatedObjectQuery and RelationshipQuery types are very useful. However, in my opinion, these types have little value for the purposes of retrieving the data. Although it is entirely possible to read and analyze just about any kind of relationship information using either RelatedObjectQuery or RelationshipQuery along with ManagementObjectSearcher, there are better ways of achieving the same goal. For instance, you may remember the GetRelated and GetRelationships methods of the ManagementObject type, as well as the GetRelatedClasses and GetRelationshipClasses methods of the ManagementClass type, described in the previous chapter. Consider the following example:

```
ManagementObject mo = new ManagementObject("Win32_Process=100");
foreach(ManagementObject o in mo.GetRelationships("CIM_ProcessExecutable")) {
    Console.WriteLine(o["__PATH"]);
}
```

Functionally, this code is equivalent to the previous example involving RelationshipQuery and ManagementObjectSearcher types. However, the code here is much clearer and easier to read. Interestingly, all four methods—GetRelated, GetRelationships, GetRelatedClasses and GetRelationshipClasses—are implemented in terms of ASSOCIATORS OF and REFERENCES OF WQL queries, although these implementation details are hidden from a casual user. Basically, unless you need to parse an existing query, consider using the relationship methods of either the ManagementObject or ManagementClass types before you resort to queries. You will end up with much simpler code, or at least save yourself some typing.

Summary

WQL and the associated query support functionality of the System.Management namespace are extremely powerful and, on occasion, simply indispensable. Having read this chapter and worked though the code examples, you should be able to

- Understand the fundamental concepts, structure, and syntax of WQL.

- Create fairly complex queries using SELECT, ASSOCIATORS OF, and REFERENCES OF statements.

- Effectively use the ManagementObjectSearcher type to retrieve the management data via WQL queries.

- Utilize query support types, such as SelectQuery, RelatedObjectQuery, and RelationshipQuery to parse, assemble, and analyze WQL queries.

You should now possess enough information to build sophisticated applications that are capable of retrieving and analyzing any kind of management data that is accessible through WMI.

CHAPTER 4

Handling WMI Events

WEBSTER'S COLLEGIATE DICTIONARY defines an *event* as "a noteworthy happening." This general definition, in addition to conveying the meaning of the word in its social sense, is also remarkably precise when it comes to describing the fairly abstract concept referred to as an event in computer parlance. For software developers an event means exactly this: a "noteworthy happening" within the realm of a particular software system. Event-driven programming is a very popular type of software development model that is widely employed throughout the industry.

As a result, nearly every GUI development toolkit in existence today is structured around some kind of an *event loop*, where custom event handling code is invoked automatically by the toolkit in response to some external actions, such as mouse movements or keystrokes. Although, GUI-based systems are the most natural candidates for applying event-driven programming techniques due to the highly irregular patterns of human interaction with computers, the event-driven model is highly beneficial even when it comes to building noninteractive, batch-mode software.

Consider, for instance, a messaging system. A conventional message-processing program would have to continuously monitor the input queue, checking for newly received messages. An event-driven program, on the other hand, would install a message handling callback and rely on the messaging infrastructure to raise an event upon the arrival of a new message. Clearly, an event-driven approach is far superior because it relieves the developer from the duty of writing often convoluted polling code, and it also increases runtime efficiency and potentially lessens resource utilization.

In the arena of system management, event-enabled architecture is often a critical success factor. While old-fashioned monitoring techniques that are based on periodic polling may be adequate for a standalone, simple computer system, today's enterprise installations rarely fit such a profile. Instead, a typical modern system may easily include dozens of geographically distributed computing nodes and hundreds of individually managed elements, thus rendering conventional monitoring methods completely impractical. Therefore, an ability to disseminate the management information via events is no longer a luxury; it is now a requirement for a robust management system.

Because it is the leading enterprise management framework, WMI features extensive support for event-driven programming. As you can imagine, the WMI eventing mechanism is fairly complex and requires an extensive infrastructure to function in a reliable and efficient fashion. Fortunately, the event-related types of the System.Management namespace hide a great deal of complexities associated with handling management events in a distributed environment. This chapter is dedicated to explaining the basic principles of WMI eventing and illustrating the most fundamental techniques for building powerful event-driven monitoring tools with System.Management types.

WMI Event Basics

Just like anything else in WMI, an event is represented by an instance of a WMI class. Unlike other WMI objects, instances of event classes are transient—they are created dynamically by an event provider or the WMI itself and only exist while they are being consumed by a client application. Ultimately, all event classes are derived from a single root—a system class called __Event. This is an abstract class, intended to serve as a basis for defining more specific event types, and as such, it does not have any nonsystem properties. All event classes derived from __Event are categorized as either intrinsic, extrinsic, or timer events.

Intrinsic Events

Intrinsic events are the most interesting and generic category of events that are supported by WMI. The idea behind intrinsic events is simple, yet elegant and powerful; it revolves around the assumption that WMI object instances depict the current state of the associated managed elements. An event, therefore, can be viewed as a change of state that is undergone by a particular WMI object. For instance, creation of an operating system process can be modeled as creation of an instance of the Win32_Process class, while the death of the process can be represented by the deletion of a corresponding Win32_Process object.

Besides the intrinsic events that represent the changes of state of an arbitrary WMI object, there are events that reflect the changes that are undergone by the CIM Repository, such as the addition and deletion of classes or namespaces. Thus, to model the intrinsic events, __Event class has three subclasses: __InstanceOperationEvent, __ClassOperationEvent, and __NamespaceOperationEvent. These subclasses are designed to represent state transitions for WMI instances, classes, and namespaces respectively.

The `__InstanceOperationEvent` class encompasses all kinds of state changes that a single instance of a WMI class may go through, such as creation, modification, and deletion. It has a single nonsystem property, `TargetInstance`, which refers to a WMI object that is affected by the event. Thus, whenever a new instance is created, `TargetInstance` points to a newly created object; when an object is changed, this property is set to the new, modified version of the object; and finally, when an instance is deleted, `TargetInstance` refers to the deleted object.

The `__ClassOperationEvent` class is an umbrella for all class-related operations. Just like its instance counterpart, it has a single property called `TargetClass`, which identifies a WMI class that is affected by the event. This property points to a newly created class, a modified class, or a deleted class for the creation, modification, and deletion of events correspondingly.

Finally, `__NamespaceOperationEvent` is a class that embodies all events that affect WMI namespaces. Again, it has a single, nonsystem property, `TargetNamespace`, which, depending on the event, refers to a newly created, modified, or deleted namespace. Note that this property does not just contain the name of the affected namespace, but a namespace object. As you may remember, WMI namespaces are modeled as instances of the WMI class `__Namespace`, thus, the data type of the `TargetNamespace` property is `__Namespace`.

Although more specific than their `__Event` superclass, `__InstanceOperationEvent`, `__ClassOperationEvent` and `__NamespaceOperationEvent` are much too general to be effective. These classes simply do not convey enough information to unambiguously differentiate between specific types of events, such as creation, deletion, or modification. Such design is intentional because none of these three classes are intended to have instances—in fact, all of them are just superclasses for more specialized event classes that zero in on the particulars of the operation that triggers the event. Table 4-1 presents a complete list of the intrinsic events that are supported by WMI.

Table 4-1. WMI Intrinsic Events

EVENT NAME	EVENT CLASS NAME	BASE CLASS	DESCRIPTION
Class Creation	__ClassCreationEvent	__ClassOperationEvent	Raised whenever a new WMI class definition is added to the CIM Repository.
Class Deletion	__ClassDeletionEvent	__ClassOperationEvent	Raised whenever a WMI class definition is deleted from the CIM Repository.
Class Modification	__ClassModificationEvent	__ClassOperationEvent	Raised whenever an existing WMI class definition is changed.
Instance Creation	__InstanceCreationEvent	__InstanceOperationEvent	Raised whenever a new WMI instance is created.
Instance Deletion	__InstanceDeletionEvent	__InstanceOperationEvent	Raised whenever an existing WMI instance is deleted.
Instance Modification	__InstanceModificationEvent	__InstanceOperationEvent	Raised whenever an existing WMI instance is changed.
Namespace Creation	__NamespaceCreationEvent	__NamespaceOperationEvent	Raised whenever a new WMI namespace is added to the CIM Repository.

(continued)

Table 4-1. WMI Intrinsic Events

EVENT NAME	EVENT CLASS NAME	BASE CLASS	DESCRIPTION
Namespace Deletion	__NamespaceDeletionEvent	__NamespaceOperationEvent	Raised whenever a namespace is deleted.
Namespace Modification	__NamespaceModificationEvent	__NamespaceOperationEvent	Raised whenever a WMI namespace is modified.

The first three classes listed in Table 4-1—__ClassCreationEvent, __ClassDeletionEvent and __ClassModificationEvent—are used to communicate to the consumer the details of an operation that affect an arbitrary WMI class definition. __ClassCreationEvent and __ClassDeletionEvent are exact copies of their superclass, __ClassOperationEvent, and they do not define any additional nonsystem properties. __ClassModificationEvent, on the other hand, adds a property, called PreviousClass, which refers to the copy of the class definition prior to the modification. Thus, a consumer application that handles __ClassModificationEvent can compare the new and the original class definitions that are pointed to by the TargetClass and PreviousClass properties and determine the exact nature of the modification.

Similarly, __InstanceCreationEvent and __InstanceDeletionEvent do not have any additional nonsystem properties, with the exception of TargetInstance, which is inherited from their superclass __InstanceOperationEvent. __InstanceModificationEvent defines an additional property, called PreviousInstance, which refers to a copy of WMI object that reflects its state prior to the modification operation. The original and the modified instances pointed to by PreviousInstance and TargetInstance properties respectively, can be compared to obtain the details of the modification.

Subclasses of __NamespaceOperationEvent also follow the same pattern so that only __NamespaceModificationEvent defines a new property, PreviousNamespace, in addition to TargetNamespace, which it inherited from the superclass. The PreviousNamespace property points to a copy of the namespace object prior to its modification.

Since the __Namespace WMI class has a single nonsystem property, Name, you may assume that __NamespaceModificationEvent is generated whenever a namespace is renamed—every time its Name property is modified. However, this is not actually the case because the Name property is a key and, therefore, it is immutable.

In fact, the only way to rename a namespace is to delete the original namespace and create a new one; this will trigger __NamespaceDeletionEvent followed by __NamespaceCreationEvent, rather than a single __NamespaceModificationEvent. You may also expect __NamespaceModificationEvent to be raised whenever any of the namespace contents are changed in some way. After all, a namespace is a container for WMI classes and objects; therefore, a change of state that is undergone by a WMI instance or a class definition constitutes a modification to a namespace that houses such an instance or a class. But this does not happen either; instead, changes to the WMI entities within a namespace are reflected by the appropriate subclasses of __ClassOperationEvent or __InstanceOperationEvent. Thus, __NamespaceModificationEvent may seem rather useless until you recall that a WMI class may have numerous class and property qualifiers. Thus, __NamespaceModificationEvent will be triggered every time a qualifier is added, deleted, or modified.

Furthermore, since WMI namespaces are represented by instances of the __Namespace class, adding or deleting a namespace is, in fact, equivalent to adding or deleting a WMI instance. Thus, in theory, adding or deleting a namespace should trigger __InstanceCreationEvent or __InstanceDeletionEvent respectively. This, however, does not happen, and __NamespaceCreationEvent or __NamespaceDeletionEvent is raised instead.

As with most WMI system classes, the intrinsic event classes that are listed in Table 4-1 cannot be extended. Thus, an event provider that wishes to support an intrinsic event must use predefined classes.

Extrinsic Events

Certain management events do not easily lend themselves to being modeled as changes of state that are undergone by arbitrary WMI objects. An example of such an event is a power shutdown. You may argue that such an event can also be represented by deleting some hypothetical WMI object that embodies a running computer system, but such an approach seems a bit awkward. Moreover, there are cases when an event corresponds to some actions taking place outside of the managed environment that render the intrinsic event mechanism unusable. Finally, WMI extension developers may find intrinsic events too rigid and not flexible enough for accomplishing their goals.

To provide a flexible and generic solution for the potential problems mentioned above, WMI offers an alternative approach to modeling events. Another category of events, referred to as *extrinsic events*, exists for the sole purpose of building user-defined event classes that may represent just about any kind of action that occurs within, or outside of, the boundaries of the managed environment. The basis for deriving all user-defined event classes is an abstract class __ExtrinsicEvent, which is also a subclass of __Event. By default, only a few subclasses of `__ExtrinsicEvent` are loaded into CIM Repository during WMI installation. One of these subclasses is another abstract class, called `__SystemEvent`, which encompasses several events that are raised by WMI itself. These events, modeled using `__EventDroppedEvent` class and its subclasses `__EventQueueOverflowEvent` and `__EventConsumerFailureEvent`, have to do with WMI failing to deliver some other event to an event consumer.

Yet another subclass of `__ExtrinsicEvent` is `Win32_PowerManagementEvent`, which represents power management events that result from power state changes. Such state changes are associated with either the Advanced Power Management (APM) protocol or the Advanced Configuration and Power Interface (ACPI) protocol. This class has two properties that detail the specifics of the power management event: `EventType` and `OEMEventCode`. `EventType` describes the type of the power state change, and it may take values such as "Entering Suspend," "Resume Suspend," "OEM Event," and so on. Whenever the `EventType` property is set to "OEM Event," the `OEMEventCode` fields contains the original equipment manufacturer event code.

WMI distribution comes with a number of event providers that are capable of raising other extrinsic events, although these providers may not be installed by default. One such example is registry event provider that triggers various events associated with changes to the system registry. Installing this provider is trivial: you just compile and load the regevent.mof file—which contains the definitions for registry-extrinsic events as well as provider registration classes—and register the provider DLL stdprov.dll. Both the MOF file and the DLL can be found in the `%SystemRoot%\WBEM` directory.

Once installed, the registry event provider offers three extrinsic event classes that are derived from `__ExtrinsicEvent`: `RegistryKeyChangeEvent`, `RegistryTreeChangeEvent`, and `RegistryValueChangeEvent`. These classes let you monitor the changes to a hierarchy of registry keys, a single key, or a single value respectively. All three of these classes have the `Hive` property, which specifies the hierarchy of keys to be monitored, such as `HKEY_LOCAL_MACHINE`. The `KeyPath` property of `RegistryKeyChangeEvent`, the `RootPath` property of `RegistryTreeChangeEvent`, as well as the `KeyPath` and `ValueName` properties of `RegistryValueChangeEvent` all identify the specific registry key, tree, or value to be monitored.

Extrinsic events afford unlimited flexibility to extensions developers, and while you are exploring WMI, you will certainly come across many useful extrinsic event providers, or perhaps, even try to roll your own. One thing you should keep in mind is that there are some restrictions when it comes to defining the extrinsic event classes.

Naturally, in your attempt to follow the best practices of object-oriented design, you may wish to organize your event classes into a hierarchy similar to that of the registry event provider. Although it is possible to derive an extrinsic event class via multilevel inheritance, only the lowest level classes—classes with no subclasses—

are allowed to have instances. For example, the base class of all registry event classes, RegistryEvent, is abstract and cannot be instantiated directly in order to be delivered to the consumer. Instead, one of its subclasses (RegistryKeyChangeEvent, RegistryTreeChangeEvent, or RegistryValueChangeEvent) must be provided. Furthermore, once a provider is registered for an extrinsic event class, this class may not be used as a superclass. Thus, you cannot derive you own event class from, say, RegistryKeyChangeEvent.

Timer Events

Timer events are simply notifications that are generated as a result of a timer interrupt. These events are very straightforward and are modeled via a single class __TimerEvent that descends directly from __Event class. __TimerEvent has two properties: TimerId and NumFirings. TimerId is simply a string that uniquely identifies an instance of the __TimerInstruction subclass that caused the timer to fire. NumFirings is a counter that indicates how many times a timer interrupt took place before the notification was delivered to the consumer. Normally NumFirings is always set to 1, however, if a notification cannot be delivered to the consumer for some time, WMI will automatically merge multiple timer events into one and increment NumFirings to reflect that. This may happen if, for instance, a timer interval is small, which causes the timer to fire at the rate that cannot be sustained by the consumer, or when a consumer is down and unreachable for a period of time.

For timer events to be useful, there has to be a way to set off the timer. This is achieved by creating an instance of the __TimerInstruction subclass. __TimerInstruction is an abstract superclass used as a base for specifying how the timer interrupts should be generated. The class has two properties: TimerId and SkipIfPassed. TimerId is a string that uniquely identifies an instance of __TimerInstruction subclass. SkipIfPassed is a Boolean flag that indicates if a timer interrupt should be suppressed in case WMI is unable to generate it at the appropriate time or if a consumer is unreachable. The default setting is FALSE, which causes the WMI to buffer the timer events, if it is unable to deliver them, until the delivery is possible. The TRUE setting will result in the event being suppressed.

Conceptually, there can be two types of timer interrupts: those that occur once at a predefined time during the day, and those that take place repeatedly at certain fixed intervals. Both types can be set up using the __AbsoluteTimerInstruction or __IntervalTimerInstruction subclasses of __TimerInstruction. The former defines one property, called EventDateTime, in addition to the properties inherited from __TimerInstruction. EventDateTime is a string that specifies an absolute time when the event should fire. As is true for all dates and times in WMI, this string must adhere to the Distributed Management Task Force (DMTF) date-time format:[1]

`yyyymmddHHMMSS.mmmmmmsUUU`

where

- `yyyy` is a four-digit year (0000 through 9999)

- `mm` is a two-digit month (01 through 12)

- `dd` is a two-digit day (01 through 31)

- `HH` is a two-digit hour using a military clock (00 through 23)

- `MM` is a two-digit minute in the hour (00 through 59)

- `SS` is a two-digit second in the minute (00 through 59)

- `mmmmmm` is a six-digit number of microseconds in the second (000000 through 999999)

- `s` is a plus (+) or minus (–) sign that indicates a positive or negative offset from Universal Time Coordinates (UTC)

- `UUU` is a three-digit offset in minutes of an originating time zone from UTC

In order to generate an absolute timer event, a client application must create an instance of the `__AbsoluteTimerInstruction` class and set its `EventDateTime` property appropriately. The event will be generated once when the indicated time of day is reached.

`__IntervalTimerInstruction` is another subclass of `__TimerInstruction`; it is used to generate periodic timer events based on a predefined time interval. In addition to properties inherited from `__TimerInstruction`, this class defines the `IntervalBetweenEvents` property, which is the number of milliseconds between individual timer interrupts. To set up an interval timer, a client application must create an instance of the `__IntervalTimerInstruction` class and set its `IntervalBetweenEvents` property accordingly. One thing to keep in mind when you are creating interval timers is that the interval setting should be sufficiently large. On some platforms, WMI may not be able to generate interval timer events if an interval is too small. Additionally, although the timer interval can be controlled with millisecond precision, there is no guarantee that WMI will be able to deliver timer events to consumers at the exact intervals specified by the

---

1. The latest version of FCL distributed with .NET Framework and Visual Studio .NET code named "Everett" includes the ManagementDateTimeConverter type, which allows for converting between DMTF-formatted time strings and .NET date and time types.

IntervalBetweenEvents property. Due to some platform's limitations, system load, and other conditions, event delivery may be delayed.

Lastly, just like most of the system classes, neither the __TimerEvent nor the subclasses of the __TimerInstruction can be extended. However, this is not a severe restriction because the timer classes provide enough flexibility and do not really warrant extension under any circumstances.

Event Delivery Mechanism

In order to start receiving event notifications, a client application must initiate an event subscription, or, in other words, it must register with WMI as an event consumer. An *event subscription* is essentially a contract between WMI and an event consumer that specifies two things: in what types of events a consumer is interested, and what actions WMI is being requested to perform on behalf of the client when an event of interest takes place. When initiating an event subscription, it is the responsibility of the event consumer to supply the filtering criteria for events as well as the code, to be executed by WMI upon the arrival of an event.

You can specify the event filtering criteria with a WQL query, which unambiguously identifies types and even specific properties of those events that a client application intends to handle. In fact, all that you need is a familiar WQL SELECT statement, which may occasionally utilize one or two clauses designed specifically to facilitate event filtering. The details of how WQL is used for event filtering will be covered later in this chapter.

Instructing WMI which actions to take when the event of interest arrives is a bit more involved. Conventionally, event-handling applications can register the address of a custom event handler routine, or *callback,* with a server so that the server can invoke that callback whenever an event of interest is triggered. This is certainly possible with WMI. Client applications that wish to receive asynchronous event notifications may simply implement the IWbemObjectSink interface and then pass the interface pointer to WMI while registering for event processing. Then, whenever an event of interest is triggered, WMI calls the IWbemObjectSink::Indicate method, thus executing the custom event handling code.

The apparent downside of such approach is that management events are only being processed while the consumer application is active. Although this may be satisfactory under certain circumstances, in those environments where round-the-clock monitoring is required, constantly running a consumer program may impose an unnecessarily heavy load on the managed computer systems. Additionally, it is an issue of reliability since the consumer may simply crash and not be restarted fast enough, which could cause some events to be dropped.

An ideal solution would involve relying on WMI itself to correctly take appropriate actions when certain events arrive, regardless of whether a consumer application is active or not. This is exactly what is achieved via the WMI permanent event consumer framework. Essentially, this framework makes it possible to configure WMI to carry out certain predefined actions, such as sending an email, or executing an application program when some event of interest occurs. While an out-of-the-box WMI installation is equipped with only a handful of such predefined actions referred to as event consumer providers, the framework can easily be extended. Thus, if you are familiar with the fundamentals of COM programming, you can build custom event consumer providers that are capable of doing just about anything. Although WMI permanent event consumer architecture has little to do with the primary focus of this book, for the sake of completeness, I will provide more details on this subject later in this chapter.

Consuming events is just one piece of the puzzle. Events have to originate somewhere; in other words, something has to act as an event source. Normally, this role is reserved for event providers. In the spirit of extensibility, WMI event providers are simply COM servers that are responsible for monitoring the underlying managed environment, detecting changes to the managed entities, and providing event notifications to WMI correspondingly. Besides implementing the provider-standard `IWbemProviderInit` initialization interface, such providers must implement the `IWbemEventProvider` interface with its single method `ProvideEvents`.

When the provider initialization is complete, WMI calls the `ProvideEvents` method to request that a provider starts providing event notifications. One of the arguments of this method is a pointer to the `IWbemObjectSink` interface that is used by the provider to forward its events to a consumer. In essence, WMI registers its event handling code (represented by the `IWbemObjectSink` pointer) with a provider, so that the provider calls the `IWbemObjectSink::Indicate` method each time an event is triggered. Note that when sending its event notifications to WMI, the provider does not perform any filtering; in fact, all events are forwarded to WMI regardless of whether there is an interested event consumer. Thus, it is the responsibility of WMI to analyze its outstanding event subscriptions and forward appropriate events to registered consumers.

Despite its simplicity, such an approach is often inefficient due to a potentially large number of unneeded event notifications generated by the provider. Thus, to reduce the traffic of event notifications and increase the overall performance, event providers have the option of implementing an additional interface, `IWbemEventProviderQuerySink`. Using this interface, WMI can notify a provider of all active event filters so that a provider can generate its notifications selectively—only if an interested event consumer is available.

Event providers are the primary, but not the only source of management events. Depending on the type of event and the availability of an event provider, WMI may assume the responsibility of generating event notifications. One, perhaps the most obvious example of WMI acting as an event source is when it generates timer events. Once an instance of the `__TimerInstruction` subclass is created and saved into CIM Repository, it is the responsibility of WMI to monitor the system clock and trigger the appropriate event notification. Timer events are not an exception and, as a matter of fact, it is WMI that raises events based on changes to any kind of static data stored in CIM Repository. For instance, all namespace operation events represented by subclasses of __NamespaceOperationEvent are monitored for and triggered by WMI since each WMI namespace is represented by a static copy of the __Namespace object stored in CIM Repository. The same is true for most of the class operation events, as long as the class definitions are static, and even certain instance operation events, given that instances are stored in the CIM Repository as opposite to being generated dynamically by an instance provider. One notable exception is extrinsic events. These events are, essentially, user-defined, and as such, they are undetectable by WMI. Therefore, all extrinsic events must be backed by an event provider.

Even the intrinsic instance operation events for dynamic WMI class instances may originate from WMI rather than from an event provider. Whenever an event provider for intrinsic events is not available, WMI employs a polling mechanism to detect changes to managed elements and to raise appropriate events. *Polling* assumes that the dynamic classes or instances are periodically enumerated and their current state is compared to previously saved state information in order to sense changes that warrant triggering events. Apparently, polling may be prohibitively expensive and, therefore, it is not initiated by WMI automatically in response to an event subscription request. Instead, an event consumer must request polling explicitly using a special WQL syntax, which will be covered later in this chapter. Despite its versatility, polling can amount to a performance nightmare, especially in a widely distributed environment that is interconnected by a slow or congested network. Therefore, it is a good idea to stay away from polling altogether, or at least exhibit caution when you are forced to resort to it.

Temporary Event Consumers

One approach you can use to monitor management events is build a custom consumer application that would initiate a subscription for certain events of interest on startup and remain listening to event notifications until shutdown. Such an event consumer, which only handles events as long as it is active, is referred to as a *temporary event consumer.* A typical example of a temporary consumer would be a graphical application that is only interested in receiving WMI events as long as there is a user interacting with the program.

Temporary event consumers may register to receive events in either a synchronous or asynchronous fashion. Synchronous event notification is, perhaps, the simplest event-processing technique offered by WMI. Event consumers register for synchronous event delivery by calling the IWbemServices::ExecNotificationQuery method, which, among other parameters, takes a WQL query string and returns a pointer to the IWbemEnumClassObject interface. This interface is an enumerator, used to iterate through the events of interest. Contrary to what you may assume, ExecNotificationQuery does not block until an appropriate event notification arrives. Instead, this method returns immediately, letting the consumer poll for events via the pointer to the returned IWbemEnumClassObject interface. Thus, whenever a consumer attempts to invoke the Next method of IWbemEnumClassObject, the call may block, waiting for events to become available. Releasing the IWbemEnumClassObject interface pointer cancels the query and deregisters the event consumer.

As simple as it is, synchronous event notification has its share of problems, the most significant of which is the performance penalty incurred as a result of the polling for notification status. As a result, it is better if event consumers use the asynchronous event delivery mechanism, which eliminates the need to continuously poll WMI for events through the Next method of IWbemEnumClassObject interface. Asynchronous event notification is initiated by calling IWbemServices::ExecNotificationQueryAsync. Similar to its synchronous counterpart, this method takes a WQL query string parameter that specifies the event filtering criteria. However, rather than returning an enumerator, the method also takes an additional input parameter—the IWbemObjectSink interface pointer. This interface, which must be implemented by an event consumer in order to engage in asynchronous event processing, allows WMI to forward event notifications to the client as they arrive. IWbemObjectSink has two methods: SetStatus, which informs the client on the progress of asynchronous method call and signals its completion; and Indicate, which provides the actual event notifications to the consumer.

Since asynchronous event subscriptions are endless —they do not terminate until explicitly cancelled—WMI never calls SetStatus while delivering events. Thus, the Indicate method is the main workhorse of asynchronous event processing; WMI calls it each time an event of interest is raised. This method takes two arguments: an array of IWbemClassObject interface pointers, and a count that reflects the number of elements in the array. Normally the array would contain just one element, a single event, returned by WMI; however, there is a provision for delivering multiple notifications in a single invocation of the Indicate method. An asynchronous event subscription remains active until it is explicitly cancelled via the IWbemServices::CancelAsyncCall method call.

In addition to providing a relatively simple implementation, temporary event consumers offer you nearly unlimited flexibility. After all, it is completely up to you to implement whatever event-handling logic you think you need. However, you pay a price because such consumers are only capable of listening to event notifications while they are active. Thus, if you need to monitor events round-the-clock, you may find that using temporary event consumers is not an adequate solution.

Permanent Event Consumers

Every once in a while, you may want certain management events handled continuously, regardless of whether a specific management application is active. You can accomplish this using the WMI permanent event consumer framework. Unlike temporary consumer registrations, where the event subscription information is stored in memory, permanent consumer registrations are persisted in CIM Repository, and therefore, they survive system reboots.

The centerpiece of WMI permanent consumer architecture is a component called the event consumer provider. This is a regular COM server that implements a standard provider initialization interface, IWbemProviderInit, as well as two other interfaces specific to event consumer providers: IWbemConsumerProvider and IWbemUnboundObjectSink. The former is used by WMI to locate an appropriate consumer for a given event and to retrieve a pointer to its IWbemUnboundObjectSink interface. Once a consumer is identified, WMI invokes its IWbemUnboundObjectSink::IndicateToConsumer method every time an event of interest is raised.

Although you can develop a custom event consumer provider, WMI SDK ships with a number of useful consumer provider components, which typically satisfy most of your event monitoring requirements. One such ready-to-use component is the Event Viewer consumer provider, which is implemented as the COM EXE server—wbemeventviewer.exe. As its name implies, the Event Viewer provider is designed to display management events using a graphical interface. The program can be started manually via the WMI Event Viewer shortcut in the WMI SDK program group, although it is not necessary—once event subscription is set up, WMI will automatically launch Event Viewer when qualifying events arrive. The Event Viewer graphical interface is shown in Figure 4-1.

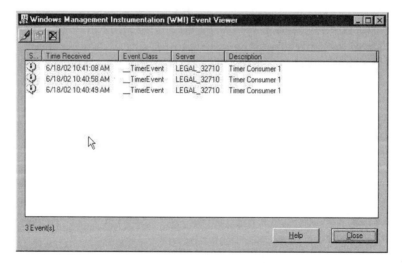

Figure 4-1. Event Viewer graphical interface

Another example of a permanent event consumer provided as part of WMI SDK is the Active Script Event Consumer that is implemented as the COM EXE server scrcons.exe. This component lets you invoke a custom script when an arbitrary event arrives. A script can be written in any scripting language that can be consumed by the Microsoft Scripting Engine, including VBScript and JavaScript. The scripting code has access to the instance of the respective event class through the environment variable TargetEvent.

Yet another example of a permanent consumer is smtpcons.dll. The SMTP event consumer provider is capable of generating and sending out email messages when the event notifications are received from WMI. This component is fairly flexible because it lets you assemble an email message using standard string templates. The templates utilize a notation, similar to one used for specifying Windows environment variables, to refer to the properties of an event. Thus, for handling process creation events, for instance, the body of the email message may include a string %TargetInstance.ExecutablePath%. Since the TargetInstance property of the _InstanceCreationEvent object always points to a newly created WMI object, this string template will be expanded to the actual path of the process executable.

A few more standard consumer providers are available, such as the Command Line Event Consumer, which launches an arbitrary process upon the arrival of an event; or the NT Log Event Consumer, which writes an entry into Windows NT Event Log as the result of a management event. In general, there is rarely a need to create a new consumer provider, since most of the event-handling functionality is already embedded in the standard consumer providers.

Although the purpose of event consumer providers should be fairly obvious at this point, one thing may still remain unclear. How does WMI locate an appropriate consumer for a given event? Just like all other COM components, consumer providers are registered in the system registry; however, such registration has little relevance as far as WMI is concerned. It turns out that all event consumer providers are registered as such in the CIM Repository. You can register an event consumer provider by creating instances of two system classes: _Win32Provider and _EventConsumerProviderRegistration. You will need the _Win32Provider object to register any kind of WMI provider; it contains mainly the basic information, such as the provider identification and CLSID. The _EventConsumerProviderRegistration, on the other hand, is specific to event consumer providers and it is used to link the physical provider that is implemented by the COM server with the logical event registration. This class has two properties: Provider, which points to an instance of the _Win32Provider class; and ConsumerClassNames, which is an array of logical consumer class names supported by the provider. A consumer class is a derivative of the system class _EventConsumer that is specific to an individual event consumer provider and, as a result, may contain properties that facilitate arbitrary event handling activities. For instance, the SMTP Event Consumer Provider comes with the SMTPEventConsumer class, which is defined as follows:

```
class SMTPEventConsumer : __EventConsumer {
    [key, Description(
        "A unique name identifying this instance of the SMTPEventConsumer.")]
    string Name;
    [Description("Local SMTP Server")]
    string SMTPServer;
    [Description("The subject of the email message.")]
    string Subject;
    [Template, Description("From line for the email message. "
        "If NULL, a from line will be constructed"
        "of the form WinMgmt@MachineName")]
    string FromLine;
    [Template, Description("Reply-To line for the email message. "
        "If NULL, no Reply-To field will be used.") ]
    string ReplyToLine;
    [Template, Description("The body of the email message.")]
    string Message;
    [Template, Description("The email addresses of those persons to be "
        "included on the TO: line. Addresses must be "
        "separated by commas or semicolons.")]
    string ToLine;
    [Template, Description("The email addresses of those persons to be "
        "included on the CC: line.")]
    string CcLine;
    [Template, Description("The email addresses of those persons to be "
        "included on the BCC: line.")]
    string BccLine;
    [Description("The header fields will be inserted into the "
        "SMTP email header without interpretation.")]
    string HeaderFields[];
};
```

As you can see, the individual properties of this class correspond to the elements that constitute a typical email message. Note that most of these properties are marked with the Template qualifier indicating that their contents may contain standard string templates to be expanded by the event processor.

Each instance of such a consumer class, often referred to as a logical consumer, represents an individual event subscription, or, more precisely, describes a particular action to be taken when an event arrives. Although logical consumers provide enough information to handle an event, there is one more piece of information that WMI requires in order to dispatch the notifications to appropriate consumers. More specifically, there has to be a specification as to what types of events are handled by a given consumer, or, in other words, there has to be an event filter. Such a specification is provided by instances of the __EventFilter system class. This class has three properties: Name, which is nothing more than just a unique instance identifier; Query, which is an event query string; and QueryLanguage, which, as its name implies, identifies the query language. At the time of this writing, WQL is the only query language available, so the Query property should always contain a valid WQL event query.

These two pieces of information—the logical consumer and the event filter—are all you need to route and handle any event. However, you may still be unclear on how they are linked. Let me try to clarify this. In the true spirit of CIM object modeling, the logical consumer and event filter classes are connected via an association class, __FilterToConsumerBinding. Two properties of this class, Filter and Consumer, refer to the __EventFilter object and a derivative of the __EventConsumer classes respectively. An instance of __FilterToConsumerBinding, which binds two valid instances of __EventFilter and a subclass of __EventConsumer, constitutes a valid and complete event subscription. Events will be delivered to a consumer as long as such instance exists and the only way to deactivate the subscription is to physically delete the instance.

You can create a permanent event registration in a few different ways. The most straightforward technique requires you to build a MOF file, which defines all necessary classes and instances. You should then compile the file using mofcomp.exe, and load it into the CIM Repository, thus creating the required event registration. Yet, another way to create a permanent event registration is to build the instances of the required classes programmatically using one of the WMI APIs. Both these techniques, although effective, are a bit tedious and error-prone. Fortunately, you can accomplish the task without writing a single line of code; just use the WMI SDK Event Registration Tool. Figure 4-2 shows its graphical interface.

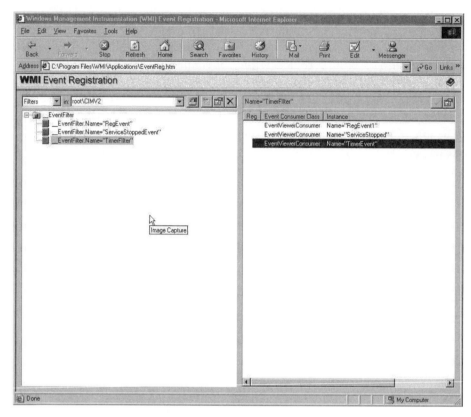

Figure 4-2. Event Registration graphical interface

This tool is extremely easy to use because it lets you create the necessary
instances of event filters and consumer classes with just a few key stokes and
mouse clicks. These instances can subsequently be linked together to create a
__FilterToConsumerBinding object, thus completing the event subscription.

Forwarding WMI Events

While the event monitoring mechanism nearly tops the list of the most exciting
features of WMI, you may not fully appreciate its versatility until you start managing a large-scale distributed system. Just imagine an environment with dozens
of computing nodes that need to be monitored on a regular basis. Setting up
event consumers locally on each of the computers is a tedious and thankless job,
which gets worse and worse as the environment grows larger. An ideal management system should allow you to intercept the events taking place on remote
computing nodes and carry out the appropriate actions in a somewhat centralized fashion.

Generally, you can handle management events, which occur on remote computer systems, in a few different ways. For instance, temporary event consumers may explicitly initiate subscriptions to events that are fired on a particular remote machine. This is the easiest approach, although it requires a consumer to manage multiple concurrent event registrations—one per each remote computer of interest.

Listening to remote events is also possible with permanent event consumers. The definition for the system class __EventConsumer, which all permanent consumers are based upon, has the following form:

```
class __EventConsumer : __IndicationRelated {
    string MachineName;
    uint32 MaximumQueueSize;
    uint8 CreatorSID[];
};
```

The first thing to notice here is the MachineName property, which is usually set to blank for locally handled events. However, it is possible to route the event notifications to a remote computer by setting the MachineName property to the name of a machine designated for handling events. After all, an event consumer provider is just a COM server that can be activated remotely using nothing but the conventional DCOM infrastructure. There are essentially two things, required for remote activation: the CLSID of the object to be created, and the name of the machine on which to instantiate the object. As you may remember, the CLSID of a consumer COM server is specified by the CLSID property of the instance of the __Win32Provider class, which describes the event consumer provider. Thus, by combining the value of the CLSID property of the __Win32Provider object with the value of the MachineName property of the instance of the __EventConsumer class, WMI is capable of connecting to an appropriate event consumer on a designated remote machine and forwarding the event notifications there.

Although such a setup is fairly straightforward, it lacks some flexibility. First, you must be able to configure the appropriate permanent event consumer registrations on all monitored machines, which may be quite a nuisance, especially in a sufficiently large managed environment. Second, forwarding event notifications to multiple remote computers at the same time significantly complicates the configuration. As you just saw, with an individual instance of __EventConsumer you can send events to a single remote computer. Thus, in order to enable WMI to route events to more than one machine, you must create multiple __EventConsumer objects—one for each receiving computer. Finally, event forwarding is achieved at the consumer provider level. In other words, WMI's ability to route notifications to remote computers depends on the availability of the appropriate event consumer providers on those machines. Moreover, if you ever need to change the way events are handled (by switching from Event Viewer consumer to Active Script consumer, for example), you have to reconfigure each monitored machine.

Fortunately, WMI provides a better way to set up permanent event forwarding. The solution lies in the forwarding event consumer provider, which intercepts the events, raised locally, and routes them to the remote computer, where they are raised again. Just like with any other event consumer, you will need a valid event registration for the forwarding consumer to work correctly. Therefore, you still need to carry out certain configuration tasks on each of the machines you want monitored. The configuration, though, is cleaner, since it has built-in provisions for routing the notifications to multiple remote computers simultaneously and does not enforce a particular event-handling technique.

To better understand how the forwarding consumer operates, consider this simple example. The following MOF definition shows the elements that make up a registration for a forwarding consumer that sends process creation event notifications to several remote machines:

```
instance of __EventFilter as $procfilter {
    Name = "Process Filter";
    Query = "SELECT * FROM __InstanceCreationEvent WITHIN 10
              WHERE TargetInstance ISA 'Win32_Process'";
    QueryLanguage = "WQL";
    EventNamespace = "root\\CIMV2";
};
instance of MSFT_ForwardingConsumer as $procconsumer {
    Name = "Forwarding process consumer";
    Authenticate = TRUE;
    Targets = { "MACHINE1", "MACHINE2", "MACHINE3" };
};
instance of __FilterToConsumerBinding {
    Consumer = $procconsumer;
    Filter = $procfilter;
};
```

The instances of the __EventFilter and __FilterToConsumerBinding classes, which are only shown here for completeness, are identical to those you would set up for local event registrations. The logical consumer definition, however, is quite different from that of a local consumer. An instance of the MSFT_ForwardingConsumer class is used by a physical forwarding consumer provider to route the notifications to appropriate remote computers.

Similar to the rest of the consumer classes, MSFT_ForwardingConsumer is a derivative of the __EventConsumer system class and, as such, it has MachineName property. However, this property does not have to be set in order to enable the event forwarding. Instead, this class defines a new property, Targets, which is an array of machine names or addresses that receive the event notifications. Thus, in the preceding example, all process creation events will be forwarded to MACHINE1, MACHINE2, and MACHINE3.

As I mentioned earlier, such an event registration has to be created on each of the machines that are to forward events, which may be a bit tedious. However, once created, these registrations should rarely change, since, as you will see in a moment, the particulars of event handling can be controlled from the monitoring machines that are receiving the events.

What really sets the forwarding consumer apart from the rest of the consumer providers is its ability to reraise the events on a remote machine so that the event can be handled just like any other WMI event that is local to that machine. The only catch is that the event will be represented via an instance of a special MSFT_ForwardedEvent class rather than a regular intrinsic or extrinsic event class. MSFT_ForwardedEvent has the following definition:

```
class MSFT_ForwardedEvent : MSFT_ForwardedMessageEvent {
    uint8 Account[];
    boolean Authenticated;
    string Consumer;
    __Event Event;
    string Machine;
    string Namespace;
    datetime Time;
};
```

where

> **Account**: Account used by the forwarding consumer that sent the event notification

> **Authenticated**: Boolean that indicates whether the event notification is authenticated

> **Consumer**: Name of the forwarding consumer that sent the event notification

> **Event**: Original event that caused the forwarding consumer to send the notification

> **Machine**: Name of the machine from which the event originates

Namespace: Namespace of a forwarding consumer that sent the event notification

Time: Time that the event notification was sent by the forwarding consumer

Although all properties of `MSFT_ForwardedEvent` provide a wealth of useful information regarding the origins of a forwarded event, its `Event` property is the most interesting. `Event` points to an embedded event object that corresponds to an original WMI event intercepted by the forwarding consumer. Therefore, if the consumer is set up to forward all process creation events, the `Event` property of the `MSFT_ForwardedEvent` object will contain an `__InstanceCreationEvent` with its `TargetInstance` property set to an instance of `Win32_Process`. By registering for `MSFT_ForwardedEvent` notifications and filtering based on the properties of the associated event objects, a remote consumer may carry out just about any monitoring task.

Event forwarding is a very powerful feature, much superior to all other remote notification techniques. Unfortunately, the forwarding consumer provider is only available under Windows XP and later, so users of older systems may have to resort to other event forwarding solutions.

WQL for Event Queries

The WMI event filtering mechanism is based on WQL queries. Queries are used by both parties engaged in event processing: event consumers and event providers. Event providers utilize WQL queries to publish their capabilities; in other words, they use them to specify what types of events they supported. Thus, the `EventQueryList` property of the `__EventProviderRegistration` class, which is used to define event providers in WMI, houses an array of WQL queries that are supported by the provider. Event consumers, on the other hand, use WQL queries to initiate an event subscription and to indicate to WMI in which types of events they are interested. There is no difference in the syntax of WQL queries used by providers and consumers, although there is a conceptual distinction, since such queries are used for different purposes. Since provider development has little to do with .NET and `System.Management`, the remainder of this chapter will look at WQL event queries from the prospective of an event consumer.

Rather than inventing a brand new syntax specifically for the purpose of handling event queries, WQL offers a specialized form of the `SELECT` statement. (For a formal definition of WQL `SELECT`, refer to Listing 3-1 in the last chapter.) The simplest form of the WQL `SELECT` query is as follows:

```
SELECT * FROM <event_class_name>
```

As you can see, the only thing that sets this query above apart from a regular data query is the class name in the FROM clause. A data query that specifies an event class name in its FROM clause is meaningless because instances of event classes are transient and only exist while the corresponding event is being delivered to a consumer. Thus, a query that uses an event class name in its FROM clause is automatically recognized as an event query.

Let us look at a very simple example:

```
SELECT * FROM __TimerEvent
```

This is certainly an event query, since it features a name of an event class, __TimerEvent, in the FROM clause. In fact, this query can be used to initiate a subscription to timer events, generated by any timer, that exist in CIM Repository.

Just like the data queries, event queries do not have to use the * placeholder; it is perfectly valid to specify a property list instead:

```
SELECT TimerId FROM __TimerEvent
```

Interestingly, in respect to returning system properties, this query behaves similarly to the way that a comparable data query would. If the '*' placeholder is used as a property list in a SELECT statement, each event object received by the event consumer will have most of its system properties properly populated, with the exception of __RELPATH and __PATH. The latter two properties are always set to NULL due to the inherently transient nature of event objects. However, if a SELECT statement contains a list of nonsystem properties like the query above, the only system properties populated by WMI for each output event are __CLASS, __DERIVATION, __GENUS, and __PROPERTY_COUNT. Note that __PROPERTY_COUNT will reflect the actual number of properties selected rather than total number of properties in the class definition.

The previous query is not very useful. This is because it is very likely that there is more then just one outstanding timer instruction active at any given time, which means that timer events may come from several different sources simultaneously. Since the query does not have selection criteria, it will pick up all timer interrupts, regardless of their source. You can easily solve this problem by rewriting the query as follows:

```
SELECT * FROM __TimerEvent WHERE TimerId = 'Timer1'
```

Here, the WHERE clause will ensure that only events that originate from the timer instruction, identified by TimerId of 'Timer1', are received by the consumer. In fact, using the WHERE clause to limit the scope of event subscriptions is strongly recommended because it greatly reduces the number of unneeded event notifications that are forwarded to event consumers. The syntax of the WHERE clause for event queries is exactly the same as that of the regular WQL SELECT queries and the same restrictions apply.

Subscribing to events other than timer events is very similar, although there are a few special considerations. Receiving extrinsic events is almost as trivial as getting the timer event notification. For example, the following query can be used to initiate a subscription to RegistryValueChangeEvent that is raised by the registry event provider every time a certain registry value is changed:

```
SELECT * FROM RegistryValueChangeEvent WHERE Hive = 'HKEY_LOCAL_MACHINE' AND
KeyPath = 'SOFTWARE\\MICROSOFT\\WBEM\\CIMOM' AND
ValueName = 'Backup Interval Threshold'
```

Note that in the case of the registry event provider, the WHERE clause is mandatory rather than optional. Thus, the provider will reject the following query with an error code of WBEMESS_E_REGISTRATION_TOO_BROAD (0x 80042001):

```
SELECT * FROM RegistryValueChangeEvent
```

In fact, even if there is a WHERE clause, but its search criteria do not reference all of the event class properties, the query would still be rejected:

```
SELECT * FROM RegistryValueChangeEvent WHERE Hive = 'HKEY_LOCAL_MACHINE' AND
KeyPath = 'SOFTWARE\\MICROSOFT\\WBEM\\CIMOM'
```

If a value for a given event class property is not explicitly supplied, the provider cannot deduce the finite set of registry entries to be monitored, and therefore, it rejects the query. Thus, when subscribing to an arbitrary registry event, the query should provide search arguments for each of the event class properties. Although this may seem like a rather severe restriction, there is an easy work around. The registry event provider offers a choice of three events: RegistryTreeChangeEvent, RegistryKeyChangeEvent, and RegistryValueChangeEvent. Therefore, the preceding query, which essentially attempts to monitor changes to a particular key rather than to the value, can be rewritten using RegistryKeyChangeEvent as follows:

```
SELECT * FROM RegistryKeyChangeEvent WHERE Hive = 'HKEY_LOCAL_MACHINE' AND
KeyPath = 'SOFTWARE\\MICROSOFT\\WBEM\\CIMOM'
```

This query will result in a subscription for all events generated as a result of a change to any of the values under the HKEY_LOCAL_MACHINE\SOFTWARE\MICROSOFT\WBEM\CIMOM key. The only downside is that the RegistryKeyChangeEvent class does not have the ValueName property, thus, the event objects received by the consumer cannot be used to identify a value that was changed to trigger the event. Assuming that you can identify a finite set of values to be monitored, you can easily solve this problem:

```
SELECT * FROM RegistryValueChangeEvent WHERE Hive = 'HKEY_LOCAL_MACHINE' AND
KeyPath = 'SOFTWARE\\MICROSOFT\\WBEM\\CIMOM' AND
( ValueName = 'Backup Interval Threshold' OR ValueName = 'Logging' )
```

Using the same technique of combining multiple search criteria, you can also monitor changes to registry values that reside under different keys or hives.

Subscribing to intrinsic events is a bit trickier. Although the same WQL SELECT statement is used, there are a couple of things you should watch out for. Generally, if an event of interest is backed up by an event provider, the event query remains essentially the same as the one used to register for extrinsic or timer events. Take a look at the intrinsic events supplied by Windows Event Log provider. This provider, when it is acting in the capacity of an event provider, triggers intrinsic instance operation events whenever changes that affect the Windows Event Log take place. An arbitrary Windows Event Log event is represented by an instance of the Win32_NTLogEvent class, shown here:

```
class Win32_NTLogEvent {
    [key] uint32 RecordNumber;
    [key] string Logfile;
    uint32 EventIdentifier;
    uint16 EventCode;
    string SourceName;
    [ValueMap{"1", "2", "4", "8", "16"}] string Type;
    uint16 Category;
    string CategoryString;
    datetime TimeGenerated;
    datetime TimeWritten;
    string ComputerName;
    string User;
    string Message;
    string InsertionStrings[];
    Uint8 Data[];
};
```

Note that this class represents a Windows event that is recorded into the system event log and it is not associated in any way with WMI event classes. Instead, a management event, raised as a consequence of a Windows event, is modeled as a subclass of the __InstanceOperationEvent system class. For instance, whenever an event record is written into the Windows Event Log, the Event Log provider raises __InstanceCreationEvent so that the TargetInstance property of an event object refers to an associated instance of the Win32_NTLogEvent class. Thus, all you need to register to receive such events is a SELECT query that features __InstanceCreationEvent in its FROM clause and has a WHERE criteria that narrows the scope of the registration down to Windows Event Log events. The latter can be achieved by examining the TargetInstance property of the __InstanceCreationEvent class. Theoretically, the following query should do the job:

```
SELECT * FROM __InstanceCreationEvent WHERE TargetInstance = 'Win32_NTLogEvent'
```

In fact, that query is almost correct, but not quite. Since the idea here is to limit the scope of the query based on the class of the embedded object that is pointed to the TargetInstance property, the = operator will not work. Instead, the ISA operator, which is specifically designed for dealing with embedded objects, should be used:

```
SELECT * FROM __InstanceCreationEvent WHERE TargetInstance ISA 'Win32_NTLogEvent'
```

Although this query is absolutely syntactically correct, an attempt to execute it will most likely result in WMI rejecting the query with the error code of WBEM_E_ACCESS_DENIED (0x80041003). Such behavior is puzzling at best, but there is a perfectly logical explanation. Using a query such as this one, a consumer essentially requests to be notified whenever any event is recorded into any of the Windows Event Logs, including System, Application, and Security logs. The Security log is protected and any user wishing to access it must enable SeSecurityPrivilege (which gives the user the right to manage audit and security log). In fact, this privilege should first be granted to a user and then enabled on a per-process basis. Later in this chapter I will demonstrate how to ensure that a privilege is enabled; meanwhile, there is a simple workaround. If you are only interested in Application events, the scope of the query can be narrowed down even further:

```
SELECT * FROM __InstanceCreationEvent WHERE TargetInstance ISA 'Win32_NTLogEvent'
AND TargetInstance.Logfile = 'Application'
```

Since this query only requests the events from the Windows Application Log, access control is no longer an issue, so no special privileges need to be enabled.

To summarize, there is nothing special about handling the intrinsic events backed up by event providers, except for the few possible idiosyncrasies that a given provider may exhibit. Thus, you should study the documentation that comes with the provider before you attempt to set up event registrations.

Events that are generated by WMI and are based on the changes to static data that resides in CIM Repository are also fairly straightforward. This typically applies to all namespace operation events as well as class operation events, unless the class definitions are dynamic. For instance, the following query may be used to subscribe to any modification to a namespace, called 'default':

```
SELECT * FROM __NamespaceModificationEvent WHERE TargetNamespace.Name = 'default'
```

Handling changes to a WMI class definition is no different. The following query will allow you to monitor all changes to a definition of the WMI class Win32_Process:

```
SELECT * FROM __ClassModificationEvent WHERE TargetClass ISA 'Win32_Process'
```

The situation is a bit more complicated when it comes to handling the instance operation events for dynamic objects, which are not backed up by event providers. For instance, consider an instance creation event for a Win32_Process object. First, it is a dynamic object, so it is not stored in CIM Repository. Second, there is no event provider capable of raising the instance creation event whenever a process is launched. It sounds as if subscribing to such an event is not even possible, but luckily, WMI comes to the rescue. As I already mentioned, WMI is capable of periodically polling the instance providers to detect changes and to raise the appropriate intrinsic events. Polling is an expensive procedure and therefore, is not done automatically. In fact, WMI has to be explicitly instructed to poll instance providers at certain time intervals. You can do this by including a WITHIN clause in the event query, so that the SELECT statement will take the following form:

```
SELECT * FROM <intrinsic_event_class> WITHIN <interval> WHERE <criteria>
```

The WITHIN clause must be placed immediately before the WHERE clause and has to specify an appropriate value for the polling interval. The polling interval is specified in units of seconds, although it is a floating point rather than an integer number, so it is possible to give it a value of fractions of a second. Due to the extremely resource-intensive nature of polling, make sure that you use sufficiently large polling intervals. In fact, if the interval value is too small, WMI may reject the query as invalid.

For example, the following query initiates a subscription to instance creation events for objects of the Win32_Process class and instructs WMI to poll the instance provider at 10-second intervals:

```
SELECT * FROM __InstanceCreationEvent WITHIN 10
WHERE TargetInstance ISA 'Win32_Process'
```

It is not always clear which events are backed up by providers and which are not. As a result, to determine whether you need a `WITHIN` clause in your query is an empirical process. WMI can provide assistance in this mater—if a query does not contain a `WITHIN` clause where it is required, WMI will reject it with the `WBEMESS_E_REGISTRATION_TOO_PRECISE` (0x80042002) error code. Such an error code has a corresponding error message that reads "`A WITHIN clause was not used in this query`". However, if `WITHIN` clause is specified where it is not required, the query will work just fine. Therefore, it is a good idea to always attempt to execute event queries without `WITHIN` clause first, and then only add it if necessary.

Sometimes it helps to be able to monitor all three instance operation events—`_InstanceCreationEvent`, `_InstanceModificationEvent`, and `_InstanceDeletionEvent`—using a single event query. This can easily be achieved by substituting the superclass `_InstanceOperationEvent` for the name of a specific subclass in the FROM clause:

```
SELECT * FROM __InstanceOperationEvent WITHIN 10
WHERE TargetInstance ISA 'Win32_Process'
```

Of course, the events, returned by such a query would belong to one of the three subclasses of `_InstanceCreationEvent`, because the latter is an abstract class, and therefore, it cannot have instances. The actual class of these events can easily be determined by examining the `_CLASS` system property of each received event object. Interestingly, if there is an event provider for intrinsic events, such a generalized query may not work. For instance, the following legitimate looking query fails:

```
SELECT * FROM __InstanceOperationEvent WHERE TargetInstance ISA 'Win32_NTLogEvent'
```

The reason for the failure is simple: the Event Log Event provider only supports `_InstanceCreationEvent`, not `_InstanceModificationEvent` or `_InstanceDeletionEvent`. This becomes obvious if you look at the instance of the `_EventProviderRegistration` class for Event Log Event provider:

```
Instance of __Win32Provider as $EventProv {
    Name = "MS_NT_EVENTLOG_EVENT_PROVIDER";
    ClsId = "{F55C5B4C-517D-11d1-AB57-00C04FD9159E}";
};

Instance of __EventProviderRegistration {
    Provider = $EventProv;
    EventQueryList = {"select * from __InstanceCreationEvent
                      where TargetInstance isa \"Win32_NTLogEvent\""};
};
```

Here, the `EventQueryList` property of the provider registration object clearly shows the supported query types.

This seems like a rather severe limitation because `__InstanceDeletionEvent` for Windows log events is quite useful in detecting when the event log is cleared. This is where WMI comes to the rescue again. The error code, returned by the query above is the already-familiar error `WBEMESS_E_REGISTRATION_TOO_PRECISE` (0x80042002), which implies that adding a WITHIN clause to the query may solve the problem:

```
SELECT * FROM __InstanceOperationEvent WITHIN 10
WHERE TargetInstance ISA 'Win32_NTLogEvent'
```

Indeed, this query works perfectly now. In this case, WMI and the event provider work together so that `__InstanceCreationEvent` is supplied by the provider, while the two remaining events are generated by WMI using the polling technique.

Specifying the polling interval is not the only use for the `WITHIN` clause. It also works in concert with the `GROUP BY` clause to indicate the grouping interval. The idea behind the `GROUP BY` clause revolves around WMI's ability to generate a single notification that represents a group of events. In its simplest form, the `GROUP BY` clause can be used as follows:

```
SELECT * FROM __InstanceCreationEvent WITHIN 10
WHERE TargetInstance ISA 'Win32_Process'
GROUP WITHIN 10
```

This particular query instructs WMI to batch together all process-creation events that occur within 10-second intervals that start as soon as the first event is triggered. Note that there are two `WITHIN` clauses, contained in this query: one that requests polling at 10-second intervals, and the other that specifies the event grouping within 10-second intervals. These clauses and their respective interval values are completely independent.

The `GROUP` clause can be used together with an optional BY clause; this allows for finer control over the grouping of event notifications. For instance, the following query batches events together based on the value of the `ExecutablePath` property of the `Win32_Process` object that is associated with the `__InstanceCreationEvent` object:

```
SELECT * FROM __InstanceCreationEvent WITHIN 10
WHERE TargetInstance ISA 'Win32_Process'
GROUP WITHIN 10 BY TargetInstance.ExecutablePath
```

Thus, no matter how many actual process creation events take place within a 10-second interval, the number of event notifications that is sent to the consumer will always be equal to the number of distinct executables that are used to launch processes within that interval.

Finally, an optional HAVING clause offers even more control over the process of event delivery. To better understand the mechanics of the HAVING clause, first look at how the aggregated events are delivered to consumers. Contrary to what you may think, the preceding query, or any query that features the GROUP BY clause, will not result in __InstanceCreationEvent objects being forwarded to the client. Instead, WMI will assemble an instance of the __AggregateEvent class that is representative of all instance creation events that took place within the grouping interval. The __AggregateEvent class has the following definition:

```
class __AggregateEvent : __IndicationRelated {
    uint32 NumberOfEvents;
    object Representative;
};
```

The NumberOfEvents property contains a total number of underlying intrinsic or extrinsic events that are combined to produce a given __AggregateEvent object. Representative is a property that refers to an embedded event object that is a copy of one of the underlying events used in the aggregation. Thus, for the query just listed, the Representative property will contain one of the __InstanceCreationEvent objects, which contributed to the resulting __AggregateEvent object. Note that there is no guarantee that a particular underlying event object will be linked to the aggregate event. For instance, given the following query, it is not possible to predict whether the Representative property of __AggregateEvent will contain the __InstanceCreationEvent, __InstanceModificationEvent, or __InstanceDeletionEvent object:

```
SELECT * FROM __InstanceOperationEvent
WITHIN 10 WHERE TargetInstance ISA 'Win32_Process'
GROUP WITHIN 10
```

All of these query examples, even those that result in event aggregation, use the WHERE clause to specify search criteria for the underlying event objects. The query above, for example, references the TargetInstance property of the __InstanceOperationEvent class, even though the event consumer receives __AggregateEvent objects rather than instance operation events. It is, however, possible to supply a search condition, based on the properties of the resulting __AggregateEvent object, and this is where the HAVING clause comes in handy. Consider the following query example:

```
SELECT * FROM __InstanceCreationEvent WHERE TargetInstance ISA 'Win32_NTLogEvent'
GROUP WITHIN 10 HAVING NumberOfEvents > 5
```

This query requests only those __AggregateEvent objects that are composed of more than five underlying instance creation events. In other words, an aggregate event will only be delivered to the consumer if more than five Windows log events take place within a 10-second time interval.

Handling Events with System.Management

The majority of event monitoring scenarios can easily be covered using the WMI permanent event consumer framework. This approach is clearly superior under many circumstances because it alleviates many concerns typically associated with a custom monitoring tool. It is simple from both the conceptual and the implementation prospective. It is also reliable because instead of relying on an application program, the monitoring task is done by WMI. Finally, it is extremely cost-effective because no, or very little, development effort is required. Although you may argue that a custom event consumer provider may have to be developed to satisfy certain monitoring needs, standard consumer providers, which are distributed as part of the WMI SDK, are usually adequate. Thus, building an event-handling utility is rarely required because there are very few compelling reasons to engage into such activity.

Nevertheless, the System.Management namespace comes well equipped for handling management events. The functionality afforded by System.Management event-handling types, however, is intended to support temporary, rather than permanent event consumers. Although it is theoretically possible to implement an event consumer provider using FCL and the .NET languages, System.Management does not include any facilities that are specifically designed to address consumer provider development. Therefore, the rest of this chapter will concentrate on explaining the mechanics of event handling from the prospective of temporary event consumers.

ManagementEventWatcher Type

The entire event-handling mechanism is packaged as a single System.Management type called ManagementEventWatcher. This type is solely responsible for handling all types of WMI events in both synchronous and asynchronous fashion. Just like most of the FCL types, ManagementEventWatcher is fairly straightforward and self-explanatory.

Perhaps, the simplest thing that can be achieved with ManagementEventWatcher is handling management events in synchronous mode.

For example, the following code snippet initiates the subscription for all process creation events and then polls for notification in a synchronous fashion:

```
ManagementEventWatcher ew = new ManagementEventWatcher(
    @"SELECT * FROM __InstanceCreationEvent WITHIN 10
      WHERE TargetInstance ISA 'Win32_Process'");
while( true ) {
    ManagementBaseObject mo = ew.WaitForNextEvent();
    Console.WriteLine("Event arrived: {0}", mo["__CLASS"]);
    mo = (ManagementBaseObject)mo["TargetInstance"];
    Console.WriteLine("Process handle: {0}. Executable path: {1}",
        mo["Handle"], mo["ExecutablePath"]);
}
```

Here, the instance of ManagementEventWatcher is created using a constructor that takes a single query string parameter. The code than enters an endless loop and starts polling for events using the WaitForNextEvent method. This method is built around the IWbemServices::ExecNotificationQuery method, which is what WMI uses to initiate synchronous event subscriptions. If you remember the discussion of synchronous query processing, you may assume that WaitForNextEvent essentially mimics the functionality of IWbemServices::ExecNotificationQuery by returning an instance of ManagementObjectCollection immediately after it is invoked. If this were true, the consumer would iterate through the collection so that each request for the next collection element would block until an event notification arrives. This, however, is not the case. Instead, WaitForNextEvent blocks until an appropriate event is triggered, and then it returns a single instance of the ManagementBaseObject type, which represents the delivered event. Such an approach, while certainly simpler, lacks some flexibility because events are always delivered one by one. The COM API IWbemServices::ExecNotificationQuery method, on the other hand, leaves enough room for delivering events in blocks, which may contribute to some performance gains.

Be careful when you are examining the delivered event. For the code above, the returned ManagementBaseObject embodies an instance of __InstanceCreationEvent. As you may remember, the TargetInstance property of the event object refers to an embedded object that triggers the event—in this case, an instance of the Win32_Process class. This instance can be retrieved by accessing the TargetInstance property through the ManagementBaseObject indexer or its Properties collection and casting the result back to ManagementBaseObject.

If you bother to compile and run the code above, it may produce an output similar to the following, assuming you launch a notepad.exe process:

```
Event arrived: __InstanceCreationEvent
Process handle: 160. Executable path: C:\WINNT\System32\notepad.exe
```

The preceding code example sets up the event registration for those events that occur on a local computer. It is, however, entirely possible to initiate a subscription to events that takes place on a remote machine. All that you need to do to listen to remote events is set up an instance of ManagementEventWatcher that is bound to a remote computer. This can be achieved by using an alternative version of its constructor, which, in addition to the query strings, takes a scope string that identifies the target machine and namespace:

```
ManagementEventWatcher ew = new ManagementEventWatcher(
    @"\\BCK_OFFICE\root\CIMV2",
    @"SELECT * FROM __InstanceCreationEvent WITHIN 10
      WHERE TargetInstance ISA 'Win32_Process'");
while( true ) {
    ManagementBaseObject mo = ew.WaitForNextEvent();
    Console.WriteLine("Event arrived: {0}", mo["__CLASS"]);
    mo = (ManagementBaseObject)mo["TargetInstance"];
    Console.WriteLine("Process handle: {0}. Executable path: {1}",
        mo["Handle"], mo["ExecutablePath"]);
    Console.WriteLine("Originating Machine: {0}", mo["__SERVER"]);
}
```

The code above registers for receiving the events that take place on a remote machine BCK_OFFICE. Note that the origins of an event can be traced by interrogating the __SERVER system property of the received event object.

As I mentioned earlier, there are certain security implications involved when you subscribe for specific categories of management events. For instance, in order to receive Windows log events, SeSecurityPrivilege must be granted and enabled. Granting the privilege is a task that should be carried out using an appropriate user management tool. Enabling the privileges, however, should be done on a per process basis, and therefore, your management code should include enough provisions to get the security issues out of the way.

Assuming that all the right privileges are granted, clearing WMI security is remarkably easy. Thus, the following code snippet successfully sets up a subscription for Windows log events, assuming that a user is granted SeSecurityPrivilege:

```
ManagementEventWatcher ew = new ManagementEventWatcher(
    @" SELECT * FROM __InstanceCreationEvent
        WHERE TargetInstance ISA 'Win32_NTLogEvent'");
ew.Scope.Options.Impersonation = ImpersonationLevel.Impersonate;
```

```
ew.Scope.Options.EnablePrivileges = true;
while( true ) {
    ManagementBaseObject mo = ew.WaitForNextEvent();
    Console.WriteLine("Event arrived: {0}", mo["__CLASS"]);
}
```

The only difference here is the two lines of code that follow the construction
of the ManagementEventWatcher object. It turns out that all security-related settings are packaged into an instance of the ConnectionOptions class. The
ConnectionOptions object, which controls the security context of the WMI connection, is contained in the instance of the ManagementScope class, which is
associated with ManagementEventWatcher object. The code above simply sets two
of the properties of ConnectionOptions object—Impersonation and
EnablePrivileges—which control the COM impersonation level and security
privileges respectively. Once these two properties are set correctly, the code is
granted the required access level. Although the detailed overview of WMI security
will not be presented until Chapter 8, the technique just demonstrated, should
allow you to get around most of the security-related issues that you may
encounter.

Although synchronous mode is definitely the simplest event-processing
option available to the developers of management applications, it is not very
flexible and not all that efficient. Its main drawback is that it needs to continuously poll WMI using the WaitForNextEvent method. A much better approach
would be to register for events once and then handle the notifications as they
arrive. This is where the asynchronous mode proves to be very helpful, although
setting up an asynchronous event subscription may require just a bit more
coding.

The following code snippet duplicates the functionality of the previous
example, but this time in asynchronous mode:

```
class Monitor {
    bool stopped = true;
    public bool IsStopped {
        get { return stopped; }
        set { stopped = value; }
    }
    public void OnEventArrived(object sender, EventArrivedEventArgs e) {
        ManagementBaseObject mo = e.NewEvent;
        Console.WriteLine("Event arrived: {0}", mo["__CLASS"]);
        mo = (ManagementBaseObject)mo["TargetInstance"];
        Console.WriteLine("Process handle: {0}. Executable path: {1}",
            mo["Handle"], mo["ExecutablePath"]);
    }
```

```
public void OnStopped(object sender, StoppedEventArgs e) {
    stopped = true;
}
public static void Main(string[] args) {
    Monitor mon = new Monitor();
    ManagementEventWatcher ew = new ManagementEventWatcher(
        @"SELECT * FROM __InstanceCreationEvent WITHIN 10
            WHERE TargetInstance ISA 'Win32_Process'");
    ew.EventArrived += new EventArrivedEventHandler(mon.OnEventArrived);
    ew.Stopped += new StoppedEventHandler(mon.OnStopped);
    ew.Start();
    mon.IsStopped = false;
    while( true ) {
        // do something useful..
        System.Threading.Thread.Sleep(10000);
    }
}
}
```

This code is fairly straightforward and should remind you of the techniques used to perform asynchronous operations with the ManagementOperationObserver type. Essentially, the ManagementEventWatcher type exposes two events: EventArrived is raised whenever a management event notification is received from WMI, and Stopped is triggered when a given instance of ManagementEventWatcher stops listening for management events. Thus, setting up an asynchronous event subscription comes down to hooking up an event handler for at least the EventArrived event. The EventArrivedEventArgs object, passed as an argument to the event handler method, has one property, NewEvent, which points to an instance of the ManagementBaseObject class that represents the management event.

An asynchronous event subscription is initiated by calling the Start method of the ManagementEventWatcher type. This is the method that internally invokes IWbemServices::ExecNotificationQueryAsync, which registers a consumer for asynchronous event delivery. Once started, ManagementEventWatcher continues listening for management events until stopped, either explicitly or implicitly. To explicitly terminate an event registration, consumers may call the Stop method, which internally invokes the IWbemServices::CancelAsyncCall method. Implicit termination may occur for a variety of reasons. Perhaps, the most obvious one is that the ManagementEventWatcher variable goes out of scope. This may happen as a result of a premature program termination or a function return, or simply because a programmer forgot to explicitly call Stop. Another reason is any kind of error condition detected by WMI, such as an invalid event query or some internal error. In order to cleanly shut down any outstanding event subscriptions,

ManagementEventWatcher is equipped with a destructor method, Finalize, which is invoked automatically by .NET runtime. Although destructors are not very popular when it comes to garbage-collecting architectures, in this particular case, having one is a necessity. After all, leaving dangling event registrations around is not a very good idea.

For obvious reasons Finalize invokes the same old Stop method, which in turn, fires the Stopped event. Thus, it is pretty much a guarantee that a Stopped event will be raised regardless of whether the subscription is terminated explicitly or implicitly. The event carries enough useful information to be able to diagnose a problem, if there is any. The StoppedEventArgs object, passed as a parameter to the handler for the Stopped event, has a single property, Status, of type ManagementStatus. This is an enumeration that contains all currently defined WMI error codes. To illustrate how it works, I will change the event handler for the Stopped event so that it will print out the value of Status property:

```
public void OnStopped(object sender, StoppedEventArgs e) {
    Console.WriteLine("Stopped with status {0}", e.Status.ToString());
    stopped = true;
}
```

Assuming that the ManagementEventWatcher object is created with an event query that references a nonexisting event class in its FROM clause, the code will produce the following output:

```
Stopped with status NotFound
```

The string "NotFound" is a textual description associated with the ManagementStatus.NotFound enumeration member, which in turn, corresponds to the WBEM_E_NOT_FOUND (0x80041002) WMI error code. In this case a ManagementException will be thrown as soon as the Start method is invoked, but the Stopped event is still triggered.

Just as it is the case with synchronous event processing, asynchronous events are always delivered one-by-one. This is a bit less efficient than the native IWbemServices::ExecNotificationQueryAsync model, which allows several events to be received at once. Curiously, there is a separate type, called EventWatcherOptions, which, like all other options types, is designed to control various aspects of event processing. Besides the Context and Timeout properties inherited from its superclass ManagementOptions, EventWatcherOptions has the BlockSize property, which seems to be designed for batching the events together. However, this property is not used by any code in the System.Management namespace and it appears to have no effect on event handling. Moreover, the design of the ManagementEventWatcher type does not really support receiving multiple events at once, thus making the BlockSize option fairly useless.

EventQuery Type

An event query does not have to be represented by a plain string. There is a special type, called EventQuery, that is dedicated to handling event queries. However, unlike the other query classes described in Chapter 3, EventQuery is neither sophisticated nor very useful. In fact, it is just a container for the query string and, as such, it does not provide for query building or parsing.

In addition to a default parameterless constructor, the EventQuery type has two parameterized constructor methods: one that takes a query string, and the other that takes a language identifier and a query string. Thus, a simple query object can be created as follows:

```
EventQuery q = new EventQuery(
   @"SELECT * FROM __InstanceCreationEvent WITHIN 10
   WHERE TargetInstance ISA 'Win32_Process'");
```

While the first constructor automatically assumes that the language of the query is WQL, the second one allows the language to be set explicitly:

```
EventQuery q = new EventQuery("WQL",
   @"SELECT * FROM __InstanceCreationEvent WITHIN 10
   WHERE TargetInstance ISA 'Win32_Process'");
```

The problem is that WQL is the only language supported at this time. So, if you attempt to create a query with a language string of, say, "XYZ", and then you feed it into ManagementEventWatcher, an exception will be thrown.

Using the EventQuery type with ManagementEventWatcher is also very straightforward. The latter offers a constructor method that takes an object of EventQuery type, rather than a query string:

```
EventQuery q = new EventQuery(
   @"SELECT * FROM __InstanceCreationEvent WITHIN 10
    WHERE TargetInstance ISA 'Win32_Process'");
ManagementEventWatcher ew = new ManagementEventWatcher(q);
```

A query can also be explicitly associated with an instance of ManagementEventWatcher by setting its Query property. Thus, the following code is equivalent to the previous example:

```
EventQuery q = new EventQuery(
   @"SELECT * FROM __InstanceCreationEvent WITHIN 10
    WHERE TargetInstance ISA 'Win32_Process'");
ManagementEventWatcher ew = new ManagementEventWatcher();
ew.Query = q;
```

Besides the properties inherited from its base type `ManagementQuery` such as `QueryString` and `QueryLanguage`, the `EventQuery` type does not offer any additional functionality, and therefore, it is not very useful.

Summary

The WMI eventing mechanism is extremely powerful and, on occasion, simply indispensable, since in a well-oiled managed environment, the entire chore of system monitoring can be reduced to watching for management events. Fortunately, the functionality WMI offers to facilitate the tasks of event-based monitoring is rich and versatile enough to satisfy just about any taste. This chapter provided a fairly complete and accurate description of the capabilities and inner workings of the event-handling machinery. Having studied the text carefully, you should be in a position to

- Understand the object model behind the WMI eventing mechanism and be able to identify its main elements.

- Recognize the difference between intrinsic and extrinsic events and be able to use the appropriate event categories as necessary.

- Comprehend the fundamentals of WMI event delivery and be aware of the traps and pitfalls associated with handling certain types of event notifications.

- Understand the difference between temporary and permanent event consumers and be able to identify the major components of the WMI permanent consumer architecture.

- Be familiar with the `System.Management` types that support event processing and be capable of writing powerful temporary event consumers using the `ManagementEventWatcher` and `EventQuery` types.

This chapter effectively concludes the overview of the functionality WMI provides to the developers of management client applications. The rest of this book will concentrate on the issue of extending the capabilities of WMI to account for unique management scenarios.

CHAPTER 5

Instrumenting .NET Applications with WMI

THE MATERIAL PRESENTED up to this point has been primarily concerned with consuming the management data for the purposes of either retrieving or modifying the system configuration information, or for proactively monitoring and troubleshooting various aspects of systems behavior. While on several occasions I mentioned the WMI data providers that are responsible for maintaining the management data exposed through WMI, I have not yet focused on the gory details of provider implementation and operations. Although it is not in my nature to withhold information, in the first four chapters, I consciously avoided delving into the provider machinery for a few reasons.

First, conventional provider programming is complex. The complexity stems mainly from the choice of available programming languages and tools; until the introduction of .NET and FCL, this choice was pretty much limited to C++. Though a hard core developer may feel very much at home implementing COM interfaces with C++, cautious system administrators who wish to remain sane often walk away as soon as somebody as much as mentions IUnknown. Even with the help of various utilities and wizards distributed with WMI SDK, C++ provider programming still remains outside the realm of most system managers.

Yet another reason for taking providers for granted is the versatility of WMI and the Windows Operating Environment, both of which come equipped with enough WMI providers to monitor just about any aspect of systems operations. Thus, if you are only concerned with monitoring the health of the operating system and its services, you may never need to bother learning the provider framework. After all, understanding the WMI client API is often all that is required to accomplish the majority of monitoring and configuration tasks, and the rest of the WMI infrastructure may as well be viewed as a black box.

Your perspective may change, however, as soon as you face the necessity of administering the numerous custom applications and third-party software packages that are spread across dozens of computing nodes. On a rare occasion, you may get lucky and find out that your favorite third-party software is already outfitted with a provider and can be managed with WMI. More often, you will have to deal with in-house developed systems, which are, at best, equipped with some rudimentary logging facilities but have no provisions for remote monitoring and administration. This is where you may roll up your sleeves and turn your undivided attention to the subject of WMI provider development. Unfortunately, this is also where you discover that the WMI Client API is just a small tip of a very large iceberg.

Although the complexity of provider programming may be the main reason for the slow acceptance of WMI as a primary instrumentation framework for vendor software systems, the current state of affairs is somewhat reassuring. The gloomy prospect of digging into the nuts and bolts of the WMI provider architecture became much less gloomy once Microsoft introduced .NET and FCL. Besides the elegant interface to WMI Client API that is housed in the System.Management namespace, FCL offers extensive functionality for exposing application events and data for management in an easy and trouble-free manner. This functionality, designed specifically to instrument .NET applications for WMI, is packaged into the System.Management.Instrumentation namespace and distributed within the System.Management.dll module.

System.Management.Instrumentation types are envisioned as a collection of helpers and attributes intended to simplify the process of exposing management events and data to WMI, and as such, they nearly completely shield the developer from the intricacies of provider programming. In fact, the preferred instrumentation model is declarative so that the bulk of management data can be made available through WMI with very little coding.

Although the types of System.Management.Instrumentation namespace are the primary focus of this chapter, I will also touch upon some aspects of WMI provider programming and deployment. Not only will this discussion help you appreciate the simplicity and elegance of .NET instrumentation types, but it will also shed some light onto the underpinnings of System.Management.Instrumentation types.

Fundamentals of Provider Programming

A provider is nothing but a COM server that implements a slew of WMI interfaces. Depending on the expected functionality and type of the provider, you may be required to supply an implementation for different provider interfaces and methods. However, one interface, which must be implemented by absolutely all providers, is IWbemProviderInit. This interface has a single method, Initialize, which is invoked by WMI following the successful load of a provider COM server. As its name implies, Initialize is designed to let the providers initialize themselves and report the initialization status back to WMI so that CIMOM may start forwarding client requests to the provider. IWbemProviderInit::Initialize has the following signature:

```
HRESULT IWbemProviderInit::Initialize(
    LPWSTR                 wszUser,
    LONG                   lFlags,
    LPWSTR                 wszNamespace,
    LPWSTR                 wszLocale,
    IWbemServices          *pNamespace,
    IWbemContext           *pContext,
    IWbemProviderInitSink  *pInitSink
);
```

where the parameters are defined as follows:

> **wszUser**: A pointer to a user name. This parameter is only used if the PerUserInitialization property of the corresponding __Win32Provider registration instance is set to TRUE. If PerUserInitialization is FALSE, the provider is initialized once for all users, in which case, wszUser should be set to NULL.

> **lFlags**: This parameter is reserved for future use and must be set to zero.

> **wszNamespace**: A pointer to the name of the namespace for which a provider is being initialized.

> **wszLocale**: A pointer to the name of the locale for which the provider is being initialized. The locale name has the format of MS_XXXX, where XXX is a standard Microsoft LCID, such as MS_409. This parameter is optional and may be set to NULL.

> **pNamespace**: A pointer to IWbemServices that a provider may use to call into WMI during its initialization.

> **pContext**: A pointer to IWbemContext used to communicate provider-specific information between a provider and WMI.

> **pInitSink**: A pointer to IWbemProviderInitSink used by the provider to report its initialization status back to WMI.

Depending on its type, the provider may carry out different operations during its initialization. For instance, a push provider will store its data into the CIM Repository and shut down, while a pull provider may just set up its execution environment. Typically, an implementation of IWbemProviderInit::Initialize will look somewhat similar to the following code:

```
HRESULT SampleProvider::Initialize(
    LPWSTR                 wszUser,
    LONG                   lFlags,
    LPWSTR                 wszNamespace,
    LPWSTR                 wszLocale,
    IWbemServices         *pNamespace,
    IWbemContext          *pContext,
    IWbemProviderInitSink *pInitSink
) {
    if (pNamespace)
        pNamespace->AddRef();
    m_pNamespace = pNamespace;
    // perform other initialization activities
    pInitSink->SetStatus(WBEM_S_INITIALIZED,0);
    return WBEM_S_NO_ERROR;
};
```

Note that if a provider intends to use the pointer to `IWbemServices` to make calls into WMI, it must call `AddRef` on it. After it has finished its initialization, the provider must report the status back to WMI by calling the `IWbemProviderInitSink::SetStatus` method. This method takes two parameters: the provider's initialization status and an unused `LONG`, which is commonly set to zero. The status may take one of the following values: `WBEM_S_INITIALIZED` and `WBEM_E_FALIED`. The former indicates that the provider has completed its initialization sequence and is ready to service the client's requests. The latter is a sign of initialization failure and marks the provider as not functional. Interestingly, if the provider initialization fails, `IWbemProviderInit::Initialize` does not have to invoke `IWbemProviderInitSink::SetStatus`; instead it may simply return the `WBEM_E_FAILED` return code.

As I mentioned before, a push provider does not have to implement any interfaces other than `IWbemProviderInit`. When it comes to building instance, class, event, method, and property providers, however, the situation is much more complicated. Table 5-1 lists the interfaces that must be implemented depending on the provider type.

Table 5-1. Provider Primary Interfaces

PROVIDER TYPE	INTERFACE	COMMENTS
Class Provider	IWbemServices	Only asynchronous methods of IWbemServices need to be implemented.
Instance Provider	IWbemServices	Only asynchronous methods of IWbemServices need to be implemented.
Property Provider	IwbemPropertyProvider	N/A
Method Provider	IWbemServices	Only IWbemServices::ExecMethodAsync needs to be implemented.
Event Provider	IwbemEventProvider	N/A
Event Consumer Provider	IwbemConsumerProvider	N/A

The easiest to implement and, perhaps, the predominant type of WMI provider is an instance provider. After all, most application monitoring and configuration issues can often be reduced to retrieving and modifying the instance-level management data. When instrumenting an application, you are most likely to build a custom instance provider, which would act as an intermediary between WMI and your application environment. Thus, for the sake of providing a reasonably complete example while keeping the size of this chapter reasonable, I will concentrate on developing a simple instance provider. Those of you who are interested in implementing other provider types will have to dig into the WMI SDK documentation, although, the following text should supply enough background information to ease the pain a bit.

Since an instance provider is responsible for retrieving the management data, which represents an individual instance, one of the primary methods, to be implemented while developing such a provider is IWbemServices::GetObjectAsync. The method has the following signature:

```
HRESULT IWbemServices::GetObjectAsync(
    const BSTR       bstrObjPath,
    LONG             lFlags,
    IWbemContext     *pContext,
    IWbemObjectSink  *pObjSink
);
```

where the parameters are defined as follows:

bstrObjPath: A path to the instance to be retrieved.

lFlags: One or more bit flags that affect the behavior of the method. See the WMI SDK for details.

pContext: A pointer to IWbemContext used to communicate provider-specific information between a provider and WMI.

pObjSink: A pointer to IWbemObjectSink interface used to return the retrieved instance data to WMI and report on the status of the operation.

A typical implementation of IWbemServices::GetObjectAsync may resemble the following code:

```
HRESULT SampleProvider::GetObjectAsync(
    const BSTR         bstrObjPath,
    LONG               lFlags,
    IWbemContext     *pContext,
    IWbemObjectSink *pObjSink
) {
    IWbemClassObject *pObj = NULL;
    if (bstrObjPath == NULL || pObjSink == NULL || m_pNamespace == NULL)
        return WBEM_E_INVALID_PARAMETER;
    // retrieve instance based on path
    if (RetrieveInstanceByPath(bstrObjPath, &pObj) == S_OK) {
        pObjSink->Indicate(1, &pObj);
        pObj->Release();
        pObjSink->SetStatus(WBEM_STATUS_COMPLETE, WBEM_S_NO_ERROR, NULL, NULL);
        return WBEM_S_NO_ERROR;
    } else {
        pObjSink->SetStatus(WBEM_STATUS_COMPLETE, WBEM_E_NOT_FOUND, NULL, NULL);
        return WBEM_E_NOT_FOUND;
    }
};
```

Here the most interesting thing is the call to IWbemObjectSink::Indicate method, which is used to pass the retrieved instance back to WMI. This method takes two parameters: a count that indicates how many objects are being returned, and an array of pointers to IWbemClassObject interfaces. Each interface pointer is a handle to the instance that is discovered by the retrieval operation and passed back to WMI.

Following the completion of IWbemObjectSink::Indicate the status of the operation is reported back to WMI via the IWbemObjectSink::SetStatus method. This method takes four parameters: a bitmask status of the operation, an HRESULT of the operation, a string, and an object parameter. The bitmask status indicates whether an operation is still in progress or completed and may be one of the following: WBEM_STATUS_COMPLETE or WBEM_STATUS_PROGRESS. The HRESULT parameter is simply an error code, if there is any, generated by the retrieval operation. The string parameter is optional and is only used when an operation is expected to return a string. For instance, when updating or creating an instance, IWbemObjectSink::SetStatus may be called with this parameter set to the object path of an updated or newly created instance. Finally, the last parameter, the pointer to the IWbemClassObject interface, is used whenever it is necessary to report any extended status information. In such cases, the pointer may be associated with an instance of the __ExtendedStatus WMI class.

Besides returning individual instances directly based on the object path, instance provides are expected to be able to enumerate all management objects. This is achieved via IWbemServices::CreateInstanceEnumAsync method:

```
HRESULT IWbemServices::CreateInstanceEnumAsync(
    const BSTR        bstrClass,
    LONG              lFlags,
    IWbemContext     *pContext,
    IWbemObjectSink  *pObjSink
);
```

where the parameters are defined as follows:

bstrClass: The name of the class for which instances are being retrieved. This is a mandatory parameter and cannot be set to NULL.

lFlags: One or more bit flags that affect the behavior of the method. See the WMI SDK for details.

pContext: A pointer to IWbemContext used to communicate provider-specific information between a provider and WMI.

pObjSink: A pointer to IWbemObjectSink interface used to return the retrieved instance data to WMI and report on the status of the operation.

`IWbemServices::CreateInstanceEnumAsync` can be implemented as follows:

```
HRESULT SampleProvider::CreateInstanceEnumAsync(
    const BSTR        bstrClass,
    LONG              lFlags,
    IWbemContext      *pContext,
    IWbemObjectSink   *pObjSink
) {
    IWbemClassObject *pClass = NULL;
    IWbemClassObject *pInst  = NULL;
    HRESULT          hr      = S_OK;
    // retrieve class definition using IWbemServices pointer cached
    // during initialization
    hr = m_pNamespace->GetObject(strClass, 0, NULL, &pClass, 0);
    if (hr != S_OK)
        return hr;
    while(GetNextInstance(pClass, &pInst, pContext)) {
        pObjSink->Indicate(1, &pInst);
        pInst->Release();
    }
    pObjSink->SetStatus(WBEM_STATUS_COMPLETE, WBEM_S_NO_ERROR, NULL, NULL);
    return WBEM_S_NO_ERROR;
};
```

As you can see, the implementation is very similar to that of
`IWbemServices::GetObjectAsync`. The only difference here is that instead of
retrieving an object based on its path, the code continuously calls a hypothetical
function `GetNextInstance`, which assembles new WMI objects based on some
kind of management data. These objects are then returned to WMI one-by-one
using the `IWbemObjectSink::Indicate` method. When the enumeration completes
(`GetNextInstance` returns a FALSE value), WMI is notified on the operation's status via a call to `IWbemObjectSink::SetStatus`.

Once `IWbemProviderInit::Initialize`, `IWbemServices::GetObjectAsync`, and
`IWbemServices::CreateInstanceEnumAsync` are implemented, the provider is functional and ready to be deployed. However, it will only be able to provide the
management data to WMI in a read-only fashion. In order for a provider to support updates to the instances that it manages, it must implement both the
`IWbemServices::PutInstanceAsync` and `IWbemServices::DeleteInstanceAsync`
methods.

`IWbemServices::PutInstanceAsync` is used to create or update an instance of
a given WMI class. The method has the following signature:

```
HRESULT IWbemServices::PutInstanceAsync(
    IWbemClassObject *pInstance,
    LONG             lFlags,
    IWbemContext     *pContext,
    IWbemObjectSink  *pObjSink
);
```

where the parameters are defined as follows:

> **pInstance**: A pointer to the IWbemClassObject interface that represents an instance to be created or updated.

> **lFlags**: One or more bit flags that affect the behavior of the method. See the WMI SDK for details.

> **pContext**: A pointer to IWbemContext used to communicate provider-specific information between a provider and WMI.

> **pObjSink**: A pointer to the IWbemObjectSink interface used to report on the status of the operation.

Implementing IWbemServices::PutInstanceAsync is trivial since the structure of this method is very similar to one of the methods described earlier, such as IWbemServices::GetObjectAsync. One thing you should keep in mind, though, is that for instances of subclasses, an update operation is compound. In other words, if pInstance points to an object of a class that has nonabstract super-classes, WMI automatically invokes IWbemServices::PutInstance for each of these superclasses starting from the top of the hierarchy. The update operation succeeds only if all the providers responsible for each of the classes within the inheritance tree handle the update successfully. You may assume that the same principle works for subclasses as well, meaning that whenever an instance of a class is updated, the update is propagated to instances of all its subclasses. Unfortunately, this is not the case—instead, if an application updates properties of an object, which are inherited by subclass instances, it must explicitly call IWbemServices::PutInstance on each of the affected subclass instances.

IWbemServices::DeleteInstanceAsync deletes an instance of a designated class, residing in a current namespace. The method has the following signature:

```
HRESULT IWbemServices::DeleteInstanceAsync(
    IWbemClassObject *pInstance,
    LONG             lFlags,
    IWbemContext     *pContext,
    IWbemObjectSink  *pObjSink
);
```

where the parameters are defined as follows:

> **pInstance**: A pointer to the IWbemClassObject interface that represents an instance to be deleted.

> **lFlags**: One or more bit flags that affect the behavior of the method. See the WMI SDK for details.

> **pContext**: A pointer to IWbemContext used to communicate provider-specific information between a provider and WMI.

> **pObjSink**: A pointer to IWbemObjectSink interface used to report on the status of the operation.

Again, implementing IWbemServices::DeleteInstanceAsync is very similar to coding the other provider methods that were described earlier. Similarly to IWbemServices::PutInstanceAsync, WMI automatically invokes IWbemServices::DeleteInstance for each of the superclass instances. It starts from the top of the hierarchy in case pInstance points to an object of a class that has nonabstract superclasses. However, the success of the delete operation depends only on the success of the IWbemServices::DeleteInstance call for the top-level nonabstract class.

Optionally, instance providers may support query processing. When a provider elects to handle queries, it must implement the IWbemServices::ExecQueryAsync method:

```
HRESULT IWbemServices::ExecQueryAsync(
    const BSTR          bstrQueryLangauge,
    const BSTR          bstrQuery,
    LONG                lFlags,
    IWbemContext      *pContext,
    IWbemObjectSink   *pObjSink
);
```

where the parameters are defined as follows:

> **bstrQueryLanguage**: A string that contains the name of one of the query languages supported by WMI. Currently, the only supported language is WQL, thus, the value of this parameter should always be set to WQL.

> **bstrQuery**: A string that contains the text of the query. This is a mandatory parameter that cannot be NULL.

lFlags: One or more bit flags that affect the behavior of the method. See the WMI SDK for details.

pContext: A pointer to IWbemContext used to communicate provider-spccific information between a provider and WMI.

pObjSink: A pointer to the IWbemObjectSink interface used to deliver the results of the query back to WMI and report on the status of the operation.

A typical implementation of IWbemServices::ExecQueryAsync must be capable of parsing the query test, retrieving the qualifying objects, and returning the results back to WMI. If for some reason, a provider cannot handle the query, it may choose to refuse the query by returning the WBEM_E_PROVIDER_NOT_CAPABLE result code. In such cases, WMI may attempt to either simplify the query and resend it to the provider, or just enumerate all instances of a class, for which the query is invoked.

Other types of providers, such as event or method providers, may need to implement additional interfaces and interface methods. For instance, in order to allow a client to execute object methods, a provider must implement the IWbemServices::ExecMethodAsync method. However, supporting the interfaces and methods described above, is usually sufficient for a provider that satisfies the majority of typical system management needs.

Once a provider COM server is coded and compiled, it must be registered just like any other COM object. To register a provider, use regsvr32.exe as follows:

```
regsvr32.exe SampleProvider.DLL
```

COM registration, although required, is not the only piece of information that WMI needs in order to use the provider. As I mentioned earlier, WMI maintains its own provider registration information in the CIM Repository. A provider is described by an instance of the __Win32Provider system class and an instance of a subclass of __ProviderRegistration. For example, in order to register an instance provider "SampleProvider", the following two instances must be added to the repository:

```
instance of __Win32Provider as $Prov {
    Name  = "SampleProvider";
    ClsId = "{fe9af5c0-d3b6-11ce-a5b6-00aa00680c3f}";
};
instance of __InstanceProviderRegistration {
    Provider = $Prov;
```

```
        InteractionType = 0;
        SupportsPut = TRUE;
        SupportsGet = TRUE;
        SupportsDelete = TRUE;
        SupportsEnumeration = TRUE;
        QuerySupportLevels = {"WQL:UnarySelect"};
};
```

This first instance of the __Win32Provider class simply describes the provider to WMI and establishes a link to an external COM server by setting the ClsId property to the Class ID of the COM object. To allow for finer control over the provider initialization, __Win32Provider offers a few other properties, such as PerLocaleInitialization and PerUserInitialization, which indicate whether a provider is initialized only one time or once per each locale and user. However, under normal circumstances the defaults are usually sufficient so that Name and ClsId are the only properties that need to be set. Because Name is a key, it cannot be left blank. WMI also needs ClsId to load the appropriate provider COM server.

The __InstanceProviderRegistration object serves as a description of the provider's capabilities. Most of its properties are self-explanatory, with the exception of InteractionType and QuerySupportLevels. The former identifies the type of the provider—the value of zero (default) stands for pull providers, while the value of one is associated with push providers. QuerySupportLevels is a bit more complex. As its name implies, this property indicates what kind of query support the provider guarantees. Setting this property to NULL would mark the provider as not capable of processing any queries. For those providers that do support query processing, this property may be set to one or more of the following values: WQL:UnarySelect, WQL:References, WQL:Associators, and WQL:V1ProviderDefined. Under the current release, WMI only delivers simple unary SELECT WQL queries to providers, hence the WQL:UnarySelect designation. Interestingly, marking the provider as capable of handling only the unary SELECT queries does not seem to preclude it from processing the REFERENCES OF or ASSO-CIATORS OF queries. WMI takes care of translating such queries into simple SELECT statements before sending them to providers, which enables the providers to handle all types of queries in a uniform fashion.

As you can see, building a provider, while not terribly complex, involves a fair amount of low-level coding and assumes working knowledge of COM. To make provider programming more appealing for a less sophisticated audience, Microsoft developed the Provider Framework, which ships as a part of the WMI SDK. The Provider Framework is nothing but a set of C++ classes that encapsulate most of the boilerplate code necessary to create an instance or method provider. The good thing about the Provider Framework is that it completely shields the developer from the intricacies of COM programming because it handles all interactions with COM. The bad thing, of course, is that it still requires fairly sophisticated C++ coding skills.

The Provider Framework includes a set of classes that implement IWbemProviderInit, IWbemServices, and IWbemClassObject interfaces (such as CWbemProviderGlue, Provider, and CInstance respectively), as well as some utility classes, which facilitate time conversions, time span calculations, string operations, and more. Typically, a developer will create a new provider class by subclassing the Provider class and overriding some of its methods. The base class supplies a default implementation for all of its methods that simply returns WBEM_E_PROVIDER_NOT_CAPABLE when invoked.

Still, coding a provider by hand, even with the help of the Framework classes, is quite an effort. That is why WMI SDK includes a handy utility called the Provider Code Generator wizard, which spits out the stab implementation for all required C++ classes and methods and creates all necessary MOF definitions. The Provider Code Generator wizard is shown in Figure 5-1.

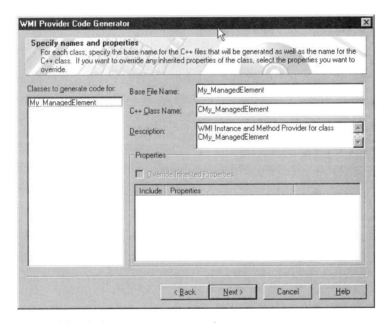

Figure 5-1. Provider Code Generation wizard

You can access the Provider Code Generator through the CIM Studio interface. In order to generate the code for a provider, you must select one of the existing classes and then invoke the wizard by clicking a button in the upper-right corner of the CIM Studio GUI. The wizard will output several CPP files, a header file, a makefile, a MOF definition, and a DEF file. Most files will be named after the initially selected WMI class (although this base name can be overridden) and will have the appropriate extensions. For instance, if you select a hypothetical class My_ManagedElement, the wizard will produce the following files:

My_ManagedElement.CPP: C++ source file that contains the stab implementation for the provider.

My_ManagedElement.H: C++ header file that contains the declaration of the provider class.

Maindll.CPP: C++ source file that contains the implementation for the DllMain, DllGetClassObject, DllCanUnloadNow, DllRegisterServer, and DllUnregisterServer functions.

My_ManagedElementProv.DEF: A definition file with the list of exports.

My_ManagedElementProv.MAK: A makefile used to compile and link the provider DLL.

My_ManagedElementProv.MOF: A MOF file that contains the MOF declarations necessary to register the provider with WMI. This file would create instances of the __Win32Provider class as well as instances of the __InstanceProviderRegistration and __MethodProviderRegistration classes.

Once the source files are generated, all that you have left to do is fill out the blanks in the default method implementations and then build and register the provider DLL. As you can see, with the help of the Provider Code Generation wizard, developing a working WMI provider is trivial, although there are still a few things left to be desired. First, the resulting provider does not allow you to expose management events, which can be a severe limitation for some managed environments. Second, you still need to engage in some, although much less complex, C++ coding exercises. As a result, despite all the nifty WMI SDK utilities, WMI provider development is often perceived as one of the more advanced subjects, and as a result, it remains largely unexplored.

Exposing Applications for Management with System.Management.Instrumentation

The goal of the System.Management.Instrumentation namespace is to make instrumenting .NET applications easier by providing extensive support for exposing the application data and events for management. However, rather than following

the familiar path of supplying the helper and utility types for provider development, the designers of the System.Management.Instrumentation namespace took
a completely different and quite innovative approach. The idea behind .NET application instrumentation is very simple, yet elegant, and it revolves around some
common traits that are shared by .NET and WMI. Both platforms are based on the
same object-oriented design principle and operate in terms of the same entities—
classes, objects, properties, and so on. Therefore, you can establish a mapping
between the managed elements modeled as .NET types, and WMI schema elements so that an arbitrary .NET type would correspond to a WMI class and its
properties, and events would map to corresponding facets of a WMI class.

Thus, once a translation scheme between the .NET application types and the
WMI classes is defined, any software system can be instrumented for WMI simply
by creating the metadata, which describes the .NET-to-WMI mapping. Naturally,
such a concept of mapping metadata fits very well with the overall philosophy of
.NET and can easily be supported through the .NET Framework attribution capabilities. Rather than coding to WMI interfaces, you may decorate the existing
.NET application types, properties, and events with the appropriate attributes so
that the .NET Framework itself takes care of all the necessary translation and
marshalling of the application data.

The instrumentation model employed by the designers of
System.Management.Instrumentation namespace is largely declarative. This
means that the namespace contains mostly the .NET attribute types that are used
to mark up the appropriate .NET assemblies, types, properties, and events.
Besides the attributes, there are a few helper types. These can be used to cus-
tomize the process of exposing the application data to WMI and to account for
complex situations that cannot be easily handled through attribution. The
remainder of this chapter is dedicated to addressing various scenarios for exposing the data and events for management using the attributes as well as the helper
types.

Instrumentation Basics

When you are instrumenting a particular .NET application, you must first mark
the application's assembly as capable of providing the management data to WMI.
You can achieve this with the custom attribute type InstrumentedAttribute,
which is a part of System.Management.Instrumentation namespace:

```
using System.Management;
using System.Management.Instrumentation;

[assembly:Instrumented(@"root\CIMV2")]
namespace InstrumentedApplication {
```

```
// instrumented application types go here
...
};
```

There are a few things happening here. First, when you look at its disassembly listing, you can easily deduce that InstrumentedAttribute is an assembly-level attribute:

```
.class public auto ansi beforefieldinit InstrumentedAttribute
    extends [mscorlib]System.Attribute {
    .custom instance void [mscorlib]System.AttributeUsageAttribute::.ctor(
        valuetype [mscorlib]System.AttributeTargets) = ( 01 00 01 00 00 00 00 00 )
}
```

Here, the definition for the InstrumentedAttribute type is decorated with another attribute, AttributeUsageAttribute, which defines a set of elements to which a given attribute can be applied. The hexadecimal string, used to initialize the AttributeUsageAttribute represents the bytes in the InstrumentedAttribute value blob. In this case, the sequence of hexadecimal digits corresponds to the Assembly member (with a value of 0x00000001) of the AttributeTargets enumeration, which is used as a parameter to the constructor of the AttributeUsageAttribute type. Thus, InstrumentedAttribute can only be applied to an assembly—if you try to use it any place else, it will trigger a compiler error. This attribute should be marked with the assembly keyword and placed at the assembly level, prior to all type definitions.

Yet another thing you should notice is the parameter that is passed to the constructor of InstrumentedAttribute. This is a string that represents the target namespace for the instrumented types contained within the assembly. In this particular case, all management classes, instances, and events will be imported into the root\CIMV2 WMI namespace. In fact, the constructor, which takes the namespace parameter, is not the only constructor featured by InstrumentedAttribute. There is also a parameterless constructor that causes all instrumented entities to be loaded into the root\default namespace. Finally, there is a constructor that takes not only the namespace parameter, but also a security descriptor (SD) that specifies the security restrictions for the instrumented assembly. The security descriptor parameter is a string formatted using the Security Description Definition Language (SDDL). The SDDL is a special notation that allows components of a SD to be represented in a textual form. Essentially, this parameter is a sequence of tokens that correspond to the four components of a SD: owner, primary group, discretionary access control list (DACL), and system access control list (SACL). Thus, a security descriptor string may take the following form:

```
O:<owner_sid>G:<group_sid>D:<dacl_flags>(ace1)(ace2)...↩S:<sacl_flags>(ace1)(ace2)...
```

where the individual elements are defined as follows:

> **O:**: Designates the owner portion of a SD string.

> **owner_sid**: A security identifier (SID) string that represents the owner of an object. A SID string can be encoded either using a standard notation (S-R-I-S-S...) or one of the string constants, defined in the sddl.h header file. Thus, AO stands for `Account operators`, AU for `Authenticated users`, and so on.

> **G:**: Designates the group portion of a SD.

> **group_sid**: A SID string that represents the object's primary group. This component uses the same encoding scheme as the `owner_sid`.

> **D:**: Designates the DACL portion of a SD.

> **dacl_flags**: A combination of SD control flags that apply to DACL. For a complete description of these flags, see the MSDN documentation.

> **S:**: Designates the SACL portion of a SD.

> **sacl_flags**: A combination of security descriptor control flags that apply to SACL. For a complete description of these flags, see MSDN documentation.

> **ace**: An access control list entry (ACE) encoded as string. This is a sequence of semicolon-separated tokens that represent various components of an ACE. For more information on ACE string encoding, see the MSDN documentation.

Assembling such string security descriptors by hand is rather convoluted and error-prone. A better idea is to use the ConvertSecurityDescriptorToStringSecurityDescriptor function, which takes a regular Windows SD (SECURITY_DESCRIPTOR structure) and outputs its string representation. The downside, of course, is that typing the name of this function is nearly as cumbersome as assembling a string SD manually.

Once the application's assembly is decorated with the InstrumentedAttribute attribute, its manifest will include the information necessary for the Framework to detect an instrumented application:

```
.assembly InstrumentedApplication {
...
.custom instance void
[System.Management]
System.Management.Instrumentation.InstrumentedAttribute::.ctor(string)
    = ( 01 00 0A 72 6F 6F 74 5C 43 49 4D 56 32 00 00 )    //...root\CIMV2..
...
}
```

The next step is to ensure that the application is registered and its schema is published in the CIM Repository. This is achieved using the standard installer mechanism, which is a part of .NET Framework. Typically, whenever the .NET Framework encounters a type that is a subclass of the System.Configuration.Install.Installer type such that this type is decorated with System.ComponentModel.RunInstallerAttribute, it checks the attribute's properties to determine whether the installation is requested. To request the installation services, the RunInstallerAttribute attribute's constructor has to be invoked with the Boolean TRUE value, which sets its RunInstaller property to TRUE. Thus, in order to ensure that all necessary installation steps are taken, an instrumented application would include some code similar to the following:

```
using System.ComponentModel;
using System.Configuration.Install;

[RunInstaller(true)]
public class MyInstaller : Installer {
...
};
```

Given such code, it is your responsibility as a developer to override the Install, Commit, and Uninstall methods of the Installer type and manually code all the installation procedures, such as publishing the application schema into the CIM Repository and registering all required components. This may get quite tricky because some of the installation steps may involve nontrivial coding. Fortunately, the System.Management.Instrumentation namespace offers a helper type, DefaultManagementProjectInstaller, which takes upon itself the task of analyzing the application's assembly and fulfilling all installation requirements. Therefore, the code just shown can be simplified as follows:

```
using System.ComponentModel;
using System.Configuration.Install;
using System.Management.Instrumentation;
```

```
[RunInstaller(true)]
public class MyInstaller : DefaultManagementProjectInstaller {};
```

Note that you are no longer required to override the methods of the
Installer type and supply your own implementation of the installation procedures. DefaultManagementProjectInstaller already contains all the necessary
implementation code, which takes care of the registration and schema publishing. Curiously, if you look at the disassembly listing of
DefaultManagementProjectInstaller, you will see that this type does not override
any of the Installer methods. Instead, its constructor does the following:

```
.method public hidebysig specialname rtspecialname
        instance void  .ctor() cil managed {
  .maxstack  2
  .locals init (class System.Management.Instrumentation.ManagementInstaller V_0)
  IL_0000:  ldarg.0
  IL_0001:  call       instance void
    [System.Configuration.Install]System.Configuration.Install.Installer::.ctor()
  IL_0006:  newobj     instance void
    System.Management.Instrumentation.ManagementInstaller::.ctor()
  IL_000b:  stloc.0
  IL_000c:  ldarg.0
  IL_000d:  call       instance class
    [System.Configuration.Install]
    System.Configuration.Install.InstallerCollection
    [System.Configuration.Install]
    System.Configuration.Install.Installer::get_Installers()
  IL_0012:  ldloc.0
  IL_0013:  callvirt   instance int32
    [System.Configuration.Install]
    System.Configuration.Install.InstallerCollection::Add(
      class [System.Configuration.Install]System.Configuration.Install.Installer)
  IL_0018:  pop
  IL_0019:  ret
}
```

Without going into too much detail, suffice it to say that this code simply creates an instance of another instrumentation helper type, ManagementInstaller,
and adds this newly created instance to the Installers collection of the
Installer object. Whenever the installation services are invoked, the Install,
Rollback, or Commit methods iterate through the Installers collection and
invoke the respective methods of each installer object found in the collection.
The ManagementInstaller type houses the implementations for the Install,

Rollback, and Commit methods that are suitable for publishing the application's schema to the CIM Repository and registering all the necessary application's components. Thus, whenever the installation services are requested, the respective methods of the ManagementInstaller object are called to carry out the necessary installation steps.

The technique demonstrated by the preceding code brings up an interesting thought. Say that your instrumented application already has an installer that takes care of all installation chores, such as copying the binaries, setting up configuration files, and so on. Then, in order to ensure that WMI-related installation steps are taken at the appropriate time, you may want to add the following line of code to the existing project installer's constructor:

```
Installers.Add(new ManagementInstaller());
```

This has exactly the same effect as the earlier code—it adds an instance of the ManagementInstaller type to the Installers collection of the project installer.

However, just having an installer embedded into your instrumented application is not enough. Somehow, the appropriate methods of the installer must be invoked at the right time to ensure that the instrumented application is correctly registered and its schema is published to the CIM Repository. The simplest and most versatile way of performing the installation is with the help of the .NET SDK utility installutil.exe. This is a command-line program that can be invoked simply with the name of the assembly to be installed. Thus, in order to install the assembly contained in the InstrumentedApplication.exe file, you can issue the following command:

```
installutil.exe InstrumentedApplication.exe
```

When this command finishes, the CIM Repository will be updated with the application's schema and provider registration information.

The complete list of command-line options for installutil.exe is shown in Table 5-2.

Table 5-2. installutil.exe Command-Line Options

OPTION	DESCRIPTION
/h[elp]	Prints syntax and command-line option information.
/help <assemblypath>	Prints any additional command-line options that are honored by individual installers contained within the assembly pointed to by the <assemblypath> parameter.
/logFile=<filename>	Causes installutil.exe to record the progress of the installation to a file pointed to by the <filename> parameter. If this option is omitted, the progress of the installation is recorded into a file called the <assemblyname>.InstallLog.
/logToConsole=<true|false>	Instructs installutil.exe to output the progress messages to the system console (true) or suppress the output altogether (false). By default, the output is suppressed.
/showCallStack	Causes installutil.exe to dump the call stack to the log file whenever an exception occurs.
/u[ninstall]	Requests uninstallation of the specified assembly.
/? <assemblypath>	Same as /help <assemblypath>.
/?	Same as /h.

Note that you can install multiple assemblies at once by specifying several assembly files on the command line. The command-line options that occur within the command line prior to the name of the assembly will apply to that assembly's installation. When multiple assemblies are installed, the installation process is transactional—if one assembly fails to install, the utility performs a rollback for all the assemblies installed up to that point. On the other hand, uninstallation is not transactional.

If installutil.exe is invoked without any command-line options, when it is finished it outputs the following files into the current directory:

InstallUtil.InstallLog: Contains the general description of the installation steps.

assemblyName.InstallLog: Contains information regarding the commit phase of the installation process for a particular assembly.

assemblyName.InstallState: Contains uninstallation information for a particular assembly.

An assembly can also be installed programmatically. For example, the following code, if placed at the beginning of the `Main` function of your instrumented application, will invoke the installation services:

```
Type t = typeof(InstrumentedClass);
string[] args = new string[] { t.Assembly.Location };
System.Configuration.Install.ManagedInstallerClass.InstallHelper(args);
```

Here, I assume that the instrumented application contains a type called `InstrumentedClass`. The first line of code obtains the `System.Type` object, associated with `InstrumentedClass`, which is subsequently utilized to get the location of the instrumented assembly. The location string is then packaged into the arguments array and passed to the `InstallHelper` method of the `System.Configuration.Install.ManagedInstallerClass` type, which actually invokes the installers. The location of the instrumented assembly is not the only argument taken by the `InstallHelper` method—in fact, you can use the same parameters as you would use for installutil.exe:

```
Type t = typeof(InstrumentedClass);
string[] args = new string[] {
    "/logFile=MyLogFile.Log",
    "/showCallStack",
    t.Assembly.Location
};
System.Configuration.Install.ManagedInstallerClass.InstallHelper(args);
```

You will find that invoking the installers programmatically is very straightforward and does not involve extensive coding. There is, however, a downside. For obvious reasons, the application's schema as well as its registration information will not be available in the CIM Repository until the first time the application is run. Thus, it is probably not a good idea to use this approach for production application deployment. Moreover, supplying such installation code is not really necessary. In fact, whenever an instrumented application first publishes an instance or raises an event, the .NET Framework performs auto-installation, which takes care of application and schema registration. Note that auto-installation only succeeds if the user running the application belongs to the Local Administrators group. Again, this is intended as a convenience to facilitate rapid prototyping and testing, and relying on this feature when deploying an application is generally not recommended.

There are also other ways to perform an installation of an instrumented application. For instance, when an application is distributed as an MSI package, the application's installers will be invoked automatically as long as the option of running .NET installers is turned on.

Lastly, there is a question of how the application's management information is actually fed into WMI. Under normal circumstances, a provider (for instance, a COM server managed by WMI itself) would interact with its associated application and gather the appropriate management data. This is not the case when it comes to instrumenting .NET applications. Here, the provider is embedded into the application itself, which allows WMI to interact with the managed subsystem directly rather than having the provider communicate with the application via the application's API. An added benefit of this approach is the degree of control the application has over the provider's life span. Since the provider is no longer controlled by WMI, it is up to the application to determine when to expose its data and events to WMI.

A provider embedded into an application is referred to as a decoupled provider. Each decoupled provider must implement two special interfaces: `IWbemDecoupledRegistrar` and `IWbemDecoupledEventProvider`. The former allows the provider to register itself with WMI and define its life span. The latter facilitates the forwarding of management events to WMI.

Even a decoupled provider has to be registered in the CIM Repository. You may find registering the decoupled provider a bit tricky because the process differs from that of registering a regular provider. For instance, rather than using a conventional class `__Win32Provider`, for this type of registration you must use a brand new class, `MSFT_DecoupledProvider`, which is the derivative of `__Win32Provider`. Fortunately, the .NET Framework generates all the necessary registration entries automatically. Although a description of the decoupled provider registration details is beyond the scope of this book, those of you who are curious may want to take a look at the generated MOF files. These files are typically placed into the `%SystemRoot%\WINNT\System32\WBEM\Framework\root\<namespace>` directory, where the namespace is the target namespace for the application's schema; and the name is based on the name of the instrumented application's assembly.

Exposing Management Data

Exposing an application's type for management is beyond simple—all you have to do is mark the type with `InstrumentationClassAttribute`, and pass the `InstrumentationType.Instance` enumeration member to its constructor. The following code demonstrates how to expose an arbitrary `MyManagedClass` to WMI:

```
using System.ComponentModel;
using System.Configuration.Install;
using System.Management.Instrumentation;

[assembly:Instrumented(@"root\CIMV2")]
namespace InstrumentedApplication {
    [RunInstaller(true)]
    public class MyInstaller : DefaultManagementProjectInstaller {};

    [InstrumentationClass(InstrumentationType.Instance)]
    public class MyManagedClass {
        public int     Prop1;
        public string Prop2;
        public static void Main(string[] args) {}
    }
}
```

If you save this code to a file, compile it, and run installutil.exe, your CIM Repository will contain the following WMI class definition in the root\CIMV2 namespace:

```
class MyManagedClass {
    [key] string ProcessId;
    [key] string InstanceId;
    sint32 Prop1;
    string Prop2;
};
```

As you can see, both the int `Prop1` and string `Prop2` properties of `MyManagedClass` type are translated into the respective properties of the WMI class. However, the WMI class has two more properties, marked with the Key qualifier: `ProcessID` and `InstanceID`. These properties are added automatically to ensure the uniqueness of any instance of the class, which may be subsequently created.

Mapping .NET Types to WMI Classes

So how do .NET types and type members map to their respective entities within WMI? Fortunately, there is striking similarity between .NET and WMI types, which makes this mapping trivial. Actually, all .NET primitive value types map one-to-one to the corresponding CIM types. Certain reference types, such as String, DateTime, and TimeSpan also map to CIM string, CIM datetime in DMTF date and time format, or datetime in DMTF interval format, respectively. Mapping .NET arrays is also straightforward—they are translated into WMI arrays of appropriate types. For example, the following .NET type

```
public class MyManagedClass {
    public string[] StrProp;
    public static void Main(string[] args) {}
}
```

has the following MOF representation:

```
class MyManagedClass {
    [key] string ProcessId;
    [key] string InstanceId;
    string StrProp[];
};
```

The situation is a bit more complex when it comes to embedded objects and references. The latest release of System.Management.Instrumentation only supports WMI embedded objects; it is impossible to generate a WMI class definition with properties of a reference type. Thus, any .NET type members of reference types other than String, DateTime, and TimeSpan, are mapped to embedded objects in WMI. Consider the following .NET types:

```
[InstrumentationClass(InstrumentationType.Instance)]
public class EmbeddedClass {
    public int EmbProp;
}
```

```
[InstrumentationClass(InstrumentationType.Instance)]
public class MyManagedClass {
    public EmbeddedClass EmbClassProp;
    public static void Main(string[] args) {}
}
```

The .NET Framework will translate these .NET types into the following WMI definitions:

```
class EmbeddedClass {
    [key] string ProcessId;
    [key] string InstanceId;
    sint32 EmbProp;
};
class MyManagedClass {
    [key] string ProcessId;
    [key] string InstanceId;
    EmbeddedClass EmbClassProp;
};
```

Interestingly, both EmbeddedClass and MyManagedClass types have to be decorated with the InstrumentationClass attribute. If, for some reason, you forget to mark the embedded type with this attribute, any property of the embedded type will simply be ignored. Thus, in the example above, if EmbeddedClass does not have the InstrumentationClass attribute, the EmbClassProp property will not be included in the CIM definition for MyManagedClass. This seemingly odd behavior actually makes sense—in order to support the definition for MyManagedClass, the CIM Repository has to contain the definition for its dependency, EmbeddedClass.

There is another caveat, which has to do with property access modifiers. Only public members of an instrumented type are mapped to WMI class properties. Take a look at the following example:

```
[InstrumentationClass(InstrumentationType.Instance)]
public class MyManagedClass {
    public string PublicProp;
           string PrivateProp;
    public static void Main(string[] args) {}
}
```

The corresponding MOF definition will be the following:

```
class MyManagedClass {
    [key] string ProcessId;
    [key] string InstanceId;
    string PublicProp;
};
```

As you may see, only the `PublicProp`, which has a `public` access modifier, is mapped to WMI class definition. The private field `PrivateProp` is simply ignored. This brings up another interesting thought. Normally, the .NET Framework does not distinguish between fields and properties—i.e., both are mapped to WMI class properties. Thus, if a given property is based upon a member field, both the property and the field will be translated into WMI class properties, essentially creating duplicate fields. This point is illustrated the following example:

```
[InstrumentationClass(InstrumentationType.Instance)]
public class MyManagedClass {
    public string StrPropertyField;
    public string StrProperty {
        get {return StrPropertyField; }
        set {StrPropertyField = value; }
    }
    public static void Main(string[] args) {}
}
```

The resulting MOF definition is the following:

```
class MyManagedClass {
    [key] string ProcessId;
    [key] string InstanceId;
    string StrPropertyField;
    string StrProperty;
};
```

When translating .NET fields and properties, the .NET Framework has no knowledge of any relationship between `StrPropertyField` and `StrProperty`, therefore both these elements end up as properties of the corresponding WMI class. By declaring `StrPropertyField` as private, which is a normal practice for property definitions, you ensure that only `StrProperty` is exposed to WMI, thus eliminating duplication.

Using access modifiers is not the only way to exclude certain .NET type members from the corresponding WMI class definition. In fact, there is a much cleaner approach based on the `System.Management.Instrumentation.IgnoreMemberAttribute` custom attribute. All type members that you decorate with this attribute will not be considered when their respective .NET type is mapped to WMI. Thus, the example above can be changed as follows:

```
[InstrumentationClass(InstrumentationType.Instance)]
public class MyManagedClass {
    [IgnoreMember]
    public string StrPropertyField;
    public string StrProperty {
        get {return StrPropertyField; }
        set {StrPropertyField = value; }
    }
    public static void Main(string[] args) {}
}
```

In fact it is a good idea to always use IgnoreMemberAttribute not only for public type members, which are to be excluded from the WMI class, but also for the private type elements. Although decorating private type members with IgnoreMemberAttribute is redundant, it does not hurt and may certainly add clarity to your code.

Normally, an instrumented .NET type is translated into a WMI class that has the same name. Thus, in the example above, MyManagedClass maps to a WMI class also called MyManagedClass. Every once in a while, you may want to create a WMI class with a different name from that of the corresponding .NET type. For instance, it is a good idea to prefix all WMI classes that belong to a particular application with some kind of schema name to provide for logical grouping. Of course, you could use the same prefix for the respective .NET application types, but it would be a bit inconvenient and just plain ugly. A better approach is to use the ManagedNameAttribute custom attribute to rename .NET types and type members while you are translating them to WMI. Consider the following example:

```
[InstrumentationClass(InstrumentationType.Instance)]
[ManagedName("MYAPP_MyManagedClass")]
public class MyManagedClass {
    [ManagedName("MYAPP_StrProp")]
    public string StrProp;
    public static void Main(string[] args) {}
}
```

Here, the MyManagedClass .NET type is exposed to WMI as MYAPP_MyManagedClass so that the schema name of MYAPP is added to the class name. At the same time, its property, StrProp, is translated into the corresponding WMI class property, MYAPP_StrProp:

```
class MYAPP_MyManagedClass {
    [key] string ProcessId;
    [key] string InstanceId;
    string MYAPP_StrProp;
};
```

Mapping .NET Type Hierarchies to WMI

Normally, all .NET types, even those that are subclasses of some other .NET types, are translated into root-level WMI classes. Consider the following example:

```
public class MyBaseClass {
    public int IntField;
}
[InstrumentationClass(InstrumentationType.Instance)]
public class MyManagedClass : MyBaseClass {
    public string StrProp;
    public static void Main(string[] args) {}
}
```

Contrary to what you may expect, MyManagedClass will be translated to WMI as follows:

```
class MyManagedClass {
    [key] string ProcessId;
    [key] string InstanceId;
    string StrProp;
};
```

As you may see, the base type MyBaseClass is ignored and the resulting WMI class definition does not include IntField, which is inherited from the superclass. An obvious remedy for this seems to be marking the base type with InstrumentationClassAttribute:

```
[InstrumentationClass(InstrumentationType.Instance)]
public class MyBaseClass {
    public int IntField;
}
```

```
[InstrumentationClass(InstrumentationType.Instance)]
public class MyManagedClass : MyBaseClass {
    public string StrProp;
    public static void Main(string[] args) {}
}
```

Unfortunately, when you attempt to install the compiled assembly, installutil.exe will produce the following error message:

```
An exception occurred during the Install phase.
System.Exception: Instance instrumentation classes must ↵
derive from abstract WMI classes.
```

It turns out that only leaf-level .NET types—types that do not have any subclasses—can publish instances to WMI. This means that applying InstrumentationClassAttribute with InstrumentationType.Instance to a base class is illegal. Somehow, the base class should be marked as abstract to indicate that it cannot expose any of its instances to WMI. You can achieve this by using another member of InstrumentationType enumeration, Abstract:

```
[InstrumentationClass(InstrumentationType.Abstract)]
public class MyBaseClass {
    public int IntField;
}
[InstrumentationClass(InstrumentationType.Instance)]
public class MyManagedClass : MyBaseClass {
    public string StrProp;
    public static void Main(string[] args) {}
}
```

Now the installation process will complete just fine and the CIM Repository will be updated with the following class definitions:

```
[abstract]
class MyBaseClass {
    sint32 IntField;
};
class MyManagedClass : MyBaseClass {
    [key] string ProcessId;
    [key] string InstanceId;
    string StrProp;
};
```

Note that the InstrumentationClassAttribute attribute is inherited by sub-classes, so if a type hierarchy includes more than two types, only the root-level type and the leaf-level type should be decorated with InstrumentationClassAttribute. To clarify this point, look at the following example:

```
[InstrumentationClass(InstrumentationType.Abstract)]
class RootLevelClass {
}
class IntermediateLevelClass : RootLevelClass {
}
[InstrumentationClass(InstrumentationType.Instance)]
class LeafLevelClass : IntermediateLevelClass {
}
```

Here, IntermediateLevelClass inherits InstrumentationClassAttribute from its parent, and therefore, it is considered abstract. The attribute, however, has to be overridden for the leaf-level type LeafLevelClass, otherwise, this type will be translated into an abstract WMI class.

Deriving from Existing WMI Classes

So far, we have discussed mapping .NET type hierarchies to WMI class hierarchies. However, what if you want to produce a WMI class that is derived from one of the existing classes that are not related to any of the instrumented application's types? For instance, how can you map an application type to a WMI class that is derived from CIM_ManagedSystemElement? This is, actually, surprisingly simple. It turns out that InstrumentationClassAttribute has an alternative constructor that not only takes the InstrumentationType parameter, but also takes a name of the existing base class. Thus, to create a WMI class MyManagedClass, which is a derivative of CIM_ManagedSystemElement, you may write the following code:

```
[InstrumentationClass(InstrumentationType.Instance, "CIM_ManagedSystemElement")]
class MyManagedElement {
}
```

Curiously, if you attempt to supply the name of a nonexistent WMI class to the constructor of InstrumentationClassAttribute, the installutil.exe will fail and produce an error message similar to the one shown earlier. Furthermore, if the name of a nonabstract WMI class such as Win32_Process is used as a parameter to the InstrumentationClassAttribute constructor, the installation will still fail with the same error message. The bottom line is that every class that supports instance instrumentation must either be a root-level class, or derive from an abstract WMI class.

There is, however, one exception to this rule. It turns out that you can define a .NET type marked with the `InstrumentationClass(InstrumentationType.Instance)` attribute as a derivative of another type that is also attributed for instance instrumentation. As the following disassembly listing demonstrates, the `System.Management.Instrumentation.Instance` type is decorated with the `InstrumentationClass(InstrumentationType.Instance)` attribute; the hexadecimal initialization string corresponds to the `InstrumentationType.Instance` enumeration member (int32 value 0x00000000):

```
.class public abstract auto ansi beforefieldinit Instance
   extends [mscorlib]System.Object
   implements System.Management.Instrumentation.IInstance {
   .custom instance void
   System.Management.Instrumentation.InstrumentationClassAttribute::.ctor(
   valuetype System.Management.Instrumentation.InstrumentationType) =
   ( 01 00 00 00 00 00 00 00 )
}
```

Nevertheless, the following compiles and passes the installation process just fine:

```
[InstrumentationClass(InstrumentationType.Instance)]
public class MyManagedElement : Instance {
   public static void Main(string[] args) {}
}
```

However, the outcome may be a bit surprising. Rather than creating two WMI classes: one that corresponds to the .NET `Instance` type, and the other as the subclass of this class, the .NET Framework updates the CIM Repository with the following class definition:

```
class MyManagedElement {
   [key] string ProcessId;
   [key] string InstanceId;
};
```

So why is this possible and how does the `Instance` type differ from all the other application types? Well, as I said before, this is a special case—the Framework simply ignores the `Instance` type when it is used as a base class. This brings up another couple of questions: what is the purpose of `Instance` and why

is it a part of the System.Management.Instrumentation namespace? As you may
remember, the InstrumentationClass attribute propagates from the base class to
its subclasses, which means that a subclass of Instance does not have to be
decorated with this attribute to indicate its ability to support instance instrumentation. Therefore, it is, possible to expose a given class for management by
simply deriving it from Instance:

```
public class MyManagedElement : Instance {
    public static void Main(string[] args) {}
}
```

Thus, the only purpose of Instance type is to provide a nice alternative to the
declarative instrumentation model, used throughout the
System.Management.Instrumentation namespace. If, for some reason, you are not
fond of custom attributes, you can always achieve the same effect by using
Instance as a base for your application types.

When modeling type hierarchies with Instance, there is again a caveat. Since
Instance is decorated with InstrumentationClass(InstrumentationType.Instance),
which propagates to its subclasses, this attribute must be explicitly overridden for
all intermediate and leaf-level types. Consider the following example:

```
[InstrumentationClass(InstrumentationType.Abstract)]
public class MyIntermediateClass1 : Instance {
}
public class MyIntermediateClass2 : MyIntermediateClass1 {
}
[InstrumentationClass(InstrumentationType.Instance)]
public class MyLeafClass : MyIntermediateClass2 {
}
```

Here, MyIntermediateClass1, which has subclasses and therefore
cannot support instance instrumentation, has to be marked with
InstrumentationClass(InstrumentationType.Abstract) to override
the InstrumentationClass(InstrumentationType.Instance) attribute inherited
from Instance. MyIntermediateClass2 is fine because it inherits
InstrumentationClass(InstrumentationType.Abstract) from its parent. Lastly,
MyLeafClass is a leaf-level type that can support instance instrumentation and,
therefore, has to be explicitly marked as such in order to override the inherited
attribute.

As you can see, using Instance to instrument single, top-level types is
straightforward. However, when it comes to type hierarchies, you still have to
resort to using attributes, which, sort of defeats the purpose of using Instance in
the first place.

Providing Instance Data to WMI

So far, I have talked about mapping .NET application types to WMI classes. Although important, having a WMI schema that reflects the instrumented types within an application by itself is not sufficient. The schema is just a skeleton, and the meat is the instance-level management data, which somehow has to be exposed to WMI. In other words, once the schema mapping is complete, there has to be a way to create instances of the application types and make them accessible to management clients just like instances of regular WMI classes.

The process of providing the instance-level data to WMI is surprisingly simple. All you have to do is create an instance of an appropriate .NET type and invoke certain helper methods to make such instances visible to management clients. The following is a complete (although fairly useless) example of creating and publishing an instance of an instrumented application type MyManagedElement:

```
using System;
using System.Management;
using System.ComponentModel;
using System.Configuration.Install;
using System.Management.Instrumentation;

[assembly:Instrumented(@"root\CIMV2")]
namespace InstrumentedApplication {
    [RunInstaller(true)]
    public class MyInstaller : DefaultManagementProjectInstaller {}

    [InstrumentationClass(InstrumentationType.Instance)]
    public class MyManagedElement {
        public string Description;
        public int    Count;
        public static void Main(string[] args) {
            MyManagedElement el = new MyManagedElement();
            el.Description = "SAMPLE INSTANCE";
            el.Count       = 256;
            Instrumentation.Publish(el);
            Console.ReadLine();
            Instrumentation.Revoke(el);
        }
    }
}
```

When this code is complied and run, a console window will pop up and wait for the user input. The program will terminate whenever any key is pressed. For the duration of this code's run, the CIM Repository will contain a single instance of MyManagedElement class, which, when expressed in MOF, will look similar to the following:

```
instance of MyManagedElement {
    Count = 256;
    Description = "SAMPLE INSTANCE";
    InstanceId = "3839";
    ProcessId = "3c702745-c84b-11d6-9159-000255f41c79";
};
```

As you can see, the Count and Description properties of this instance reflect the initialization values for their respective .NET fields. Two other mysterious properties—InstanceID and ProcessID—represent the unique identifier for the newly created instance and the process identity of the running .NET application respectively. The InstanceID is just a sequence number that is incremented automatically for each published instance. The ProcessID, contrary to what you may think, has nothing to do with OS process ID (PID) of the running program. It is just a GUID generated once per process so that it guarantees the uniqueness of a particular application's session in time and space. The choice of GUIDs vs. conventional PIDs is obvious: PIDs are recycled by the operating system and may, therefore, cause collisions. The .NET Framework automatically adds these two properties to any WMI class that represents a .NET type and automatically assigns the appropriate values when an instance is published. This is done to ensure that any instance created by a .NET application always has a unique identifier; as you may remember, these two properties are marked with the Key qualifier within the WMI class definition.

The code used to publish the instance of a .NET type is remarkably simple. In fact, there are only two lines that may look somewhat new: calls to Publish and Revoke methods of the helper type Instrumentation. As its name implies, Publish takes an instance of a .NET type as a parameter and makes it visible through WMI. Once published, the instance remains accessible to WMI clients until the application exits or the Revoke method is called. Revoke is the opposite of Publish; it essentially erases all traces of a given instance from the CIM Repository. If an instance is to remain visible for the entire lifetime of the application, calling Revoke is optional—the .NET Framework cleans up after itself automatically when an application shuts down.

When you are managing multiple instances, sometimes you may want to keep track of which of these instances are published. Generally, the .NET Framework is

very good about ensuring that a given instance is not duplicated in the CIM
Repository. Even if you invoke `Publish` on a particular instance more than once, all
but the first invocation will have no effect and the CIM Repository will only contain
a single version of the instance. Nevertheless, to avoid confusion and application
errors, it might be a good idea to somehow record that a particular instance has
been exposed to WMI. To do so, you can add a Boolean flag to your instances and
set it to TRUE every time an instance is published, but unfortunately, it is easy to
make a mistake that may eventually wreak havoc on your application. This is
where subclassing `System.Management.Instrumentation.Instance` rather than
using custom attributes may prove to be advantageous. All subclasses of `Instance`
will automatically inherit its `Published` property, which is set to TRUE by the .NET
Framework as soon as the instance is published, and updated back to FALSE whenever the Revoke is called on this instance. Consider the following code:

```
using System;
using System.Management;
using System.ComponentModel;
using System.Configuration.Install;
using System.Management.Instrumentation;

[assembly:Instrumented(@"root\CIMV2")]
namespace InstrumentedApplication {
    [RunInstaller(true)]
    public class MyInstaller : DefaultManagementProjectInstaller {}

public class MyManagedElement : Instance {
        public string Description;
        public int     Count;
        public static void Main(string[] args) {
            MyManagedElement el = new MyManagedElement();
            el.Description = "SAMPLE INSTANCE";
            el.Count       = 256;
            Instrumentation.Publish(el);
            Console.WriteLine( "Instance published (true/false): {0}", el.Published);
            Console.ReadLine();
            Instrumentation.Revoke(el);
            Console.WriteLine( "Instance published (true/false): {0}", el.Published);
        }
    }
}
```

Upon its invocation, this code will print the following message on the console:

```
Instance published (true/false): True
```

Once a key is pressed, the program will terminate and print another message:

```
Instance published (true/false): False
```

Exposing Management Events

Although exposing the application's data for management through WMI is invaluable, being able to send out notifications when some application-specific events occur is even more important. Thus, you may rightly expect the System.Management.Instrumentation namespace to provide extensive functionality in support of management events. This is indeed the case, and armed with .NET instrumentation types, you can easily outfit your applications with full-fledged event notification capabilities.

Generating management events is as easy (if not easier) as supporting instance instrumentation. Working in concert with the principles of the declarative instrumentation model, you can simply mark the application types with the appropriate attributes and then use helper methods to route the notifications to WMI. For instance the following snippet of code, creates the application-defined event and sends it to the consumers:

```
using System;
using System.Management;
using System.ComponentModel;
using System.Configuration.Install;
using System.Management.Instrumentation;

[assembly:Instrumented(@"root\CIMV2")]
namespace InstrumentedApplication {
    [RunInstaller(true)]
    public class MyInstaller : DefaultManagementProjectInstaller {}

[InstrumentationClass(InstrumentationType.Event)]
public class MyManagementEvent {
        public string Description;
        public int     EventNo;
```

```
public static void Main(string[] args) {
    MyManagementEvent ev = new MyManagementEvent();
    ev.Description      = "SAMPLE MANAGEMENT EVENT";
    ev.EventNo          = 256;
    Instrumentation.Fire(ev);
    Console.ReadLine();
  }
 }
}
```

This code has a lot in common with the previous code fragment that was used to supply instance-level data to WMI. The first noticeable difference is the InstrumentationType enumeration member that is passed to the constructor of the InstrumentationClass attribute, which decorates MyManagementEvent type. To indicate that a certain application type represents a management event, such a type must be marked with InstrumentationClass(InstrumentationType.Event) attribute.

If you save this code to a file and then compile and install it using installutil.exe, the CIM Repository will contain the following definition for the application event class:

```
class MyManagementEvent : __ExtrinsicEvent {
    string Description;
    sint32 EventNo;
};
```

The first thing to notice here is that the event class is derived from the system class __ExtrinsicEvent. This is logical because all application event classes are, indeed extrinsic events. Although it is certainly possible to create application-specific event hierarchies by building the respective hierarchies of .NET types, the top-level class of the resulting WMI event tree will always be __ExtrinsicEvent.

Another aspect of this generated event class definition that makes it different from the previously shown WMI classes that were generated in support of instance instrumentation is the absence of the ProcessID and InstanceID properties. Since WMI events are transient, they do not have to be stored in the CIM Repository, and therefore, they do not need unique identities.

The process of routing an application event to a consumer is also very similar to publishing an instance. The difference here is that rather than using the Publish method of the Instrumentation helper type, you must use the Fire method that belongs to the same type. Just like Publish, Fire takes a single parameter—an object that represents an application event to be sent to the consumers. Note that a call to Fire does not have to be followed by a call to Revoke; the events are transient and do not have to be unpublished.

Similar to the Instance type, which can be used as a superclass for management types, this process uses a BaseEvent type that is designed as a top-level type for modeling events. Subclassing BaseEvent is a nice alternative to decorating the event types with the InstrumentationClass(InstrumentationType.Event) attribute—the base type is already marked with this attribute, which propagates down to its children. Thus, the code example shown earlier can be rewritten as follows:

```
using System;
using System.Management;
using System.ComponentModel;
using System.Configuration.Install;
using System.Management.Instrumentation;

[assembly:Instrumented(@"root\CIMV2")]
namespace InstrumentedApplication {
    [RunInstaller(true)]
    public class MyInstaller : DefaultManagementProjectInstaller {}

public class MyManagementEvent : BaseEvent {
    public string Description;
    public int     EventNo;
    public static void Main(string[] args) {
        MyManagementEvent ev = new MyManagementEvent();
        ev.Description       = "SAMPLE MANAGEMENT EVENT";
        ev.EventNo           = 256;
        ev.Fire();
        Console.ReadLine();
    }
}
}
```

The effect of this code is exactly the same as that of the earlier code and the generated WMI definition for the event class remains unchanged. The only substantial difference here is that to fire an event that is a subclass of BaseEvent, you no longer need to use Instrumentation.Fire method. Instead, you can use the Fire method inherited from BaseEvent.

Using BaseEvent as a base type is especially convenient when it comes to modeling complex event hierarchies. Consider the following:

```
public class MyTopLevelEvent : BaseEvent {
};
public class MyIntermediateLevelEvent : MyTopLevelEvent {
};
public class MyLeafLevelEvent : MyIntermediateLevelEvent {
};
```

Since `BaseEvent` is marked with the
`InstrumentationClass(InstrumentationType.Event)` attribute, which is applicable to all of its children, the attribute does not have to be overridden anywhere within the type hierarchy. By the same token, when you are using the declarative approach, you only have to apply the attribute to the top-level type:

```
[InstrumentationClass(InstrumentationType.Event)]
public class MyTopLevelEvent {
};
public class MyIntermediateLevelEvent : MyTopLevelEvent {
};
public class MyLeafLevelEvent : MyIntermediateLevelEvent {
};
```

This makes modeling event hierarchies a bit less complex than building instance inheritance trees, which is a big help, considering that event hierarchies often come in handy. The apparent value of having all application events be subclasses of a common base event type comes from the ability to issue catch-all event queries against the root-level event class. Thus, given the event tree, shown earlier, you may write the following query to subscribe to all three of the events, `MyTopLevelEvent`, `MyIndermediateLevelEvent`, and `MyLeafLevelEvent`:

```
SELECT * FROM MyTopLevelEvent
```

By issuing such a generalized event query, you ask an application to instruct WMI to route to it not only the events that belong to the class that is specified in the query, but also all other events that are the subclasses of that class.

Summary

Instrumenting applications is a notoriously complex task that many developers and system administrators have been dreading for years. Fortunately, even the first release of FCL and the `System.Management.Instrumentation` namespace has made a significant number of the challenges commonly associated with exposing custom programs for management simply go away. Nowadays, it is possible to publish the management data and distribute management events through WMI with minimal coding effort.

This chapter has been a comprehensive introduction to the subject of instrumenting .NET applications with `System.Management.Instrumentation` types. Although, the scope of this book does not allow me to delve deeper into the guts of the .NET instrumentation framework, after having read the material presented here, you should be at least aware of

- The fundamentals and mechanics of the WMI provider framework

- The basics of publishing a .NET application's schema to the CIM Repository

- The techniques you can use to expose an application's data and events for management using either the declarative model or the base types that are provided as part of `System.Management.Instrumentation` namespace

Although extremely helpful, the `System.Management.Instrumentation` namespace is not perfect. There are no major issues and it is fair to say that Microsoft developers did a great job, especially considering that this is the first release of the .NET Framework. Nevertheless, there are a few things that need improvement:

The schema publishing and installation facilities, although very robust and easy to use, do not provide a way to easily uninstall the schema once it is registered in the CIM Repository. In fact, running installutil.exe with the /u switch does not seem to do anything useful. This means that all the application's class definitions and provider registration information have to be removed from the CIM Repository manually.

Certain aspects of WMI class modeling cannot be represented through their respective .NET types. For instance, due to the lack of support for reference data types, it is impossible to model the association classes. Yet, another deficiency is the lack of support for defining the default values for class properties, since the .NET field initializers are simply ignored by the .NET Framework. Finally, there is no support for building method providers. Although, some people may consider the ability to invoke an application's methods through WMI an unnecessary luxury, methods often come in handy and may, on occasion, streamline the process of designing an instrumentation model for a particular application.

The auto-generated key object properties, `ProcessID` and `InstanceID`, make for a very poor instance identification scheme. Since the values for these properties are system-generated rather than application-supplied, retrieving an instance based on the values of its key properties is virtually impossible. Thus, in most cases, the only way to retrieve an instance of a WMI class that is backed by a .NET application is by using complex WQL queries, which are bound to cause substantial performance degradation. Moreover, such an auto-generated identity is contradictory to one of the most basic principles of CIM modeling—using natural object keys. It is conceivable that handing excessive control over the process of generating object identities out to developers is dangerous and may result in CIM Repository corruption. Nevertheless, there has to be a reasonable compromise to allow for easier and faster object lookup.

Although `System.Management.Instrumentation` custom attributes are extremely simple and easy to use, they may not always provide the necessary degree of control over the generated WMI class definitions. For instance, it is impossible to directly assign certain qualifiers to the generated WMI classes and class properties. While fairly minor, this restriction may seriously complicate the development of some management functionality, and it may make the existing management applications unusable for managing the classes and instances that are backed by .NET applications.

Despite all the deficiencies, `System.Management.Instrumentation` is still a great framework for instrumenting custom applications. Its most attractive characteristic is simplicity and, even if it does not satisfy all your instrumentation needs, it is still a big step forward. Again, its goal is to bring the joy of instrumenting .NET applications to a wider audience and it is fair to say that it achieves this.

Of course, there will always be people reaching out for more control or flexibility, or there will be those who try to cater to a unique management situation, not covered by the `System.Management.Instrumentation` framework. Hopefully, such people will represent just a small percentage of the developers and system administrators, but even for them, .NET has something to offer.

In fact, Visual Studio .NET offers two new ATL wizards to make the conventional COM-based provider development more accessible: the WMI Event Provider Wizard and the WMI Instance Provider Wizard. These wizards generate most of the code required to get a full-fledged event, instance, or method provider up and operational in a reasonably short time with minimal coding efforts. Unfortunately, digging into the practical aspects of these wizards is well beyond the scope of this book, so the adventurous reader will have to resort to Visual Studio .NET documentation.

CHAPTER 6

The WMI Schema

STRICTLY SPEAKING, THE **WMI** schema is a logical grouping of classes and instances that constitute a particular managed environment. Thus, the WMI SDK comes, equipped with two schemas: the CIM schema and the Win32 schema. The former includes class and instance definitions for those managed entities that are common to all managed environments regardless of the underlying hardware and OS platform. As you may remember from Chapter 1, the CIM schema essentially covers two layers of CIM model: the core model and the common model. The Win32 schema contains classes and instances specific to Win32 environments; and, in CIM parlance, is said to be an extension model schema.

Extension schemas are the cornerstones of the WMI extensibility model. In fact, the only two things that are necessary to make WMI aware of vendor-specific extensions to a managed environment are an appropriate extension schema, which describes custom managed entities, and a provider, which is responsible for handling the underlying management data. Thus, there is a very clear parallel between the WMI schema and COM interface definitions. Both schemas and component interface specifications describe the capabilities of a particular component, or, in case of WMI, a provider. Both essentially represent a contract that a particular component or provider agrees to fulfill on behalf of its clients. Finally, the process of extending WMI is very similar to that of building a COM server—the first step always involves designing the interface or, in other words, devising the schema.

Contrary to what you may expect, this chapter is not about the extension schemas. It is about the schema in general. As opposed to the formal definition of the term "schema," I tend to use it to refer not to a particular set of WMI classes and instances, but rather to a general mechanism for defining the properties of an arbitrarily managed environment. Just like any serious COM developer must be ultimately familiar with the Interface Definition Language (IDL), anyone planning to become a WMI guru must thoroughly understand the WMI schema and have a working knowledge of the tools and facilities used to manage the schema elements. It is, therefore, a goal of this chapter to acquaint you with the Managed Object Format (MOF) Schema Definition Language that is used to describe the schema elements; to provide an overview of the schema management facilities that are available through the .NET System.Management namespace; and, finally, to discuss some of the alternate schema definitions and management techniques, such as XML representation for management information and the XML encoder component.

Managed Object Format Basics

The CIM specification prescribes that any management information be described in the Managed Object Format (MOF) language. MOF is a derivative of Interface Definition Language (IDL), and as such, it utilizes essentially the same syntactic structure. Just like IDL, MOF is declarative rather than procedural—its primary purpose is to define classes and instances, which represent the managed entities. Therefore, it is not possible to produce any executable code with MOF; the language simply does not include any syntactic elements that support procedural coding.

Compiling MOF

MOF is a compiled language. Typically, MOF class and instance definitions are saved in a text file subsequently processed by a MOF Compiler. The compiler parses the MOF file and adds the appropriate classes and objects to a CIM Repository. MOF definitions that make up such MOF file can be encoded in either Unicode or UTF-8. To avoid localization-related problems, all MOF files distributed with WMI are encoded in Unicode. In fact, it is encouraged that Unicode be used at all times for all MOF definitions.

The first two bytes of a Unicode MOF file must contain a valid signature of either U+FFFE or U+FEFF; these identify the byte ordering of a file as little- or big-endian respectively. All keywords and punctuation symbols used within MOF definitions are not locale-specific and must fall into the Unicode character range of U+0000 to U+007F. The identifiers, such as namespace, class, and property names must either start with an alphabetic character or an underscore (these must be the Unicode values of U+005F, U+0041 to U+005A, U+0061 to U+007A, U+0080 to U+FFEF). All the following characters of the identifier must be alphabetic characters, Arabic numerals (0 through 9), or underscores (previous set of Unicode ranges plus U+0030 to U+0039). All nonidentifier string values must be surrounded with the delimiter Unicode character U+0027 (double quote), and the characters within the quotation marks (U+0027) may fall into the Unicode character range of U+0001 to U+FFEF.

All these encoding rules may sound terribly complicated at first, but luckily, most Windows tools have built-in Unicode support. Thus even the ultra-popular notepad.exe has the appropriate provisions for creating and editing Unicode files in a manner that is nearly transparent to the user. However, if for some sentimental reason you insist on using an ASCII-based text editor you still will not have a problem. The MOF Compiler utility mofcomp.exe, which ships as part of WMI SDK, is perfectly capable of processing plain ASCII files just as well as Unicode files.

mofcomp.exe is designed to run manually from the command line so that the name of the MOF file to be compiled is passed as a parameter. Thus, the following command will compile and install the regevent.mof file, which contains the definitions for all the classes and instances required by the Registry Provider:

```
mofcomp.exe  C:\WINNT\SYSTEM32\WBEM\regevent.mof
```

The operation of the mofcomp.exe can be controlled via a number of command-line switches; these are listed in Table 6-1.

Table 6-1. mofcomp.exe Command-Line Switches

COMMAND-LINE SWITCH	DESCRIPTION
-autorecover	Instructs mofcomp.exe to add the file to the list of files automatically compiled during the repository recovery.
-check	Instructs mofcomp.exe to perform a syntax check only and print out the appropriate error messages. This switch cannot be used in combination with any other command-line option.
-N:<namespacepath>	Instructs the compiler to load the contents of the file into a namespace specified by the parameter. By default, the contents of an arbitrary MOF file are loaded into the root\default namespace, unless instructed otherwise by either the command-line switch or the #pragma namespace directive contained in the MOF file. If both the command-line switch and the #pragma namespace are specified, the latter takes precedence.
-class:createonly	Instructs the compiler not to make any changes to classes that already exist in the CIM Repository. The compilation terminates when it encounters a class that already exists in the repository.
-class:forceupdate	Instructs mofcomp.exe to proceed with updating a class when conflicting child classes exist. If, for instance, a base class tries to add a qualifier that already exists on one of its child classes, the compiler resolves the conflict by removing the child class qualifier. Such an update only succeeds if a child class has no instances.

(continued)

Table 6-1. mofcomp.exe Command-Line Switches (continued)

COMMAND-LINE SWITCH	DESCRIPTION
-class:safeupdate	Allows for updates of base classes that have child classes as long as there are no conflicts. For instance, this option will permit the compiler to add a new property to a base class even though there are existing child classes. Such an update only succeeds if a child class has no instances.
-class:updateonly	Instructs mofcomp.exe not to create any new classes. If this flag is specified, compilation terminates when the compiler encounters a class that does not already exist in the CIM Repository.
-instance:updateonly	Requests that the compiler not create any new instances. If this flag is specified, compilation terminates when the compiler encounters an instance that does not already exist in the CIM Repository.
-instance:createonly	Instructs the compiler not to make any changes to existing instances. If this flag is specified, compilation terminates when the compiler encounters an instance that already exists in the CIM Repository.
-B:<filename>	Instructs mofcomp.exe to create a binary version of the MOF file and save it into a file identified by the filename parameter. When this flag is specified, no changes are made to the CIM Repository.
-WMI	Instructs the compiler to perform a WMI syntax check when it is building binary MOF files for use by WDM device drivers. This switch must be used together with the -B switch. When the -WMI switch is supplied, mofcomp.exe invokes a separate binary MOF file checker after the binary version of MOF file is generated.
-U:<user>	Specifies the name of the user to use when logging on to WMI.
-P:<password>	Specifies the password to use when logging on to WMI.
-A:<authority>	Specifies the domain name to use when logging on to WMI.

(continued)

Table 6-1. mofcomp.exe Command-Line Switches (continued)

COMMAND-LINE SWITCH	DESCRIPTION
-AMENDMENT:<locale>	Instructs the compiler to split the MOF file into language-neutral and language-specific versions. The language-neutral version has all MOF definitions with all localized qualifiers removed. The localized version, which is saved into a separate file with the MFL extension, contains the class definitions localized for the locale, which is identified by the locale parameter. The locale parameter is a hexadecimal string that represents the Windows LCID. For more information on WMI Localization, see Chapter 2.
-MOF:<filename>	This switch is used together with the -AMENDMENT switch and specifies the name of the MOF file that will contain language-neutral MOF definitions.
-MFL:<filename>	This switch is used together with the -AMENDMENT switch and specifies the name of the MOF file that will contain locale-specific MOF definitions.

The first phase of the MOF compilation is a syntax check. If any syntax errors are encountered, the compiler prints an error message on the console and terminates the compilation. To indicate the success or failure of a compilation when used in batch files, mofcomp.exe produces an exit code; the possible exit codes are shown in Table 6-2.

Table 6-2. mofcomp.exe Exit Codes

EXIT CODE	DESCRIPTION
0	Successful compilation.
1	Compiler is unable to connect to WMI. This may be because the version of mofcomp.exe and the version of the CIM Repository are not compatible. The same exit code will also be produced if the WMI service is not running.
2	Usage error. Indicates that mofcomp.exe has been invoked with command-line arguments that are not valid.
3	A MOF syntax error has been detected.

There are cases when a MOF file parses correctly, but some of the repository updates, warranted by the MOF code, conflict with command-line arguments passed to mofcomp.exe. For instance, if the repository already contains the classes and instances that are generated as a result of a compilation of regevent.mof mentioned earlier, attempting to invoke a compiler for this file with the -class:createonly switch will result in error. Let us see how this works:

```
mofcomp.exe -class:createonly C:\WINNT\SYSTEM32\WBEM\regevent.mof
```

The command above will produce the following message on the console:

```
Parsing MOF file: C:\winnt\system32\wbem\regevent.mof
MOF file has been successfully parsed
Storing data in the repository...
An error occurred while processing item 1 defined on lines 4 - 6 in file
C:\winnt\system32\wbem\regevent.mof:
Error Number: 0x80041019, Facility: WMI, Description: Object or property already
 exists
Compiler returned error 0x80041001
```

Contrary to what you may expect, the exit code produced by the compiler will not fall into the range of values listed in Table 6-2. Instead, a WMI error code will be returned. In this particular case, mofcomp.exe will output the exit code of 0x80041001 (WBEM_E_FAILED).

The compiler has no built-in rollback capabilities. If a compilation aborts for whatever reason, the repository may be left in an undefined state. Thus, in the example above, any classes or instances defined in the MOF file prior to the point where the compiler detected a conflict would be created and stored in the repository. In such case, the repository may have to be rebuilt from scratch. To accomplish this, the WMI service (winmgmt.exe) has to be stopped and then run manually to restore the Repository from the latest backup file:

```
winmgmt.exe /restore backup.rep
```

Note that those MOF files, which were loaded after the last backup was taken, might not be restored correctly. As you may remember, only the files on the autorecover list are automatically recompiled whenever the repository is rebuilt. To place a file on the autorecover list, either invoke mofcomp.exe with the -autorecover switch, or specify #pragma autorecover in the MOF file itself.

As a convenient alternative to command-line compilation, there is a graphical MOF Compiler wizard that is accessible through the CIM Studio. This simple tool, shown in Figure 6-1, can be used to specify the compilation options in a hassle-free fashion, so you do not have to remember the usage syntax of the command-line utility.

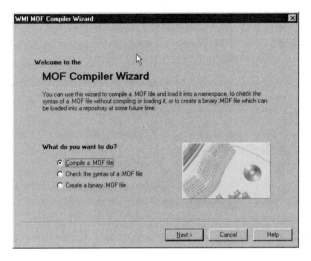

Figure 6-1. MOF Compiler Wizard

The MOF Compiler Wizard is not a separate compiler but rather a graphical interface to the same command-line mofcomp.exe.

MOF Intrinsic Data Types

Just like IDL, MOF offers a wide range of intrinsic data types for defining the properties of managed classes and instances. Table 6-3 contains a complete list of these data types.

Table 6-3. MOF Intrinsic Data Types

DATA TYPE	DESCRIPTION
uint8	Unsigned 8-bit integer.
sint8	Signed 8-bit integer.
uint16	Unsigned 16-bit integer.
sint16	Signed 16-bit integer.
uint32	Unsigned 32-bit integer.
sint32	Signed 32-bit integer.
uint64	Unsigned 64-bit integer, encoded as string that is compliant with ANSI C decimal/hexadecimal number encoding format.
sint64	Signed 64-bit integer, encoded as string that is compliant with ANSI C decimal/hexadecimal number encoding format.

(continued)

Table 6-3. MOF Intrinsic Data Types (continued)

DATA TYPE	DESCRIPTION
real32	IEEE 4-byte floating-point number.
real64	IEEE 8-byte floating-point number.
boolean	Boolean logical TRUE or FALSE value.
char16	Single 16-bit Unicode character in Universal Character Set-2 (UCS-2) format.
string	Unicode character string.
datetime	Fixed length date-time string that is compliant with the DMTF date/time format. Example: yyyymmddhhmmss.mmmmmmsutc where: yyyy—4-digit year mm—2-digit month dd—2-digit day hh—2-digit hour (24-hour clock) mm—2-digit minute ss—2-digit second mmmmmm—6-digit number of milliseconds s—+ or – sign of the offset from the Universal Time Coordinates (UTC) utc—Offset from UTC in minutes
void	Used in method declarations to indicate that a method has no return value. Cannot be used for property declarations.

Additional type semantics can be expressed via qualifiers. Thus, rather than treating the popular management types such as Gauge and Counter as separate intrinsic types, the MOF specification prescribes that the type usage be expressed via appropriate qualifiers at a time of property declaration:

```
class TypeSemanticsExample {
   [counter]
   uint32 SamlpeCounter;
   [gauge]
   uint32 SampleGauge;
};
```

This approach is very logical because both Gauge and Counter are just simple unsigned integers with clearly defined semantic properties.

MOF Embedded Objects

In certain cases, instances of management classes can be contained within other objects. Such contained objects are often referred to as *embedded objects.* MOF syntax fully supports declarations of embedded classes and instances.

Class properties, referring to embedded objects, can be declared as strongly or weakly typed. A property that references an embedded object in a strongly typed fashion has a data type that corresponds to the class that is being referred to:

```
class InnerClass {
    uint32 prop1;
    uint32 prop2;
};
class OuterClass {
    InnerClass embedProp1;
    InnerClass embedProp2;
};
```

Here, the properties `embedProp1` and `embedProp2` of class `OuterClass` reference the embedded objects of type `InnerClass`.

A weakly typed embedded object is declared using the `object` keyword in place of the class name:

```
class OuterClass {
    object embedProp1;
    object embedProp2;
};
```

Here, the properties `embedProp1` and `embedProp2` of class `OuterClass` refer to an embedded object of an unspecified class.

Note that at the time of this writing, MOF does not support embedding objects within other embedded objects. In other words, only one level of embedding is allowed.

MOF References

Those interobject relationships that do not fall into the category of containment are expressed in MOF using the `ref` data type. A property of the `ref` data type essentially contains a string that represents an *object path*—a symbolic or "soft" reference to an object that exists independently somewhere in the CIM Repository (see Chapter 1 for an exhaustive explanation of object path syntax).

In fact, this is how all WMI association classes are implemented. As you may remember, an association object represents a link between two arbitrary instances of WMI classes. Thus, an association class would typically contain at least two properties, each of an appropriate `ref` data type, so that each property references a single WMI object.

Just as it is the case with embedded objects, MOF supports strongly and weakly typed references. A strongly typed reference points to an object of a specific class, which in MOF syntax is expressed via a combination of the `ref` keyword and an appropriate class name. Thus, to declare a class property as a reference to class Foo (assuming that such class Foo exists) you may use the following MOF code:

```
class Bar {
    // refClassFoo is a strongly typed reference
    Foo ref refClassFoo;
    ...
};
```

A weakly typed reference points to an object of an unspecified class. In MOF, this is expressed via a combination of the `ref` and `object` keywords. For example, the following code declares a class property as a weak reference, which may point to an object of any class:

```
class Bar {
    // refAnyClass is a weakly typed reference
    object ref refAnyClass;
    ...
};
```

Very often, especially when it comes to defining association classes, properties of reference type act as object keys. In such case, WMI uses the string value of the reference property rather than the contents of the referenced object to identify an instance.

MOF Arrays

In addition to the intrinsic data types, embedded object types, and references, MOF syntax supports different types of arrays. An array can be declared using notation similar to that of ANSI C—square brackets following the property identifier. An array can be of fixed or variable length. Fixed-length arrays are identified by an unsigned integer constant within the square brackets that represents the total length of the array. If the length specification is omitted, an array is assumed to be of variable length:

```
uint32[10] Array1; // 10-element uint32 array
uint32[]   Array2; // variable-length uint32 array
```

The current CIM standard supports only one-dimensional arrays, although it is possible that support for n-dimensional array types will be added in the near future.

Semantically, arrays can act as bags and ordered or indexed lists. The array type is designated by the ARRAYTYPE qualifier, which may take the values of Bag, Ordered, or Indexed to indicate the respective semantics of the array. In case the ARRAYTYPE qualifier is omitted, an array is considered to be of type Bag—an unordered list of values that allows duplicates. By definition, the order of elements is not defined for a bag-type array, meaning that accessing such an array twice with the same index may not yield the same element. By the same token, there is no guarantee that the array elements will always be returned in the same order when iterating through the array.

An ordered list array is really just a special case of a bag. It also allows for duplicate values, but, unlike the bag, it preserves the order of elements. Thus, if no elements are added or deleted, an array access through the same index will always yield the same element. The same applies to iterating through an array—elements are always returned in the same order.

Finally, an indexed array always maintains a correlation between individual element values and their positions so that accessing an array via an index or iterating through it will always yield the same elements in the same order. Elements of an indexed array can be overwritten but cannot be deleted.

The following code snippet illustrates how different types of arrays are declared using the ARRAYTYPE attribute:

```
class ArrayExample {
    // Bag array - implicit declaration
    uint32 BagArray1[];
    // Another bag array - explicit declaration
    [ArrayType("Bag")] uint32 BagArray2[];
    // Ordered list array
    [ArrayType("Ordered")] uint32 OrderedArray[];
    // Indexed Array
    [ArrayType("Indexed")] uint32 IndexedArray[];
};
```

Curiously, the CIM Documentation states that only the arrays of basic types are valid. WMI, however, supports arrays of embedded objects and references just fine. Thus, the following MOF code should compile without any problems:

```
class ComplexArrayExample {
    // Array of references
    object ref RefArray[];
    // Array of embedded objects of class Foo
    Foo EmbedObjArray[];
};
```

The only tricky thing about reference and object arrays is providing the default initialization values. Ordinarily, an array of basic types can be initialized as follows:

```
// initialized uint32 array
uint32 IntArray[] = {1,2,3,4,5,6,7,8,9,10};
// initialized string array
string StringArray[] = {"first", "second", "third"};
```

Here the initialization is accomplished by supplying a list of integral values within the curly brackets as part of the array declaration. The problem with object and reference types, however, is that it is unclear how to represent instances of such types within the initialization list. As you may remember, references are really just strings that represent the appropriate object paths. Therefore, an arbitrary array of references to objects of type Win32_Process, can be initialized as follows:

```
Win32_Process ref RefArray[] = {
    "Win32_Process.Handle=100", "Win32_Process.Handle=101"};
```

Here, the initialization list contains a sequence of quoted object path strings that refer to valid instances of the Win32_Process class.

The situation is similar with embedded object arrays, although the initialization syntax is just a bit more complex. Since objects are not strings and cannot really be represented as strings, a special keyword, instance of, has to be used to convert an arbitrary object path into an appropriate object. Thus, the following code initializes an array of embedded Win32_Process objects:

```
#pragma namespace("\\\\.\\Root\\CIMV2")
...
Win32_Process EmbedObjArray[] = {
    instance of Win32_Process{Handle="100";},
```

```
    instance of Win32_Process{Handle="101";}
};
```

Be careful when you are supplying default initialization values for arrays of embedded objects. Since references to objects used as initialization values are resolved at the time of compilation, these instances have to be accessible from the namespace into which a given MOF code is being compiled. In the preceding example, because Win32_Process objects used to initialize the array reside in the root\CIMV2 namespace, the pragma namespace compiler directive is added to ensure that the code is compiled into the same namespace.

Although MOF arrays are homogeneous and cannot contain elements of different types at the same time, it is entirely valid to construct an array of objects that belong to completely unrelated classes. To achieve this, an array has to be declared of type object:

```
object ObjArray[] = {
    instance of Win32_Process{Handle="100";},
    instance of Win32_Service{Name="WinMgmt";}
};
```

Similarly, if an array is declared to be of a specific type, it may contain objects that belong not only to this class, but also to any of its subclasses. Thus, an array of CIM_Service objects may house instances of Win32_Service and Win32_SystemDriver, as shown here:

```
CIM_Service ObjArray[] = {
    instance of Win32_SystemDriver{Name="atapi";},
    instance of Win32_Service{Name="WinMgmt";}
};
```

Class Declarations

A management class can be declared using the MOF class keyword followed by the name of the class and an optional list of properties and methods enclosed in curly brackets. Thus, the most basic class declaration may look like the following:

```
class SimpleClass {
};
```

The name of the class is case-insensitive and must start with a letter. The rest of the class name may be composed of letters, digits, and underscores. Note that no leading or trailing underscores are allowed, although embedded underscores are used quite often. It is, in fact, a common practice to compose a class identifier from two components—the name of the schema, which the class belongs to, and the actual class name—separated by an underscore.

The CIM model relies heavily on class inheritance and it is conceivable that a typical extension schema would also enforce some kind of hierarchical structure by deriving specialized classes from common ancestors. Declaring a derived class in MOF is extremely easy; you just define a subclass by including the name of a base class, preceded by a colon, immediately following the class name:

```
class MyManagedElement : CIM_ManagedSystemElement {
};
```

Here a new class `MyManagedElement` is declared as a subclass of `CIM_ManagedSystemElement`. Note that a class, used as a base, must either be already registered in the namespace where the derived class is being defined, or it must precede the declaration of the derived class in the same MOF file.

Class definitions may optionally contain property and method declarations. A property declaration consists of a data type, a property identifier, and an optional default value, followed by a semicolon. As discussed above, array property declarations must include square brackets and an optional array size designation as part of the property identifier. The rules for choosing the property identifiers are the same as those for class names—an identifier is case insensitive and must start with a letter, followed by any number of letters, digits, and underscores. The following code snippet illustrates how class properties are defined:

```
class PropertyDeclarationExample {
    uint32 IntProperty;   // uint32 property
    string StrProperty;   // string property
    uint32 ArrProperty[]; // variable-length array property
};
```

A property may optionally be assigned a default initialization value. To assign a property of basic type a default value, simply follow the property identifier with an equal sign and the appropriate representation of the value:

```
// default uint32 value
uint32 IntProperty = 128;
// default string value
string StrProperty = "STRING";
// default boolean value
boolean BoolProperty = true;
```

```
// default object value
object ObjProperty = instance of Win32_Process{Handle=100;};
// default reference value
object ref RefProperty = "Win32_Process.Handle=100";
```

As discussed earlier, setting the default value for array properties requires specialized syntax:

```
string ArrProperty[] = {"ONE", "TWO", "THREE"};
```

Whenever a class is instantiated, its properties are automatically assigned the appropriate default values, unless the instance declaration explicitly overrides the default value specification. Instance declarations will be covered in the "Instance Declarations" section later in this chapter.

Besides properties, a class definition may include method declarations. A method declaration consists of a method identifier, a return type, and a possibly empty parameter list enclosed in parentheses. Both the return type and the method parameters can be of any basic MOF data type, although arrays constitute an exception. Although it is entirely legal to use an array as a method parameter, declaring a method that returns an array is not supported. Thus, a method return type should always be one of the integral, non-array data types. If a method does not return a value, a special keyword, void, can be used as the return type.

The following MOF code is an example of method declaration:

```
// parameterized method returning uint32
uint32 Method1(uint32 parm1, string parm2);
// parameterless method not returning a value
void Method2();
```

Although the preceding declaration fails to do so, all method parameters must be marked as either input or output using the In or Out qualifiers. Thus, the declaration for Method1 should be rewritten as follows:

```
uint32 Method1([In]uint32 parm1, [Out]string parm2);
```

Here, parm1 is designated as input and parm2 is designated as output. In certain cases, a parameter may act as both input and output. As the following example shows, this can be achieved in a couple of different ways:

```
uint32 Method1([In,Out]uint32 parm1);
uint32 Method2([In]uint32 parm1, [Out]uint32 parm1);
```

The declaration for `Method1` is fairly self-explanatory—a parameter is simply marked with both `In` and `Out` qualifiers to designate it as input/output. `Method2`, however, is a bit trickier. Here, the same parameter `parm1` is listed twice: once with the `In` qualifier and once with `Out`. This does not mean that the method has two parameters: it just indicates that `parm1` is used for both input and output. Note that if separate input and output declarations for a single parameter are used, all aspects of such declarations must match exactly, including the identifier, data type, and number and type of all other qualifiers. The other requirement is that the `ID` qualifier is explicitly supplied for both input and output declarations. Normally, the `ID` qualifier, which is used to uniquely identify each parameter's position within the method parameter list, is automatically assigned by the compiler. However, when you are using separate input and output parameter declaration, it is your responsibility to mark the parameters appropriately. For instance, you would rewrite the declaration for `Method2` shown in the preceding code snippet as follows:

```
uint32 Method2([In, ID(0)]uint32 parm1, [Out, ID(0)]uint32 parm1);
```

Here the `ID` qualifier with the value of zero (first parameter) is explicitly added to both input and output parameter definitions, stating that the same parameter is being defined in both cases.

Instance Declarations

An instance of a class is declared using the `instance of` keyword followed by the name of the class, curly brackets that enclose an optional list of property value assignments, and a semicolon. Thus, an instance of an arbitrary class Foo can be created as follows:

```
instance of Foo {
};
```

When an instance is created, it contains all properties of its immediate class as well as all superclass properties. Ordinarily, only those properties, which have default values assigned within the class declaration, are initialized at a time of instance creation. However, you can supply an initialization value or even override the default initialization value within the `instance of` statement. Consider the following example:

```
class SampleClass {
    [key]
    uint32  Prop1;
    boolean Prop2 = true;
```

```
    string  Prop3[] = {"ONE", "TWO", "THREE"};
};

instance of SampleClass {
    Prop1 = 128;
    Prop3 = {"UNO", "DUE", "TRE", "QUATTRO"};
};
```

Here the class SampleClass has three properties: Prop1, Prop2, and Prop3, where the latter is assigned a default initialization value within the class declaration. At a time of instance creation, Prop1 is assigned a new integer value of 128, Prop2 gets to keep its default initialization value of true, and the default value of Prop3 is overridden.

While it is legal to supply a new value or override a default initialization value at a time of instance creation, the value assignment should conform to the data type of the property to which it is being assigned. For instance, if you attempt to initialize an integer property with a string value, mofcomp.exe will flag that as an error. Thus, if you rewrite the preceding example as follows, the compiler will abort the compilation and spit out an error message:

```
instance of SampleClass {
    Prop1 = "ONE TWENTY EIGHT";
    Prop3 = {"UNO", "DUE", "TRE", "QUATTRO"};
};
```

If you actually try to compile this code, you are likely to see output, similar to the following:

```
An error occurred while creating object 2 defined on lines 10 - 13:
0X80041005 The value specified for property 'Prop1' conflicts with the
declaration of the property.
Compiler returned error 0x80041001
```

Properties do not have to be assigned a value during instance creation. Even when certain properties do not have a default initialization value, it is perfectly legal to create an instance without initializing such properties. Uninitialized properties would simply contain a special NULL value, which essentially indicates the absence of value. There is, however, one exception. Unless a class is marked as a singleton, it must have a key property, which has to be assigned a unique value for every instance of the class. As you may remember, a property is designated as a key by attributing it with the key qualifier within the class declaration. Thus, in the example above, Prop1 is a key property, and failure to supply a unique value for it when creating an instance of SampleClass will cause the compiler to abort the compilation complaining about an illegal NULL value.

System properties of a class constitute another special case. As you may remember, these properties cannot be explicitly declared within a class definition. Instead, WMI automatically adds them whenever a class is registered, and provides the appropriate initialization values when a class is instantiated. Consequently, you cannot assign system properties a value when you are creating instances. If you attempt to do so, this action will be flagged as an error by the compiler.

Instance Aliasing

When initializing object references, you often need to type lengthy object paths; this process is not only tedious but also error prone. Fortunately, MOF offers a convenient feature, called *instance aliasing*, which is designed to simplify the process of reference initialization. An instance alias is just a symbolic reference to an instance declared somewhere else within the same MOF file. You can create an instance alias by adding a special keyword, as, followed by the alias name, to the instance declaration:

```
instance of SampleClass as $SampleInstanceAlias {
...
};
```

The rules for choosing an alias name are the same as those for the class and instance identifier with one exception—an alias name always has to be prefixed with a dollar sign.

Once an alias is declared, you can use it in place of an explicit object path to initialize a reference. Consider the following example:

```
class Foo {
    [key]
    uint32 KeyProp;
    string OtherProp;
};
class FooRef {
    [key]
    uint32  KeyProp;
    Foo ref RefProp;
};
instance of Foo as $FooInstance {
    KeyProp = 100;
};
instance of FooRef {
```

```
    KeyProp = 200;
    RefProp = $FooInstance;
};
```

Here, an alias $FooInstance is established for an instance of class Foo. This alias is then used to initialize a reference property RefProp of the instance of class FooRef. This reference property can also be initialized with a conventional object path as follows:

```
instance of FooRef {
    KeyProp = 200;
    RefProp = "Foo.KeyProp=100";
};
```

However, using aliases is much more convenient, especially if a certain object is referred to more than once throughout the MOF file.

An alias can be declared not only for instances, but for classes as well. In fact, the following code is perfectly legal and will compile just fine:

```
class Foo as $FooClass {
    [key]
    uint32 KeyProp;
    string OtherProp;
};
class FooRef {
    [key]
    uint32  KeyProp;
    Foo ref RefProp;
};
instance of FooRef {
    KeyProp = 200;
    RefProp = $FooClass;
};
```

Conceptually, an alias can be viewed as an immutable string variable that is initialized to a path of the object being aliased. Therefore, it is valid to use an alias to initialize a string rather than a reference property:

```
class Foo as $FooClass {
    [key]
    uint32 KeyProp;
    string OtherProp;
};
```

```
class FooRef {
    [key]
    uint32 KeyProp;
    string StrProp;
};
instance of FooRef {
    KeyProp = 200;
    StrProp = $FooClass;
};
```

When the `FooRef` object is instantiated, its `StrProp` property will be set to a string value of `"\\.\root\default:Foo"`, assuming that the MOF code is loaded into `root\default` namespace.

Note that aliases are only valid within the scope of a single MOF file. Thus, it is impossible to alias a class or instance that is not defined within the same compilation unit as an alias. It is, however, legal to use *forward referencing*—an alias can be referenced at a point in a MOF file that precedes the alias declaration.

Qualifiers

Qualifiers are special attributes that can be used to associate certain semantics with managed classes, instances, methods, and properties. MOF is a fairly generic declarative language and often a class, method, or property definition alone does not convey enough information about the purpose or behavior of a particular managed entity.

Recall the example of the `Counter` or `Gauge` properties, presented earlier in this chapter. A definition for such a property would have a data type of `uint32`, which alone is not sufficient to express its behavioral characteristics. Alternatively, a naming convention may be used to provide a hint regarding the purpose of the property. The problem, however, is that the standard does not prescribe any definitive property naming conventions (besides the identifier naming rules, outlined earlier in the "Compiling MOF" section), so that making any assumptions regarding the property purpose based solely on its name is, at best, unreliable. The solution is to decorate such a property with some additional attributes that fully describe the intentions of the designer. Thus, the `Counter` or `Gauge` qualifiers act as metadata and express the special semantics associated with an arbitrary property.

All qualifiers are broadly divided into four categories: meta, standard, optional, and user-defined. Meta-qualifiers are used to clarify the usage of a particular class or property, declared with MOF. For instance, all association classes must be marked with the `Association` qualifier to indicate the intended usage. Currently, there are only two meta-qualifiers, defined by the CIM standard:

`Association` and `Indication`. These qualifiers must be declared for those CIM classes that are used as associations or indications, respectively.

Standard qualifiers are those that all CIM-compliant implementations are required to support. This is the largest category, and it includes most of the qualifiers described so far in this book. The `Counter` and `Gauge` qualifiers just described, are the examples of standard qualifiers. The `Abstract` qualifier, used to mark CIM classes as abstract, is another example of a standard qualifier. The usage of standard qualifiers is governed by a set of rules that outline the applicability of qualifiers to certain CIM model constructs as well as other constraints. The complete list of standard qualifiers along with extensive usage notes can be found in the CIM Specification Version 2.2 (`www.dmtf.org`).

Optional qualifiers are designed to account for various situations that are not common to all CIM-compliant implementations. Such implementations, therefore, are not required to handle optional qualifiers and, for the most part, simply ignore them. In fact, the idea behind optional qualifiers is to prevent the proliferation of random user-defined qualifiers, which address some fairly common, but not very generic aspects of CIM modeling. An example of such a qualifier is `Expensive`, which is used to indicate that accessing an arbitrary property or class may involve substantial computations. Again, the complete list of currently defined optional qualifiers is a part of CIM Specification Version 2.2.

Finally, a CIM designer is free to define custom qualifiers, although, for obvious reasons, it is not recommended. Declaring a qualifier involves determining certain characteristics that a qualifier should possess. First, just like properties, qualifiers have a data type. Table 6-4 presents a complete list of the CIM data types that can be used with qualifiers. Note that homogeneous arrays of the following types are also supported as qualifier data types.

Table 6-4. Qualifier Data Types

CIM DATA TYPE	DESCRIPTION
string	CIM string
uint16	Unsigned 16-bit integer
uint32	Unsigned 32-bit integer
sint32	Signed 32-bit integer
uint64	Unsigned 64-bit integer
sint64	Signed 64-bit integer
real32	IEEE 4-byte floating-point number
real64	IEEE 8-byte floating-point number
boolean	Boolean

Besides the data type, every qualifier has a clearly defined scope. Scope indicates to which elements of the schema the qualifier is applicable. A scope specification may identify a qualifier as relevant to classes, properties, methods, associations, and indications.

Finally, qualifiers have flavors that describe certain qualifier characteristics, such as localizability, propagation, and overriding rules. Qualifier flavors are described in detail in Chapter 2 (see Table 2-7).

Once all features of a qualifier are determined, it can be declared using the qualifier keyword. For instance, the following code snippet declares a qualifier, called MyQualifier:

```
qualifier MyQualifier :string = null, scope(class), flavor(DisableOverride);
```

This qualifier, which has a data type of string, applies to classes only and cannot be overridden by subclasses. Note that the qualifier is assigned a default value of null. This ability to specify a default qualifier value may come in very handy because MOF syntax allows a qualifier to be specified without an explicit value. For instance, the Association qualifier is usually used as follows:

```
[Association]
class FooAssoc {
...
};
```

Since, this qualifier is Boolean, its value is automatically assumed to be TRUE. A similar principle applies to qualifiers of other data types—numeric and string qualifiers are implicitly set to NULL and arrays are, by default, empty.

Although the ability to declare qualifiers as well as the qualifier keyword is part of the CIM standard, they are not supported under the current release of WMI. If you attempt to compile a MOF file, which contains a qualifier declaration, you are likely to see the following error message:

```
error SYNTAX 0X00af: CIM V2.2 feature not currently ⤶
supported for qualifier declaration
```

This, however, does not mean that custom qualifiers cannot be declared in WMI. In fact, creating a WMI user-defined qualifier is surprisingly easy—all you have to do is use the qualifier within a MOF declaration in the same way you would use a standard qualifier. WMI is smart enough to figure out the qualifier scope and the data type based on the placement of the qualifier within a MOF construct and the specified qualifier value.

Normally, a qualifier is enclosed in square brackets and placed right before the MOF keyword or identifier to which it applies. If multiple qualifiers apply, you can place them within a single set of square braces with a comma acting as a separator. Thus, the following code creates and utilizes a Boolean qualifier, MyQualifier, which applies to classes:

```
[MyQualifier]
class Foo {
...
};
```

Here, the value for the qualifier is not supplied explicitly, therefore, WMI makes an assumption that MyQualifier is a Boolean, set to TRUE. Optionally, a qualifier can be declared with an explicit value, as shown here:

```
[MyStringQualifier("CUSTOM QUALIFIER")] //creates string qualifier
class Foo {
...
};
[MyIntQualifier(1024)]                   //creates integer qualifier
class Foo {
...
};
```

The data type of a qualifier is determined based on the data type of the value, which is supplied as part of the qualifier declaration. Thus, in the preceding example, MyStringQualifier is of string data type, while MyIntQualifier is sint32.

Similarly, a qualifier can be declared as an array of values. In this case, the list of values is enclosed in curly brackets. The underlying data type is determined based on the data type of the supplied values, which implies that all of these values should be of the same type. Thus, the following fragment declares qualifiers that are typed as string and integer arrays:

```
//creates string array qualifier
[MyStringArrayQualifier{"VALUE 1", "VALUE 2", "VALUE 3"}]
class Foo {
...
};
//creates integer array qualifier
[MyIntArrayQualifier{1024, 2048, 4096}]
class Foo {
...
};
```

In the absence of formal qualifier declarations, required qualifier flavors must be included in the qualifier specification as follows:

```
[MyFlavoredQualifier("VALUE") : DisableOverride ToSubclass]
class Foo {
...
};
```

Note that it is legal to include multiple qualifier flavors in the specification, in which case the flavor identifiers must be separated by one or more blanks.

Not having to declare qualifiers explicitly in WMI creates a bit of a problem. It is entirely possible for a user-defined qualifier to collide with one of the standard or optional WMI qualifiers and cause undesirable side effects. Unfortunately, WMI makes such problems hard to detect because a qualifier, intended as user-defined, will most likely be interpreted as an existing one. It is, therefore, recommended that you prefix custom qualifier names with the name of the schema of which the qualifier is a part.

Compiler Directives

Although most of the mofcomp.exe behavior can be controlled via command-line switches, the CIM standard provides for an implementation-independent way of supplying the directives for compilation. Such directives, referred to as preprocessor commands or pragmas, are introduced into the MOF file by means of the pragma keyword, prefixed by a hash mark (#). Most pragmas may only appear at the beginning of the MOF file, preceding all other MOF constructs, but there are exceptions. Thus, pragma namespace may be specified at any point within a MOF compilation unit. The pragma directive has the following syntax:

```
#pragma <command>[(<value>)]
```

Table 6-5 lists all available pragma commands.

Table 6-5. MOF Pragma Commands

COMMAND	DESCRIPTION
amendment(locale)	Instructs a MOF compiler to separate the MOF file into the locale-neutral and local-specific portions. The locale value is an identifier of a locale that is used to create a language-specific MOF file. For details of WMI Localization, see Chapter 2.

(continued)

Table 6-5. MOF Pragma Commands (continued)

COMMAND	DESCRIPTION
autorecover	Instructs the compiler to add the MOF file to the list of files that are automatically compiled during the repository recovery. This autorecover file list is stored in the system registry under the key HKLM\Software\Microsoft\WBEM\CIMOM\ Autorecover MOFS.
classflags(flag)	Affects the way WMI classes are created and updated. The flag value may be one of the following: createonly, forceupdate, safeupdate, or updateonly. The effect of each of these flags is described in detail in Table 6-1.
deleteclass(name,failflag)	Instructs the compiler to delete a class, specified by the name parameter. The failflag controls the behavior of the compiler in case the specified class does not exist in the repository. If set to FAIL, the compiler aborts the compilation and prints an error message. If set to NOFAIL, the compilation continues. Note, if a target class has instances, these instances are deleted along with the class definition.
include(moffile)	Causes the compiler to include the contents of the MOF file, specified by the moffile parameter, into the current compilation unit.
instanceflags(flag)	Affects the way WMI instances are created and updated. The flag value may be one of the following: createonly, or updateonly. The effect of each of these flags is described in detail in Table 6-1.
namespace(path)	Instructs the compiler to save classes and instances into the namespace specified by the path parameter. By default, all classes and instances are saved into the root\default namespace. Note, if this directive appears in the middle of a MOF file, it does not affect the classes and instances that are defined prior to the command.

Interestingly, all of these commands, with the exception of `include` and `namespace`, are WMI specific and are not a part of CIM standard. Conversely, the CIM Specification defines a few other pragmas, which do not seem to be supported under WMI. For a complete list of standard pragma commands, see CIM Specification Version 2.2 (`www.dmtf.org`).

Comments

Similarly to most other computer languages, MOF allows you to specify comments. Comments may appear anywhere within a MOF compilation unit and are introduced via either a pair of leading forward slashes (//), or by a pair of matching /* and */ sequences.

A // comment spans a single line in a MOF file and does not have to be terminated explicitly. Instead, a carriage return provides an implicit termination. Thus, the following is an example of a single-line comment:

```
// This is a single-line comment.
```

A pair of /* and */ sequences is used to introduce a multiline comment. The following text illustrates how multiple lines are commented at once:

```
/* This is a first line of a multi-line comment.
   This is a second line of a multi-line comment.
   This is a last line of a multi-line comment. */
```

WMI Schema and System.Management Namespace

Although mofcomp.exe is the ultimate tool for manipulating the WMI Schema, sometimes you may want to carry out some schema modifications programmatically. Perhaps, the main reason for programmatic manipulation of the schema is the relative complexity of the MOF syntax, which is often enough to make schema administration a challenge for less experienced or less sophisticated system managers and administrators. Instead, you can develop a user-friendly GUI interface to obtain greater control over the schema extension and modification. This would allow you to carry out the required administrative tasks in a graphical fashion, thus, obviating the need to learn the MOF grammar.

One such GUI tool, the already familiar CIM Studio, comes as a part of WMI SDK. CIM Studio offers a convenient and simple graphical interface, which makes the task of managing WMI classes and instances very easy and straightforward.

Nevertheless, you may find that, under certain circumstances, neither CIM Studio nor mofcomp.exe is an ideal solution for schema management.

For instance, some management applications may, restrict the schema management activities such that only a subset of operations is allowed. Others may simply require you to build a schema administration tool into the applications UI. Under these conditions, the developers will need to program directly against the schema management API offered by WMI. Fortunately, the System.Management namespace comes well equipped with features that effectively hide the low-level details of schema manipulation APIs while working in concert with the rest of the .NET system management services.

Extracting MOF Definitions

You will often need to extract an arbitrary MOF definition from the CIM Repository. This may have to be done for several reasons. For example, when you extend the schema, sometimes you may find it easier to extract the definition of an existing class, alter it, and load it back into the repository, rather than, say, define a class from scratch. Alternatively, you may want to implement a custom backup tool, which would allow you to create logical, class- or instance-level backups of the schema. Finally, you may just be curious to find out how the definition of a particular class looks.

There are a few ways you can go about extracting the MOF code for a given instance or class. Perhaps, the easiest is to use the MOF Generation Wizard, accessible though the CIM Studio GUI. A bit more complicated approach involves using the wbemdump.exe command-line utility. This utility is a multipurpose tool, capable of not only displaying the class and instance information, but also running queries and executing methods. In order to print out a MOF definition of an arbitrary class, you have to invoke wbemdump.exe with the /M switch, the namespace path, and the name of the class. Thus, the following command will dump the MOF source for the Win32_Process class in the root\CIMV2 namespace:

```
wbemdump.exe /m root\CIMV2 Win32_Process
```

You can find the complete description of the functionality afforded by wbemdump.exe can in WMI SDK documentation.

Finally, the most flexible way to extract the MOF source from the CIM Repository is programmatically using the WMI API. The COM API offers two different ways to obtain the MOF text for a class or instance: by using the IWbemClassObject::GetObjectText method or the IWbemObjectTextSrc interface.

The GetObjectText method of the IWbemClassObject interface has the following definition:

```
HRESULT IWbemClassObject::GetObjectText(
    LONG lFlags,
    BSTR *pstrObjectText

);
```

The lFlags parameter controls several aspects of MOF generation. There are two allowable values for this parameter: WBEM_FLAG_NO_FLAVORS and WBEM_FLAG_NO_SEPARATORS. The former requests that the returned MOF text not include the qualifier propagation or flavor information. The latter suppresses the trailing semicolon after the class or instance declarations. The resulting MOF text is placed into a location, pointed to by pstrObjectText parameter, which must be initialized to NULL prior to calling the method.

In the System.Management namespace, the GetObjectText method is mapped to the GetText method of the ManagementBaseObject type. This method has a single parameter of type enumeration TextFormat. Currently, the TextFormat enumeration contains a single member TextFormat.Mof, which instructs the method to return a MOF-formatted representation of a WMI object.[1]

Retrieving the MOF source with the GetText object is very straightforward. For instance, the following code, extracts and prints on the console the MOF declaration of WMI class Win32_Process:

```
ManagementClass mc = new ManagementClass("Win32_Process");
Console.WriteLine(mc.GetText(TextFormat.Mof));
```

Extracting instance declarations is also extremely simple:

```
ManagementObject mo = new ManagementObject("Win32_Process.Handle=100");
Console.WriteLine(mo.GetText(TextFormat.Mof));
```

If you examine the output of these code fragments, you will notice that all the qualifiers are listed along with their respective flavor and propagation information, and all class and instance declarations are terminated with a semicolon. When you look at the disassembly of the System.Management.dll more closely, you will see that the GetText implementation unconditionally sets the lFlags parameter of the IWbemClassObject::GetObjectText method to zero, thus making it impossible to refine the aspects of MOF generation mentioned previously.

At this point, you may be asking, "What is the purpose of the GetText method's TextFormat parameter?" Since the TextFormat enumeration contains a single member, Mof, you cannot produce a textual representation of a WMI object in a format other than MOF. Moreover, if you look at the disassembly of

---

1. The TextFormat enumeration distributed with the latest version of .NET framework and Visual Studio .NET code named "Everett" includes two additional members: TextFormat.CimDtd20 and TextFormat.WmiDtd20. These flags are used to produce XML-formatted representations of WMI objects compliant with either CIM or WMI DTD, respectively.

GetText, you will definitely notice that the TextFormat parameter is ignored altogether. Again, this is easy to explain because the underlying IWbemClassObject::GetObjectText method does not offer you a choice of output formats. So why have a parameter that seemingly serves no purpose?

The answer is easy to guess. The parameter is there for the sake of future expansion. Not just hypothetical future expansion, but something, which, hopefully, will be a part of System.Management namespace in the very near future. Starting with Windows XP, WMI offers an alternative interface for generating textual representations of management objects. The interface, IWbemObjectTextSrc, is designed specifically to retrieve and format the declarations of WMI entities, and as a result it allows for more than one output format.

Again, the question is what other formats or encoding standards can be used to represent the structure of management information? After all, MOF is designed specifically for describing the managed entities and their interrelationships, but what are the alternatives? Today, when just about everything is encoded in XML, it would be surprising if somebody did not at least try to come up with a suitable XML representation for CIM objects and classes. Indeed, the first draft of the specification, entitled "XML As a Representation for Management Information," was produced and published by DMTF quite some time ago—in September of 1998 (www.dmtf.org/standards/xmlw.php). Microsoft, driven by their commitment to the XML initiative, rushed to produce an XML encoder for WMI entities, which became a part of the Windows XP distribution. The encoder, accessible through the above-mentioned IWbemObjectTextSrc interface, is capable of representing WMI objects using either the CIM-compliant or the extended WMI DTD.

Unfortunately, the IWbemObjectTextSrc interface is not utilized by the current release of FCL and is not accessible through any elements in the System.Management namespace.[2] As the disassembly of System.Management.dll shows, there is a wrapper for IWbemObjectTextSrc, but it does not appear to be used in any way, even on Windows XP systems. Nevertheless, the intentions of Microsoft developers seem to be clear, which probably means that XML encoding capabilities will make it into the next release of FCL.

Altering the Schema

As I mentioned previously, the System.Management namespace contains enough features to carry out just about any modification to the WMI schema, without ever resorting to MOF. For instance, to create a brand new class, you may simply use the Derive method of the ManagementClass type as follows:

---

2. The latest version of FCL distributed with "Everett" utilizes the IWbemObjectTextSrc interface on Windows XP systems. This interface is engaged by the ManagementBaseObject.GetText method if this method is called with a parameter other than TextFormat.Mof.

```
ManagementClass mc = new ManagementClass("CIM_ManagedSystemElement");
ManagementClass nc = mc.Derive("My_ManagedElement");
nc.Put();
```

This method has to be invoked on the instance of the `ManagementClass` type that is bound to an existing WMI class. When this operation completes successfully, the method returns an instance of the `ManagementClass` type, bound to a newly created class definition, derived from the class for which the method is invoked, and named according to the string parameter. Thus, the code above will create the `My_ManagedElement` class as a subclass of `CIM_ManagedSystemElement`. Note that the new class definition has to be committed to the CIM Repository using the `Put` method of `ManagementClass` type.

At first, the `Derive` method of the `ManagementClass` type may appear as the only way to create a new class definition with `System.Management`. This may seem to be a gap in functionality because `Derive` does not provide for creating a class that does not have any superclasses. After all, the necessity of resorting to MOF every time you need to create a root-level class, apart from simply being annoying, may severely cripple the functionality of management applications developed with .NET. Therefore, you may expect to see some kind of static `ManagementClass.Create` method, which would return a blank instance of the WMI class ready to be populated and saved into the CIM Repository. Unfortunately, no such method exists. It is also not possible to alter the behavior of the `Derive` method and force it to create a root-level class. Internally, `Derive` calls the `IWbemClassObject::SpawnDerivedClass` method, which is designed specifically to create subclasses of a given class rather than root-level classes.

Nevertheless, if you examine WMI COM API documentation, you will find out that it is indeed possible to create a root-level class programmatically using the `IWbemServices::PutClass` method. As you may remember, `IWbemServices::PutClass` is invoked by the `Put` method of the `ManagementClass` type and is used primarily to save changes to the CIM Repository. Thus, in theory, it should be possible to produce a root-level class definition as long as you can obtain a blank, unbound instance of a `ManagementClass` type. Coincidentally, such an unbound `ManagementClass` object is returned by the parameterless version of the `ManagementClass` constructor:

```
ManagementClass nc = new ManagementClass();
nc.SystemProperties["__CLASS"].Value = "My_ManagedElement";
nc.Put();
```

This code works just fine, although it is necessary to explicitly name the newly created class by setting its system property __CLASS. In fact, assigning the __CLASS property is the easiest way to copy a class definition. For instance, the following code fragment will create a new class, `My_Process`, by copying the definition of the existing `Win32_Process` WMI class:

```
ManagementClass nc = new ManagementClass("Win32_Process");
nc.SystemProperties["__CLASS"].Value = "My_Process";
nc.Put();
```

Note that the resulting class definition will be absolutely identical to the definition of Win32_Process with the exception of the class name. The values of system properties other than __CLASS will remain the same so that My_Process will share the same parent class and derivation tree as Win32_Process.

Apparently, a class is fairly useless unless it is decorated with qualifiers, properties, and methods. Adding a class qualifier is just a matter of invoking the Add method of the QualifierDataCollection type, exposed through the Qualifiers property of ManagementClass. Thus, the following code will mark the newly created class as singleton by adding the Singleton qualifier:

```
ManagementClass nc = new ManagementClass();
nc.SystemProperties["__CLASS"].Value = "My_ManagedElement";
nc.Qualifiers.Add("Singleton", true);
nc.Put();
```

The simplest version of the Add method takes two parameters: the string qualifier name and the object qualifier value. Since Singleton is a Boolean qualifier, the code above sets the second parameter to TRUE. As simple as it is, this version of Add has one downside—it does not allow you to specify qualifier flavors. That is why the QualifierDataCollection type exposes an overloaded version of Add, which takes not only the qualifier name and value parameters, but also a slew of Boolean values that indicate whether the qualifier is amended, whether it propagates to instances and subclasses, and whether it is overridable:

```
public virtual void Add(
    string qualifierName,
    object qualifierValue,
    bool   isAmended,
    bool   propagatesToInstance,
    bool   propagatesToSubclass,
    bool   isOverridable
);
```

For example, this code marks the Singleton qualifier as nonamended and nonoverridable and allows propagation to instances and subclasses:

```
ManagementClass nc = new ManagementClass();
nc.SystemProperties["__CLASS"].Value = "My_ManagedElement";
nc.Qualifiers.Add("Singleton", true, false, true, true, false);
nc.Put();
```

You can add an amended qualifier, although the results may not be exactly what you would expect. Thus, the following code sample adds a localizable `Description` qualifier to the definition for the `My_ManagedElement` class:

```
ManagementClass nc = new ManagementClass();
nc.SystemProperties["__CLASS"].Value = "My_ManagedElement";
nc.Qualifiers.Add("Description", "Sample Class", true, true, true, false);
nc.Put();
```

Although this code correctly creates a definition for `My_ManagedElement` and stores it in the CIM Repository, it does not automatically produce a definition for an amendment class. The `Description` qualifier is stored along with the class definition in the `root\CIMV2` namespace and, although it is marked as amended, it is not really localized. Thus, in order to produce a truly localized version of a class, you would have to create the language-specific class definition separately and save it into the localization namespace as described in Chapter 2.

Adding properties to a class is similar to adding qualifiers. The `PropertyDataCollection` type, exposed through the `Properties` property of `ManagementClass`, offers an overloaded `Add` method, which is suitable for creating just about any kind of class property. The first version of `Add` takes three parameters: a string property identifier, a member of the `CimType` enumeration that specifies the property data type, and a Boolean that indicates whether a property is an array:

```
public void Add(
    string   propertyName,
    CimType  propertyType,
    bool     isArray
);
```

For example, the following code snippet adds two properties to a definition of the `My_ManagedElement` class: a string `Property1` and an unsigned 32-bit integer array `Property2`:

```
ManagementClass nc = new ManagementClass();
nc.SystemProperties["__CLASS"].Value = "My_ManagedElement";
nc.Properties.Add("Property1", CimType.String, false);
nc.Properties.Add("Property2", CimType.UInt32, true);
nc.Put();
```

The resulting class definition, expressed in MOF, will look like the following:

```
class My_ManagedElement {
    string Property1;
    uint32 Property2[];
};
```

One obvious problem with this method is that it does not have any provisions for specifying the default property values. Of course, it is possible to manually set the value, once the property is added to the class definition:

```
nc.Properties.Add("Property1", CimType.String, false);
nc.Properties.Add("Property2", CimType.UInt32, true);
nc.Properties["Property1"].Value = "DEFAULT VALUE";
```

Nevertheless, this approach requires at least one extra line of code and, under certain circumstances, it may not be the most desirable way of doing things. Conveniently, there is another version of Add that takes a parameter of type object housing the default value for the property:

```
public void Add(
    string   propertyName,
    object   propertyValue,
    CimType propertyType
);
```

Thus, the code above can be simplified as follows:

```
nc.Properties.Add("Property1", "DEFAULT VALUE", CimType.String);
nc.Properties.Add("Property2", CimType.UInt32, true);
```

Unfortunately, it looks as if there is another problem—the second version of Add does not seem to allow you to mark a property as an array. In fact, this statement is not true because the type of the property is derived from the propertyValue parameter. Thus, passing an array of values to the Add method will automatically mark the property as an array:

```
nc.Properties.Add("Property2", new int[] {10, 15, 20, 25}, CimType.UInt32);
```

Note that values passed to Add through the propertyValue parameter of type object must be compatible with the CimType value specification. As a result, the following code will generate an exception since negative integer values cannot be coerced into UInt32:

```
nc.Properties.Add("Property2", new int[] {-10, 15, -20, 25}, CimType.UInt32);
```

Finally, there is another, even simpler overload of the Add method that takes a string property name parameter and a property value of type object:

```
public void Add(
    string  propertyName,
    object  propertyValue
);
```

In this case, the WMI property data type is guessed, based on the type of value, passed as a parameter. For instance, the following code will create a property, typed as an array of SInt32:

```
nc.Properties.Add("Property2", new int[] {10, 15, 20, 25});
```

When using this method, you should always supply a valid, non-null value of the type that can be converted to one of the CIM data types. See the WMI SDK documentation for conversion guidelines between CIM and Automation data types.

Adding properties of reference or object type is technically the same, although some special considerations apply. To add a reference property, use the Reference member of the CimType enumeration for the property data type as follows:

```
nc.Properties.Add("RefProperty", CimType.Reference, false);
```

Only weakly typed references can be created programmatically. Therefore, the preceding code will result in the following property definition:

```
class My_ManagedElement {
    object ref RefProperty;
};
```

Even if you supply a default value that indicates the type of the reference, this value would only be used for initialization purposes and its data type will be ignored. In other words, this code

```
ManagementObject mo = new ManagementObject("Win32_Process.Handle=100");
nc.Properties.Add("RefProperty", mo, CimType.Reference);
```

will generate the following property definition:

```
class My_ManagedElement {
    object ref RefProperty = "Win32_Process.Handle=100";
};
```

Adding properties that refer to embedded objects is very much the same. Just as it is not possible to create a strongly typed reference, it is impossible to define a strongly typed embedded object property. Take a look at the following snippet of code:

```
ManagementObject mo = new ManagementObject("Win32_Process.Handle=100");
nc.Properties.Add("ObjProperty", mo, CimType.Object);
```

The definition, produced by this code, will resemble the following:

```
class My_ManagedElement {
    object ObjProperty = instance of Win32_Process {
                            Handle = "100";
                        ...
                    };
};
```

In all, if you need to create strongly typed reference or object properties, MOF seems to be the only choice.

Similarly to classes, properties may have qualifiers. The process of adding a property qualifier is the same as it is for adding a class qualifier; the only difference is that property qualifiers are added to the QualifierDataCollection, which is exposed through the Qualifiers property of the PropertyData type. For instance, to decorate a property with the Description qualifier, you may use code similar to the following:

```
ManagementClass nc = new ManagementClass();
nc.SystemProperties["__CLASS"].Value = "My_ManagedElement";
nc.Properties.Add("Property1", CimType.String, false);
nc.Properties["Property1"].Qualifiers.Add("Description", "Qualified Property");
nc.Put();
```

Finally, a class can be outfitted with methods. As you may remember, methods are accessible through the Methods property of the ManagementClass type, which houses a collection of MethodData objects. This collection of type MethodDataCollection also exposes two variations of the Add method, thus allowing you to create method definitions programmatically. The simplest version of Add takes a single string parameter that denotes the name of the method to be added to the class definition:

```
ManagementClass nc = new ManagementClass();
nc.SystemProperties["__CLASS"].Value = "My_ManagedElement";
nc.Methods.Add("Method1");
nc.Put();
```

The method definition, produced by the preceding code, will have no parameters and a return type of void:

```
class My_ManagedElement {
    void Method1();
};
```

To add a method with parameters, use another version of Add, which takes two additional parameters of type ManagementBaseObject:

```
public virtual void Add(
    string              methodName,
    ManagementBaseObject inParameters,
    ManagementBaseObject outParameters
);
```

The two instances of the ManagementBaseObject type represent input and output parameter collections respectively. Thus, it seems that all you need to do is create two ManagementBaseObjects and add the appropriate properties to represent the parameters. In other words, if you want to add a method with a string input parameter and an integer output parameter, the following code sequence should work just fine:

```
ManagementClass nc = new ManagementClass();
nc.SystemProperties["__CLASS"].Value = "My_ManagedElement";
ManagementBaseObject inp = new ManagementBaseObject();
inp.Properties.Add("StrParm", CimType.String, false);
ManagementBaseObject outp = new ManagementBaseObject();
outp.Properties.Add("IntParm", CimType.SInt32, false);
nc.Methods.Add("ParameterizedMethod", inp, outp);
nc.Put();
```

Unfortunately, it does not. There are a few reasons for this. First, the parameterless constructor of ManagementBaseObject type is private and therefore, it cannot be used here. Using the ManagementObject type instead is not a very good option because you cannot add properties to an instance. In fact, your only option is to use the ManagementClass type, but, even if you change the code as follows, it will still not work:

```
ManagementClass nc = new ManagementClass();
nc.SystemProperties["__CLASS"].Value = "My_ManagedElement";
ManagementBaseObject inp = new ManagementClass();
inp.Properties.Add("StrParm", CimType.String, false);
```

```
ManagementBaseObject outp = new ManagementClass();
outp.Properties.Add("IntParm", CimType.SInt32, false);
nc.Methods.Add("ParameterizedMethod", inp, outp);
nc.Put();
```

Instead, it will throw `ManagementException` and complain about missing parameter IDs. As you may remember, each of the method parameters must have an ID qualifier, which uniquely identifies the parameter's position within the method signature. It is, therefore, necessary to decorate each parameter with the ID qualifier as follows:

```
ManagementClass nc = new ManagementClass();
nc.SystemProperties["__CLASS"].Value = "My_ManagedElement";
ManagementBaseObject inp = new ManagementClass();
inp.Properties.Add("StrParm", CimType.String, false);
inp.Properties["StrParm"].Qualifiers.Add("ID", 0);
ManagementBaseObject outp = new ManagementClass();
outp.Properties.Add("IntParm", CimType.SInt32, false);
outp.Properties["IntParm"].Qualifiers.Add("ID", 1);
nc.Methods.Add("ParameterizedMethod", inp, outp);
nc.Put();
```

The preceding code will produce the correct definition for `ParameterizedMethod`:

```
class My_ManagedElement {
    void ParameterizedMethod([in] string StrParm, [out] sint32 IntParm);
};
```

Note, the parameter IDs must be consecutive numbers starting from zero. If you attempt to use nonconsecutive ID qualifiers, you will get a `ManagementException`. However, if a parameter is used as both input and output, it may be added to both input and output `ManagementBaseObjects` with the same value of ID qualifier:

```
ManagementClass nc = new ManagementClass();
nc.SystemProperties["__CLASS"].Value = "My_ManagedElement";
ManagementBaseObject inp = new ManagementClass();
inp.Properties.Add("StrParm", CimType.String, false);
inp.Properties["StrParm"].Qualifiers.Add("ID", 0);
ManagementBaseObject outp = new ManagementClass();
outp.Properties.Add("StrParm", CimType.String, false);
outp.Properties["StrParm"].Qualifiers.Add("ID", 0);
```

```
nc.Methods.Add("ParameterizedMethod", inp, outp);
nc.Put();
```

This will produce the following method definition:

```
class My_ManagedElement {
    void ParameterizedMethod([in,out] string StrParm);
};
```

In this case, the name and data type of the parameter properties for input and output ManagementBaseObjects must match exactly, otherwise WMI will complain about duplicate parameters.

So far you have seen the technique for adding method parameters; however, there doesn't appear to be a way to specify the method return value. In fact, all the methods that I have defined up until now, had the return type of void. As you may remember from Chapter 2, the return value of a method is identified by a special ReturnValue property, which is a member of output parameters collection. Thus, to produce a definition for a method that takes a string parameter and returns an integer, you may use the following code:

```
ManagementClass nc = new ManagementClass();
nc.SystemProperties["__CLASS"].Value = "My_ManagedElement";
ManagementBaseObject inp = new ManagementClass();
inp.Properties.Add("StrParm", CimType.String, false);
inp.Properties["StrParm"].Qualifiers.Add("ID", 0);
ManagementBaseObject outp = new ManagementClass();
outp.Properties.Add("ReturnValue", CimType.SInt32, false);
nc.Methods.Add("ParameterizedMethod", inp, outp);
nc.Put();
```

Since the return value parameter is not a part of the method parameter list, it may not be decorated with the ID qualifier. If you attempt to add this qualifier, WMI will throw ManagementException.

Methods and method parameters may have qualifiers. You already know how to add a method parameter qualifier since the preceding code dealt extensively with parameter IDs specified by ID qualifiers. Adding a method qualifier is just as trivial. The Qualifiers collection of the MethodData type houses an already familiar QualifierDataCollection object, which offers several overloads of the Add method, described earlier. Thus, the following code adds a definition for a QualifiedMethod method and decorates it with the Description qualifier:

```
ManagementClass nc = new ManagementClass();
nc.SystemProperties["__CLASS"].Value = "My_ManagedElement";
```

```
nc.Methods.Add("QualifiedMethod");
nc.Methods["QualifiedMethod"].Qualifiers.Add("Description", "Qualified Method");
nc.Put();
```

As a final comment on generating method definitions, I must mention that using the parameterless constructor of the ManagementClass type to initialize the input and output ManagementBaseObjects is probably not such a great idea. It works just fine, but there is a certain danger in using an anonymous, unbound class. This is because it is entirely possible that future releases of WMI may require bound parameter classes in order to operate correctly, which will certainly break some legacy code. As you may remember, the CIM Repository contains a special system class __PARAMETERS, designed specifically to represent method parameter definitions. Using an instance of ManagementClass type, bound to the definition for __PARAMETERS class is, therefore, a superior and certainly more portable approach:

```
ManagementBaseObject inp = new ManagementClass("__PARAMETERS");
```

If you attempted to compile and run the earlier code examples, by now, your CIM Repository probably contains quite a few useless classes. You can fire up CIM Studio and delete these classes manually one by one, but you can also accomplish the same thing programmatically. Deleting a class is extremely simple: you just create an instance of ManagementClass that is bound to a given WMI class definition, and then call its Delete method. For example, to delete the previously created definition for the My_ManagedElement class from the CIM Repository, use the following code:

```
ManagementClass mc = new ManagementClass("My_ManagedElement");
mc.Delete();
```

The Delete method, inherited from the ManagementObject type, may also be invoked in an asynchronous fashion by calling it with an instance of the ManagementOperationObserver type as a parameter. Yet another overload of Delete accepts a parameter of type DeleteOptions, which lets you have some control over the delete operation. Both asynchronous programming and the DeleteOptions type are described in Chapter 2.

Note, Delete does not have to be followed by a call to Put because internally, it invokes the IWbemServices::DeleteClass method, which updates the CIM Repository instantly. If a class has instances, these instances are deleted along with the class definition.

Schema Management Miscellany

Once a class definition is created and saved into the CIM Repository, it can be used to create instances. An instance is created by invoking the `CreateInstance` method on a `ManagementClass` object that is bound to an arbitrary WMI class:

```
ManagementClass mc = new ManagementClass("My_ManagedElement");
ManagementObject o = mc.CreateInstance();
o.Put();
```

To save a newly created instance into the repository, you must call its `Put` method, which would internally invoke the `IWbemServices::PutInstance` method. There are a few things to watch out for when you are committing a new instance to the repository. Generally, every WMI object must either have a unique identity or be a single instance of a singleton class. Thus, the code above will actually fail unless the class is marked with a `Singleton` qualifier. Interestingly, if you attempt to create multiple instances of a singleton class, your code will most likely execute just fine; however, upon completion, the repository will contain a single instance. Such behavior is understandable because object identity is ignored for singletons, so once the first instance is created, every subsequent call to `IWbemServices::PutInstance` will be assumed to be an update to that instance.

In order to successfully create an instance of a non-singleton class, the class must have a property that is decorated with the Key qualifier. Moreover, before saving an instance to the repository, this key property should be assigned a value, which uniquely identifies an object. Thus, assuming that `My_ManagedElement` class has a key property, `KeyProp`, of type `string`, its instance can be created as follows:

```
ManagementClass mc = new ManagementClass("My_ManagedElement");
ManagementObject o = mc.CreateInstance();
o.Properties["KeyProp"].Value = "element1";
o.Put();
```

Strictly speaking, assigning an identity value to a key property is not mandatory. In a case where a class has a property marked with the Key qualifier, and such a property has a data type of `string`, `IWbemServices::PutInstance` will automatically generate a GUID to be used as an object identity as long as the property is set to `NULL`. The upside of this approach is, of course, the simplicity and guaranteed unique identity of a new object; but unfortunately, it comes at the price of usability. GUIDs are not smart identifiers and do not convey any information about an object, which makes them quite difficult to memorize and use. Just imagine constructing an object path, which is based on a GUID—not only is it extremely error prone, it also involves typing many meaningless hexadecimal digits. Thus, it is probably a good idea to always assign proper identity values to a key property manually before saving the object to the repository. Moreover, if a key property is of a type other than string, WMI will not attempt to generate an identity value for it. If such property is left NULL, Put will trigger an exception stating that the object's key property contains an illegal null value.

An existing instance can be deleted by invoking the Delete method of the ManagementObject type. The following code deletes the previously created My_ManagedElement object:

```
ManagementObject o = new ManagementObject("My_ManagedElement.KeyProp='element1'");
o.Delete();
```

Again, the call to Delete does not have to be followed by Put because it invokes IWbemServices::DeleteInstance internally, which automatically updates the CIM Repository.

Classes and instances are not the only elements of the WMI schema that can be deleted. Class properties and methods, as well as class, property, and method qualifiers can be deleted as well. However, instead of providing the Delete method, PropertyDataCollection, QualifierDataCollection, and MethodDataCollection types offer the Remove method. For instance, the following code fragment removes a property, a qualifier and a method of My_ManagedElement type, assuming that such schema elements exist:

```
ManagementClass mc = new ManagementClass("My_ManagedElement");
// removes Property1 from class definition
mc.Properties.Remove("Property1");
// removes Singleton qualifier from class definition
mc.Qualifiers.Remove("Singleton");
// removes Method1 from class definition
mc.Methods.Remove("Method1");
mc.Put();
```

In order to save the changes to a class definition to the CIM Repository, the invocation of Remove has to be followed by a call to Put.

Besides Add and Remove methods, PropertyDataCollection, QualifierDataCollection, and MethodDataCollection types provide the CopyTo method, which allows you to copy the respective PropertyData, QualifierData, or MethodData objects into another collection object. CopyTo has two overloads: one that allows you to copy the elements of the respective collection into a generic Array object, and another, which uses an array of PropertyData, QualifierData, or MethodData objects as a target.

For example, the following snippet of code copies all properties of the Win32_Process class into an array of objects that iterates through this array and prints out property names and values:

```
ManagementClass mc = new ManagementClass("Win32_Process");
object[] arr = new object[mc.Properties.Count];
mc.Properties.CopyTo(arr, 0);
foreach(PropertyData pd in arr) {
    Console.WriteLine("{0} = {1}", pd.Name, pd.Value);
}
```

The last parameter to CopyTo is an index into the target array at which copying is to start. Thus, it is possible to, say, combine properties of several classes into one array and then iterate through it once:

```
ManagementClass mc1  = new ManagementClass("Win32_Process");
ManagementClass mc2 = new ManagementClass("Win32_Service");
object[] arr = new object[mc1.Properties.Count + mc2.Properties.Count];
mc1.Properties.CopyTo(arr, 0);
mc2.Properties.CopyTo(arr, mc1.Properties.Count);
```

The same operation can be performed on methods and qualifiers—the only difference is that CopyTo will be applied to the MethodDataCollection or QualifierDataCollection objects respectively.

An alternative version of CopyTo is not much different. For example, the following code works in the same fashion as the previous code fragment: it prints out all property names and values for the Win32_Process class:

```
ManagementClass mc = new ManagementClass("Win32_Process");
PropertyData[] arr = new PropertyData[mc.Properties.Count];
mc.Properties.CopyTo(arr, 0);
foreach(PropertyData pd in arr) {
    Console.WriteLine("{0} = {1}", pd.Name, pd.Value);
}
```

Similar to the previously shown version of CopyTo, the last parameter is an index into the target array at which the copy operation is to start.

Apart from being occasionally useful for combining properties, methods, and qualifiers of multiple objects into a single collection for subsequent iteration, CopyTo is not very interesting and has limited value when it comes to schema manipulation.

Summary

This chapter provided a fairly detailed and comprehensive overview of the schema management facilities available through WMI and the

System.Management namespace. Having read the material and worked through the example code, you should now be familiar with the following:

- Fundamentals of the Managed Object Format (MOF) language that are used to declare CIM managed entities

- Techniques for creating new WMI classes and objects using the mofcomp.exe utility

- Methods for extracting MOF definitions for WMI classes from the CIM Repository

- How to use System.Management types to create, remove, and modify various elements of the WMI schema

With this kind of information in your pocket, you should be well positioned to define and deploy custom extension schemas or manipulate the elements of the existing management schemas.

CHAPTER 7

WMI Providers

MICROSOFT FAVORS PROVIDER-based architectures. There are OLE DB providers, cryptographic providers that are designed to work together with Microsoft Crypto API, and finally, there are WMI providers. The reasons for Microsoft's affection are more than just sentimental. Today's competition-driven world of software development is ridiculously diverse when it comes to technology, which often renders conventional architectures useless.

Take relational databases, for instance. Over the past few years, fierce competition has successfully annihilated many aspiring database vendors; however, there are still enough database products around to turn the lives of IT strategists into a never-ending nightmare. While this market segment is certainly dominated by such giants as Microsoft SQL Server and Oracle, die-hard Sybase is still out there, holding many Wall Street firms hostage, and even DB2, despite its Jurassic mainframe past, is making headway in the modern computing world. Moreover, regardless of the market dynamics, databases tend to have a much longer life span when compared to other software products. Once committed to a particular database infrastructure, you are basically trapped, since replacing such an infrastructure is generally a very time-consuming and extremely expensive exercise.

For in-house software developers, database independence may remain a subject for a theoretical discussion. However, for numerous commercial software vendors, it is a constant source of grief. Database affinity severely limits the product's market penetration abilities and may easily amount to an extensive loss of revenue.

This is where provider-based architectures come to the rescue. By building a layer of abstraction between the underlying database API and the application, you can afford the luxury of coding to a standard set of interfaces and then rely on plug-in components or providers to translate the application's requests into the database API calls. The advantages are apparent—an application, which utilizes such a provider architecture, can be ported from one database to another in seconds, without changing a single line of code. All you need to do is replace the database provider component—this can usually be achieved simply by changing a configuration file.

When it comes to database access, provider-based frameworks do not surprise anyone. In fact, many such frameworks have existed for years, especially on Windows platforms. OLE DB and its predecessor, ODBC, have always been, and remain, the primary vehicles for dealing with relational and non-relational data sources for just about any Windows-based software system. These technologies have proven themselves to be so successful that many software vendors, in addition to Microsoft, have made numerous attempts to utilize the same architectural principles. Thus, Rogue Wave Software offers the SourcePro DB (and now-defunct DBTools++) library, which is designed to solve the database independence problem through the use of plug-in database drivers. The Perl DBI database interface is built upon the same idea of providing a generalized interface that internally communicates with database-specific replaceable components. Even Sun Microsystems ported ODBC to their premier Solaris operating environment.

Today the apparent success of provider-based architectures has attracted the close attention of many software engineers who are looking to solve problems other than those of database access. Although this architectural principle may easily and beneficially be applied to many aspects of modern software development, the area of systems management certainly deserves special attention. By definition, a good management system must be able to deal with the wide variety of hardware and software technologies that make up today's complex computing universe. Unfortunately, inventing a generalized approach to managing thousands of dissimilar entities is extremely difficult; that is why most management systems tend to concentrate on certain aspects of the managed universe. For example, the Simple Network Management Protocol (SNMP) is almost solely dedicated to network management and most of the attempts to adopt it to address other areas of systems management never gained much popularity.

WMI is unique in that its goal is to cover all aspects of the management domain. The industry experience accumulated over the last couple of years indicates that WMI is fairly successful at achieving this goal. You should understand that one of the critical factors that determines WMI's success is its provider-based architecture. WMI itself is just a framework for collecting, disseminating, and managing the data, and its value is directly related to the availability of providers that are capable of dealing with various facets of the management domain.

Fortunately, there are plenty of providers. First, the WMI SDK includes a number of providers that allow you to manage the most common aspects of computer systems, such as disks, networks, processors and so on. To address more esoteric management needs, there are providers that collect various systems statistics; providers that allow you to integrate legacy systems, such as SNMP into WMI; and providers that deal with specific Windows technologies, such as Active Directory. Finally, there are tools and wizards for building custom providers that can do just about anything imaginable. The fact that WMI makes such diverse and versatile providers available is the main reason for its growing popularity.

As you may have guessed by now, this chapter is all about WMI providers. However, it does not recap the material presented in Chapter 5. This time, rather than focusing on the subject of custom provider development, I will attempt to provide an overview of some of the existing providers distributed with WMI. Covering every single existing provider is well outside the scope of this book, so I will only address a few—primarily those that do not seem to receive the coverage they deserve elsewhere.

Performance Data Providers

Monitoring system and application performance is one of the most critical tasks with which many system managers concern themselves. Although there are many performance monitoring tools available, you will find that being able to review the performance data via WMI is very attractive. First, you can effectively use the existing WMI-based management tools, such as WMI Studio, to monitor the performance. Second, once you become familiar with various WMI client APIs, you will learn to appreciate the unlimited flexibility of programmatic access to the performance data that they afford.

The system and application performance data is delivered to WMI by several providers. In fact, there are three available providers that can collect the performance data from local or remote computers:

> **Performance Monitoring provider:** This provider supplies performance information in the form of instances of CIM classes that represent the performance counters of interest.

> **Performance Counter provider:** This provider supplies raw performance counter data so that the management applications often have to apply special calculation algorithms to derive meaningful performance data.

> **Cooked Counter provider**: This provider supplies calculated or "cooked" performance data, similar to the data that appears in the System Performance Monitor.

Although all of these providers can be used to retrieve just about any kind of system or application performance information, there are certain advantages and disadvantages in using a particular provider to satisfy certain monitoring requirements. The remainder of this section is dedicated to providing more details on the operations and the usage patterns of each of these providers.

The Performance Monitoring Provider

The Performance Monitoring provider is a conventional WMI provider that is
available under Windows NT 4.0 and Windows 2000 platforms. It is not available
on Windows 95, Windows 98, or Windows Me platforms. The Performance
Monitoring provider is comprised of two WMI providers: instance and property
providers. The instance provider supplies the performance data in the form of
instances of CIM classes. The property provider updates the properties of the
specific instances of these classes.

Installing the Performance Monitoring Provider

This provider is not registered by default when the WMI SDK is installed. In order
to request its services, you have to carry out all registration-related tasks by hand.
Since there are really two providers—instance and property—you can perform
the registration in two ways. To register the provider as instance provider, you
must create instances of two WMI classes, __Win32Provider and
__InstanceProviderRegistration, and save them to the CIM Repository. The fol-
lowing MOF code can be used to register the Performance Monitoring provider
as an instance provider:

```
instance of __Win32Provider as $ProvInstance {
    Name = "PerformanceMonitorProvider";
    ClsId = "{f00b4404-f8f1-11ce-a5b6-00aa00680c3f}";
};
instance of __InstanceProviderRegistration {
    Provider = $ProvInstance;
    SupportsPut = FALSE;
    SupportsGet = TRUE;
    SupportsDelete = FALSE;
    SupportsEnumeration = TRUE;
};
```

Note that the ClsId property of the __Win32Provider instance refers to the
provider's COM object, which is implemented within stdprov.dll. This DLL, which
can be found in the %SystemRoot%\System32\WBEM directory, has to be correctly
registered on your system for the provider to function.

Registering the provider as a property provider is very similar to registering
the instance provider. In fact, the only difference is that you need to use an
instance of the __PropertyProviderRegistration system class instead of the
__InstanceProviderRegistration instance:

```
instance of __Win32Provider as $ProvInstance {
    Name = "PerformanceMonitorPropProvider";
    Clsid = "{72967903-68EC-11d0-B729-00AA0062CBB7}";
};
instance of __PropertyProviderRegistration {
    Provider = $ProvInstance;
    SupportsGet = TRUE;
    SupportsPut = FALSE;
};
```

Here, the ClsId property of the __Win32Provider instance also refers to a COM object implemented within the same stdprov.dll.

Once registration is complete, the provider is fully operational. However, you will find that it is not obvious how to access the performance data since the CIM Repository does not seem to contain any classes that are backed by the Performance Monitoring provider. It turns out that these classes also have to be created manually. Depending on whether the instance or property provider is used, the definition for a class, which represents a performance counter, may be different.

Using the Performance Monitoring Provider as an Instance Provider

When the Performance Monitoring provider is being used as an instance provider, the WMI class that is to house the performance data should roughly correspond to a given Performance Monitor object. Therefore, if your objective is to monitor the CPU performance, a WMI class should look like the Processor object in Performance Monitor. Then each property of the WMI class will relate to the respective counter name within the Processor object. For instance, in order to be able to retrieve the value of the "% User Time" counter, the WMI class definition should contain a property that corresponds to this counter.

Although you can certainly look up the counter names and their associated descriptions using the Performance Monitor GUI, doing this programmatically is a lot more fun. Coincidentally, the System.Diagnostics namespace contains a few types that come in very handy when you are working with performance counters. For example, the following code snippet will print out the names and descriptions of all performance counters that make up the Processor object:

```
using System;
using System.Diagnostics;
```

```
class CounterHelper {
    public static void Main(string[] args) {
        PerformanceCounterCategory cat =
            new PerformanceCounterCategory("Processor");
        foreach(PerformanceCounter cntr in cat.GetCounters("0")) {
            Console.WriteLine("{0}: {1}", cntr.CounterName, cntr.CounterHelp);
        }
    }
}
```

This code is extremely simple. First, it creates an instance of PerformanceCounterCategory type, which refers to the Processor object of Performance Monitor. It then enumerates all counters within the Processor object that are returned by the GetCounters method of the PerformanceCounterCategory object. This method takes a single string parameter, which represents the name of the performance object instance. It is always safe to use "0" when dealing with Processor objects because any machine will always have at least one CPU. Finally, for each counter object returned, the code prints out the values of two properties: CounterName, which contains the display name of the counter, and CounterHelp, which is essentially a counter description. The output produced by this code resembles the following:

```
% Processor Time: Processor Time is expressed as a percentage of the elapsed
time that a processor is busy executing a non-Idle thread. It can be viewed as
the fraction of the time spent doing useful work. Each processor is assigned an
Idle thread in the Idle process, which consumes those unproductive processor
cycles not used by any other threads.
% User Time: User Time is the percentage of processor time spent in User Mode in
non-Idle threads. All application code and subsystem code executes in User
Mode. The graphics engine, graphics device drivers, printer device drivers,
and the window manager also execute in User Mode. . . .
```

Once all required properties of a WMI class are identified, the class can be defined as follows:

```
[Dynamic, Provider("PerformanceMonitorProvider"),
 ClassContext("local|Processor")]
class PerfMon_Processor {
    [key]
    string Processor;
    [PropertyContext("% Processor Time")]
    real32 ProcessorTime;
    [PropertyContext("% User Time")]
    real32 UserTime;
```

```
    [PropertyContext("% Privileged Time")]
    real32 PrivilegedTime;
    [PropertyContext("Interrupts/sec")]
    real32 Interrupts;
    [PropertyContext("% DPC Time")]
    real32 DPCTime;
    [PropertyContext("% Interrupt Time")]
    real32 InterruptTime;
    [PropertyContext("DPCs Queued/sec")]
    real32 DPCsQueued;
    [PropertyContext("DPC Rate")]
    real32 DPCRate;
    [PropertyContext("DPC Bypasses/sec")]
    real32 DPCBypasses;
    [PropertyContext("APC Bypasses/sec")]
    real32 APCBypasses;
};
```

Note, it is not really necessary for a WMI class definition to include the properties that refer to each and every counter within a given performance object. You can simply pick just those properties in which you are interested.

You may have noticed a couple of class and property qualifiers here that may seem unfamiliar. The first one is the Dynamic class qualifier; it simply indicates that a provider backs instances of a particular class. The Provider qualifier establishes the binding between the class and its provider; its string parameter refers to the name of __Win32Provider instance, which represents the provider registration. The ClassContext qualifier establishes the mapping between the WMI class and a particular performance object. Its parameter is a string that may contain a number of tokens separated by a vertical bar (|). The first token represents the name of the computer that houses the performance object of interest. The second token is the name of the performance object to bind to. Finally, there is the PropertyContext qualifier, which establishes the binding between a particular property of the WMI class and its respective performance counter. This qualifier's parameter is a display name of the associated performance counter.

Yet another thing to notice is the Processor property, marked with the Key qualifier. Since performance objects are represented by instances of WMI classes, every such instance must have a unique identity. Thus, the Performance Monitoring provider will automatically set the Processor property to the instance ID of the respective CPU. For instance, on a dual-CPU machine, the provider will create two instances of the PerfMon_Processor class, with their Processor properties set to 0 and 1 respectively.

Once compiled and saved into the CIM Repository, the PerfMon_Processor class is ready to be used. Accessing the performance data is no different from accessing instances of any other WMI classes. Thus, the following snippet of code continuously prints out some statistics for CPU 0:

```
using System;
using System.Management;

class CPUMonitor {
    public static void Main(string[] args) {
        while(true) {
            ManagementObject mo = new ManagementObject("PerfMon_Processor='0'");
            Console.WriteLine("% Processor Time: {0}", mo["ProcessorTime"]);
            Console.WriteLine("% User Time: {0}", mo["UserTime"]);
            Console.WriteLine("% Privileged Time: {0}", mo["PrivilegedTime"]);
            System.Threading.Thread.Sleep(5000);
        }
    }
}
```

Note that every iteration of the while loop recreates the instance of ManagementObject type. Although seemingly inefficient at first, this is necessary in order to refresh the performance data. As you may remember, a property access operation invokes the IWbemClassObject::Get method, which always fetches the locally cached property value. Therefore, unless the instance of the ManagementObject type is rebound to its underlying WMI object, its properties will not be refreshed.

Generally, mapping performance objects to WMI classes is straightforward—a particular performance object category corresponds to a WMI class, counters correspond to the class properties, and performance objects map to instances of WMI classes. However, there are certain performance objects that do not easily yield themselves to this kind of modeling. The TCP object, for instance, which contains a slew of TCP/IP statistical counters, does not have any instances. Consider the following WMI class, which may be used to retrieve TCP/IP performance data:

```
[Dynamic, Provider("PerformanceMonitorProvider"), ClassContext("local|TCP")]
class PerfMon_TCP {
    [Key]
    string KeyProp;
    [PropertyContext("Segments/sec")]
    real32 Segments;
    [PropertyContext("Connections Established")]
    real32 ConnectionsEstablished;
    [PropertyContext("Connections Active")]
```

```
    real32 ConnectionsActive;
    [PropertyContext("Connections Passive")]
    real32 ConnectionsPassive;
    [PropertyContext("Connection Failures")]
    real32 ConnectionFailures;
    [PropertyContext("Connections Reset")]
    real32 ConnectionsReset;
    [PropertyContext("Segments Received/sec")]
    real32 SegmentsReceived;
    [PropertyContext("Segments Sent/sec")]
    real32 SegmentsSent;
    [PropertyContext("Segments Retransmitted/sec")]
    real32 SegmentsRetransmitted;
};
```

The class definitions in this code look very similar to those for the performance Processor object; however, it is unclear how you can access the individual instances of this class since the TCP performance object is global. One way to do this is to bind to a class and then enumerate its instances:

```
using System;
using System.Management;

class TCPMonitor {
    public static void Main(string[] args) {
        ManagementClass mc = new ManagementClass("PerfMon_TCP");
        foreach(ManagementObject mo in mc.GetInstances()) {
            Console.WriteLine("Key: {0}", mo["KeyProp"]);
        }
    }
}
```

Running the preceding code reveals a single instance with its KeyProp key property set to @. This means that the TCP performance object essentially maps to a singleton WMI class. Therefore, the WMI class definition above should be changed as follows:

```
[Singleton, Dynamic, Provider("PerformanceMonitorProvider"), ClassContext("local|TCP")]
class PerfMon_TCP {
    [PropertyContext("Segments/sec")]
    real32 Segments;
    [PropertyContext("Connections Established")]
```

```
    real32 ConnectionsEstablished;
    [PropertyContext("Connections Active")]
    real32 ConnectionsActive;
    [PropertyContext("Connections Passive")]
    real32 ConnectionsPassive;
    [PropertyContext("Connection Failures")]
    real32 ConnectionFailures;
    [PropertyContext("Connections Reset")]
    real32 ConnectionsReset;
    [PropertyContext("Segments Received/sec")]
    real32 SegmentsReceived;
    [PropertyContext("Segments Sent/sec")]
    real32 SegmentsSent;
    [PropertyContext("Segments Retransmitted/sec")]
    real32 SegmentsRetransmitted;
};
```

There are two things to notice here: first, the class is marked with the Singleton qualifier; second, there is no key property because singletons are not required to have a unique identity. Therefore, the code to retrieve the TCP performance data can be simplified as follows:

```
using System;
using System.Management;

class TCPMonitor {
    public static void Main(string[] args) {
        while(true) {
            ManagementObject mo = new ManagementObject("PerfMon_TCP=@");
            Console.WriteLine("Connections Established: {0}",
                mo["ConnectionsEstablished"]);
            Console.WriteLine("Connections Active: {0}", mo["ConnectionsActive"]);
            Console.WriteLine("Connections Passive: {0}", mo["ConnectionsPassive"]);
            System.Threading.Thread.Sleep(5000);
        }
    }
}
```

Using the Performance Monitoring Provider as a Property Provider

An interesting alternative to the instance-centric approach, outlined above, is using the Performance Monitoring provider as a property provider. Just as it is the case with the instance provider, to make the property provider work, you have to define the WMI classes to represent the performance data. Additionally, instances of these classes also have to be defined manually, since the property provider is not capable of returning the instance-level data to its clients. Consider the following sample MOF code:

```
class PerfMonProp_TCP {
    [Key]
    string KeyProp;
    real32 ConnectionsEstablished;
    real32 ConnectionsActive;
    real32 ConnectionsPassive;
};
[DYNPROPS]
instance of PerfMonProp_TCP {
    KeyProp = "tcp1";
    [PropertyContext("local|TCP|Connections Established"),
     Dynamic, Provider("PerformanceMonitorPropProvider")]
    ConnectionsEstablished;
    [PropertyContext("local|TCP|Connections Active"),
     Dynamic, Provider("PerformanceMonitorPropProvider")]
    ConnectionsActive;
    [PropertyContext("local|TCP|Connections Passive"),
     Dynamic, Provider("PerformanceMonitorPropProvider")]
    ConnectionsPassive;
};
```

The class definition for PerfMonProp_TCP is fairly straightforward and does not include any special qualifiers. The class has a key property KeyProp, although it is not, strictly speaking, necessary. Since properties of this class refer to global performance counters, the class may as well be marked as a singleton.

The instance definition is a bit more interesting. First, the instance is decorated with the DYNPROPS qualifier, which simply indicates that the instance is to house the values, backed by a property provider. The KeyProp property is initialized to an arbitrary value to guarantee the uniqueness of the instance identity. Finally, each of the instance's properties is marked with the already familiar

PropertyContext qualifier. However, rather then simply referring to the display names of the associated performance counters, these PropertyContext qualifiers include the machine and performance object names as part of their initialization strings. This information is necessary in order for the property provider to bind to a correct performance object for each property. Additionally, each property is decorated with the Dynamic qualifier to indicate that a property provider backs it, and with the Provider qualifier, which refers to the proper provider registration entry.

Using the PerfMonProp_TCP class is no different than using the previously defined PerfMon_TCP class. There is, however, an interesting twist. Since the performance data is provided at the property level rather than the instance level, the WMI class definition no longer has to correspond to a single performance object. In fact, it is perfectly legitimate to define a class that combines the performance counters from multiple categories into a single package:

```
class PerfMonProp_Combo {
    [Key]
    string KeyProp;
    real32 ConnectionsEstablished;
    real32 AvailableBytes;
};
[DYNPROPS]
instance of PerfMonProp_Combo {
    KeyProp = "combo1";
    [PropertyContext("local|TCP|Connections Established"),
     Dynamic, Provider("PerformanceMonitorPropProvider")]
    ConnectionsEstablished;
    [PropertyContext("local|Memory|Available Bytes"),
     Dynamic, Provider("PerformanceMonitorPropProvider")]
    AvailableBytes;
};
```

This is certainly convenient because the management application is afforded the luxury of defining its single performance monitoring class, which includes all counters of interest. Unfortunately, there does not appear to be a way to retrieve nonglobal performance counters with the property provider. For instance, it is not possible to alter the definition of the WMI class above to refer to, say, the "% Processor Time" counter for CPU 0.

Usage Considerations

The Performance Monitoring provider often comes in very handy when you are reading the performance data. There are, however, a few drawbacks. First, WMI class definitions for performance objects have to be created by hand, which is not only tedious but also error-prone. The second and the most disappointing issue is the suboptimal performance of this provider, especially when you are retrieving large amounts of data on a regular basis. That is why Microsoft offers a couple of alternatives for retrieving the performance counter values.

The Performance Counter Provider

Perhaps, the most significant performance implication of using the Performance Monitoring provider is the necessity to marshal fairly large amounts of data. The Performance Monitoring provider is a conventional, old-fashioned WMI provider that is always loaded out-of-process respective to the client application, hence the need for marshalling the performance data across the process boundaries.

High-Performance Providers

To alleviate the performance problem often associated with conventional providers, Microsoft introduced a so-called high-performance provider API— a set of interfaces designed to increase the efficiency of communication between a client WMI application and a data provider. The basic idea behind the high-performance provider API is simple. As opposed to conventional providers, high-performance providers, if located on the same machine as the client application, are loaded in-process to the client, thus eliminating the need for cross-process data marshalling. Even when a client and a provider are located on different computers, the high-performance API is still a superior communication vehicle because it allows for caching the data on the remote machine and transmits only the minimal required data back to the client.

Because performance data providers need to handle vast amounts of frequently changing statistical data, choosing them to be implemented as high-performance providers is a good idea. Thus, starting with Windows 2000, the WMI distribution includes a high-performance alternative to the Performance Monitoring provider: the Performance Counter provider, also referred to as the Raw Performance Counter provider.

The Performance Counter Provider and the ADAP Process

Besides addressing performance issues, the Performance Counter provider eliminates the need to manually define the WMI classes that represent various performance objects. More precisely, it is not the provider itself, but rather the WMI AutoDiscovery/AutoPurge (ADAP) process that allows you to automatically import the definitions for Windows performance objects into the CIM Repository. The sole purpose of ADAP is to monitor the state of performance objects on a given computer and ensure that the definitions for these objects remain synchronized with their respective WMI performance class definitions.

On Windows 2000 and XP platforms, the ADAP process is launched automatically as soon as the WinMgmt service starts; unfortunately, neither the ADAP functionality nor the Performance Counter provider are available on any other Windows platforms. Upon startup, ADAP examines all currently installed performance DLLs and generates a list of all currently available performance objects. This list is then compared to a list of WMI performance classes and necessary adjustments are made.

Under Windows 2000 and XP, you can add custom performance objects and counters by implementing a performance DLL and registering it using lodctr.exe utility. Obviously, installing a new performance library is likely to render the WMI performance class definitions outdated or incomplete. That is why lodctr.exe and its counterpart unlodctr.exe, which is used to de-register the performance libraries, both invoke the ADAP process, thus making sure that WMI's CIM Repository remains synchronized with the actual performance objects.

ADAP can also be invoked manually via the /resyncperf command-line switch of winmgmt.exe:

```
winmgmt.exe /resyncperf <winmgmt service process id>
```

On Windows 2000, ADAP is implemented as part of winmgmt.exe; however, under Windows XP, it is a separate executable called wmiadap.exe. Table 7-1 lists all command-line parameters taken by wmiadap.exe:

Table 7-1. wmiadap.exe Command-Line Options

COMMAND-LINE SWITCH	DESCRIPTION
/f	Instructs wmiadap.exe to parse all performance DLLs on a given system and synchronize the WMI performance class definitions
/c	Causes wmiadap.exe to clear the status of all currently available performance libraries
/r	Instructs wmiadap.exe to parse all the Windows Driver Model (WDM) drives on a given system and synchronize the WMI performance class definitions
/t	Throttles the ADAP process as soon as the user operates a keyboard or mouse

It is, therefore, possible to invoke the ADAP process manually as follows:

```
wmiadap.exe /f
```

The ADAP process maintains an error log, which can be found in %SystemRoot%\System32\Wbem\Logs\Wmiadap.log. The log is used to record various events triggered during the execution of the ADAP process, such as indications of the process's startup and shutdown as well as certain error conditions. In addition to the log file, all errors related to loading and parsing the performance DLLs are recorded in the Windows event log and can be viewed with the Event Viewer (eventvwr.exe). ADAP error messages can be found in the application log—you can filter errors based on the value of the Source column, which should be set to WinMgmt for ADAP messages. The application log messages are worth looking at because, on occasion, they may explain why certain performance counters are not being correctly transferred to the CIM Repository.

Finally, WMI system class, __ADAPStatus, located in the root\DEFAULT namespace, offers a way to programmatically determine the status of the ADAP process. This class has the following definition:

```
class __ADAPStatus : __SystemClass {
    uint32   Status;
    datetime LastStartTime;
    datetime LastStopTime;
};
```

Its `LastStartTime` and `LastStopTime` properties are self-explanatory and reflect the last time the ADAP process was started and shut down respectively. The `Status` property is a bit more interesting—it is an integer value that defines the current state of the ADAP process. The allowable values for this property are shown in Table 7-2:

Table 7-2. `__ADAPStatus.Status` *Constants*

VALUE	DESCRIPTION
0	The ADAP process has never been run on the computer.
1	The ADAP process is currently running.
2	The ADAP process is currently processing a performance library.
3	The ADAP process is currently updating the CIM Repository.
4	The ADAP process has finished.

To programmatically determine the status of the ADAP process, you can write code similar to the following:

```
using System;
using System.Management;

class ADAPStatus {
    public static void Main(string[] args) {
        ManagementObject mo =
            new ManagementObject(@"\\.\root\DEFAULT:__ADAPStatus=@");
        Console.WriteLine("Status: {0}", mo["Status"]);
        Console.WriteLine("Last started: {0}", mo["LastStartTime"]);
        Console.WriteLine("Last stopped: {0}", mo["LastStopTime"]);
    }
}
```

The only thing to notice here is that the `__ADAPStatus` object is singleton and, therefore, has to be accessed using the @ symbol.

When the ADAP process successfully finishes, the WMI CIM Repository will be updated with the definitions of WMI classes that represent the performance objects. All such WMI classes will be derived from either `Win32_PerfRawData` or `Win32_PerfFormattedData`—preinstalled abstract classes that are used as superclasses for raw and "cooked" performance objects. The majority of the performance classes will be imported into the `root\CIMV2` namespace; however, those classes that represent the performance objects for WDM drivers will be loaded into the `root\WMI` namespace, instead.

The remainder of this section will concentrate on non-WDM performance objects that are backed by the Raw Performance Counter provider and derived from the Win32_PerfRawData class. The following section will cover the Cooked Counter provider, which supports the classes, derived from Win32_PerfFormattedData.

Understanding the Performance Counter Provider

To better understand how the Performance Counter provider works, take a close look at one of the performance classes imported into the CIM Repository by the ADAP process. The Win32_PerfRawData_PerfOS_Processor class relates to the Processor Performance category and each of its instances corresponds to one of the Processor performance objects:

```
[perfdefault, dynamic, provider("Nt5_GenericPerfProvider_V1"),
 registrykey("PerfOS"), perfindex(238), helpindex(239),
 perfdetail(100), genericperfctr]
class Win32_PerfRawData_PerfOS_Processor : Win32_PerfRawData {
    [key] string Name = NULL;
    [perfdefault, DisplayName("% Processor Time"),
     countertype(558957824), perfindex(6), helpindex(7),
     defaultscale(0), perfdetail(100)]
    uint64 PercentProcessorTime;
    [DisplayName("% User Time"), countertype(542180608),
     perfindex(142), helpindex(143),
     defaultscale(0), perfdetail(200)]
    uint64 PercentUserTime;
    [DisplayName("% Privileged Time"), countertype(542180608),
     perfindex(144), helpindex(145),
     defaultscale(0), perfdetail(200)]
    uint64 PercentPrivilegedTime;
    [DisplayName("Interrupts/sec"), countertype(272696320),
     perfindex(148), helpindex(149), defaultscale(-2),
     perfdetail(100)]
    uint32 InterruptsPersec;
    [DisplayName("% DPC Time"), countertype(542180608),
     perfindex(696), helpindex(339),
     defaultscale(0), perfdetail(200)]
    uint64 PercentDPCTime;
    [DisplayName("% Interrupt Time"), countertype(542180608),
     perfindex(698), helpindex(397),
     defaultscale(0), perfdetail(200)]
```

```
    uint64 PercentInterruptTime;
    [DisplayName("DPCs Queued/sec"), countertype(272696320),
     perfindex(1334), helpindex(1335),
     defaultscale(0), perfdetail(200)]
    uint32 DPCsQueuedPersec;
    [DisplayName("DPC Rate"), countertype(65536),
     perfindex(1336), helpindex(1337),
     defaultscale(0), perfdetail(200)]
    uint32 DPCRate;
    [DisplayName("DPC Bypasses/sec"), countertype(272696320),
     perfindex(1338), helpindex(1339),
     defaultscale(0), perfdetail(200)]
    uint32 DPCBypassesPersec;
    [DisplayName("APC Bypasses/sec"), countertype(272696320),
     perfindex(1340), helpindex(1341),
     defaultscale(0), perfdetail(200)]
    uint32 APCBypassesPersec;
};
```

At first glance, the definition for this class seems to be very similar to that of the PerfMon_Processor class used earlier in this chapter to illustrate the operations of the Performance Monitoring provider. Indeed, the concept is the same—the class itself corresponds to the Process Performance category, while each of its properties relates to a single performance counter within the category. Yet another similarity is a key property, Name, which is set to the unique ID of the Processor instance by the provider.

However, this class, as well as all of its properties, is decorated with various qualifiers that are different from those of the PerfMon_Processor class. These qualifiers are required by the Performance Counter provider in order to locate the respective performance objects and associate them with the properties of the WMI class. The list of class qualifiers along with their descriptions is presented in Table 7-3.

Table 7-3. Class Qualifiers Used by the Performance Counter Provider

QUALIFIER	DESCRIPTION
Costly	If set, indicates that retrieving instances of this class is an expensive operation in terms of resource consumption. ADAP automatically adds this qualifier to a WMI class definition for a performance object that is marked as costly (see the Platform SDK documentation for more information on creating Performance Extension DLLs). Additionally, ADAP adds the _Costly suffix to the name of the WMI class. Example: Win32_PerfRawData_PerfProc_ThreadDetails_Costly.
GenericPerfCounter	If set, indicates that the WMI class corresponds to a performance object backed by a legacy performance DLL.
HelpIndex	Specifies the index of the object's help text in the performance names database.
HiPerf	Marks the WMI class as a high-performance class.
PerfDefault	If set, indicates that the WMI class is to be used as a default selection in a list box in a graphical application.
PerfDetail	Indicates the level of knowledge the audience is required to possess. This qualifier can take the following values: PERF_DETAIL_NOVICE (0x00000064)—For novice users PERF_DETAIL_ADVANCED (0x000000C8) —For advanced users PERF_DETAIL_EXPERT (0x0000012C) —For expert users PERF_DETAIL_WIZARD (0x00000190) —For system designers
PerfIndex	Specifies the index of the object's display name in the performance names database.
RegistryKey	Specifies the name of the registry subkey under HKLM\System\CurrentControlSet\Services under which the performance counter definitions are located.

Besides the qualifiers specific to the Performance Counter provider the class is marked with the Dynamic qualifier, indicating that its instances are supplied dynamically by the provider; as well as by the Provider qualifier, which establishes the link to the appropriate provider registration entry.

The actual binding between the WMI class and the respective performance counters is achieved through the property qualifiers that ADAP adds to the class definition. Table 7-4 lists all the property qualifiers specific to the Performance Counter provider.

Table 7-4. Property Qualifiers Used by the Performance Counter Provider

QUALIFIER	DESCRIPTION
CounterType	Indicates the type of performance counter associated with a given property. Since the Performance Counter provider exposes raw, uncalculated performance data, the CounterType qualifier is used by WMI clients to determine the formula for calculating the performance values that are meaningful to the end users. A detailed description of the available counter types is presented later in this section.
DefaultScale	The scale value used by graphical display applications such as System Performance Monitor to scale the performance chart lines.
DisplayName	Although this qualifier is not really specific to the Performance Counter provider, here it plays dual role. In addition to specifying the UI display name for the property, it is used to establish an association between a performance counter object and a property of its respective WMI class.
HelpIndex	Specifies the index of the object's help text in the performance names database.
PerfDefault	If set, indicates that WMI class property is to be used as a default selection in a list box in a graphical application.
PerfDetail	Indicates the level of knowledge the audience is required to possess. See Table 7-3 for the complete list of allowed values.
PerfIndex	Specifies the index of the object's display name in the performance names database.

Most of these qualifiers are fairly self-explanatory. CounterType, however, is a key to deciphering the performance data exposed by the Performance Counter provider, and so it is a bit more complicated. As I already mentioned, this provider supplies uncalculated data, which, in its raw form, does not make much sense to the end users. For instance, the Interrupts/sec performance counter has the type of PERF_COUNTER_COUNTER (with a CounterType of 272696320), which means that at any given time, it will hold a value that reflects the total rate of interrupts for a processor. Thus, to derive the interrupt rate per second, you would have to take snapshots of the counter value over some time interval and perform the calculation based on the following formula:

```
Interrupts/sec = (V1 - V0)/((T1 - T0)/TB)
```

where

V1: Counter value at the end of the monitoring interval

V0: Counter value at the beginning of the monitoring interval

T1: Number of processor ticks at the end of the monitoring interval

T0: Number of processor ticks at the beginning of the monitoring interval

TB: Time base or frequency of the processor ticks

In this case, the expression (V1 - V0) evaluates to the number of interrupts that take place within a certain monitoring interval. The other expression, (T1 - T0), reflects the length of the monitoring interval in units of processor ticks. Considering that tick frequency is expressed in numbers of ticks per second; ((T1 - T0)/TB) evaluates to the number of seconds elapsed during the monitoring interval. Thus, the entire calculation yields a value that reflects an average number of processor interrupts per second.

There are many different counter types that govern the calculations of the performance values. Based on the counter usage pattern and required computation algorithm, all counter types can be divided into the following categories:

- Noncomputational counters

- Base counters

- Basic Algorithm counters

- Counter Algorithm counters

- Timer Algorithm counters

- Precision Timer Algorithm counters

- Queue-Length Algorithm counters

- Statistical counters

Each of these categories will now be described in detail.

Noncomputational Counters

The noncomputational counters are the easiest to understand because their values can be used "as is" without applying any computational algorithms. Table 7-5 lists all noncomputational counter types along with their descriptions.

Table 7-5. Noncomputational Performance Counter Types

COUNTER	DESCRIPTION
PERF_COUNTER_TEXT (2816)	Variable-length Unicode text string. This counter does not require any calculations.
PERF_COUNTER_RAWCOUNT (65536)	Raw counter that represents the last observed value. This counter does not require any calculations.
PERF_COUNTER_LARGE_RAWCOUNT (65792)	Similar to PERF_COUNTER_RAWCOUNT, but uses 64-bit representation, which allows very large values to be stored.
PERF_COUNTER_RAWCOUNT_HEX (0)	Raw counter that represents the last observed value in HEX format. This counter does not require any calculations.
PERF_COUNTER_LARGE_RAWCOUNT_HEX (256)	Similar to PERF_COUNTER_RAWCOUNT_HEX, but uses 64-bit representation, which allows very large values to be stored.

Base Counters

The base counter types are not intended to be used by themselves. Instead, such counters supply base values to act as denominators in the formulas used to calculate the performance statistics for other counter types. For instance, the AvgDiskBytesPerRead property of the Win32_PerfRawData_PerfDisk_PhysicalDisk class contains the total number of bytes transferred from the disk during the read operation. Unless there is a basis for determining the number of read operations that take place over a time interval, this property is not very useful. Such a basis is provided by another property of the same class, AvgDiskBytesPerRead_Base, which reflects the total number of read operations so that the following formula can be applied to calculate the meaningful counter value:

```
Avg. Bytes/read = (V1 - V0)/(B1 - B0)
```

where

V1: Value of AvgDiskBytesPerRead at the end of the monitoring interval

V0: Value of AvgDiskBytesPerRead at the beginning of the monitoring interval

B1: Value of AvgDiskBytesPerRead_Base at the end of the monitoring interval

B0: Value of AvgDiskBytesPerRead_Base at the beginning of the monitoring interval

The base counter types are represented by the WMI class properties with the _Base suffix. Declarations of such properties must immediately follow the corresponding counter properties declarations within the WMI class definition.

Table 7-6 lists all the available base counter types along with their descriptions.

Table 7-6. Base Performance Counter Types

COUNTER	DESCRIPTION
PERF_AVERAGE_BASE (1073939458)	Represents the base value used to calculate cooked values for the PERF_AVERAGE_TIMER and PERF_AVERAGE_BULK counter types
PERF_COUNTER_MUTI_BASE (1107494144)	Represents the base value used to calculate cooked values for PERF_COUNTER_MULTI_TIMER, PERF_COUNTER_MULTI_TIMER_INV, PERF_100NSEC_MULTI_TIMER and PERF_100NSEC_MULTI_TIMER_INV counter types
PERF_LARGE_RAW_BASE (1073939715)	Represents the base value used to calculate cooked values for 64-bit PERF_RAW_FRACTION counter types
PERF_RAW_BASE (1073939459)	Represents the base value used to calculate cooked values for PERF_RAW_FRACTION counter types
PERF_SAMPLE_BASE (1073939457)	Represents the base value used to calculate cooked values for PERF_SAMPLE_COUNTER and PERF_SAMPLE_FRACTION counter types.

Basic Algorithm Counters

The basic algorithm counter types typically represent either absolute or relative (percentage) change in a measured performance value over a time interval. For instance, the `ElapsedTime` property of the `Win32_PerfRawData_PerfProc_Thread` class reflects the total number of clock ticks that correspond to the start time of the tread. Thus, to calculate the time elapsed from the moment the thread is started to a given point, you can use the following formula:

```
Elapsed Time = (TO - VO)/TB
```

where

> **VO:** Current counter value

> **TO:** Current number of clock ticks

> **TB:** Time base or number of clock ticks per second

The basic algorithm counter types employ different formulas to produce cooked counter values, and it is uncommon to see the computational algorithms that utilize the base properties. Table 7-7 lists all the available basic algorithm counter types along with their descriptions and associated computational formulas. The following is the legend for the formulas:

> **V0/V1:** Counter values at the beginning/end of the monitoring interval

> **T0/T1:** Time values (number of clock ticks) at the beginning/end of the monitoring interval

> **B0/B1:** Base property values at the beginning/end of the monitoring interval

> **TB:** Time base or number of clock ticks per second

Table 7-7. Basic Algorithm Counter Types

COUNTER	DESCRIPTION	FORMULA
PERF_RAW_FRACTION (537003008)	Current percentage value calculated as a ratio of a subset of values to its set. Such a counter usually contains an instantaneous value to be divided by the value of the corresponding base counter (PERF_RAW_BASE).	V0/B0 * 100
PERF_SAMPLE_FRACTION (549585920)	Similar to PERF_RAW_FRACTION, but represents an average percentage value calculated over a period of time. This counter also requires a base counter of type PERF_RAW_BASE.	(V1-V0) / (B1-B0) * 100
PERF_COUNTER_DELTA (4195328)	Represents an absolute change in the value of the underlying performance counter measured over a period of time.	V1 - V0
PERF_COUNTER_LARGE_DELTA (4195584)	Same as PERF_COUNTER_DELTA, but uses 64-bit representation to hold very large values.	V1 - V0
PERF_ELAPSED_TIME (807666944)	Represents the total time elapsed between the start of the process and the current point in time.	(T0 - V0) / TB

Counter Algorithm Counters

The counter algorithm counter types are used to represent rate or average values calculated either for a sample or over a certain time interval. One example of a counter that falls into this category is Interrupt/sec of the Processor performance object discussed earlier in this section. Table 7-8 shows all available counter algorithm counter types along with their descriptions and associated computational formulas. The variables, used in these formulas adhere to the previous legend.

Table 7-8. Counter Algorithm Counter Types

COUNTER	DESCRIPTION	FORMULA
PERF_AVERAGE_BULK (1073874176)	Average number of items processed per operation. This value is calculated as a ratio of items processed to the total number of completed operations. Example: the AvgDiskBytesPerTransfer property of the Win32_PerfRawData_PerfDisk_PhysicalDisk class. The calculation requires the base property of type PERF_AVERAGE_BASE.	(V1 - V0) / (B1 - B0)
PERF_COUNTER_COUNTER (272696320)	Average number of completed operations per each second in the monitoring interval.	(V1 - V0) / ((T1 - T0) / TB)
PERF_SAMPLE_COUNTER (4260864)	Average number of operations completed in one second. The computation for this counter requires a base property of type PERF_SAMPLE_BASE.	(V1 - V0) / (B1 - B0)
PERF_COUNTER_BULK_COUNT (272696576)	Same as PERF_COUNTER_COUNTER but uses 64-bit representation to hold larger values.	(V1 - V0) / ((T1 - T0) / TB)

Timer Algorithm Counters

Timer algorithm counter types are used to represent time-based performance measures, such as the average time per operation or the ratio of active time vs. total time. An example of such a counter is an object represented by the PercentPrivilegedTime property of the Win32_PerfRawData_PerfOS_Processor class. This property reflects the percentage of time the processor spends in privileged mode, and it can be calculated using the following formula:

```
PercentagePrivilegedTime = ((V1-V0)/(T1-T0))*100
```

Interestingly, this counter is of type PERF_100NSEC_TIMER, which means that its value is expressed in units of 100 nanoseconds rather than in clock ticks, and the sampling interval is measured with 100-nanosecond precision.

Table 7-9 lists all the available timer algorithm counter types along with their descriptions and associated computational formulas. The variables used in the formulas adhere to the earlier legend.

Table 7-9 Timer Algorithm Counter Types

COUNTER	DESCRIPTION	FORMULA
PERF_COUNTER_TIMER (541132032)	Percentage of time an object is active.	$((V_1 - V_0) / (T_1 - T_0)) * 100$
PERF_COUNTER_TIMER_INV (557909248)	This counter type is the opposite of PERF_COUNTER_TIMER and expresses the percentage of time an object is inactive.	$(1 - (V_1 - V_0)/(T_1 - T_0)) * 100$
PERF_AVERAGE_TIMER (805438464)	Average time per operation. This counter types requires a base counter of type PERF_AVERAGE_BASE.	$((V_1 - V_0) / T_B) / (B_1 - B_0)$
PERF_100NSEC_TIMER (542180608)	This counter is the same as PERF_COUNTER_TIMER, but it expresses the value in units of 100 nanoseconds rather than in clock ticks.	$((V_1 - V_0) / (T_1 - T_0)) * 100$
PERF_100NSEC_TIMER_INV (592512256)	This counter is the same as PERF_COUNTER_TIMER_INV, but it expresses the value in units of 100 nanoseconds rather than in clock ticks.	$(1 - (V_1 - V_0) / (T_1 - T_0)) * 100$
PERF_COUNTER_MULTI_TIMER (574686464)	Percentage of time an object (or multiple objects) is active. This counter requires a base counter of type PERF_COUNTER_MULTI_BASE.	$((V_1 - V_0) / ((T_1 - T_0) / T_B)) / B_1 * 100$
PERF_COUNTER_MULTI_TIMER_INV 591463680)	This counter type is the opposite of PERF_COUNTER_ MULTI_TIMER and expresses the percentage of time an object (or multiple objects) is inactive.	$(((B_1 - ((V_1 - V_0) / ((T_1 - T_0) / T_B))) / B_1) * 100$

(continued)

Table 7-9 Timer Algorithm Counter Types (continued)

COUNTER	DESCRIPTION	FORMULA
PERF_100NSEC_MULTI_TIMER (575735040)	This counter is the same as PERF_COUNTER_MULTI_TIMER, but it expresses the value in units of 100 nanoseconds rather than in clock ticks.	$((V_1 - V_0) / ((T_1 - T_0) / T_B)) / B_1 * 100$
PERF_100NSEC_MULTI_TIMER_INV (592512256)	This counter is the same as PERF_COUNTER_MULTI_TIMER_INV, but it expresses the value in units of 100 nanoseconds rather than in clock ticks.	$((B_1 - ((V_1 - V_0) / ((T_1 - 0) / T_B))) / B_1) * 100$

Precision Algorithm Counters

The purpose of the precision algorithm counter types is to obtain the performance measurements that are more precise than those provided by the regular counter types. When you collect the performance data using regular counter types, there is an inherent error due to a small variable delay between the point when the value of the system clock is retrieved and the point when the performance sample is read. Thus, to minimize or eliminate this delay, the precision algorithm counter types employ a base counter of type PERF_PRECISION_TIMESTAMP, which is essentially a high-precision timestamp that should be used instead of the system clock. Therefore, a property of a WMI class that corresponds to a precision counter type must be immediately followed by a base property that refers to a PERF_PRECISION_TIMESTAMP counter, as shown here:

```
class Win32_PerfRawData_PerfDisk_PhysicalDisk : Win32_PerfRawData {
    ...
    [countertype(542573824)...]  // PERF_PRECISION_100NS_TIMER
    uint64 PercentIdleTime;
    [countertype(1073939712)...] // PERF_PRECISION_TIMESTAMP
    uint64 PercentIdleTime_Base;
    ...
};
```

Table 7-10 lists all available precision algorithm counter types along with their descriptions and associated computational formulas. The variables used in the formulas adhere to the legend shown earlier.

Table 7-10. Precision Algorithm Counter Types

COUNTER	DESCRIPTION	FORMULA
PERF_PRECISION_SYSTEM_TIMER (541525248)	This counter is the same as PERF_COUNTER_TIMER, but it uses the base counter for computations rather than the system clock.	$((V_1 - V_0) / (T_1 - T_0)) * 100$
PERF_PRECISION_100NS_TIMER (542573824)	This counter is the same as PERF_PRECISION_SYSTEM_TIMER, but it uses the 100-nanosecond precision base counter.	$((V_1 - V_0) / (T_1 - T_0)) * 100$

Queue-Length Algorithm Counters

Queue-length algorithm counter types typically represent an average number of items on a queue that is calculated over a time interval. An example of such a counter is the Average Disk Queue Length of a physical disk object, which is represented by the AvgDiskQueueLength property of Win32_PerfRawData_PerfDisk_PhysicalDisk. At any given time the raw value of this counter reflects the total number of items on the queue; thus, to produce the calculated measure, you can use the following formula:

AvgDiskQueueLength = $(V_1 - V_0)/(T_1 - T_0)$

Note, this counter is of type PERF_COUNTER_100NS_QUEUELEN_TYPE, so the monitoring interval has to be measured with 100-nanosecond precision.

Table 7-11 lists all the available queue-length algorithm counter types along with their descriptions and associated computational formulas. The variables, used in the formulas adhere to the legend shown earlier.

Table 7-11. Queue-Length Algorithms Counter Types

COUNTER	DESCRIPTION	FORMULA
PERF_COUNTER_QUEUELEN_TYPE (4523008)	Average length of a queue for a resource calculated over a certain time interval.	$(V_1 - V_0) / (T_1 - T_0)$
PERF_COUNTER_LARGE_QUEUELEN_TYPE (4523264)	This counter is the same as PERF_COUNTER_QUEUELEN_TYPE, but it uses 64-bit representation to hold larger values.	$(V_1 - V_0) / (T_1 - T_0)$

(continued)

Table 7-11. Queue-Length Algorithms Counter Types (continued)

COUNTER	DESCRIPTION	FORMULA
PERF_COUNTER_100NS_QUEUELEN_TYPE (5571840)	This counter is the same as PERF_COUNTER_QUEUELEN_TYPE, but it requires the monitoring interval to be measured with 100-nanosecond precision.	$(V_1 - V_0) / (T_1 - T_0)$
PERF_COUNTER_OBJECT_TIME_QUEUELEN_TYPE (6620416)	This counter is the same as PERF_COUNTER_QUEUELEN_TYPE, but it uses an object-specific time base rather than the system clock.	$(V_1 - V_0) / (T_1 - T_0)$

Statistical Counters

Finally, the last and perhaps the most complex category of performance counter types are the statistical counter types. These counter types are not available through the WMI classes supported by the Performance Counter provider. Instead, you must use the Cooked Counter provider, described in the next section, in order to obtain the statistical performance measures. In fact, these counters are only accessible through the Cooked Counter provider and do not exist outside of WMI. Thus, it is impossible to retrieve this kind of data using conventional performance interfaces, such as the Performance Data Helper (PDH) library.

Table 7-12 lists all the available statistical counter types along with their descriptions.

Table 7-12. Statistical Counter Types

COUNTER	DESCRIPTION
COOKER_AVERAGE	Provides the statistical average of the data for a particular counter. The cooked value is calculated by repeatedly sampling the underlying raw value, summing up the results, and dividing them by the number of samples taken.
COOKER_MIN	Represents the smallest value from a set of observations of a single raw counter value.
COOKER_MAX	Represents the largest value from a set of observations of a single raw counter value.

(continued)

Table 7-12. Statistical Counter Types (continued)

COUNTER	DESCRIPTION
COOKER_RANGE	Expresses the difference between the minimum and the maximum values from a set of observations of a single raw counter value.
COOKER_VARIANCE	Expresses the variability that can be indicative of dispersion for a set of observations of a single raw counter value. The cooked value is calculated by averaging the squared deviations from the mean for each sample taken.

Identifying the Counter Type

One pretty annoying thing about working with WMI raw performance classes is that you have to lookup the counter types based on the decimal value of the CounterType property qualifier. In other words, by looking at the MOF definition for a given class, you cannot deduce the types of counters to which the properties refer, unless, of course, you memorize the decimal values that correspond to each counter type. Life can be made a lot easier with help of a simple program that translates the numeric CounterType qualifier values into the human-readable counter type constants:

```
using System;
using System.Management;

enum PerfCounterType : ulong
{
    PERF_COUNTER_RAWCOUNT_HEX  = 0,
    PERF_COUNTER_LARGE_RAWCOUNT_HEX  = 256,
    PERF_COUNTER_TEXT  = 2816,
    PERF_COUNTER_RAWCOUNT  = 65536,
    PERF_COUNTER_LARGE_RAWCOUNT  = 65792,
    PERF_DOUBLE_RAW  = 73728,
    PERF_COUNTER_DELTA  = 4195328,
    PERF_COUNTER_LARGE_DELTA  = 4195584,
    PERF_SAMPLE_COUNTER  = 4260864,
    PERF_COUNTER_QUEUELEN_TYPE  = 4523008,
    PERF_COUNTER_LARGE_QUEUELEN_TYPE  = 4523264,
    PERF_COUNTER_100NS_QUEUELEN_TYPE  = 5571840,
    PERF_COUNTER_OBJ_TIME_QUEUELEN_TYPE  = 6620416,
    PERF_COUNTER_COUNTER  = 272696320,
```

```
            PERF_COUNTER_BULK_COUNT   = 272696576,
            PERF_RAW_FRACTION  = 537003008,
            PERF_COUNTER_TIMER  = 541132032,
            PERF_PRECISION_SYSTEM_TIMER  = 541525248,
            PERF_100NSEC_TIMER  = 542180608,
            PERF_PRECISION_100NS_TIMER  = 542573824,
            PERF_OBJ_TIME_TIMER  = 543229184,
            PERF_PRECISION_OBJECT_TIMER  = 543622400,
            PERF_SAMPLE_FRACTION  = 549585920,
            PERF_COUNTER_TIMER_INV  = 557909248,
            PERF_100NSEC_TIMER_INV  = 558957824,
            PERF_COUNTER_MULTI_TIMER  = 574686464,
            PERF_100NSEC_MULTI_TIMER  = 575735040,
            PERF_COUNTER_MULTI_TIMER_INV  = 591463680,
            PERF_100NSEC_MULTI_TIMER_INV  = 592512256,
            PERF_AVERAGE_TIMER  = 805438464,
            PERF_ELAPSED_TIME  = 807666944,
            PERF_COUNTER_NODATA  = 1073742336,
            PERF_AVERAGE_BULK  = 1073874176,
            PERF_SAMPLE_BASE  = 1073939457,
            PERF_AVERAGE_BASE  = 1073939458,
            PERF_RAW_BASE  = 1073939459,
            PERF_PRECISION_TIMESTAMP  = 1073939712,
            PERF_LARGE_RAW_BASE  = 1073939715,
            PERF_COUNTER_MULTI_BASE  = 1107494144,
            PERF_COUNTER_HISTOGRAM_TYPE  = 2147483648
        };
        class PerfCounters {
        public static void Main(string[] args) {
            ManagementClass c = new ManagementClass("Win32_PerfRawData");
            foreach(ManagementClass mc in c.GetSubclasses()) {
                Console.WriteLine("Class: {0}", mc["__CLASS"]);
                foreach(PropertyData pd in mc.Properties) {
                    try {
                        PerfCounterType ct = (PerfCounterType)ulong.Parse(
                            mc.GetPropertyQualifierValue(pd.Name, "CounterType").ToString());
                        Console.WriteLine("   {0} : {1}", pd.Name, ct);
                    } catch (Exception e) {}
                }
                Console.WriteLine();
            }
        }
        }
```

The key idea behind this code involves using the enumeration PerfCounterType to translate the decimal counter type values into meaningful identifiers. As you may remember, when printing the members of an enumeration, the WriteLine method outputs a label rather than the underlying numeric value. Thus, by defining the PerfCounterType enumeration so that each of its members has an underlying value that corresponds to a single counter type value, you can simply cast the numeric value of the CounterType qualifier to an enumeration variable and print it out, letting the WriteLine method handle the conversion. Note that counter types are usually large decimal numbers; therefore, the PerfCounterType has to have an underlying type that is large enough to accommodate such values. The default underlying type is int, which is not sufficient to hold most of the counter type values; that is why the enumeration is declared with an underlying type of long.

Yet another trick is enumerating all WMI raw performance classes. Luckily, every class backed by the Performance Counter provider originates from the same ancestor: Win32_PerfRawData. As a result, the task of obtaining the performance classes can be reduced to binding to the Win32_PerfRawData class and enumerating all of its subclasses.

Finally, you may be asking, "What is the purpose of the try/catch block that surrounds the code that retrieves the value of the CounterType qualifier for each property and converts it to the associated member of the PerfCounterType enumeration?" The problem that the try/catch block is designed to solve is that certain properties of a performance class—its key, for instance—may not have the CounterType qualifier, in which case the GetPropertyQualifierValue method will throw an exception. For our purposes, such properties are of no interest and should be simply ignored, hence the empty try/catch construct in the code fragment above.

Curiously, you do not even have to define your own PerfCounterType enumeration. The System.Diagnostics namespace already contains an enumeration type, called PerformanceCounterType, which is equivalent to the PerfCounterType, shown earlier, and, therefore it can be used in the same way. The only difference is that rather than using the standard counter value constants referred to throughout the Platform SDK documentation, this enumeration introduces its own comprehensive labels. Thus, PERF_RAW_FRACTION is referred to as RawFraction, PERF_COUNTER_RAWCOUNT becomes NumberOfItems32, and so on.

Working with Raw Performance Classes

At first, raw performance classes may seem fairly incomprehensible and difficult to work with, simply due to the large amount of background information that you have to study in order to produce even a rudimentary monitoring program. However, once you develop a basic understanding of the principles that govern the collection of raw performance data, coding becomes fairly trivial. In order to put things in context, look at this simple example of monitoring the Interrupts/sec counter of the Processor object:

```
using System;
using System.Management;

class ProcessorMonitor {
public static void Main(string[] args) {
    DateTime t0 = DateTime.UtcNow;
    DateTime t1;
    ManagementObject mo =
        new ManagementObject("Win32_PerfRawData_PerfOS_Processor='0'");
    float v0 = float.Parse(mo["InterruptsPersec"].ToString());
    float v1 = 0;
    while(true) {
        System.Threading.Thread.Sleep(10000);
        t1 = DateTime.UtcNow;
        mo = new ManagementObject("Win32_PerfRawData_PerfOS_Processor='0'");
        v1 = float.Parse(mo["InterruptsPersec"].ToString());
        Console.WriteLine((v1-v0)/(t1-t0).Seconds);
        v0 = v1;
        t0 = t1;
    }
}
}
```

This code is really not complex. First, it allocated two sets of variables: two of type DateTime to hold the time measurements for the beginning and end of the monitoring interval; and two floats for recording the values of the InterruptsPersec property of Win32_PerfRawData_PerfOS_Processor also at the beginning and end of the monitoring interval. The variables that correspond to the starting time of the monitoring interval and counter value at that time are initialized appropriately. The time is read from the UtcNow property of the DateTime type, which returns the current time in Universal Time Coordinates (UTC) also known as Greenwich Mean Time (GMT). The value of the performance counter is obtained from the InterruptsPersec property of the Win32_PerfRawData_PerfOS_Processor object, which corresponds to CPU 0. Then an infinite while loop first suspends the execution of the current thread for the duration of the monitoring interval (10000 milliseconds), and when the thread returns from the Thread.Sleep method, it obtains the time and the counter value that correspond to the end of the interval.

The cooked counter value is then calculated as the difference between the counter values at the beginning and end of the interval divided by the interval duration in units of seconds ($(V1 - V0)/(T1 - T0)$) and printed on the system console. The duration of the interval is calculated using the subtraction operator (-) of DateTime type, which yields an object of type TimeSpan. To convert the TimeSpan object into an integer number of seconds, the code reads the value of its Seconds property. Finally, the code reinitializes the variables that correspond to the beginning of the monitoring interval to prepare for the next iteration of the while loop.

Despite its obvious simplicity, this code may raise a few questions. First, the formula used to calculate the cooked value of the performance counter seems to be a bit different. As you may remember, the original calculation, shown earlier, relies on recording the interval beginning and end time as a number of clock ticks and then dividing the difference between these by either the time base or clock frequency. The reality is that it does not necessarily have to be done this way. The DateTime objects records the time using a100-nanosecond precision clock. As a result, the TimeSpan object, which was obtained by subtracting the beginning time from the end time, houses the interval duration expressed in units of 100-nanosecond ticks. Thus, reading the value of the TimeSpan.Seconds property, which converts ticks to seconds, is equivalent to applying the time base to the calculation.

If the idea is to eventually calculate the duration of the interval in units of seconds, why bother recording the time? After all, the thread is suspended for 10 seconds (10000 milliseconds) using the Thread.Sleep method, so why not just divide the counter value difference by 10 and be done with it? Well, unfortunately, Thread.Sleep is imprecise and may not necessarily suspend the current thread for exactly 10 seconds. This may introduce a significant error into the calculation and skew the results.

The approach taken by the preceding code is fine and will produce fairly accurate results, especially for large monitoring intervals. However, there will always be some error, mainly due to the way the measurements are taken. The process of taking a performance measurement has two parts: recording the time, and sampling the performance counter value that corresponds to that point in time. Because there are two distinct steps involved, taking a performance measurement is not atomic as there is always a slight delay between the two operations. (Actually, this is one of the reasons why Microsoft introduced the precision algorithm counter types that rely on high-precision timestamps rather than the system clock.) Nevertheless, even when you are dealing with simple counters such as Interrupts/sec, there is a way to minimize an error that results from the nonatomic nature of the performance measurement operation.

As I already mentioned, all raw performance counter classes have a common superclass: Win32_PerfRawData. There is a reason for such design, besides just providing a convenient way to enumerate all performance classes. It turns out that Win32_PerfRawData has a few useful properties of its own that often provide a neat solution to some of the problems that may arise when you are taking the performance measurements. Take a look at the class definition:

```
class Win32_PerfRawData : Win32_Perf {
    string Name;
    string Caption;
    string Description;
    uint64 Timestamp_Object;
    uint32 Frequency_Object;
    uint64 Timestamp_PerfTime;
    uint64 Frequency_PerfTime;
    uint64 Timestamp_Sys100NS;
    uint64 Frequency_Sys100NS;
}
```

This class has the following properties:

Name: The name of the associated performance metric

Caption: A short description of the associated performance metric

Description: A long description of the associated performance metric

Timestamp_Object: An object-defined timestamp that contains a time measure expressed in units specific to a given performance object

Frequency_Object: A time base or frequency in ticks per second for the object-defined timestamp, Timestamp_Object

Timestamp_PerfTime: A timestamp expressed in units of clock ticks

Frequency_PerfTime: A time base or frequency in ticks per second for the timestamp, Timestamp_PerfTime

Timestamp_Sys100NS: A timestamp, expressed in units of 100-nanosecond clock ticks

Frequency_Sys100NS: A time base or frequency of the 100-nanosecond clock for the timestamp, Timestamp_Sys100NS

Two of the Win32_PerfRawData properties—Timestamp_PerfTime and Frequency_PerfTime—are exactly what you need to calculate the cooked value for the Interrupts/sec counter. Using the values of these properties not only alleviates the need for recording the time manually, but it also ensures the atomic nature of the operation. As you may remember, binding to a management object causes a copy of the object to be created locally, which means that all subsequent property access operations work against this local copy. Thus, once a bound instance of the ManagementObject type is created, it reflects the state of the management object at a time of creation so that the timestamp values correspond exactly to the respective counter values.

With this in mind, the code for monitoring the Interrupts/sec counter can be rewritten as follows:

```
using System;
using System.Management;

class ProcessorMonitor {
public static void Main(string[] args) {
    ulong t0, t1, tb;
    float v0, v1;
    ManagementObject mo =
        new ManagementObject("Win32_PerfRawData_PerfOS_Processor='0'");
    v0 = float.Parse(mo["InterruptsPersec"].ToString());
    t0 = ulong.Parse(mo["Timestamp_PerfTime"].ToString());
    tb = ulong.Parse(mo["Frequency_PerfTime"].ToString());
    while(true) {
        System.Threading.Thread.Sleep(5000);
        mo = new ManagementObject("Win32_PerfRawData_PerfOS_Processor='0'");
        v1 = float.Parse(mo["InterruptsPersec"].ToString());
        t1 = ulong.Parse(mo["Timestamp_PerfTime"].ToString());
        Console.WriteLine((v1-v0)/((t1-t0)/tb));
        v0 = v1;
        t0 = t1;
    }
}
}
```

This approach is not only simpler and more accurate, it is also elegant and definitely more self-contained because there is no reliance on external mechanisms for recording the time.

The Cooked Counter Provider

The Performance Counter provider is certainly a very good source of performance metrics; it affords its users a great deal of flexibility while ensuring adequate performance. There is, however, a price to pay. Using this provider is a bit tricky; a developer needs to fully understand the raw performance counter types and be proficient in applying the appropriate computations in order to derive meaningful "cooked" performance statistics. In order to shorten the learning curve and provide a way to quickly build simple performance monitoring tools, Microsoft introduced the Cooked Counter provider, which became the preferred source of performance metrics on Windows XP platforms.

Understanding the Cooked Counter Provider

The Cooked Counter provider is a high-performance provider that exposes the calculated or formatted performance statistics; as a result this provider eliminates the need to understand the differences between various counter types and to apply proper calculations to the raw data. In effect, you may think of this provider as a wrapper on top of the Performance Counter provider that encapsulates the algorithms necessary to produce the cooked performance metrics.

WMI classes, backed by the Cooked Counter provider, are created automatically and maintained by ADAP. These classes reside in the root\CIMV2 namespace and, just like the raw performance classes, have a common ancestor: Win32_PerfFormattedData. The definition for this class is identical to that of Win32_PerfRawData, which was shown earlier in this chapter. As a matter of fact, WMI classes that are exposed by the Cooked Counter provider are also very similar to their respective raw counter classes—typically, each "cooked" class would act as a wrapper for the corresponding "raw" class. For example, Win32_PerfFormattedData_PerfOS_Processor is a cooked alternative to the already familiar Win32_PerfRawData_PerfOS_Processor. What sets the cooked and raw class definitions apart is their qualifiers. Table 7-13 lists all the class qualifiers that are used for WMI classes that are backed by the Cooked Counter provider.

Table 7-13. Class Qualifiers for Cooked Performance Counter Classes

QUALIFIER	DESCRIPTION
AutoCook	This qualifier sets the cooking version of the class and essentially indicates that the provider will cook the performance data automatically based on the raw counter values. The current release of the Cooked Counter provider requires this qualifier be set to 1.

(continued)

Table 7-13. Class Qualifiers for Cooked Performance Counter Classes (continued)

QUALIFIER	DESCRIPTION
AutoCook_RawClass	Name of the underlying raw performance class used by the provider to derive the values for cooking.
AutoCook_RawDefault	This qualifier indicates that the underlying raw class has the following properties, often used in the performance measures computations: Timestamp_PerfTime, Timestamp_Sys100NS, Timestamp_Object, Frequency_PerfTime, Frequency_Sys100NS, and Frequency_Object. The current release of the Cooked Counter provider requires this qualifier be set to 1.
Base	For counters that require a base counter for computations, this qualifier indicates the name of the property of an underlying raw class that corresponds to the base performance counter.
Cooked	Boolean value that indicates whether the class contains cooked performance data.
Perf100NSTimeFreq	Name of the underlying raw class property to be used as a frequency of a 100-nanosecond clock in cooking computations.
Perf100NSTimeStamp	Name of the underlying raw class property to be used as a 100-nanosecond timestamp in cooking computations.
PerfObjTimeFreq	Name of the underlying raw class property to be used as an object frequency in cooking computations.
PerfObjTimeStamp	Name of the underlying raw class property to be used as an object timestamp in cooking computations.
PerfSysTimeFreq	Name of the underlying raw class property to be used as a frequency of a system clock in cooking computations.
PerfSysTimeStamp	Name of the underlying raw class property to be used as a system timestamp in cooking computations.

Just as is the case with raw performance classes, the properties of the cooked classes are decorated with provider-specific qualifiers as well. These qualifiers provide a "recipe" for "cooking" the raw data and obtaining the meaningful result. Table 7-14 lists all property qualifiers for the cooked performance classes.

Table 7-14. Property Qualifiers for Cooked Performance Classes

QUALIFIER	DESCRIPTION
Base	For counters that require a base counter for computations, this qualifier indicates the name of the property of an underlying raw class, which corresponds to the base performance counter.
CookingType	This qualifier identifies the formula required to produce a cooked result based on the value of the underlying raw counter. This qualifier uses the same set of values as the CounterType qualifier of the Raw Performance Counter provider. For a complete description of counter types, see Tables 7-5 through 7-12.
Counter	Name of the underlying raw class property to be used as a counter value in cooking computations.
PerfTimeFreq	Name of the underlying raw class property to be used as a clock frequency in cooking computations. If this qualifier is not present, the provider will use a default value, set by the appropriate class-level qualifier (see Table 7-13).
PerfTimeStamp	Name of the underlying raw class property to be used as a timestamp in cooking computations. If this qualifier is not present, the provider will use a default value, set by the appropriate class-level qualifier (see Table 7-13).
SampleWindow	Mainly used for statistical counter types to define a number of samples for calculating the final cooked value.

Using the Cooked Counter Provider

The best news, of course, is that an application developer does not have to know anything about these qualifiers. Unlike the Performance Counter provider, which requires the programmers to fully understand its class and property qualifiers in order to apply the proper computation to the raw values, the Cooked Counter provider does all the grunt work behind the scenes. Thus, implementing a monitoring utility based upon the cooked performance classes becomes a rather trivial coding exercise. To prove this, I will rewrite the monitor for the Interrupts/sec counter using the Win32_PerfFormattedData_PerfOS_Processor class:

```
using System;
using System.Management;

class ProcessorMonitor {
public static void Main(string[] args) {
    while(true) {
        System.Threading.Thread.Sleep(5000);
        mo = new ManagementObject("Win32_PerfFormattedData_PerfOS_Processor='0'");
        Console.WriteLine(mo["InterruptsPersec"]);
    }
}
}
```

As you can see, retrieving a performance metric basically comes down to reading the respective property of a cooked WMI object. This approach is far more advantageous than using the Performance Counter provider because it results in a more compact and simple code and leaves virtually no room for error. Unfortunately, the Cooked Counter provider is only available on Windows XP platforms, so the unfortunate users of older Windows systems are stuck with using either the slow Performance Monitoring provider or doing the computations using the raw performance data.

The SNMP Provider

The Simple Network Management Protocol (SNMP) was developed in the late 1980s in an attempt to satisfy rapidly growing demands for reliable management of heterogeneous networks. SNMP quickly gained popularity and remains the best explored management standard for TCP/IP-based internets.

The core of SNMP is the database housing the management data upon which the network management system operates. This database is commonly referred to as Management Information Base (MIB). SNMP MIB is a tree-like collection of objects, each representing a managed resource on a network. An SNMP-based network management system can monitor the state of these objects by reading their properties, and it can alter their states by modifying these properties. The organization of a MIB is governed by a standard called the Structure of Management Information (SMI), which outlines the rules for constructing and defining MIB management objects. Over the years, many different MIBs have been developed to address various aspects of network and system management; these include the Relational Database Monitoring MIB, the Mail Management MIB, and many others. However, MIB-II, which defines the second version of the management information base for TCP/IP-based internets, remains the most important and the most commonly used MIB specification. MIB-II defines the following broad groups of management information:

System: Includes general information about the networked system such as its identification information, location, and uptime

Interfaces: Houses information that describes each of the system's network interfaces

AT: Contains information pertinent to the operations of an address translation (AT) protocol—essentially the contents of the address translation table

IP: Contains information pertinent to the operations of the Internet Protocol (IP) on a given system

ICMP: Houses information pertinent to the operations of the Internet Control Message Protocol (ICMP) on a given system

TCP: Contains information pertinent to the operations of the Transmission Control Protocol (TCP) on a given system

UDP: Contains information pertinent to the operations of User Datagram Protocol (UDP) on a given system

EGP: Houses information pertinent to the operations of Exterior Gateway Protocol (EGP) on a given system

DOT3: Contains information pertinent to the transmission schemes and access protocols at each system interface

SNMP: Includes information pertinent to the operations of the Simple Network Management Protocol (SNMP) on a given system

Due to its widespread popularity and significant install base, SNMP is still a valuable source of management information, despite its fairly narrow specialization and some inherent inflexibility. As a result, when you are building a distributed enterprise management system, the ability to integrate the existing SNMP installations into the management model may be instrumental in determining your success.

WMI SNMP Provider

In a perfect world, all managed systems talk the same language or, in other words, expose the information for management in a way that complies with a common standard such as WBEM. In the real world, however, the situation is different. Thus, a typical managed environment is likely to include a number of computers that do not understand WBEM and, at best, run some legacy management system such as SNMP. My world, for instance, consists of five Sun Microsystems SPARCs running Solaris 8, two Linux machines, six Compaq servers running Windows 2000, and countless desktops with an odd mix of Windows NT, Windows 2000, and Windows XP.

Managing the Windows boxes in a centralized fashion does not seem to be a problem because they all support WMI. UNIX machines, on the other hand, are more troublesome. This does not mean that the UNIX/Linux community has been ignoring the WBEM standard altogether—in fact, a few UNIX vendors already provide WBEM-compliant management tools, such as Solaris WBEM SDK. Moreover, the latest Common Information Model (CIM) Specification version 2.6 is specifically concerned with the issue of managing UNIX platforms. The new model includes a number of elements that map to the Open Group's Single UNIX Specification and address various management aspects of UNIX systems, such as modeling of processes, threads, and filesystems. Thus, at least in theory, it should be possible to outfit the UNIX machines with WBEM capabilities, which would allow for administering them from a single centralized management console.

Unfortunately, this is where the reality kicks in. First, most UNIX WBEM implementations are nowhere near as sophisticated as WMI and do not seem to support some of its essential functionality (WQL queries, for instance). But most importantly, there does not seem to be a good way of integrating, say, the Solaris WBEM package with WMI, due to radical differences in their APIs and interfaces. To nobody's surprise, Solaris's WBEM is Java-based, and therefore, it does not lend itself easily to being integrated into a COM-centric WMI model. Perhaps in the future when all WBEM implementations are equipped with support for platform-neutral communication protocols such as the Simple Object Access Protocol (SOAP), the integration issue will go away, but the technology is not there yet.

The good news is that all UNIX flavors support SNMP. In fact, there is an SNMP implementation for just about every conceivable computing platform in existence today. Although not a match for WBEM in terms of versatility and flexibility, SNMP has a number of advantages. First, it is an old and well-understood standard, so most implementations are similar when it comes to the structure of management information and supported functionality. Second, it conveys the management information using a set of well-defined UDP-based messages, meaning that cross-platform communications are not a problem. Thus, if integrated with WMI, SNMP may be an acceptable, although not perfect, solution to the problem of managing dissimilar computing nodes in a centralized fashion.

The integration of SNMP with WMI is achieved via the SNMP provider, which essentially acts as a proxy, translating the WMI requests into SNMP messages and then converting the SNMP responses into a form that is consumable by WMI. In fact, there are several SNMP providers:

Class provider: Responsible for dynamically providing WMI class definitions that correspond to SNMP MIB objects.

Instance provider: Responsible for providing access to SNMP management data.

Event providers: Responsible for generating WMI events from SNMP traps and notifications. There are two event providers that generate WMI events in two different formats: encapsulated and referent. These formats are described in detail in the "Receiving SNMP Traps" section later in this chapter.

Mapping SNMP Objects to WMI

The most important task the providers mentioned in the previous section are required to perform is mapping the SNMP data to WMI classes and objects. So that you can understand how this is accomplished, I will first explain how SNMP MIBs are structured.

The notation used to define SNMP objects, is known as Abstract Syntax Notation One (ASN.1). This is a declarative language that was developed and standardized by the Telecommunication Standardization Sector (CCITT) of the International Telecommunications Union (ITU) and the International Standards Organization (ISO). ASN.1 provides a set of predefined primitive types, such as INTEGER or BOOLEAN and compound data types, such as SET or SEQUENCE; and it offers syntax for declaring new types, which are derived from existing types. Additionally, there is a provision for defining macros—templates that can define sets of related types. A macro definition outlines a set of legitimate macro instances and specifies the traits of a set of related types. In essence, a macro definition can be viewed as a *meta-type,* which defines characteristics of a type. A *macro instance,* produced by supplying proper arguments for the parameters of the macro, is a specification for a concrete SNMP type. Finally, a *macro instance value* represents a specific SNMP entity or object.

There are few SNMP macros used as a basis for mapping the SNMP data to WMI:

OBJECT-TYPE: Used to describe the traits of an SNMP object

TEXTUAL-CONVENTION: Used to enhance the readability of the MIB source and specify additional type semantics

TRAP-TYPE: Used to describe the characteristics of an SNMP trap or event in SNMPv1

NOTIFICATION-TYPE: Used to describe the characteristics of an SNMP trap or event in SNMPv2

When building SNMP MIBs, the only way to structure the data is by defining simple, two-dimensional tables that contain entries with scalar values. Thus, it is possible to draw a parallel between an SNMP table and a WMI class so that individual table entries correspond to specific WMI objects. For instance, the TCP Connection table, which houses the information about all TCP connections for a particular managed node, contains the following elements or columns:

tcpConnState: State of a particular TCP connection

tcpConnLocalAddress: The local IP address of a particular TCP connection

tcpConnLocalPort: The local port number of a particular TCP connection

tcpConnRemAddress: The remote IP address of a particular TCP connection

tcpConnRemPort: The remote port number of a particular TCP connection

The entire data structure is defined in SNMP MIB as a sequence of OBJECT-TYPE macros where the enclosing macro defines the tcpConnTable object itself, and individual columns are specified by inner OBJECT-TYPE macros—one for each of the elements in the preceding list.

Translated to MOF, such definition will look like the following:

```
class SNMP_RFC1213_MIB_tcpConnTable : SnmpObjectType {
    string tcpConnState;
    sint32 tcpConnRemPort;
    sint32 tcpConnLocalPort;
    string tcpConnRemAddress;
    string tcpConnLocalAddress;
};
```

Here the entire TCP Connection Table is represented by a single WMI class and the individual table columns are translated into the WMI class properties. Note that the class is derived from an abstract superclass SnmpObjectType. The superclass does not add any properties; it is only used as a vehicle for grouping the SNMP objects. The naming convention used for the generated WMI class definitions is interesting—the name of the WMI class is constructed as a name of the respective SNMP table, prefixed with "SNMP_RFC1213_MIB" string. The RFC1213_MIB portion of the prefix is actually the name of the MIB module, provided by another macro, MODULE-IDENTITY. Apparently, RFC1213 refers to Request for Comments 1213, "Management Information Base for Network Management of TCP/IP-Based Internets: MIB2," which defines the second version of the MIB.

SNMP events, referred to as traps, are mapped in a similar fashion. If a trap is defined in a MIB using the SNMPv1 TRAP-TYPE macro, it is first mapped to a newer SNMPv2 NOTIFICATION-TYPE macro and then converted to an appropriate WMI class. All WMI classes representing SNMP traps, ultimately derive from the system class, __ExtrinsicEvent, which makes subscribing for traps similar to registering for WMI extrinsic events. However, depending on the event provider, the trap classes may inherit from one of the two subclasses of __ExtrinsicEvent: SnmpNotification or SnmpExtendedNotification. The former is used to model encapsulated events, while the latter represents referent events. The difference between the two is usually in the form of some additional class properties within the referent event class; these properties allow you to establish a link to an underlying object that is responsible for generating a trap.

The MIB definitions are converted to a form consumable by WMI using the SNMP Information Module Compiler (smi2smir.exe) utility, which is distributed as part of the WMI SDK. It is a very flexible program, which can be used to not only translate MIBs, but also update the CIM Repository and produce extensive informational and diagnostic output.

Based on whether you want to use the dynamic class provider, you have two options when converting SNMP MIBs to WMI class definitions. First, you can use the Information Module Compiler to produce regular MOF files, which can then be loaded into the repository manually, using mofcomp.exe. Alternatively, you can instruct smi2smir.exe to load the generated WMI class definitions into a specially designated portion of the CIM Repository, known as SNMP Module Information Repository (SMIR). SMIR is a special namespace, which usually resides under root\SNMP\SMIR, and it is used by the dynamic class provider as a template for generating the appropriate class definitions on demand.

The following is the basic syntax for invoking smi2smir.exe:

```
SMI2SMIR.EXE <command-line options> <MIB file> <Import files>
```

Table 7-15 lists all the SMI2SMIR.EXE command-line options.

Table 7-15. SMI2SMIR.EXE Command-Line Options

OPTION	DESCRIPTION
/m <level>	Designates the level of diagnostics to output: 0—Silent 1—Fatal 2—Fatal and warnings (default) 3—Fatal, warnings, and information messages
/c	Indicates the maximum total number of fatal and warning messages to output. If omitted, there is no limit.
/v1	Enforces strict conformance to SNMPv1 and instructs the compiler to report an error if it encounters non-SNMPv1-compliant statements.
/v2c	Enforces strict conformance to SNMPv2 and instructs the compiler to report an error if it encounters non-SNMPv2-compliant statements.
/d	Deletes the module specified by the MIB file from the SMIR.
/p	Deletes all modules from the SMIR.
/l	Lists all modules in the SMIR.
/lc	Conducts a local syntax check on the module specified by the MIB file.
/ec <modifier>	Conducts a local and external syntax check on the module specified by the MIB file.
/a <modifier>	Conducts a local and external syntax check on the module specified by the MIB file and loads the module into the SMIR.
/sa <modifier>	Same as /a except that it does not produce any diagnostic output.
/g <modifier>	Generates a MOF file suitable for being loaded into the SMIR.
/gc <modifier>	Generates a static MOF file suitable for being loaded into the appropriate SNMP namespace manually. This option is very useful in situations when the dynamic class provider is not used.
/h, /?	Prints out help information.

Some command-line options may take command modifiers, as detailed in Table 7-16.

Table 7-16. SMI2SMIR.EXE Command Modifiers

MODIFIER	DESCRIPTION
/i <directory>	Specifies a lookup directory to be searched for dependent MIB files. This modifier can be used with options /a, /ec, /g, /gc, and /sa. You can use this option multiple times on a single command-line in order to specify multiple lookup directories. The order of lookup depends on the order of /i options within the command line.
/ch	Adds date, time, host, and user identifiers to the header of the generated MOF file. This modifier can be used with the /g and /gc options.
/t	Instructs the compiler to generate SnmpNotification classes. This modifier can be used with /a, /g, and /sa options.
/ext	Instructs the compiler to generate SnmpExtendedNotification classes. This modifier can be used with /a, /g, and /sa options.
/t /o	Instructs the compiler to generate only SnmpNotification classes. This modifier can be used with /a, /g, and /sa options.
/ext /o	Instructs the compiler to generate only SnmpExtendedNotification classes. This modifier can be used with /a, /g, and /sa options.
/s	Causes the compiler to ignore the text in the DESCRIPTION clause. This modifier can be used to minimize the size of the output WMI class definitions. It can be used with /a, /g, /gc, and /sa options.
/auto	Causes the compiler to rebuild the MIB lookup table before processing the command-line option. This modifier can be used with /a, /ec, /g, and /gc options.

When processing MIB files, smi2smir.exe uses a registry lookup table to search for dependent MIB files. In order to administer and maintain this table, the utility provides a few command-line options, shown in Table 7-17.

Table 7-17. smi2smir.exe Lookup Table Administration Command-Line Options

OPTION	DESCRIPTION
/pa	Adds the directory name supplied on the command line to the lookup table
/pd	Deletes the directory name supplied on the command line from the lookup table
/pl	Lists all directory names in the lookup table
/r	Rebuilds the lookup table

Finally, the smi2smir.exe utility can be used to obtain the module information (ASN.1 module names) from a MIB file. Table 7-18 shows the command-line options that instruct the compiler to extract the names from the SNMP module.

Table 7-18. smi2smir.exe Module Information Command-Line Options

OPTION	DESCRIPTION
/n	Instructs the compiler to extract and output the ASN.1 name of the MIB module pointed to by the MIB file argument.
/ni	Instructs the compiler to extract and output the ASN.1 names of all import modules, which are used by the MIB module, pointed to by the MIB file argument.

Configuring the SNMP Provider

As I already mentioned, the SNMP to WMI bridge can be configured in a couple of different ways (with or without the dynamic class provider). Perhaps the easiest way to set it up is to compile the MIB for a particular SNMP device using the smi2smir.exe with the /gc option and then load the resulting WMI class definitions into the appropriate WMI namespace. Once such static class definitions are installed, the SNMP instance provider takes care of retrieving the appropriate instance-level data.

The apparent downside of this approach is that it involves a fair amount of manual labor and leaves a lot of room for error. The problem is that SNMP devices and SNMP agents differ and they may not always possess certain capabilities. Thus, unless you load a MIB definition that is specific to the device in question, rather than a generic MIB, the repository may be polluted with unsupported SNMP classes.

This problem may easily be solved by utilizing the dynamic class provider. This provider is responsible for generating the WMI class definitions dynamically, based on the template classes, which can be found in the SMIR repository. The repository, located in the root\SNMP\SMIR namespace, usually houses the WMI class definitions that correspond to a generic MIB. In fact, if installed with SNMP support enabled, WMI automatically loads such generic classes into the SMIR, thus alleviating the need for manually compiling the MIB modules with smi2smir.exe. Once the SMIR is populated with class templates, the provider can query the SNMP agent and match the returned SNMP object IDs (OIDs) against the objects in the repository, thus determining the capabilities of the agent.

The provider is fairly flexible and can operate in two modes: correlated and noncorrelated. When enumerating classes in correlated mode, the provider traverses the SMIR and returns only the classes that are supported by the SNMP agent. In noncorrelated mode, all classes from SMIR are returned to the client. While the former is default, the mode can be controlled via the Boolean context value Correlate, which can be set through the IWbemContext interface.

Regardless of whether the class provider is utilized, there has to be a way to associate a set of WMI classes that pertain to a particular SNMP device with that device. If you recall the definition for the SNMP_RFC1213_MIB_tcpConnTable class, shown earlier, you may remember that the class does not seem to include any properties, such as host name or address, which would allow it to be bound to a specific SNMP device.

In this case, rather than associating individual WMI classes with corresponding SNMP objects that pertain to a given device, the SNMP provider relies on the association between a device and a WMI namespace, which houses the respective classes. Thus, in order to gain access to SNMP objects for a given computing node, you have to set up a separate WMI proxy namespace that is linked to the node in question. For instance, in order to see the SNMP objects pertaining to one of my UNIX hosts called "sun1", I would have to set up a separate WMI namespace and link it to the host name or address. Linking a namespace and a SNMP device is accomplished with the help of class qualifiers with which the namespace class is decorated. The following MOF code snippet shows the minimalistic declaration for the namespace class:

```
#pragma namespace("\\\\.\\root\snmp")
[AgentAddress("sun1")]
instance of __Namespace {
    Name = "sun1";
};
```

The result of compiling and loading this code with MOFCOMP.EXE is a new namespace root\SNMP\SUN1, attributed with an AgentAddress qualifier that points to the UNIX host "sun1".

The AgentAddress qualifier is not the only qualifier that may appear as part of the SNMP namespace declaration, although it is the only qualifier necessary for the SNMP provider to establish a link between WMI and the SNMP device. Table 7-19 shows all the qualifiers that are permitted to appear as part of the SNMP namespace declaration.

Table 7-19. SNMP Provider Namespace Qualifiers

QUALIFIER	DESCRIPTION
AgentAddress	Transport address (valid unicast host IP address or DNS name) associated with a specific SNMP agent.
AgentTransport	Transport protocol that is used to communicate with the SNMP agent. Currently, the only valid values are IP (Internet Protocol) and IPX (Internet Packet Exchange). The default value is IP.
AgentReadCommunityName	Variable-length octet string used by the SNMP agent to authenticate the requestor during a read operation. The default value is public.
AgentWriteCommunityName	Variable-length octet string used by the SNMP agent to authenticate the requestor during a write operation. The default value is public.
AgentRetryCount	Integer value that specifies the number of times an SNMP request can be retried before indicating failure to the client. The default value is 1.
AgentRetryTimeout	Time (in milliseconds) to wait for the response from an SNMP agent before indicating failure. The default value is 500.
AgentVarBindsPerPdu	Integer value indicating the maximum number of variables that can be included in a single request. The default value is 10.
AgentFlowControlWindowSize	Integer value indicating the maximum number of outstanding requests that can be sent to an SNMP agent while the response has not yet been received. The value of 0 indicates an infinite number of requests. The default value is 10.
AgentSNMPVersion	String specifying the version of SNMP used to communicate with an SNMP agent. The permitted values are 1 (for SNMPv1) and 2C (for SNMPv2C). The default value is 1.

In order to configure the SNMP bindings for a particular device, you have to set up not only the SNMP namespace, but also the appropriate provider registration entries, and if the class provider is not utilized, you have to load the static classes into the namespace. As I already mentioned, the simplest configuration relies on the SMIR repository and therefore, does not include the static class definitions. For instance, Listing 7-1 shows the MOF code that is sufficient to establish the link to the SNMP agent that is running on the host "sun1".

Listing 7-1. SNMP Namespace and Provider Registration

```
#pragma namespace("\\\\.\\root\\snmp")

[AgentAddress ( "sun1" )]
instance of __Namespace {
   Name = "sun1" ;
} ;


#pragma namespace("\\\\.\\root\\snmp\\sun1")

instance of __Win32Provider as $PClass {
   Name = "MS_SNMP_CLASS_PROVIDER";
   Clsid = "{70426720-F78F-11cf-9151-00AA00A4086C}";
};
instance of __ClassProviderRegistration {
   Provider = $PClass;
   SupportsGet = TRUE;
   SupportsPut = FALSE;
   SupportsDelete = FALSE;
   SupportsEnumeration = TRUE;
   QuerySupportLevels = NULL ;
   ResultSetQueries = { "Select * From meta_class Where __this isa SnmpMacro" } ;
} ;
instance of __Win32Provider as $EventProv {
   Name = "MS_SNMP_REFERENT_EVENT_PROVIDER";
   ClsId = "{9D5BED16-0765-11d1-AB2C-00C04FD9159E}";
};
instance of __EventProviderRegistration {
   Provider = $EventProv;
   EventQueryList = {"select * from SnmpExtendedNotification"} ;
};
instance of __Win32Provider as $EncapEventProv {
   Name = "MS_SNMP_ENCAPSULATED_EVENT_PROVIDER";
```

```
    ClsId = "{19C813AC-FEE7-11D0-AB22-00C04FD9159E}";
};
instance of __EventProviderRegistration {
    Provider = $EncapEventProv;
    FventOueryList = {"select * from SnmpNotification"};
};
instance of __Win32Provider as $PInst {
    Name = "MS_SNMP_INSTANCE_PROVIDER";
    Clsid = "{1F517A23-B29C-11cf-8C8D-00AA00A4086C}";
};
instance of __InstanceProviderRegistration {
    Provider = $PInst;
    SupportsGet = TRUE;
    SupportsPut = TRUE;
    SupportsDelete = TRUE;
    SupportsEnumeration = TRUE;
    QuerySupportLevels = { "WQL:UnarySelect" } ;
};
```

As you may see, in addition to creating a new namespace, root\SNMP\SUN1, this code registers the dynamic class provider, two event providers—encapsulated and referent—and the SNMP instance provider. Once compiled and loaded into the CIM Repository, this code will create all the metadata the SNMP provider needs to connect to the SNMP agent on the host "sun1" and gain access to all available SNMP objects. Note that the dynamic class provider will take upon itself the responsibility of generating dynamic WMI class definitions for the SNMP objects based on the templates found in the SMIR repository.

Accessing SNMP Data

Using the SNMP Provider to access the management data is fairly trivial once all the configuration work is completed. In order to make sure you understand how the SNMP data is retrieved through WMI, I will attempt to create a little program that mimics the functionality of the popular UNIX utility arp(1M). The arp(1M) program displays and modifies the contents of the Internet-to-Ethernet address resolution tables used by the Address Resolution Protocol (ARP). For the sake of saving space, the capabilities of our program will be limited to printing the contents of the address translation or Net-to-Media table, which is equivalent to running the arp(1M) utility with the -a command line switch. The complete source code for this program is shown in Listing 7-2.

Listing 7-2. Listing the Contents of the Internet-to-Ethernet Address Resolution Table

```
using System;
using System.Management;

public class Arp {
public static void Main(string[] args) {
    ManagementClass mc = new ManagementClass(
        @"\\.\root\SNMP\SUN1:SNMP_RFC1213_MIB_ipNetToMediaTable");
    foreach(ManagementObject mo in mc.GetInstances()) {
        Console.WriteLine("{0} {1} {2} {3}",
            mo["ipNetToMediaIfIndex"], mo["ipNetToMediaNetAddress"],
            mo["ipNetToMediaPhysAddress"], mo["ipNetToMediaType"]);
    }
}
}
```

This code first constructs a new `ManagementClass` object that is bound to the definition for the `SNMP_RFC1213_MIB_ipNetToMediaTable` WMI class, which corresponds to the SNMP Net-to-Media table. Then the program retrieves all instances of this class using the `GetInstances` method of the `ManagementClass` type. Each instance corresponds to a single entry in the Net-to-Media table, or, in other words to a single address translation mapping. Then the following properties of each retrieved object are printed out on the system console:

ipNetToMediaIfIndex: Index of the network interface for which the entry is effective.

ipNetToMediaNetAddress: IP address that corresponds to the physical address for the entry.

ipNetToMediaPhysAddress: Physical, media-dependent address for the entry. For example, for ethernets, it will contain the MAC address.

ipNetToMediaType: Dynamic or static depending of whether the particular address mapping is learned through the ARP (dynamically).

Once compiled and executed, the program will produce the output, similar to the following:

```
2 198.22.30.50 00:02:55:66:31:9c dynamic
2 198.22.31.112 08:00:20:90:cf:1c static
```

```
2 198.22.31.121 00:02:a5:87:72:72 dynamic
2 198.22.31.122 00:50:04:09:e7:9b dynamic
2 198.22.31.124 00:02:55:f4:19:b0 dynamic
2 198.22.31.151 00:e0:29:98:37:56 dynamic
...
```

It does not take a rocket scientist to dump the contents of the SNMP Net-to-Media table. To fully appreciate the capabilities of the SNMP-to-WMI bridge, let us look at a little more complex example—a rudimentary intrusion detection program.

Building reliable intrusion detection systems is somewhat of a black art and it often requires an intimate understanding of the inner workings of TCP/IP. With SNMP, however, it is possible to implement a simple monitor that would check for the most common intrusion scenarios. For instance, one of the first steps a potential intruder would take is fingerprinting your system with some kind of a port scanning utility. Actually, fingerprinting and port scanning are two different things. *Fingerprinting* involves identifying the traits of a particular computing node, such as its operating system, version of the TCP/IP stack, and so on. *Port scanning,* on the other hand, comes down to determining which networks services are running on the target machine in order to pick the most vulnerable area of the system. Once the make, release, and build of the OS are known and all network services are identified, an intruder may be able to exploit a known security hole in one of the network daemons, such as sendmail, for instance.

The good news is that most port scanning activities are easy to detect, although implementing a port scanner monitor requires a solid understanding of the TCP connection establishment process. The three-way handshake connection establishment procedure assumes that in order to initiate a connection, a client application will send a SYN (synchronize sequence numbers) segment that specifies the server port number to which this client wants to connect and the client's initial sequence number (ISN). The server then replies with a SYN/ACK packet—the segment that contains the server's initial sequence number as well as the acknowledgment of the client's SYN. Finally, the client acknowledges the server's SYN with another ACK segment. However, if a client attempts to connect to a port that no service is listening to the server will reply with an RST (reset) packet.

There are a few different techniques that port scanners utilize to produce a list of services running on a target machine. The simplest and the most basic form of TCP scanning is a *vanilla connect scan.* This technique relies on a connect system call to open a connection to each port of interest on a target machine; if the connection succeeds, there's a service listening, otherwise the port is unreachable. A TCP connect scan is very "loud" because most systems will log the failed connection attempts, and it is also very inefficient, especially over slow network links.

A much better scanning technique is *SYN* or *half-open scanning.* When using this form of scan, a client will send a SYN packet just like it would do if it were initiating a normal connection. If the server replies with SYN/ACK, the port is in service, if it sends an RST, the port is unreachable. When the client receives a reply from the server, it immediately sends back an RST packet, thus tearing down the connection so that it never goes into the established state. SYN scanning is fairly efficient, and significantly less visible than the vanilla connect scan, because the half-open connection attempts are normally not logged by the target system.

Yet, another scanning technique that is even more clandestine than SYN scanning, is *FIN scanning.* When FIN-scanning, a client sends a FIN (finish sending data) packet to a server. If the client receives the RST reply, the port of interest is closed; however, if the FIN packet is ignored altogether, the port is listening.

As you can see, regardless of the scanning technique used, the server will send RST replies out if packets arrive on a closed port. Therefore, in order to detect a port scan in progress, all you have to do is to compare the number of outgoing RST packets with a predefined threshold and report a possible port scan if this threshold is exceeded.

The number of outgoing RST packets is maintained as a value of the tcpOutRsts object in the SNMP tcp table. In WMI parlance, this is equivalent to the tcpOutRsts property of SNMP_RFC1213_MIB_tcp object. Thus, the port scanner monitor would have to bind to the aforementioned object and then continuously measure the number of RST packets sent out over a predefined time interval. Listing 7-3 shows the complete source code for this crude port scan monitoring utility.

Listing 7-3. Port Scan Monitor

```
using System;
using System.Management;

class PortScanMonitor {
public static void Main(string[] args) {
    DateTime t0 = DateTime.UtcNow;
    DateTime t1;
    ManagementObject mo = new ManagementObject(
        @"\\.\root\SNMP\localhost:SNMP_RFC1213_MIB_tcp=@");
    float v0 = float.Parse(mo["tcpOutRsts"].ToString());
    float v1 = 0;
    while(true) {
        System.Threading.Thread.Sleep(10000);
        t1 = DateTime.UtcNow;
        mo = new ManagementObject(
```

```
        @"\\.\root\SNMP\localhost:SNMP_RFC1213_MIB_tcp=@");
    v1 = float.Parse(mo["tcpOutRsts"].ToString());
    if ( (v1-v0)/(t1-t0).Seconds > 2) {
        Console.WriteLine(
            "Incoming connections refused: possible port scanner attack");
    }
    v0 = v1;
    t0 = t1;
    }
}
}
```

The structure of this program is very similar to that of the performance monitoring utility, shown earlier in this chapter. The code simply repeatedly binds to the instance of the SNMP_RFC1213_MIB_tcp class (note that this class is a singleton) and calculates the number of outgoing RST packets over a 10 second (10,000 milliseconds) interval. If the calculated number of RSTs exceeds the threshold (2 packets per 10 seconds), the program reports a possible port scan. Indeed, if you fire up your favorite port scanner (mine is Nmap from Insecure.Org— www.insecure.org), you will notice that our program detects the scanning activity immediately regardless of the scanning technique used.

Receiving SNMP Traps

In addition to monitoring the state of SNMP objects, the SNMP provider is capable of receiving and processing events generated by SNMP devices. In the SNMP world, events raised by the devices under different circumstances are referred to as *traps,* or in SNMPv2 parlance, *notifications.* All SNMP traps can be broadly subdivided into the following three categories:

Generic: Traps and notifications that are the result of named events, such as link up, link down, cold, and warm start events. In WMI, generic traps are represented by the subclasses of SnmpNotification and SnmpExtendedNotification, depending on whether the encapsulated or referent event provider is used.

Enterprise-specific: User-defined traps and notifications. WMI does not include any classes that correspond to enterprise-specific traps. In order to enable support for these traps, a user must manually define specific WMI classes and install them in the CIM Repository. Note that standard SNMP MIBs do not include any enterprise-specific trap definitions—it is the responsibility of the user to supply such definitions for all supported trap types.

Enterprise-nonspecific: Traps and events that do not correspond to either generic or enterprise-specific events. In WMI, enterprise-nonspecific traps and notifications are represented by SnmpV1Notification, SnmpV2Notification, SnmpV1ExtendedNotification, and SnmpV2ExtendedNotification classes.

Generic traps are the most widely utilized category of notifications mainly due to their platform-neutral nature. There are a handful of events that may generate generic traps. Table 7-20 lists all the available generic traps along with their descriptions and the WMI classes that represent these traps.

Table 7-20. SNMP Generic Trap Types

TRAP	DESCRIPTION	WMI CLASS
coldStart	Generated whenever the SNMP device is undergoing a reboot due to a hardware reset or power-up	SnmpColdStartNotification, SnmpColdStartExtendedNotification
warmStart	Generated whenever the SNMP agent is restarted	SnmpWarmStartNotification, SnmpWarmStartExtendedNotification
linkDown	Raised whenever a physical network link on the SNMP device is brought down	SnmpLinkDownNotification, SnmpLinkDownExtendedNotification
linkUp	Raised whenever a physical network link on the SNMP device is brought up	SnmpLinkUpNotification, SnmpLinkUpExtendedNotification

(continued)

Table 7-20. SNMP Generic Trap Types (continued)

TRAP	DESCRIPTION	WMI CLASS
authenticationFailure	Generated whenever the SNMP agent receivesa request with either an invalid community specification or a specification for a community that is not authorized to carry out the requested operation	SnmpAuthenticationFailureNotification SnmpAuthenticationFailureExtendedNotification
egpNeighborLoss	Raised whenever the peerrelationship betweentheEGP neighbor andthe EGP peer is lost	SnmpEGPNeighborLossNotification, SnmpEGPNeighborLossExtendedNotification

As you may remember, there are two SNMP event providers: encapsulated and referent. The former delivers traps to WMI clients as subclasses of the SnmpNotification class. The latter represents notifications as subclasses of the SnmpExtendedNotification class. Both these base classes are absolutely identical and contain the same properties. Their subclasses, however, may differ depending on the trap type. For instance, take a look at the definitions for SnmpLinkDownNotification and its referent counterpart SnmpLinkDownExtendedNotification:

```
class SnmpLinkDownNotification : SnmpNotification {
    sint32 ifIndex;
    string ifAdminStatus;
    string ifOperStatus;
};
```

```
class SnmpLinkDownExtendedNotification : SnmpExtendedNotification {
    SNMP_RFC1213_MIB_ifTable ifIndex;
    SNMP_RFC1213_MIB_ifTable ifAdminStatus;
    SNMP_RFC1213_MIB_ifTable ifOperStatus;
};
```

These two classes are very similar except that they derive from different bases and their properties are of different data types. SnmpLinkDownNotification conveys the information on the respective network interface using string properties for the interface index (ifIndex), the desired status of the interface (ifAdminStatus), and the current operational status of the interface (ifOperStatus). SnmpLinkDownExtendedNotification, on the other hand, represents the same information using embedded objects of type SNMP_RFC1213_MIB_ifTable. As you may remember, the SNMP interfaces table corresponds to the aforementioned WMI class and contains a single entry per network interface installed on the SNMP device.

As I already mentioned, the user defines the enterprise-specific traps and notifications. There are few steps involved in configuring WMI in order to receive these kinds of notifications. First, trap definitions for enterprise-specific events should be added to the MIB file for the SNMP device, which is capable of generating such traps. Then, the MIB should be converted to a form that is consumable by WMI (MOF) and loaded into the CIM Repository. This conversion can be performed using the smi2smir.exe utility, described earlier. The resulting WMI class definitions will be the subclasses of either SnmpNotification or SnmpExtendedNotification—the compiler actually supports a few command-line options that provide instruction on generating the trap classes (see Table 7-15). Once defined and installed, enterprise-specific traps can be subscribed to similarly to subscribing to the generic traps.

Finally, if an SNMP event provider receives a trap or notification that it cannot map to any of the existing WMI classes, it will consider the event an enterprise-nonspecific notification and deliver it using one of the following four WMI classes: SnmpV1Notification, SnmpV2Notification, SnmpV1ExtendedNotification, or SnmpV2ExtendedNotification. Interestingly, all four of these classes are exactly the same and have just one property, VarBindList, which is an array of SnmpVarBind objects. The SnmpVarBind is a WMI base class, which represents the SNMP variable binding, and it has the following definition:

```
class SnmpVarBind {
    string Encoding;
    string ObjectIdentifier;
    uint8  Value[];
};
```

where

Encoding: String that indicates the type of SNMP variable (ASN.1)

ObjectIdentifier: String that contains an SNMP object identifier (OID) for the SNMP variable

Value: Raw (octets) data for the SNMP variable

This structure makes the enterprise-nonspecific trap classes very generic and suitable for conveying the information on just about any type of event.

Having done all the necessary set up work, you can subscribe to SNMP traps in the same way you would subscribe to regular WMI extrinsic events. For instance, the following snippet of code registers for all `linkUp` traps:

```
using System;
using System.Management;

public class LinkUpMonitor {
    public static void Main(string[] args) {
        ManagementBaseObject mo;
        ManagementEventWatcher ev =
            new ManagementEventWatcher(@"\\.\root\SNMP\localhost",
                "SELECT * FROM SnmpLinkUpNotification");
        while(true) {
        mo = ev.WaitForNextEvent();
        foreach(PropertyData pd in mo.Properties) {
            Console.WriteLine("{0} {1}", pd.Name, pd.Value);
        }
    }
}
}
```

To see this code in action, you would have to find a way to generate the `linkUp` event. There are a couple of ways to go about this. The easiest and the crudest technique is to simply pull the network cable out, and then plug it back in and wait for the SNMP agent to generate the trap. Unfortunately, this approach is less than elegant and may not make you a popular person among your colleagues and coworkers. Fortunately, there is a better way to generate the traps than this brute force approach. Most SNMP implementations include the `snmptrap` command, which allows you to create any kind of SNMP trap and dispatch it to the destination of your choice. Thus, a generic `linkUp` trap can be generated as follows, using the `snmptrap` command that comes with the

University of California at Davis SNMP distribution (UCD-SNMP also known as Net-SNMP), which can be downloaded from net-snmp.sourceforge.net:

```
/usr/local/bin/snmptrap -v 2c -c public localhost '' \
    IF-MIB::linkUp RFC1213-MIB::ifIndex.1 i 1 RFC1213-MIB::ifOperStatus.1 \
    i 1 RFC1213-MIB::ifAdminStatus.1 i 1
```

The syntax of this command is fairly involved and explaining it in detail is certainly outside the scope of this chapter. Suffice it to say that this command line generates a linkUp event, sets the values of relevant SNMP variables, and dispatches the trap to the SNMP agent on the local machine. The interface index, represented by the ifIndex variable, is set to 1, pointing to the first network interface for the local host. The SNMP variables ifOperStatus and ifAdminStatus are also set to the integer value 1, which corresponds to the "up" state of the interface. Once the trap is raised and intercepted by the SNMP event provider, the preceding code will produce the following output:

```
AgentAddress 10.22.31.112
AgentTransportAddress 10.22.31.112
AgentTransportProtocol IP
Community public
Identification 1.3.6.1.6.3.1.1.5.4
ifAdminStatus up
ifIndex 1
ifOperStatus up
TimeStamp 607804475
```

If you ignore the properties inherited from the SnmpNotification class, you may notice that the interface index (ifIndex) is set to 1 and both status variables—ifOperStatus and ifAdminStatus—contain the string "up", indicating that the interface 1 has been brought to the up state.

Since the code just listed issues an event query against the SnmpLinkUpNotification class, the events are supplied by the encapsulated SNMP event provider. However, using the referent provider is just as easy. The main difference is that instead of querying the SnmpLinkUpNotification, you would have to write a query against the SnmpLinkUpExtendedNotification class:

```
using System;
using System.Management;

public class LinkUpMonitor {
    public static void Main(string[] args) {
        ManagementBaseObject mo;
```

```
        ManagementEventWatcher ev =
            new ManagementEventWatcher(@"\\.\root\SNMP\localhost",
                "SELECT * FROM SnmpLinkUpExtendedNotification");
        while(true) {
        mo = ev.WaitForNextEvent();

        ManagementBaseObject mo1 = (ManagementBaseObject)mo["ifIndex"];
        if ( mo1 != null )
            Console.WriteLine("ifIndex: {0}", mo1["ifIndex"]);
        mo1 = (ManagementBaseObject)mo["ifAdminStatus"];
        if (mo1 != null)
            Console.WriteLine("ifAdminStatus: {0}", mo1["ifAdminStatus"]);
        mo1 = (ManagementBaseObject)mo["ifOperStatus"];
        if (mo1 != null)
            Console.WriteLine("ifOperStatus: {0}", mo1["ifOperStatus"]);
        }
    }
}
```

Be careful when retrieving the values of the SnmpLinkUpExtendedNotification properties; rather than being integral values, these properties are embedded objects of the SNMP_RFC1213_MIB_ifTable class, and therefore, they have to be treated as such.

Finally, I will show you how to subscribe to the enterprise-nonspecific notifications. The code to register for such events is very similar to the event handling code you have seen so far, although there are subtle differences in the way the returned event objects are processed:

```
using System;
using System.Management;

public class NonSpecificTrapMonitor {
    public static void Main(string[] args) {
        ManagementBaseObject mo;
        ManagementEventWatcher ev =
            new ManagementEventWatcher(@"\\.\root\SNMP\localhost",
                "SELECT * FROM SnmpV2Notification");
        while(true) {
        mo = ev.WaitForNextEvent();
        foreach(ManagementBaseObject o in (
            ManagementBaseObject[])mo["VarBindLIst"]) {
            Console.Write("{0} ({1}): 0x",
                o["ObjectIdentifier"], o["Encoding"]);
```

```
    foreach(byte b in (byte[])o["Value"]) {
        Console.Write(b.ToString("X2"));
    }
    Console.WriteLine();
   }
  }
 }
}
```

You should notice a few things here. First, this code issues a WQL query against the `SnmpV2Notification` class, which is used to represent the enterprise-nonspecific notifications. All WMI classes that correspond to nonspecific traps have a single property, which is an array of `SnmpVarBind` objects. Thus, once an event is received, the code iterates through the array pointed to by the `VarBindList` property of the returned `SnmpV2Notification` instance and prints out the property values of each `SnmpVarBind` object. Outputting the `ObjectIdentifier` and `Encoding` property values is straightforward, however, handling the `Value` property is a bit involved. This property contains the raw variable value in octets, and therefore, it is represented by a byte array. Typically, your code should interrogate the `Encoding` property to determine the real data type of the variable and then cast the byte array to the appropriate type. The code fragment above simply prints the raw value in hexadecimal format.

The following UCD-SNMP command can be used in order to generate an enterprise nonspecific trap to test this code:

```
snmptrap -v 2c -c public localhost '' SNMPv2-MIB::snmpTraps.7↵
    RFC1213-MIB::ifIndex.1 i 1↵
    RFC1213-MIB::ifOperStatus.1 i 1 RFC1213-MIB::ifAdminStatus.1 i 1
```

Just like the `snmptrap` command for `linkUp` notification shown earlier, this command sets the values of `ifIndex`, `ifOperStatus`, and `ifAdminStatus` to the integer value 1. The trap type used here, however, is different and corresponds to the enterprise-nonspecific trap category. Upon receiving the trap generated by this command, the event handling code will produce the following output:

```
1.3.6.1.2.1.2.2.1.1.1 (INTEGER): 0x01000000
1.3.6.1.2.1.2.2.1.8.1 (INTEGER): 0x01000000
1.3.6.1.2.1.2.2.1.7.1 (INTEGER): 0x01000000
```

The dot-separated values are the OIDs of `ifIndex`, `ifOperStatus`, and `ifAdminStatus` SNMP objects respectively. The encoding (`INTEGER`) indicates that the values of these variables are indeed integers. Finally, the raw values printed in hexadecimal format correspond to the integer value of 1 (little-endian notation).

As you can see, SNMP provider is fairly versatile and lets you build powerful monitoring applications, even when you are dealing with legacy computing environments. Although integrating SNMP into a WMI-based management framework may be a bit laborious and may require a fair understanding of SNMP fundamentals, it is certainly worth the effort, which is guaranteed to eventually pay off.

Summary

This chapter provided an overview of some of the WMI providers that are distributed as part of the WMI SDK. Although there are many more providers available from Microsoft and third-party vendors, those described here are among the most interesting and least well known. Thus, having studied the material presented here, you should now be in position to

- Understand how the performance metrics are organized and structured on Windows platforms.

- Write simple monitoring utilities using the Performance Monitoring provider.

- Understand the difference between conventional and high-performance WMI providers.

- Comprehend the basic methodology for calculating the meaningful performance metrics from the raw values, obtained through the Performance Counter provider.

- Create simple, yet powerful, performance monitoring applications with the Cooked Counter provider on Windows XP.

- Understand the fundamentals of the Simple Network Management Protocol (SNMP).

- Comprehend the structure of a WMI SNMP provider and determine the configuration required to access specific SNMP devices from a WMI-based management console.

- Develop code for retrieving SNMP objects.

- Create simple programs to receive SNMP traps and notifications.

In addition to supplying the background information on some of the WMI providers, the goal of this chapter was also to whet your appetite so that you will want to explore other, poorly documented and little-known providers that may be available from Microsoft or other software vendors. After all, sometimes solving the most challenging system management problem can be as simple as finding an appropriate WMI provider to do the job for you.

CHAPTER 8

WMI Security

WINDOWS MANAGEMENT INSTRUMENTATION (WMI), like any power tool, is a double-edged sword. To system administrators, WMI is an indispensable part of the system management arsenal that allows them to oversee and alter all aspects of the entire management domain from a single, centralized management console. However, if misconfigured, such a system may just as easily enable a malicious hacker not only to sniff out the valuable and sensitive system configuration and operational data, but also severely disrupt the operations of the entire enterprise, and even damage or destroy some of its components. The ability to rename and delete files, start and stop services, manage processes, and reboot computers from a centralized remote location is the dream of any system manager, and although WMI certainly turns this dream into a reality, there is a clear and present danger if all this power falls into the wrong hands.

Thus, it should be clear to anyone that for a system such as WMI, strong security capabilities are not just a luxury, but an essential measure of success. In fact, a few otherwise very powerful and flexible management systems have been receiving bad press for years, solely due to their lack of sufficient security protection. For instance, many industry professionals attribute the slow adaptation of the Simple Network Management Protocol (SNMP) to its less then robust security features; in fact, some organizations and individuals consider using the SNMP-based management tools a potential security risk.

Therefore, it will not surprise you to discover that extensive support for securing access to the enterprise is built into the very core of WMI. Unlike other management solutions, WMI is not equipped with a standalone security framework; instead it relies on the security features of the Windows operating system and the Distributed Component Object Model (DCOM) security mechanism. Such an approach to securing the management operations via tight integration with Windows and DCOM security frameworks is well justified. In addition to easing the configuration and management of the system's security attributes by sharing APIs and configuration utilities, both Windows and DCOM security models are well reputed and are considered to be among the most reliable security frameworks around.

Unfortunately, flexibility and robustness often come at a price—high complexity—which is definitely the case with Windows and DCOM security. DCOM, for instance, has more security features than any other system known to man; however, it is often misunderstood and even more often misconfigured, thus creating security holes that naturally defeat its very purpose. But lowering the complexity is not an acceptable option either, since ensuring the proper degree of protection in a distributed environment is, by definition, very complex and cannot be achieved by simple means. In fact, industry experience shows that simplistic distributed security systems are either far too restrictive and inflexible, or are plainly unreliable and risky. Hence Windows and DCOM security.

Ignoring the security implications that result from using WMI as an enterprise-wide management solution is not a smart choice. Also, attempting to configure the system blindfolded without understanding its security features is not really a choice at all—it simply will not work. Thus, any system administrator searching for a successful management solution must be somewhat familiar with Windows and DCOM security and WMI's integration with these security models.

The purpose of this chapter is to expose you to the most important security features of WMI and to help you build a foundation on which to develop secure management applications. Although I will provide a basic overview of the Windows and DCOM security topics relevant to WMI, it is not my intention to turn this chapter into a tutorial on distributed security. As I already mentioned, this subject is very complex and delving into its intricacies could easily add a thousand pages to this book. Remember, the primary focus of this chapter is building secure management clients with .NET, and therefore, some WMI security issues, especially those related to provider development, will not be addressed. Fortunately, WMI and Platform SDK documentation seem to contain enough information on the most obscure aspects of WMI security that you can dig into to satisfy your curiosity.

WMI Security Fundamentals

As just mentioned, the Windows security model is the foundation of WMI security. As is true for most security frameworks in existence today, Windows security revolves around user IDs or names, and the associated passwords. Simply put, the operating system associates every object within the enterprise with a list of users authorized to access it. Every user request is checked against this list before access to the object is granted. WMI employs a similar strategy: it maintains a list of authorized users for each namespace.

In addition to controlling access to WMI namespaces, the system has to be able to verify the user's identity before allowing the client application to connect to WMI services. The process of confirming the identity of the user who is running the management client application is referred to as *authentication*. In order to authenticate the client requests for services, WMI relies on the Component Object Model (COM) authentication mechanism. The COM authentication scheme is password-based and it provides for not only verifying the identity of the requestor, but also protecting the communications between the client and the server by encrypting the network packets.

WMI is designed for remote administration, which means that management requests from a remote management client are carried out by the WMI service that is running on the local machine. Since the WMI service operates on behalf of the remote user, there has to be a way to ensure that the user possesses adequate permissions to complete certain management actions. This essentially means that each client's request has to be carried out by the WMI service under the security context of the client and perhaps by using the client's identity. This is achieved by using the COM impersonation mechanism, which allows the client to grant certain authority to the WMI service so that the latter may perform the requested operations on the client's behalf.

Securing WMI Namespaces

On Windows NT, 2000, and XP platforms, each user and group is given unique *security identifiers (SIDs)*. A SID is a variable length value that is assigned to a user or group account when such an account is created. SIDs are always unique within the scope of the account to which they belong. Thus, a SID for a local account is always unique within the computer system to which the account belongs, and a SID for a domain account is unique within that domain. SIDs are also unique in time, meaning that the system does not reuse the SID values under any circumstances. Therefore, if an account is deleted and then recreated, it is assigned a brand new SID despite the fact that the account name stays the same.

SIDs are used extensively by the Windows security framework. For instance, each *access token*—an object that described the security context of a process or a thread—has an embedded SID, which represents a user or a group associated with the token. Another security structure—the *security descriptor (SD)*, which contains all relevant security information for a securable object—also contains SIDs that identify the owner of the associated object and the primary group of the owner. Finally, *access control entries (ACEs)*, which govern access to a particular securable object, house SIDs that identify the users and groups to whom access is granted or denied.

A SD is, perhaps, the most notable structure within the Windows security model. As its name implies, it describes the security-related traits of a given object, such as its ownership and access restrictions. A Security Descriptor structure (SECURITY_DESCRIPTOR), consists of the following elements:

- SID of the object's owner

- SID of the group to which the object's owner belongs

- Discretionary access control list (DACL) that specifies the levels of access that particular users or groups may have to the object

- System access control list (SACL) that controls the generation of the audit messages, logging the attempts to access the object

- Security descriptor control information, packaged into the SECURITY_DESCRIPTOR_CONTROL structure. This is a set of bit flags that qualify the semantics of the individual components of the security descriptor.

An access control list (ACL) is a list of zero or more access control entries (ACEs) that are used as a basis for determining the access control and audit rights for a particular security principal. Each ACE contains the following information:

- A SID that uniquely identifies a security principal (user or group) to which the ACE applies.

- An access mask—a 32-bit value that specifies the rights that are denied or allowed by the ACE.

- A flag that indicates the type of the ACE: access-denied ACE, access-allowed ACE, or system-audit ACE.

- Bit flags that specify whether the child objects are allowed to inherit the ACE from the primary object to which the ACE applies.

The access rights, specified by the access mask field, can be divided into four categories: generic, standard, SACL access, and Directory Services (DS) access rights. Table 8-1 lists all access rights by category.

Table 8-1. Access Rights

CATEGORY	ACCESS RIGHT	DESCRIPTION
Generic	GENERIC_ALL	Read, write, and execute access.
Generic	GENERIC_READ	Read access.
Generic	GENERIC_WRITE	Write access.
Generic	GENERIC_EXECUTE	Execute access.
Standard	DELETE	Right to delete an object.
Standard	READ_CONTROL	Right to read the security descriptor associated with the object, excluding the SACL.

(continued)

Table 8-1. Access Rights (continued)

CATEGORY	ACCESS RIGHT	DESCRIPTION
Standard	SYNCHRONIZE	Right to use the object for thread synchronization.
Standard	WRITE_DAC	Right to modify the object's DACL in its security descriptor.
Standard	WRITE_OWNER	Right to change the owner of the object.
SACL Access	ACCESS_SYSTEM_SECURITY	Right to read and modify the SACL in the object's security descriptor.
Directory Services Access	ACTRL_DS_OPEN	Right to open a DS object.
Directory Services Access	ACTRL_DS_CREATE_CHILD	Right to create a child DS object.
Directory Services Access	ACTRL_DS_DELETE_CHILD	Right to delete a child DS object.
Directory Services Access	ACTRL_DS_LIST	Right to enumerate DS objects.
Directory Services Access	ACTRL_DS_READ_PROP	Right to read the properties of a DS object.
Directory Services Access	ACTRL_DS_WRITE_PROP	Right to modify the properties of a DS object.
Directory Services Access	ACTRL_DS_SELF	Access is allowed only after the validated rights checks supported by the object are passed.
Directory Services Access	ACTRL_DS_DELETE_TREE	Right to delete a tree of DS objects.
Directory Services Access	ACTRL_DS_LIST_OBJECT	Right to list a tree of DS objects.
Directory Services Access	ACTRL_DS_CONTROL_ACCESS	Access is allowed only after the extended rights checks supported by the object are passed.

A combination of access rights is packaged into a 32-bit field so that the low-order 16 bits of the access mask reflect the object-specific rights, the next 7 bits are reserved for the standard rights, bit 23 represents the right to access the SACL, and finally, the 4 high-order bits are used for the generic access rights.

Another structure that plays a very important role within the Windows security infrastructure is the access token. An access token is assigned to a user whenever a user logs into the system. When a logon session is initiated, the system authenticates the user's password against the security database and issues an access token, which subsequently gets attached to every process executed on behalf of the user. Then, the system uses the access token to establish the user's identity and level of access every time the user issues a request to access a securable object. An access token contains the following information:

- A SID of the user's account.

- A collection of SIDs for each group to which the user belongs.

- A logon SID that uniquely identifies the logon session.

- A list of privileges granted to a user or the user's groups.

- An owner SID.

- A SID of the primary group.

- The source of the access token.

- The flag that indicates whether it is a primary or impersonation token. The primary token is created by the Windows executive layer and typically represents the default security settings for the process. The impersonation token is created to capture the security settings of an arbitrary process, thus allowing the current process to "impersonate" the latter.

- A list of restricting SIDs. The restricting SIDs are used when a process is running under a restricted security context. In such cases, the system checks not only the primary SID but also the restricted SIDs before it grants access to a securable object.

- Current impersonation levels.

- Miscellaneous statistics.

Besides carrying the user's identity, an access token also includes all privileges granted to a user or the user's groups. A *privilege* is a right granted to a security principal that enables the latter to perform certain administrative functions on a local computer. Such administrative functions may include shutting down the system, modifying the system's date and time settings, and loading and unloading the device drivers. As opposed to access rights, which control access to securable objects, privileges govern access to system resources and tasks.

Each user and group account is associated with a set of privileges that is stored in Windows security database. Whenever a user logs into a system, the privileges are incorporated into the user's access token. Note that such privileges will only apply to a local computer system, since domain accounts may have different sets of privileges on different machines. When a user attempts to perform an operation that is marked as privileged, the system checks the privileges embedded into the user's access token. If the appropriate privileges are granted and enabled, the system allows the operation; otherwise the operation fails. Interestingly, the privileges, even if granted, are disabled by default so that the user has to explicitly enable them prior to requesting a privileged operation. A privilege can be enabled using the AdjustTokenPrivileges function of the Win32 API.

To summarize, every access check carried out by the system essentially boils down to matching the user's security information, which is encoded into the access token, against the SD of a securable object. Thus, in order to secure an arbitrary resource, the resource has to be assigned an appropriate SD that incorporates the necessary ACEs. Securing the WMI namespaces is no exception. In fact, each namespace is associated with an SD that carries all the security information needed to ensure the proper access checks.

The SD of a namespace can be manipulated using the WMI MMC snap-in, as shown in Figure 8-1.

Figure 8-1. Securing WMI namespaces

Using the security configuration page of the snap-in is as trivial as using the Properties dialog when securing files. All you need to do is select a namespace to secure and modify the associated user's or group's permissions.

In the true spirit of WMI, the SD for a namespace can also be retrieved and manipulated programmatically. A system class called __SystemSecurity provides such programmatic access to namespace security settings. This class has the following definition:

```
class __SystemSecurity {
    [Static] uint32 GetSD([out] uint8 SD[]);
    [Static] uint32 Get9XUserList([out] __ntlmuser9x ul[]);
    [Static] uint32 SetSD([in] uint8 SD[]);
    [Static] uint32 Set9XUserList([in] __ntlmuser9x ul[]);
    [Static] uint32 GetCallerAccessRights([out] sint32 rights);
};
```

This class is fairly unusual because it does not contain any properties. Rather than exposing all of the SD or its individual parts as properties of an object, the designers of WMI turned the __SystemSecurity class into a singleton and equipped it with a number of static methods for reading the security descriptor and writing the modified version of it back to the CIM Repository. As you can see in the definition above, the class has the following methods:

GetSD: Used to get an SD associated with a namespace to which the user is currently connected. The SD is returned as an array of unsigned bytes and it has to be cast into an appropriate structure to be manipulated. This method is only available on Windows NT, Windows 2000, and Windows XP platforms.

Get9XUserList: Used to retrieve a list of users who are allowed to access the namespace. This method is only available on Windows 9X platforms, and it returns an array of instances of the __Win9XUser class. This is done to simulate the functionality of SDs on Windows 9X systems.

SetSD: Writes the modified SD for a namespace back to the CIM Repository. The SD is represented by an array of unsigned bytes. This method is only available on Windows NT, Windows 2000, and Windows XP platforms.

Set9XUserList: Writes the list of users who are allowed to access the namespace back to the CIM Repository. This method is only available on Windows 9X platforms.

GetCallerAccessRights: Retrieves the access masks for a client process. The mask is a 32-bit value where each bit represents an individual access right. This method is available on all Windows platforms.

Unfortunately, the methods of the __SystemSecurity class can only be used to retrieve or save an SD, but they cannot be utilized for SD manipulation. Also, it is not recommended to manipulate the SD byte array directly. Instead, the functions of the Win32 API should be used to extract or set the individual values within an SD. For instance, to convert a binary SD into a human-consumable form (an SDDL string representation), you may use the ConvertSecurityDescriptorToStringSecurityDescriptor function (that is, if you manage to spell the name of the function correctly).

By default, the security settings for a namespace are inherited by all its children namespaces. This means that by setting the permissions for the \root namespace, you may have these permissions propagated to each WMI namespace. You can also change the default behavior and turn the inheritance off by setting the CONTAINER_INHERIT_ACE (0x2) flag in the ACEs that are associated with a security descriptor for a namespace. It is also possible to determine whether a particular ACE is inherited by checking for the INHERITED_ACE (0x10) flag within the ACE for a namespace.

WMI and COM Security

All client applications access WMI services via COM interfaces. It is true that WMI Scripting API or .NET System Management Framework may shield the developers from the complexities of COM. However, regardless of the development platform, at run time, all service requests issued by a management application are routed to WMI via an arbitrary COM interface. Thus, from the prospective of a client application, WMI security is synonymous with COM security.

COM security revolves around the concepts of *authentication* and *impersonation*. The former is a process that verifies the authenticity of the client's identity, while the latter is the ability of a thread to execute in a security context different from that of the process that owns the thread. Since different processes may require different levels of security, the authentication and impersonation requirements may vary from application to application. Therefore, COM clients are given the ability to control the security levels, or levels of authentication and impersonation, for their processes.

The default security levels for a process are set via the CoInitializeSecurity function. Among a few other parameters, this function accepts two DWORD values that specify the default authentication and impersonation levels. The first of these values controls the degree of protection applied to the communications between the COM client and the server. Currently, COM defines seven different authentication levels, listed in Table 8-2.

Table 8-2. COM Authentication Levels

AUTHENTICATION LEVEL CONSTANT	DESCRIPTION
RPC_C_AUTH_LEVEL_DEFAULT	Under Windows NT 4.0, this value defaults to RPC_C_AUTH_LEVEL_CONNECT. Under Windows 2000 and later, this value instructs COM to select an appropriate authentication level using its normal security blanket negotiation algorithm.
RPC_C_AUTH_LEVEL_NONE	Instructs COM not to perform any authentication.
RPC_C_AUTH_LEVEL_CONNECT	Causes COM to authenticate the credentials of the client only when the client establishes a session with the server.
RPC_C_AUTH_LEVEL_CALL	Instructs COM to authenticate the client at the beginning of each remote procedure call (RPC) when the server receives the request.

(continued)

Table 8-2. COM Authentication Levels (continued)

AUTHENTICATION LEVEL CONSTANT	DESCRIPTION
RPC_C_AUTH_LEVEL_PKT	Instructs COM to ensure that the data is received from the authenticated client.
RPC_C_AUTH_LEVEL_PKT_INTEGRITY	Causes COM to ensure the integrity of the data received from the client.
RPC_C_AUTH_LEVEL_PKT_PRIVACY	Instructs COM to perform all the types of authentication referred to in this table and encrypt all RPC arguments.

Again, CoInitializeSecurity sets the default authentication level for the process so that all subsequently arriving COM requests with lower authentication levels will fail.

The impersonation level specifies the amount of authority granted to the server when it performs tasks on behalf of the client. Table 8-3 lists all available impersonation levels.

Table 8-3. COM Impersonation Levels

IMPERSONATION LEVEL CONSTANT	DESCRIPTION
RPC_C_IMP_LEVEL_DEFAULT	This value can be used with Windows 2000 and later. It instructs COM to select an appropriate impersonation level using its normal security blanket negotiation algorithm.
RPC_C_IMT_LEVEL_ANONYMOUS	The client remains anonymous to the server. The impersonation is possible, but since the server's impersonation token will not contain any client security information, the server will not be able to perform any tasks under the security context of the client.
RPC_C_IMP_LEVEL_IDENTITY	The server's impersonation token will include the client's identity, which implies that the server will be able to impersonate the client during ACL checking. However, the server will not be able to access the system objects on behalf of the client.
RPC_C_IMP_LEVEL_IMPERSONATE	The server may impersonate the client's security context, but only while it accesses the resources on local machines on behalf of the client. In other words, the impersonation token cannot be used across the machines' boundaries.

(continued)

Table 8-3. COM Impersonation Levels (continued)

IMPERSONATION LEVEL CONSTANT	DESCRIPTION
RPC_C_IMP_LEVEL_DELEGATE	The server may impersonate the client's security context while accessing the resources on local or remote machines on behalf of the client. The impersonation token can be passed across the machines' boundaries. This impersonation level is available under Windows 2000 and later.

Calling `CoInitializeSecurity` is optional. If a client application chooses not to invoke this function, COM will automatically initialize and manage the security settings for a process. In such cases, in order to establish the default security settings for a process, COM uses a set of default values, stored in the system registry. Thus, the default authentication level is set based on the registry value `HKLM\SOFTWARE\MICROSOFT\OLE\LegacyAuthenticationLevel`. Similarly, the default impersonation level is chosen based on the value of `HKLM\SOFTWARE\MICROSOFT\OLE\LegacyImpersonationLevel`. If these values are not found in the registry, COM will use `RPC_C_AUTH_LEVEL_CONNECT` and `RPC_C_IMP_LEVEL_IDENTITY` for the default authentication and impersonation levels respectively.

As you may remember, once connected to WMI, a client application receives an out-of-process pointer to the `IWbemServices` interface, which can subsequently be used to engage various WMI services. This pointer has the identity of a client process rather than the WMI `IWbemServices` process. Thus, if the client attempts to use the pointer to invoke the services of WMI it may receive an access-denied error, since the access check will be carried out with the client's identity. To avoid such errors, the WMI client applications must call the `CoSetProxyBlanket` function in order to set the identity of a newly obtained pointer. Once the pointer identity is set, it can be used to call into WMI.

Finally, whenever a client attempts to perform an operation marked as privileged, such as a system reboot, it must enable its privileges. This is achieved via the `AdjustTokenPrivileges` function. This function takes the access token of the client process as a parameter and, depending on the type of the request, enables or disables the privileges associated with the token. Note that before a particular privilege can be enabled, an administrator should explicitly grant it to the user or group.

WMI Security and System.Management

The designers of the `System.Management` namespace took a somewhat simplistic approach to enveloping the security-related capabilities of WMI. They primarily focused on exposing the functionality for managing the security settings of client processes. As a result, the System.Management security model is easy to use, but it definitely lacks support for low-level manipulation of the security settings.

Establishing WMI Connections

Throughout all of the code examples, shown earlier in this book, I consistently and consciously neglected most of the issues related to WMI security, crudely assuming that these examples are being executed by a user with administrative privileges. Moreover, when I described the process of connecting to WMI, I barely scratched the surface and chose to rely on the ability of System.Management types to automatically establish a connection on an as-needed basis. Thus, all of the code examples used something similar to the following boilerplate code to bind to a WMI class or object:

```
ManagementObject mo = new ManagementObject(@"\\.\root\CIMV2:Win32_Process=100");
Console.WriteLine(mo["__CLASS"]);
...
```

This code looks deceivingly simple and you may not realize what is really going on behind the scenes.

Before the newly constructed object can be used, a valid connection to WMI must be established and the instance of the ManagementObject type must be bound to the underlying WMI object. However, the code does not seem to be doing either of these things—instead, it simply instantiates the object and prints out its properties. Such simplicity and ease of use is afforded by the ability of the System.Management ManagementObject type to initialize itself and establish the appropriate connections in a lazy fashion. In fact, none of the type constructors issue any COM API calls, and therefore, they do not even attempt to contact WMI. Instead, when an instance of a type is first accessed, it undergoes the initialization stage. The initialization code typically checks whether the instance is already connected to WMI, and if necessary, it invokes the initialization sequence. As part of the initialization, the object of type ManagementScope is created and then its initialization code is invoked. The ManagementScope's InitializeGuts method, briefly discussed in Chapter 2, obtains a pointer to IWbemLocator object and calls its ConnectServer method to retrieve the IWbemServices interface pointer. The IWbemLocator::ConnectServer method has the following signature:

```
HRESULT IWbemLocator::ConnectServer(
    const BSTR strNetworkResource,
    const BSTR strUser,
    const BSTR strPassword,
```

```
    const BSTR strLocale,
    LONG lSecurityFlags,
    const BSTR strAuthority,
    IWbemContext* pCtx,
    IWbemServices** ppNamespace
);
```

where

> **strNetworkResource**: A pointer to a valid BSTR that contains a WMI path to the target object.

> **strUser**: A pointer to a valid BSTR that contains the name of the security principal to be used to establish the connection to WMI. If this parameter is set to NULL, ConnectServer will use the name of the currently logged on user. When using the user name from a domain other than the current domain, the name should be prefixed with the domain name and a double backslash separator—i.e., <domain_name>\\<user_name>.

> **strPassword**: A pointer to a valid BSTR that contains a password to be used to establish the connection to WMI. If this parameter is set to NULL, ConnectServer will use the password of the currently logged on user. An empty string is considered to be a valid password of zero length.

> **strLocale**: A pointer to a valid BSTR that specifies the locale (i.e., MS_xxx) to be used to retrieve the information from WMI. If this parameter is set to NULL, the current locale is used.

> **lSecurityFlags**: Reserved for future use. Must be set to zero.

> **strAuthority**: A pointer to a valid BSTR that contains a designation of the authentication method to be used for establishing the connection, as well as the name of the domain in which to obtain the user information for authentication. If this parameter begins with string "Kerberos:", Kerberos authentication is used and the remainder of the string must contain a valid Kerberos principal name. If the parameter begins with "NTLMDOMAIN:", then Windows NT Challenge/Response authentication protocol (also known as Windows NT LAN Manager or NTLM protocol) is used and the remainder of the string must contain a valid NTLM domain name. If the parameter is set to NULL, ConnectServer uses NTLM authentication and the NTLM domain of the currently logged on user. Note that the name of the domain cannot be specified simultaneously in two places (i.e., strUser and strAuthority parameters); doing so will cause ConnectServer to fail.

pCtx: A pointer to the IWbemContext object used to provide additional information to certain WMI providers. This parameter is typically set to NULL.

ppNamespace: An output parameter used to receive the pointer to a valid IWbemServices object.

As you can deduce from the method signature, it is possible to control many aspects of the connection establishment process, such as the name of the connecting user and domain as well as the authentication method. Unfortunately, the lazy initialization sequence of the ManagementObject type constructs a default instance of the ManagementScope type so that the IWbemLocator::ConnectServer method is called with most of its parameters set to NULL values. Obviously, this causes WMI to use the NTLM authentication along with the name and domain of the currently logged on user. While adequate for some of the management scenarios, this may result in access-denied errors when the current user is not granted full administrative access to the target WMI resources.

The good news is that you can override the default behavior by explicitly constructing an instance of the ManagementScope type and associating it with the ManagementObject. Take a look at the following code snippet:

```
ManagementScope ms = new ManagementScope();
ms.Path = new ManagementPath(@"\\BCK_OFFICE\root\CIMV2");
ms.Options.Username = "Administrator";
ms.Options.Password = "password";
ManagementObject mo = new ManagementObject(@"Win32_Process=100");
mo.Scope = ms;
Console.WriteLine(mo["__CLASS"]);
```

Here, the Path property of the newly created ManagementScope object is assigned to the instance of the ManagementPath type, which specifies the remote WMI namespace to connect to. Then, the Username and Password properties of the ConnectionOptions object, pointed to by the Options property of the ManagementScope object, are initialized to the name of the user and the password to be used for establishing a connection. Finally, the new instance of the ManagementObject type is created and associated with the ManagementScope object by setting its Scope property. When the ManagementObject instance is accessed by the WriteLine method, rather than constructing a default ManagementScope object, the initialization code of the ManagementObject type uses the ManagementScope instance associated with the object. Interestingly, in this case, all information that pertains to the WMI connection—not only the user name and the password, but also the namespace path—is always extracted from the associated ManagementScope object. Thus, the following code is incorrect and will generate an error:

```
ManagementScope ms = new ManagementScope();
ms.Options.Username = "Administrator";
ms.Options.Password = "password";
ManagementObject mo = new ManagementObject(
    @"\\BCK_OFFICE\root\CIMV2:Win32_Process=100");
mo.Scope = ms;
Console.WriteLine(mo["__CLASS"]);
```

Here, rather than setting the Path property of the ManagementScope object, we supply a full namespace and an object path to the constructor of the ManagementObject type. Therefore, the resulting ManagementScope object contains a default namespace path \\.\root\CIMV2. Upon setting the Scope property of the ManagementObject instance, the namespace path of ManagementObject essentially is overridden by the namespace path of the associated ManagementScope object. As a result, rather than binding to the remote namespace \\BCK_OFFICE\root\CIMV2, the initialization code of the ManagementObject type binds to the local \\.\root\CIMV2 namespace. For security reasons, it is not allowed to change the user credentials when it connects to a local namespace; therefore, the preceding code throws a ManagementException, complaining that user credentials cannot be used for local connections.

The coding pattern just discussed is not the only way to create a ManagementScope object and associate it with an appropriate System.Management type. One of the constructors of the ManagementObject type, for instance, accepts the instance of ManagementScope as a parameter:

```
ManagementScope ms = new ManagementScope();
ms.Path = new ManagementPath(@"\\BCK_OFFICE\root\CIMV2");
ms.Options.Username = "Administrator";
ms.Options.Password = "password";
ManagementPath mp = new ManagementPath("Win32_Process=100");
ManagementObject mo = new ManagementObject(ms, mp, null);
Console.WriteLine(mo["__CLASS"]);
```

Here, the ManagementScope object is the first parameter of the ManagementObject type constructor. The second parameter is an object of type ManagementPath, which points to an appropriate WMI Win32_Process object to bind to. Finally, the last parameter is an instance of ObjectGetOptions type, which, for the purposes of this discussion, may simply be ignored, hence it is set to null. Note that this code behaves similarly to the code snippet, shown earlier—in other words, the namespace path of the ManagementScope instance overrides the namespace path of the ManagementPath object. Thus, if you forget to initialize the Path property of the ManagementScope object, the code will generate an error.

Since the default `ManagementScope` object is constructed during the initialization of the `ManagementObject` unless the `ManagementScope` parameter is supplied to the type constructor, it is entirely possible to use the default object rather than constructing a brand new one:

```
ManagementObject mo = new ManagementObject(
    @"\\BCK_OFFICE\root\CIMV2:Win32_Process=100");
mo.Scope.Options.Username = "Administrator";
mo.Scope.Options.Password = "password";
Console.WriteLine(mo["__CLASS"]);
```

This code is certainly more concise and, perhaps, a bit more efficient than my first example because it alleviates the need for allocating a new instance of the `ManagementScope` type.

Finally, you do not need to rely on the initialization code of the `ManagementObject` type to implicitly establish a connection to WMI. With the `ManagementScope`, you can request a connection explicitly:

```
ManagementScope ms = new ManagementScope();
ms.Path = new ManagementPath(@"\\BCK_OFFICE\root\CIMV2");
ms.Options.Username = "Administrator";
ms.Options.Password = "password";
ms.Connect();
ManagementObject mo = new ManagementObject(@"Win32_Process=100");
mo.Scope = ms;
Console.WriteLine(mo["__CLASS"]);
```

As I already mentioned, the initialization sequence of the `ManagementObject` type first checks if there is a valid WMI connection and then attempts to use it if such a connection exists. Here, since the `ManagementScope` object is already connected to WMI by the time the `ManagementObject` initialization code is invoked, the entire connection establishment process is bypassed and the `ManagementScope`'s connection is used instead. The apparent benefit of such an approach is that you can reuse a single connected `ManagementScope` object with multiple instances of the `ManagementObject`, thus achieving a marginal performance gain.

The `ManagementObject` type is not the only `System.Management` type designed to work in conjunction with `ManagementScope`. In fact, all `System.Management` types that represent WMI entities, such as `ManagementClass`, `ManagementEventWatcher`, and `ManagementObjectSearcher`, offer the same functionality. Thus, each of these types is equipped with a constructor that takes the `ManagementScope` object as a parameter and the `Scope` property, which exposes the associated instance of the `ManagementScope` type.

Securing WMI Connections

At the beginning of this chapter, I mentioned that in order to establish the proper security settings for a WMI session, the client process should call several security API functions such as CoInitializeSecurity and CoSetProxyBlanket. Fortunately, it is not something that a developer of the management applications has to do manually. Here again, the initialization logic of the ManagementScope type kindly takes care of setting the appropriate authentication and impersonation levels for the process. A developer however, is afforded the luxury of controlling both the authentication and the impersonation settings through the instance of the ConnectionOptions type, associated with the ManagementScope object. This type, briefly mentioned above, has the following properties:

> **Authentication**: Gets or sets the COM authentication level to be used for the WMI connection
>
> **Impersonation**: Gets or sets the COM impersonation level to be used for the WMI connection
>
> **Authority**: Gets or sets the authority value to be used for the WMI connection
>
> **Locale**: Gets or sets the locale value to be used for the WMI connection
>
> **Username**: Gets or sets the name of the security principal to be used for the WMI connection
>
> **Password**: Gets or sets the password to be used for the WMI connection
>
> **EnablePrivileges**: Gets or sets a Boolean flag that indicates whether the privileges are to be enabled for the WMI connection

As you can see, all of these properties, with the exception of the EnablePrivileges, which is discussed later in this chapter, map directly to the parameters of the IWbemLocator::ConnectServer method. However, these properties are also used by the private Secure method of the ManagementScope type, which, during the initialization phase, sets the appropriate authentication and impersonation levels for the process and "blesses" the retrieved IWbemServices interface pointer.

The Username, Password, Locale, and Authority properties of the ConnectionOptions type are governed by the same rules as the respective parameters of the IWbemLocator::ConnectServer method. The Impersonation and Authentication properties, however, are of enumeration types

ImpersonationLevel and AuthenticationLevel respectively, which means that you must use a member of the appropriate enumeration when initializing these properties. It should come as no surprise that the members of these enumeration types map one-to-one to the respective COM authentication and impersonation level constants listed in Tables 8-2 and 8-3. The members of the AuthenticationLevel enumeration type are shown in Table 8-4.

Table 8-4. Members of AuthenticationLevel *Enumeration*

MEMBER	COM CONSTANT	DESCRIPTION
Default	RPC_C_AUTH_LEVEL_DEFAULT	Under Windows NT 4.0, this value defaults to RPC_C_AUTH_LEVEL_CONNECT. Under Windows 2000 and later, this value instructs COM to select an appropriate authentication level using its normal security blanket negotiation algorithm.
None	RPC_C_AUTH_LEVEL_NONE	Instructs COM not to perform any authentication.
Connect	RPC_C_AUTH_LEVEL_CONNECT	Causes COM to authenticate the credentials of the client only when the client establishes a session with the server.
Call	RPC_C_AUTH_LEVEL_CALL	Instructs COM to authenticate the client at the beginning of each RPC when the server receives the request.
Packet	RPC_C_AUTH_LEVEL_PKT	Instructs COM to ensure that the data is received from the authenticated client.
PacketIntegrity	RPC_C_AUTH_LEVEL_PKT_INTEGRITY	Causes COM to ensure the integrity of the data received from the client.
PacketPrivacy	RPC_C_AUTH_LEVEL_PKT_PRIVACY	Instructs COM to perform all types of authentication referred to in this table and encrypt all RPC arguments.
Unchanged		The authentication level remains unchanged.

The members of the ImpersonationLevel enumeration type are shown in Table 8-5.

Table 8-5. Members of ImpersonationLevel *Enumeration*

MEMBER	COM CONSTANT	DESCRIPTION
Default	RPC_C_IMP_LEVEL_DEFAULT	This value can be used with Windows 2000 and later. It instructs COM to select an appropriate impersonation level using its normal security blanket negotiation algorithm.
Anonymous	RPC_C_IMT_LEVEL_ANONYMOUS	The client remains anonymous to the server. The impersonation is possible, but since the server's impersonation token will not contain any client security information, the server will not be able to perform any tasks under the security context of the client.
Identity	RPC_C_IMP_LEVEL_IDENTITY	The server's impersonation token will include the client's identity, which implies that the server will be able to impersonate the client for ACL checking. However, the server will not be able to access the system objects on behalf of the client.
Impersonate	RPC_C_IMP_LEVEL_IMPERSONATE	The server may impersonate the client's security context, but only while it is accessing the resources on the local machine on behalf of the client. In other words, the impersonation token cannot be used across the machines' boundaries.
Delegate	RPC_C_IMP_LEVEL_DELEGATE	The server may impersonate the client's security context while accessing the resources on local or remote machines on behalf of the client. The impersonation token can be passed across the machines' boundaries. This impersonation level is available under Windows 2000 and later.

By constructing an instance of the ConnectionOptions type and associating it with the management scope, you may effectively control the security settings for a WMI client process:

```
ConnectionOptions co = new ConnectionOptions();
co.Username = "Administrator";
co.Password = "password";
co.Authentication = AuthenticationLevel.PacketPrivacy;
co.Impersonation = ImpersonationLevel.Impersonate;
ManagementScope ms = new ManagementScope(@"\\BCK_OFFICE\root\CIMV2", co);
```

```
ManagementObject mo = new ManagementObject(@"Win32_Process=100");
mo.Scope = ms;
Console.WriteLine(mo["__CLASS"]);
```

Unless the ConnectionOptions object is explicitly associated with an instance of the ManagementScope, the latter constructs a default ConnectionOptions instance during its initialization. Therefore, you can use the default object to control the security settings of the process:

```
ManagementScope ms = new ManagementScope();
ms.Path = new ManagementPath(@"\\BCK_OFFICE\root\CIMV2");
ms.Options.Username = "Administrator";
ms.Options.Password = "password";
ms.Options.Authentication = AuthenticationLevel.PacketPrivacy;
ms.Options.Impersonation = ImpersonationLevel.Impersonate;
ManagementObject mo = new ManagementObject(@"Win32_Process=100");
mo.Scope = ms;
Console.WriteLine(mo["__CLASS"]);
```

Finally, the ConnectionOptions type is equipped with a convenient constructor method that allows you to set all of the object properties at once. This constructor has the following signature:

```
public ConnectionOptions (
    string                 locale,
    string                 username,
    string                 password,
    string                 authority,
    ImpersonationLevel     impersonation,
    AuthenticationLevel    authentication,
    bool                   enablePrivileges,
    ManagementNamedValueCollection context,
    TimeSpan               timeout
);
```

where

locale: A string that specifies the locale (i.e., MS_xxx) to be used for the WMI connection

username: A string that specifies the name of the user to be used for the WMI connection

password: A string that specifies the password to be used for the WMI connection

authority: A string that specifies the authority to be used for the WMI connection

impersonation: A member of the `ImpersonationLevel` enumeration that indicates the impersonation level to be used for the WMI connection.

authentication: A member of the `AuthenticationLevel` enumeration that indicates the authentication level to be used for the WMI connection

enablePrivileges: A Boolean flag that indicates whether the privileges are to be enabled for the WMI connection

context: A `ManagementNamedValueCollection` that contains provider-specific context values

timeout: A `TimeSpan` object that sets the timeout value for the connection operation

Using this constructor, the earlier code may be changed as follows:

```
ConnectionOptions co = new ConnectionOptions(
    null, "Administrator", "password", null, ImpersonationLevel.Impersonate,
    AuthenticationLevel.PacketPrivacy, false, null, new TimeSpan());
ManagementScope ms = new ManagementScope(@"\\BCK_OFFICE\root\CIMV2", co);
ManagementObject mo = new ManagementObject(@"Win32_Process=100");
mo.Scope = ms;
Console.WriteLine(mo["__CLASS"]);
```

Although using this constructor may save you a bit of typing, it certainly does not promote code readability and lacks in clarity when compared to setting the properties of the `ConnectionOptions` object explicitly.

Enabling Privileges

Some operations that can be carried out through WMI may require the user to hold certain system privileges. For instance, the ability to reboot a computer is dependent on `SeShutdownPrivilege` or `SeRemoteShutdownPrivilege`, which must not only be granted to the user, but must also be enabled for the process that is attempting the reboot. The privileges can be granted using the local security policy editor, shown in Figure 8-2.

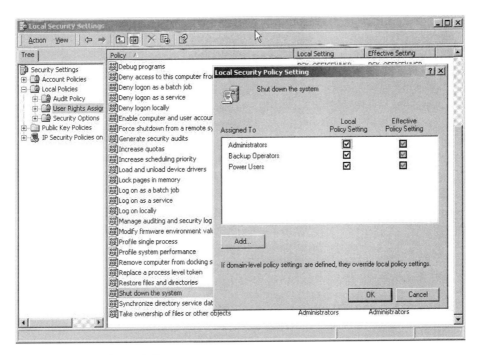

Figure 8-2. Granting privileges

Once the privileges are granted, they have to be explicitly enabled by the process attempting the privileged operation. Thus, in order to reboot a remote computer you may write code similar to the following:

```
ManagementClass mc = new ManagementClass(
    @"\\BCK_OFFICE\root\CIMV2:Win32_OperatingSystem");
foreach(ManagementObject mo in mc.GetInstances()) {
    mo.Scope.Options.Username = "username";
    mo.Scope.Options.Password = "password";
    mo.Scope.Options.EnablePrivileges = true;
    mo.InvokeMethod("Reboot", new Object [] {0});
}
```

This code binds to the Win32_OperatingSystem WMI class, enumerates its instances, and invokes the Reboot method for each operating system. Of course in most cases, there would be a single instance of the Win32_OperatingSystem class and it is probably easier to just locate such an instance directly based on its key. Unfortunately, the key of this class is the name of the OS, which is often very long and easy to mistype, therefore, I chose to use the enumeration approach. The thing you should notice here is the line of code that sets the EnablePrivileges property of the ConnectionOptions object to true. Unlike the AdjustTokenPrivileges function, which allows you to enable and disable individual privileges, setting the EnablePrivileges property to true enables all privileges granted to a given user or group. In effect, assigning this property to true is equivalent to obtaining the set of privileges associated with the access token via the GetTokenInformation function; iterating through the returned array of token privileges to set the enabled attribute for each of them; and then invoking AdjustTokenPrivileges. Here again the designers of the System.Management namespace chose to trade flexibility for simplicity by disallowing access to individual user and group privileges.

Lastly, there is still the question of figuring out which WMI operations are privileged and exactly what privileges are required to perform such operations. Although it is always possible to get the answer by digging through the mess of WMI security documentation, there is an easier way. It turns out that all WMI methods that require certain privileges are marked as such using the Privileges qualifier. For instance, take a look at the partial MOF definition for the Win32_OperatingSystem class:

```
class Win32_OperatingSystem : CIM_OperatingSystem {
  ...
    [Privileges{"SeShutdownPrivilege"}: ToSubClass]
    uint32 Reboot();
    [Privileges{"SeShutdownPrivilege"}: ToSubClass]
    uint32 Shutdown();
    [Privileges{"SeShutdownPrivilege"}: ToSubClass]
    uint32 Win32Shutdown(sint32 Flags, sint32 Reserved = 0);
};
```

Here the Privileges qualifier is parameterized with the string value of the required privilege. In reality, the qualifier value is really an array of strings, so it is possible to account for methods that require multiple privileges to be enabled. Therefore, by examining the qualifiers associated with a given method, you can determine whether it is necessary to enable the privileges before attempting to execute the method. Note that it is not even necessary to check the qualifier value (since individual privileges cannot be controlled via the System.Management types anyway)—the mere presence of the Privileges qualifier is indicative of a privileged operation.

Summary

This chapter, although fairly short, provided a comprehensive overview of the security issues pertinent to building management applications with .NET System.Management types. Having read the material presented here, you should now be able to

- Understand the fundamentals of WMI security.

- Configure WMI namespace security.

- Use the ManagementScope type to establish WMI connections.

- Alter the security settings of the client process.

- Manipulate the privileges necessary to execute the privileged operations through WMI.

Although the information covered in this chapter is sufficient for building just about any management application, WMI, COM and Windows security are extremely complex topics, which really warrant a separate book. There are a few decent Windows security books on the market, however, none of them seem to completely alleviate the need for delving into the Microsoft documentation every once in a while. Thus, the tried and true MSDN still remains the best source of information on the most obscure and confusing security issues.

Index

Symbols and Numbers

. (dot), substituting for server names, 42–43

/? <assemblypath> command-line option for installutil.exe, description of, 241

/? command-line option
of installutil.exe, 241
of MgmtClassGen.exe, 131

// (double slashes) in MOF, commenting with, 288

; (semicolon), purpose in MOF class definitions, 276

/* and */ sequences in MOF, commenting with, 288

* (asterisk) placeholder
using with SELECT statements, 143, 147, 204
using with SelectQuery type, 166

@ (at) placeholder, role in binding ManagementObject types to instances of singletons, 43–44

[] (square brackets), using with MOF qualifiers, 284–285

_ (underscore), purpose in CIM classes, 6

{ } (curly brackets), using with MOF arrays, 274

| (vertical bar), purpose in ClassContext class qualifier, 313

0–3 mofcomp.exe exit codes, table of, 267

0–4 __ADAPStatus.Status constants, descriptions of, 322

A

/a <modifier> command-line option for smi2smir.exe, description of, 353

-A:<authority> mofcomp.exe command-line switch, explanation of, 266

access modifiers, role in mapping .NET types to classes, 247

access rights
packaging of, 378
table of, 376–377

access tokens
contents of, 378–379
role in securing namespaces, 375

ACCESS_SYSTEM_SECURITY access right, description of, 377

Account parameter of MSFT_ForwardedEvent class, explanation of, 203

ACEs (access control entries)
determining inheritance of, 381
role in securing namespaces, 375–376

ACK segments, role in SNMP intrusion detection, 361

ACLs (access control lists), role in securing namespaces, 376

Active Script Event Consumer, purpose of, 197

ACTRL_*access rights, descriptions of, 377

ADAP (AutoDiscovery/AutoPurge) process and Performance Counter provider, overview of, 320–323

ADAP process error log, location of, 321

ADAP processes, determining status of programmatically, 322

__ADAPStatus system class, location and purpose of, 321–322

Add method
alternative versions of, 296–298
of PropertyDataCollection type, 294
of QualifierDataCollection type, 293

Agent* SNMP provider namespace qualifiers, descriptions of, 357

__AggregateEvent class, definition of, 212

alias names, choosing for MOF instances, 280–282

Amended qualifier, description of, 85

About Apress

Apress, located in Berkeley, CA, is a fast-growing, innovative publishing company devoted to meeting the needs of existing and potential programming professionals. Simply put, the "A" in Apress stands for *The Author's Press™*. Apress' unique approach to publishing grew out of conversations between its founders, Gary Cornell and Dan Appleman, authors of numerous best-selling, highly regarded books for programming professionals. In 1998 they set out to create a publishing company that emphasized quality above all else. Gary and Dan's vision has resulted in the publication of over 70 titles by leading software professionals, all of which have *The Expert's Voice™*.

Do You Have What It Takes to Write for Apress?

Apress is rapidly expanding its publishing program. If you can write and you refuse to compromise on the quality of your work, if you believe in doing more than rehashing existing documentation, and if you're looking for opportunities and rewards that go far beyond those offered by traditional publishing houses, we want to hear from you!

Consider these innovations that we offer all of our authors:

- **Top royalties with *no* hidden switch statements**
  Authors typically receive only half of their normal royalty rate on foreign sales. In contrast, Apress' royalty rate remains the same for both foreign and domestic sales.

- **Sharing the wealth**
  Most publishers keep authors on the same pay scale even after costs have been met. At Apress author royalties dramatically increase the more books are sold.

- **Serious treatment of the technical review process**
  Each Apress book is reviewed by a technical expert(s) whose remuneration depends in part on the success of the book since he or she too receives royalties.

Moreover, through a partnership with Springer-Verlag, New York, Inc., one of the world's major publishing houses, Apress has significant venture capital and distribution power behind it. Thus, we have the resources to produce the highest quality books *and* market them aggressively.

If you fit the model of the Apress author who can write a book that provides *What The Professional Needs To Know™*, then please contact us for more information:

editorial@apress.com